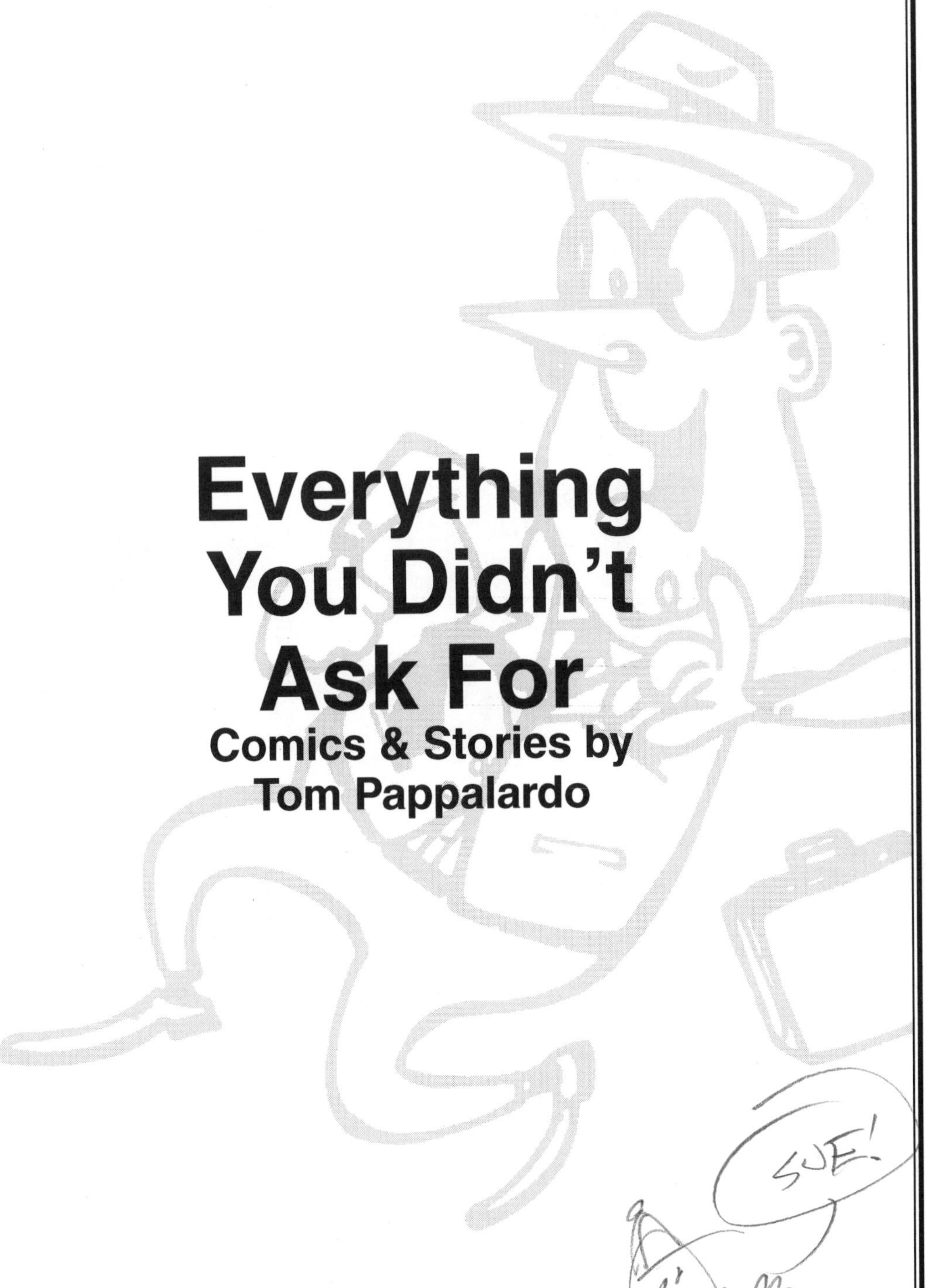

Everything You Didn't Ask For

Comics & Stories by Tom Pappalardo

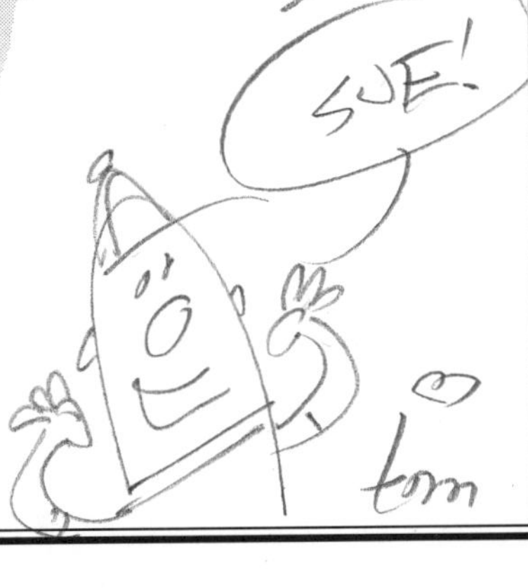
SUE!
tom

WORK HAS PREVIOUSLY APPEARED IN

Gigposters.com, I Want Your Skull, LETTER X, Lollipop magazine, Meat For Tea, Public Radio Exchange, Sierra Grille, Tom-N-Dave stickers, Tree & Hills anthologies, The Valley Advocate, VMAG, The Weekly Dig, WHMP.

APOLOGIES TO:

Samuel Beckett, Gustave Doré, Jules Feiffer, Hokusai, Wenceslas Hollar, Norton Juster, Nirvana, Ray Patin, Max Schreck, and Simon & Garfunkel.

FIRST EDITION, OCTOBER 2014

HA! HA! HA!
HA! HA!
HA! HA! HA! HA! HA! HA! HA! HA!
HA! HA! HA! HA! HA! HA! HA! HA! HA! HA!
BUS STOP
HA! HA! HA! HA! HA! HA! HA! HA! HA!
HA!
FROZEN FOOD
HA!
HA! HA! HA! HA! HA! HA!
HA! HA! HA! HA! HA! HA! HA! HA! HA! HA! HA! HA!

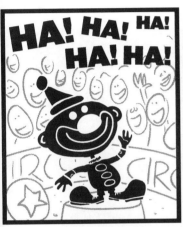

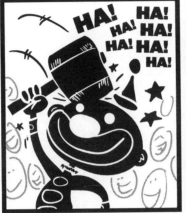

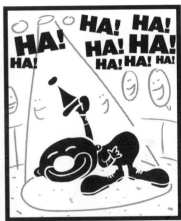

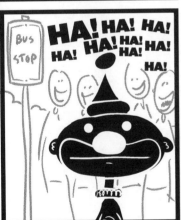

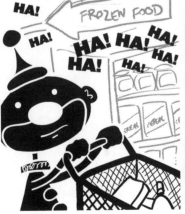

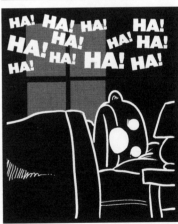

HELLO, ANN? HI, IT'S... YEAH, HI.
I WAS JUST CALLING TO ASK... HELLO?
MY PHONE'S BEEN ACTING - I WAS WONDERING IF YOU'D LIKE TO -
I SAID... HELLO? THE RECEPTION'S TERRIBLE HERE -
HELLO?
HELLO?
HELLO?
HELLO?
HELLO?
HOW CAN I MAKE YOU LIKE ME IF YOU CAN'T HEAR ME?!?!

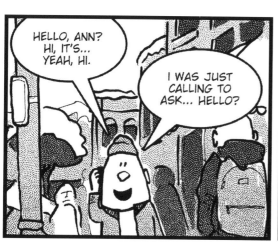

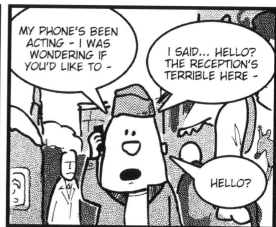

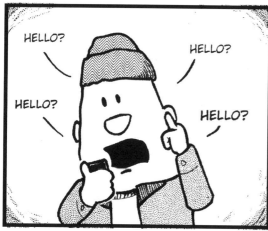

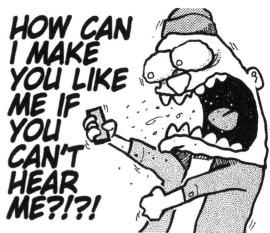

YOU'VE BEEN STARING AT THAT GIRL FOR WEEKS. GO TALK TO HER.
NAW, I'M TOO SHY.
HAVE YOU EVER STOPPED TO CONSIDER THAT WHAT YOU CALL SHYNESS MIGHT JUST BE EGO? PERHAPS YOUR ANXIETY OVER HOW OTHERS MIGHT PERCEIVE YOU IS JUST A COWARD'S VERSION OF VANITY.

"Hey asshole, perhaps you shouldn't make cartoons where you try to sound smart about topics you are clearly ignorant to."

"Fuck, I think this might be me."

"'Damn.' I audibly said to myself. Right to the point, well done."

"Fuuuuuck... I need to lie down for a bit."

"That's... strangely motivating..."

"Well... shit."

"Like a brick to the face"

"Psychologisted, bitch!"

"This just motivated me to leave a stale relationship."

"Haha. Sad."

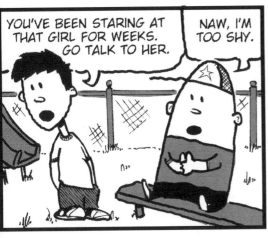

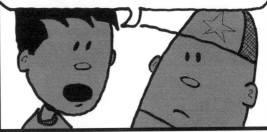

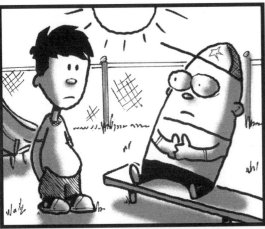

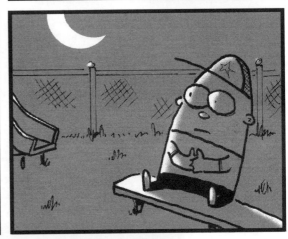

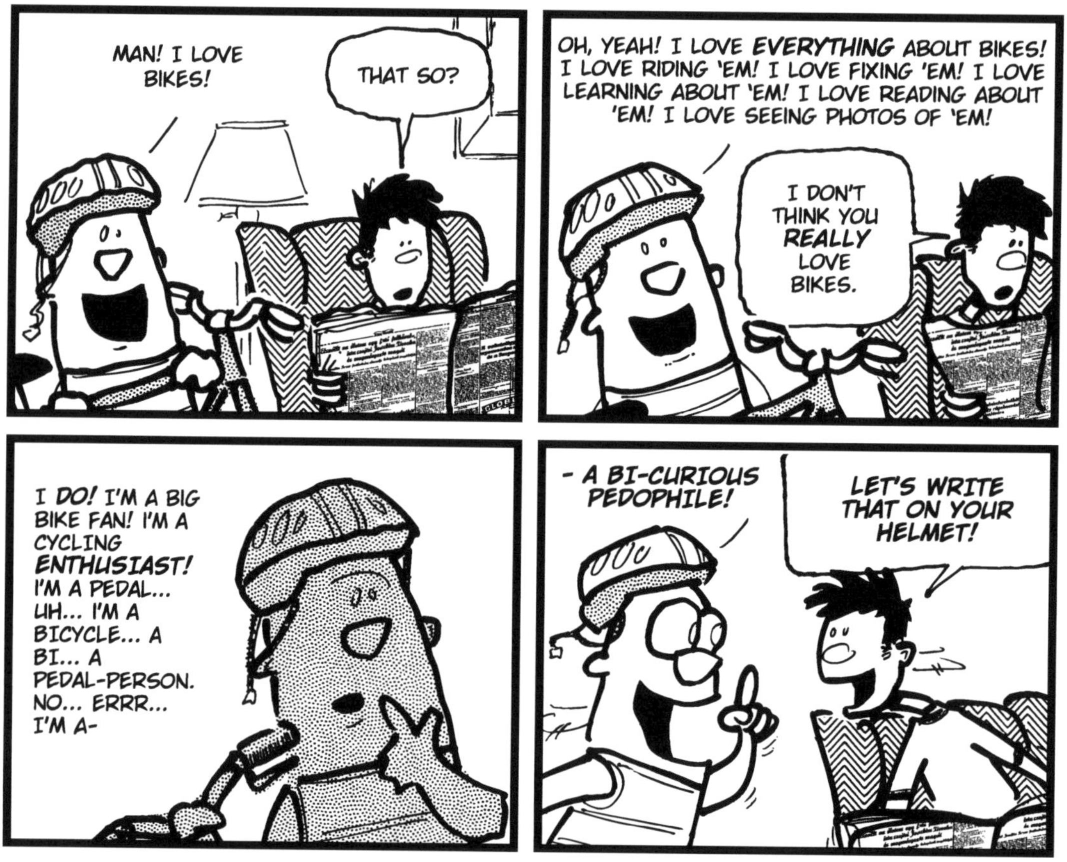
MAN! I LOVE BIKES!
THAT SO?
OH, YEAH! I LOVE EVERYTHING ABOUT BIKES! I LOVE RIDING 'EM! I LOVE FIXING 'EM! I LOVE LEARNING ABOUT 'EM! I LOVE READING ABOUT 'EM! I LOVE SEEING PHOTOS OF 'EM!
I DON'T THINK YOU REALLY LOVE BIKES.
I DO! I'M A BIG BIKE FAN! I'M A CYCLING ENTHUSIAST! I'M A PEDAL... UH... I'M A BICYCLE... A BI... A PEDAL-PERSON. NO... ERRR... I'M A-
- A BI-CURIOUS PEDOPHILE!
LET'S WRITE THAT ON YOUR HELMET!

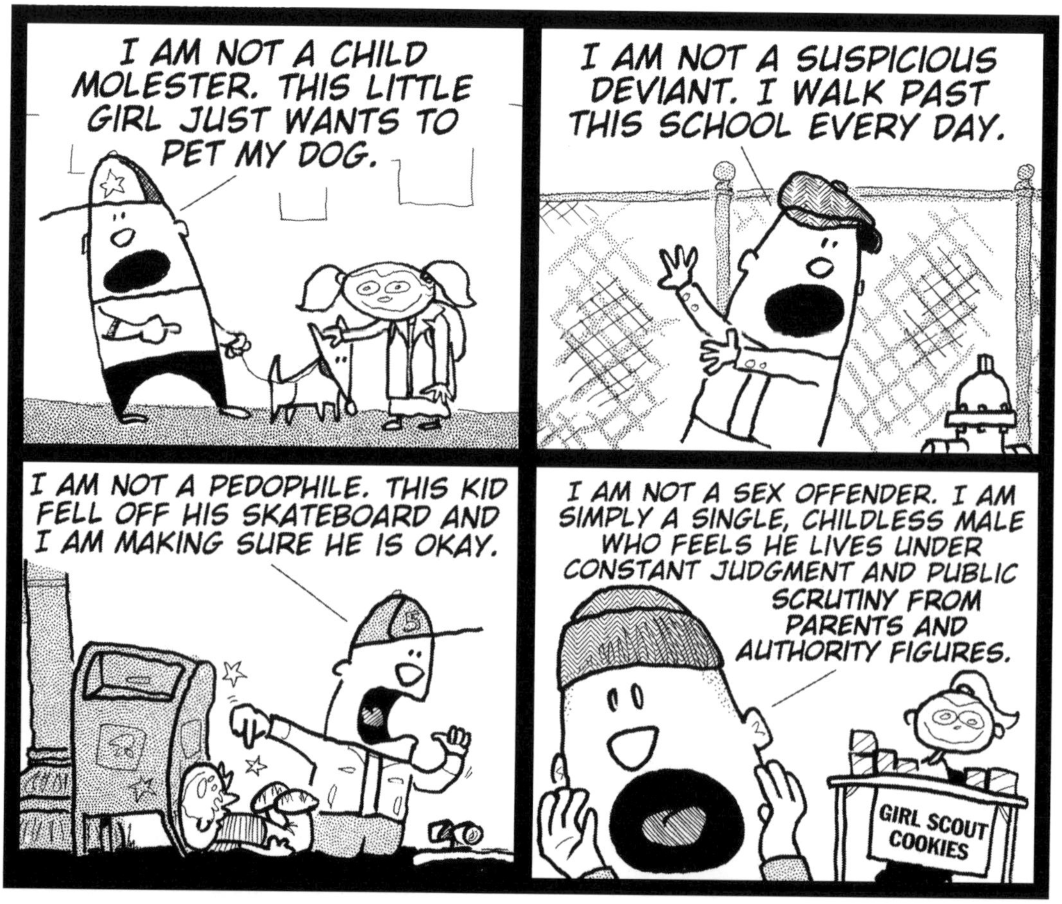
I AM NOT A CHILD MOLESTER. THIS LITTLE GIRL JUST WANTS TO PET MY DOG.
I AM NOT A SUSPICIOUS DEVIANT. I WALK PAST THIS SCHOOL EVERY DAY.
I AM NOT A PEDOPHILE. THIS KID FELL OFF HIS SKATEBOARD AND I AM MAKING SURE HE IS OKAY.
I AM NOT A SEX OFFENDER. I AM SIMPLY A SINGLE, CHILDLESS MALE WHO FEELS HE LIVES UNDER CONSTANT JUDGMENT AND PUBLIC SCRUTINY FROM PARENTS AND AUTHORITY FIGURES.
GIRL SCOUT COOKIES

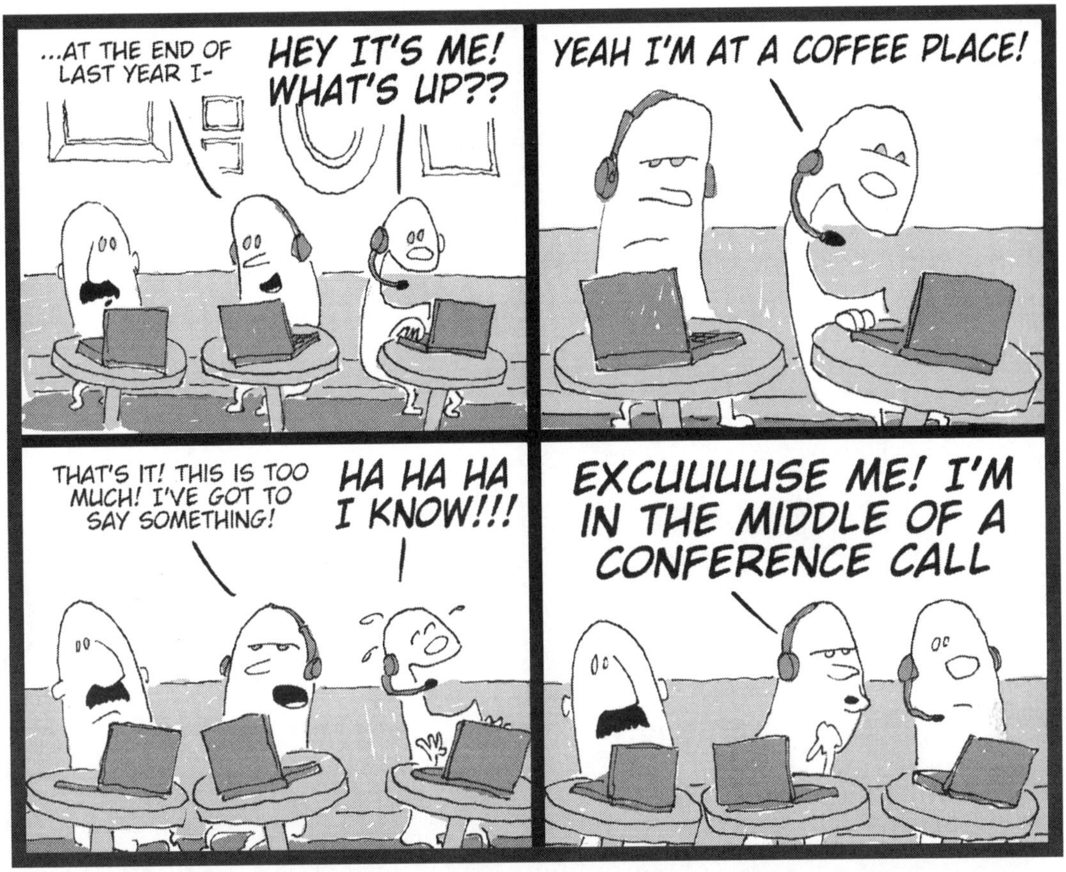
...AT THE END OF LAST YEAR I-
HEY IT'S ME! WHAT'S UP??
YEAH I'M AT A COFFEE PLACE!
THAT'S IT! THIS IS TOO MUCH! I'VE GOT TO SAY SOMETHING!
HA HA HA I KNOW!!!
EXCUUUUSE ME! I'M IN THE MIDDLE OF A CONFERENCE CALL

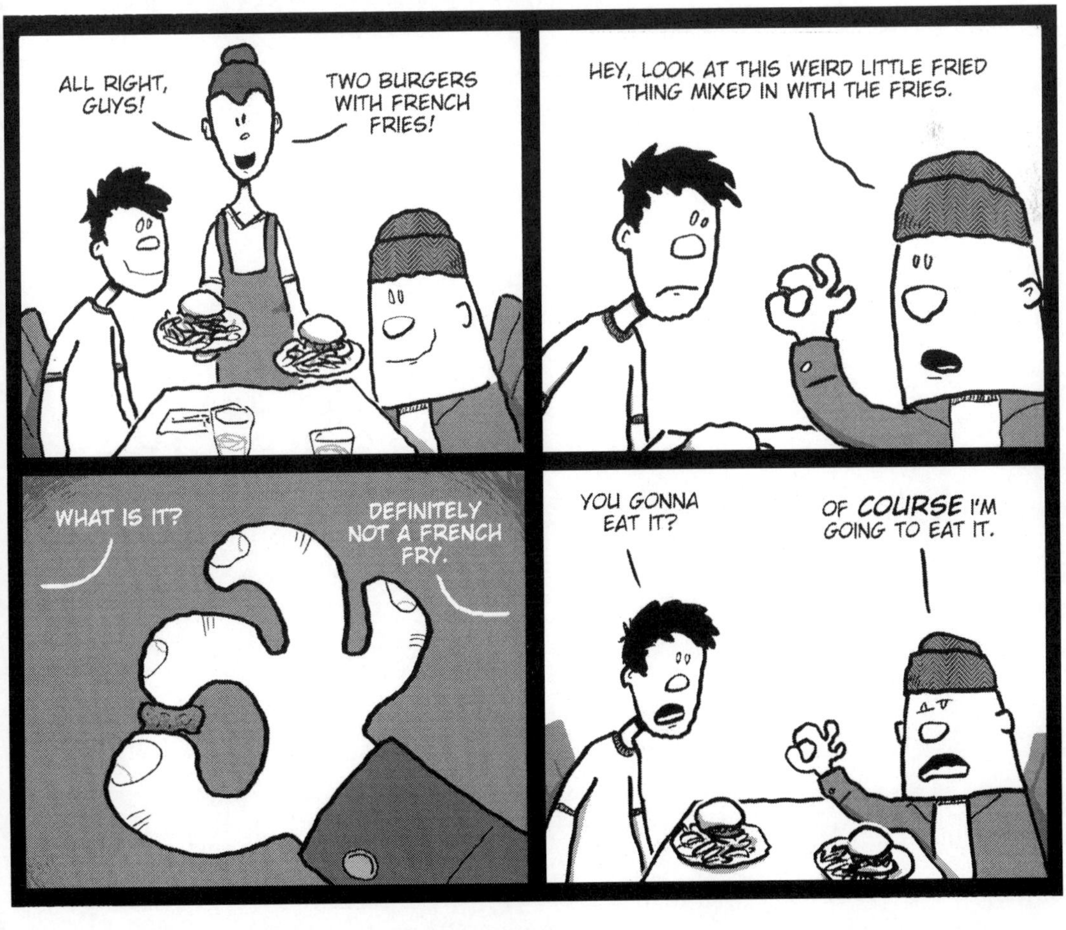
ALL RIGHT, GUYS!
TWO BURGERS WITH FRENCH FRIES!
HEY, LOOK AT THIS WEIRD LITTLE FRIED THING MIXED IN WITH THE FRIES.
WHAT IS IT?
DEFINITELY NOT A FRENCH FRY.
YOU GONNA EAT IT?
OF COURSE I'M GOING TO EAT IT.

Politically Correct
EVERYTIME I HEAR SOMEONE CALL A BLACK DUDE AN 'AFRICAN-AMERICAN'
I THINK TO MYSELF:
"WHAT IF HE'S CANADIAN?"

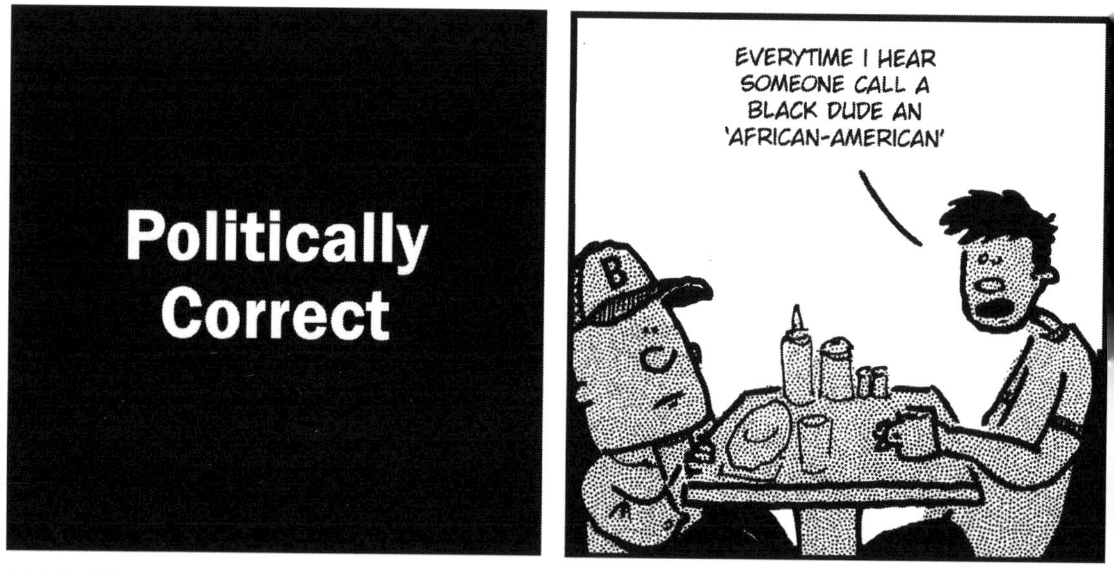

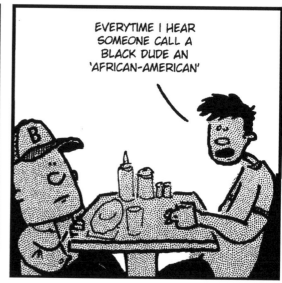

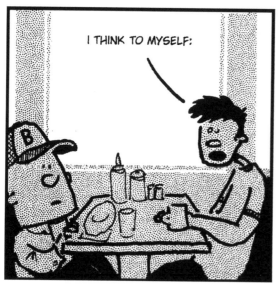

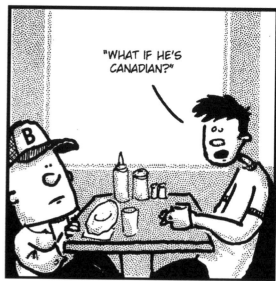

THE PHANTOM TOLLBOOTH TODAY

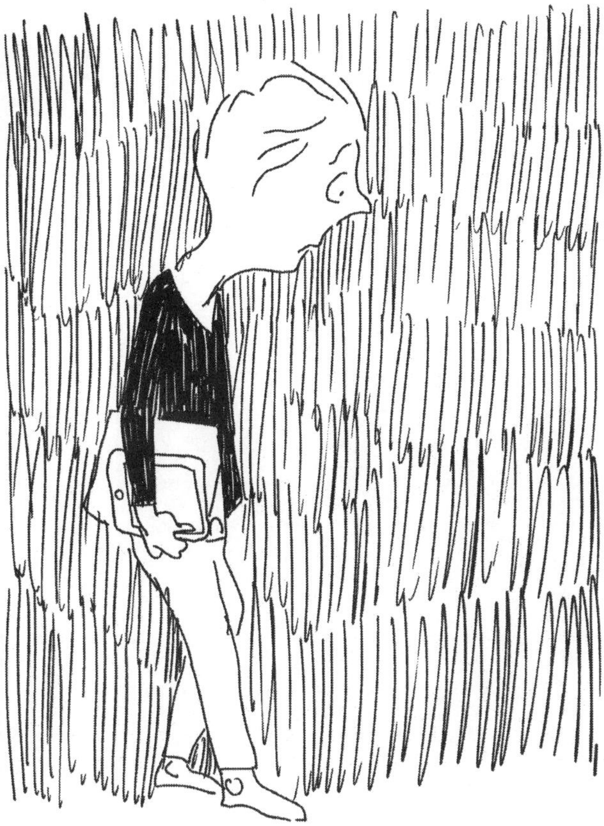

There was once a boy named Milo who didn't know what to do with himself—not just sometimes, but always.

When he was in school he longed to be out, and when he was out he longed to be in. On the way he thought about coming home, and coming he thought about going. Wherever he was he wished he were somewhere else, and when he got there he wondered why he'd bothered. Nothing really interested him—least of all the things that should have.

He was diagnosed with ADD and now he takes pills. THE END

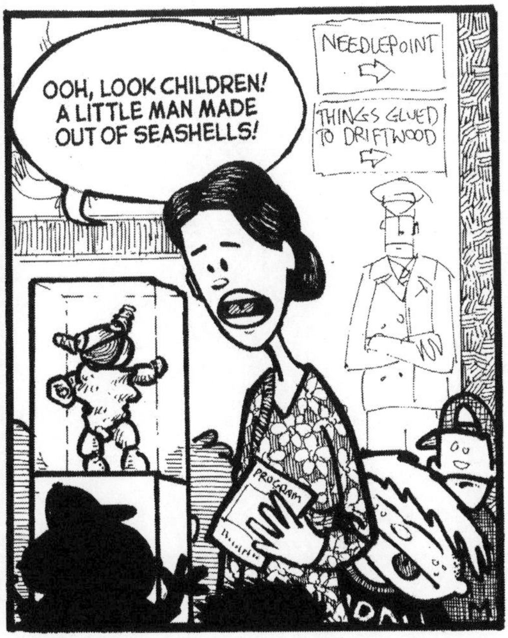
OOH, LOOK CHILDREN! A LITTLE MAN MADE OUT OF SEASHELLS!
NEEDLEPOINT
THINGS GLUED TO DRIFTWOOD
PROGRAM

The Museum of Fine Arts and Crafts

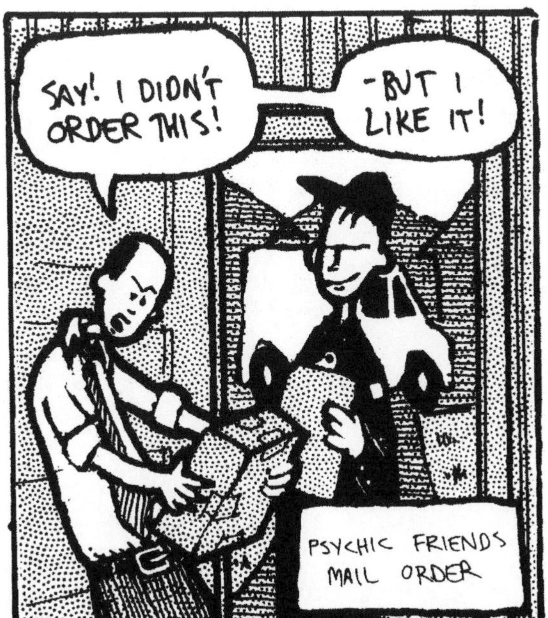
SAY! I DIDN'T ORDER THIS!
-BUT I LIKE IT!
PSYCHIC FRIENDS MAIL ORDER

CULTURAL VAMPIRISM

White culture's re-appropriation of black culture has been well-documented, but less discussed is the white mainstream's tendency to swipe from within its own counterculture. These mainstream vampiric whiteys, known as Hipsters, will absorb any subcultural artifact that can be fashionably consumed.

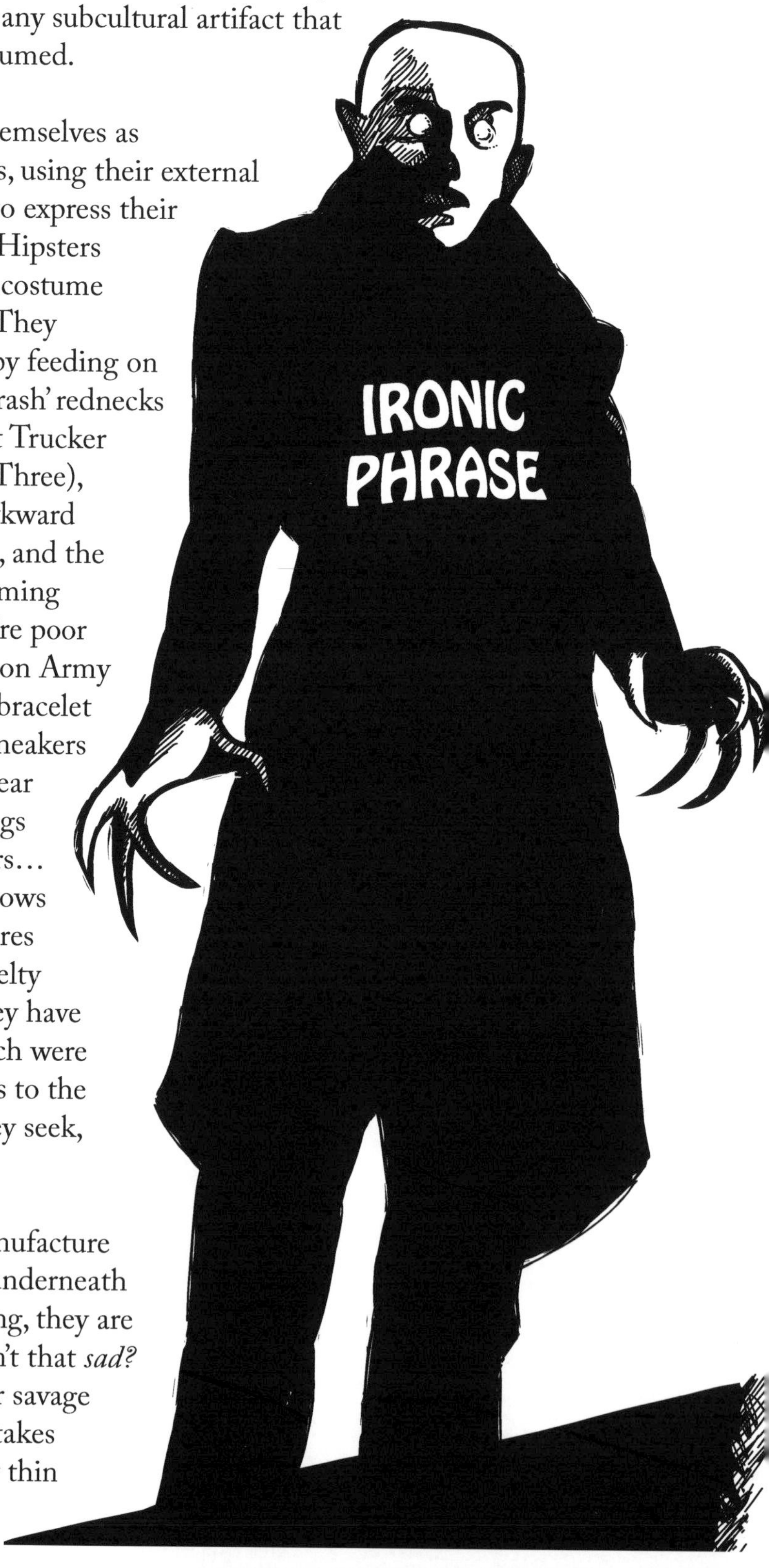
IRONIC PHRASE

Hipsters disguise themselves as nonconformist outsiders, using their external appearance as a means to express their perceived individuality. Hipsters play dress-up, and their costume is "Unique Individual." They accessorize and co-opt by feeding on subcultures like 'white trash' rednecks (belt buckles, The Great Trucker Hat Debacle of Aught-Three), the geeks and dorks (awkward eyeglasses, bad haircuts), and the ever-popular class-slumming trend of pretending you're poor (ripped clothing, Salvation Army scavenging). A studded bracelet from the headbangers, sneakers from the skaters, fixed gear bicycles and shoulder bags from the bike messengers… A Hipster's trendlust knows no bounds. These vampires feed until the ironic novelty is drained away, until they have devalued the things which were once important signifiers to the original subcultures. They seek, consume, and destroy.

Hipsters need to manufacture their rebellion, because underneath all of their cheap signaling, they are indescribably normal. Isn't that *sad?* Doesn't that explain your savage desire to drive wooden stakes through their impossibly thin T-shirts?

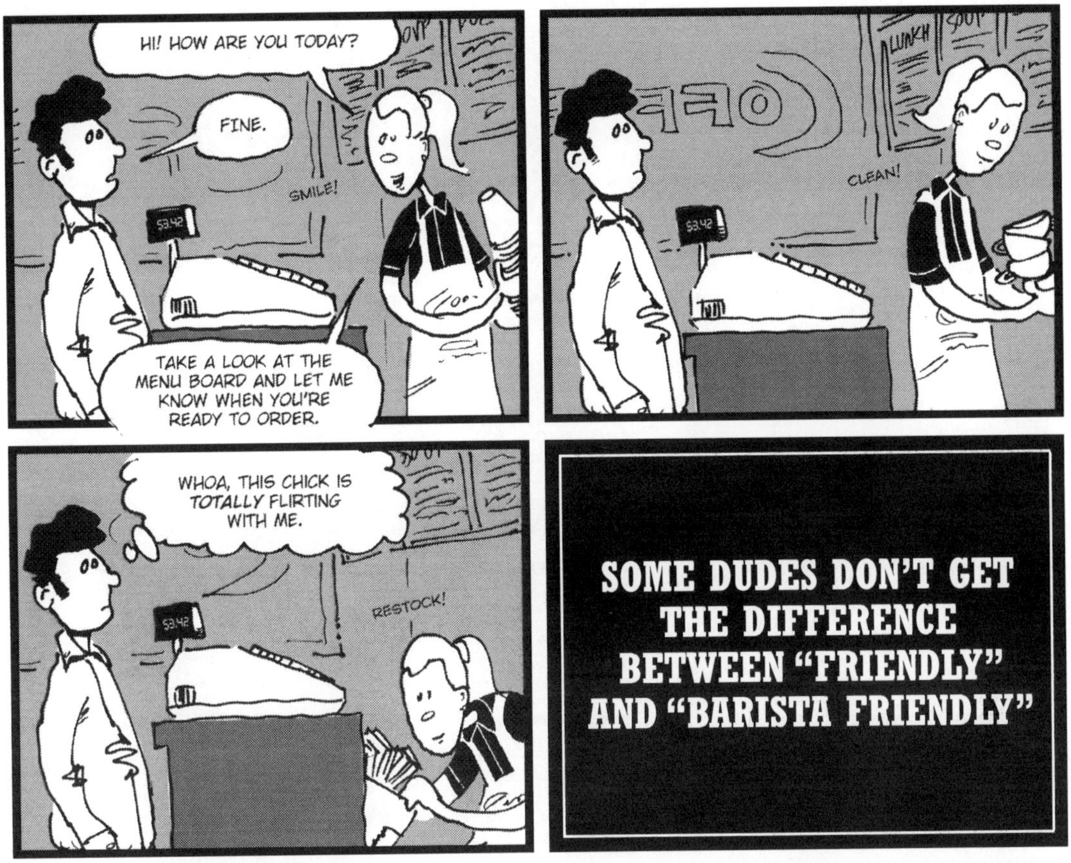
HI! HOW ARE YOU TODAY?
FINE.
SMILE!
TAKE A LOOK AT THE MENU BOARD AND LET ME KNOW WHEN YOU'RE READY TO ORDER.
CLEAN!
WHOA, THIS CHICK IS TOTALLY FLIRTING WITH ME.
RESTOCK!
SOME DUDES DON'T GET THE DIFFERENCE BETWEEN "FRIENDLY" AND "BARISTA FRIENDLY"

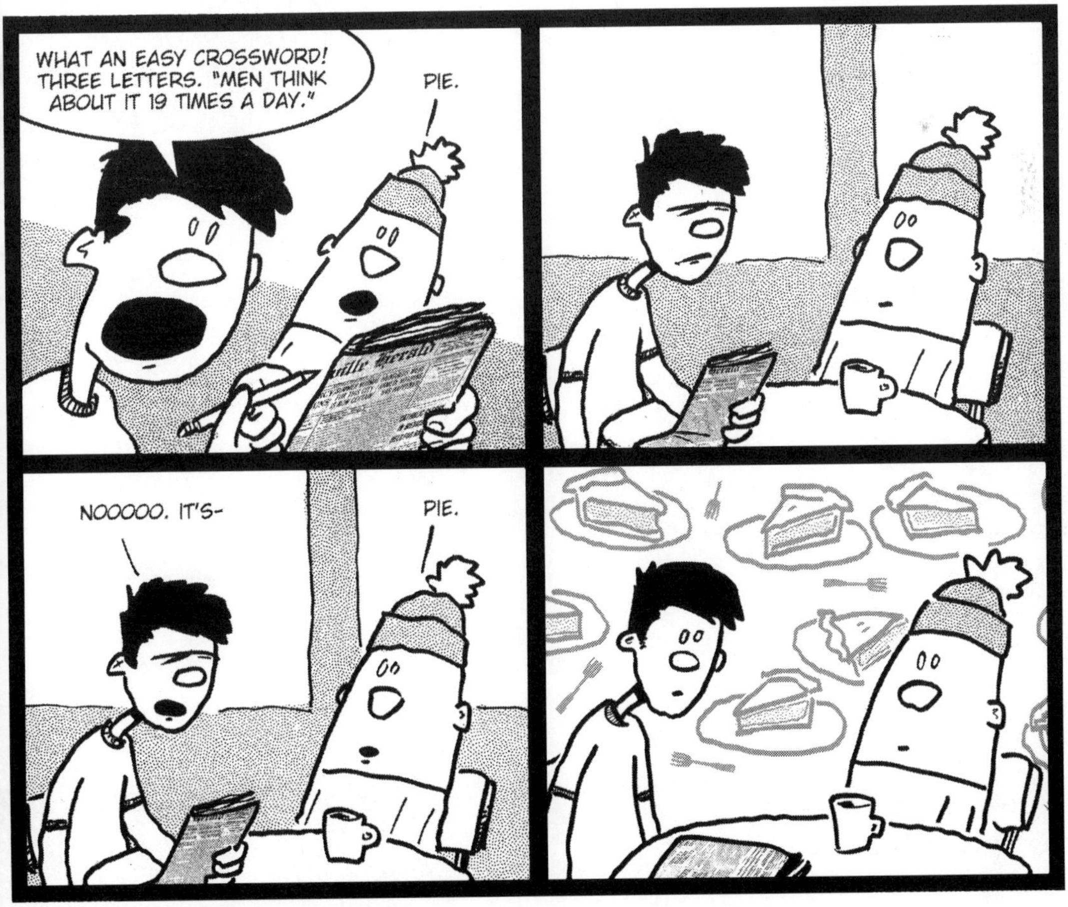
WHAT AN EASY CROSSWORD! THREE LETTERS. "MEN THINK ABOUT IT 19 TIMES A DAY."
PIE.
NOOOOO. IT'S-
PIE.

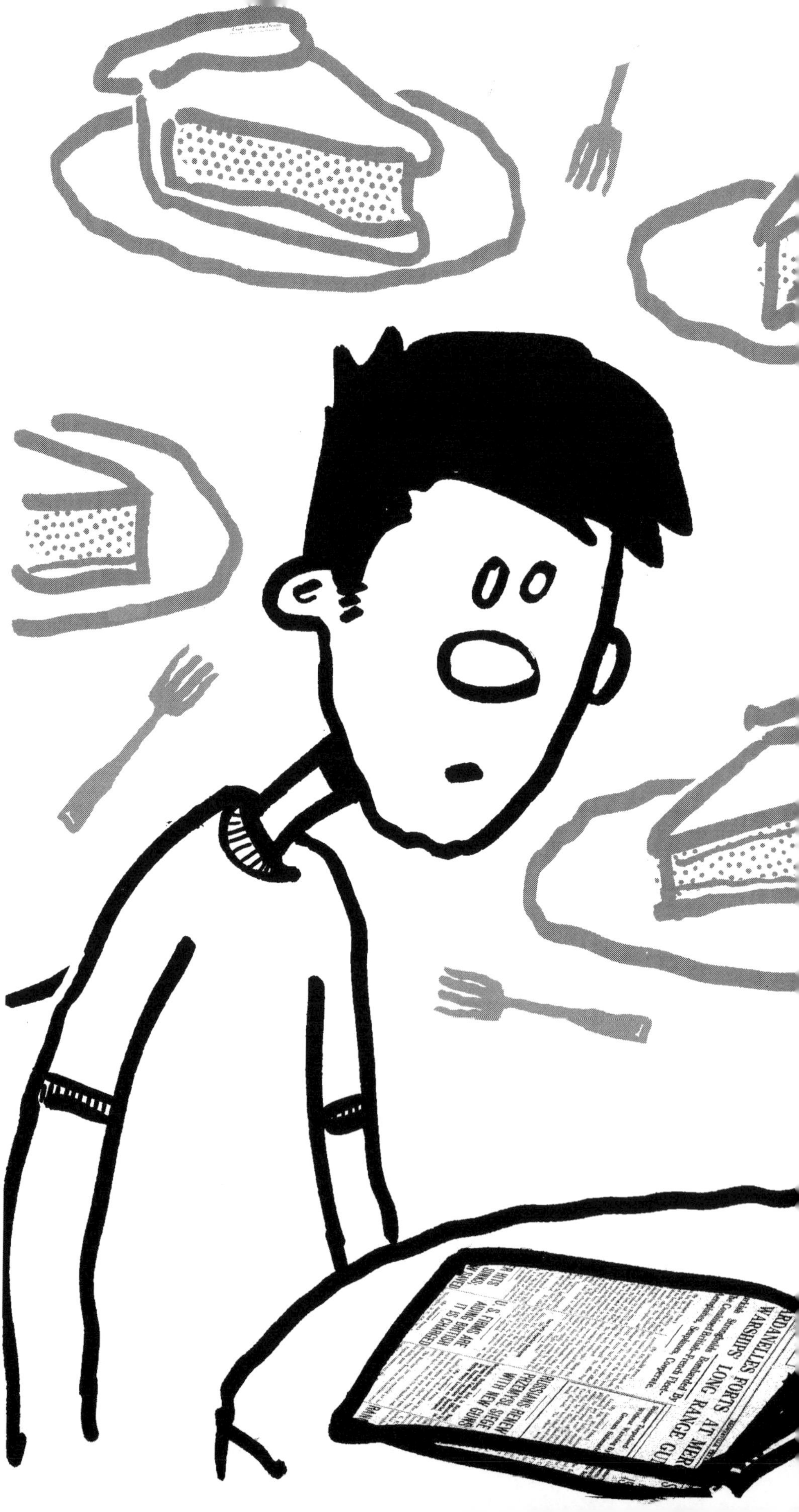
U. S. FIRMS ARE AIDING BRITISH IT IS CHARGED
RUSSIANS RENEW PRZEMYSL SIEGE WITH NEW GUNS

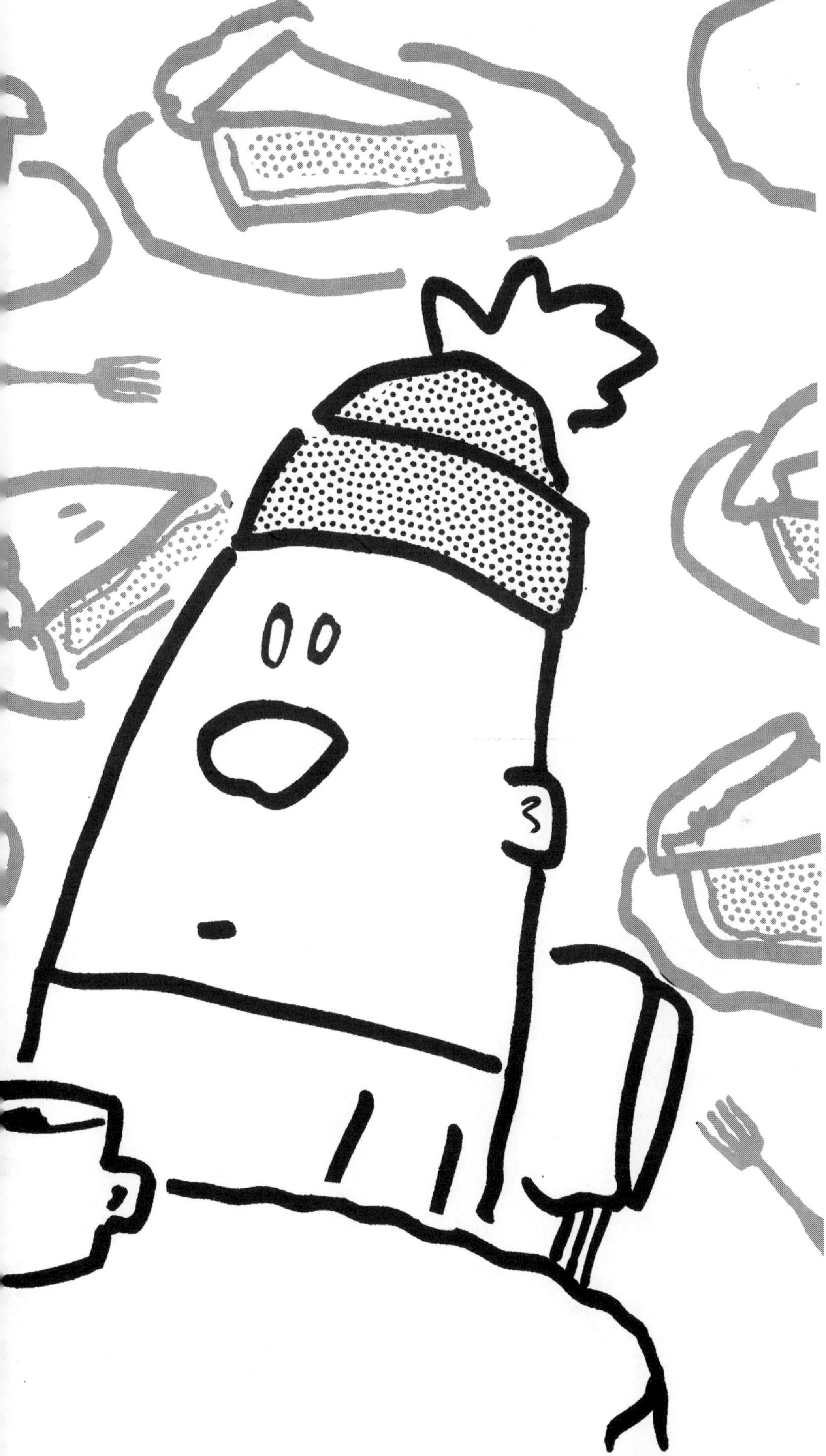

BOARD

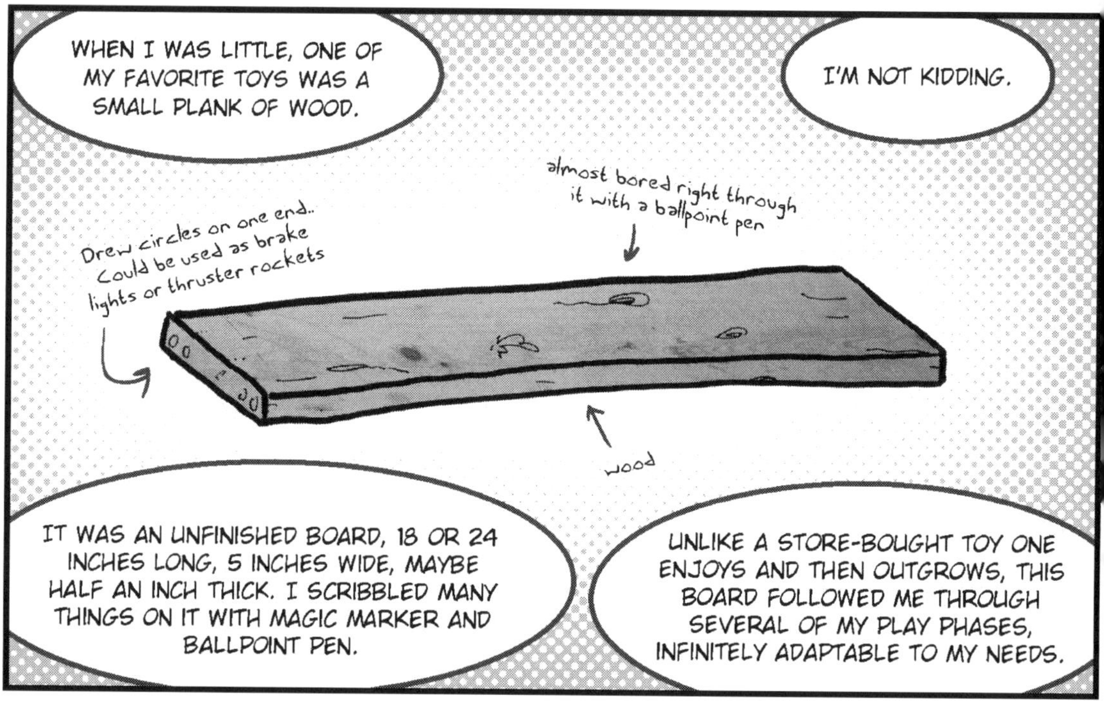
WHEN I WAS LITTLE, ONE OF MY FAVORITE TOYS WAS A SMALL PLANK OF WOOD.
I'M NOT KIDDING.
Drew circles on one end.. Could be used as brake lights or thruster rockets
almost bored right through it with a ballpoint pen
wood
IT WAS AN UNFINISHED BOARD, 18 OR 24 INCHES LONG, 5 INCHES WIDE, MAYBE HALF AN INCH THICK. I SCRIBBLED MANY THINGS ON IT WITH MAGIC MARKER AND BALLPOINT PEN.
UNLIKE A STORE-BOUGHT TOY ONE ENJOYS AND THEN OUTGROWS, THIS BOARD FOLLOWED ME THROUGH SEVERAL OF MY PLAY PHASES, INFINITELY ADAPTABLE TO MY NEEDS.

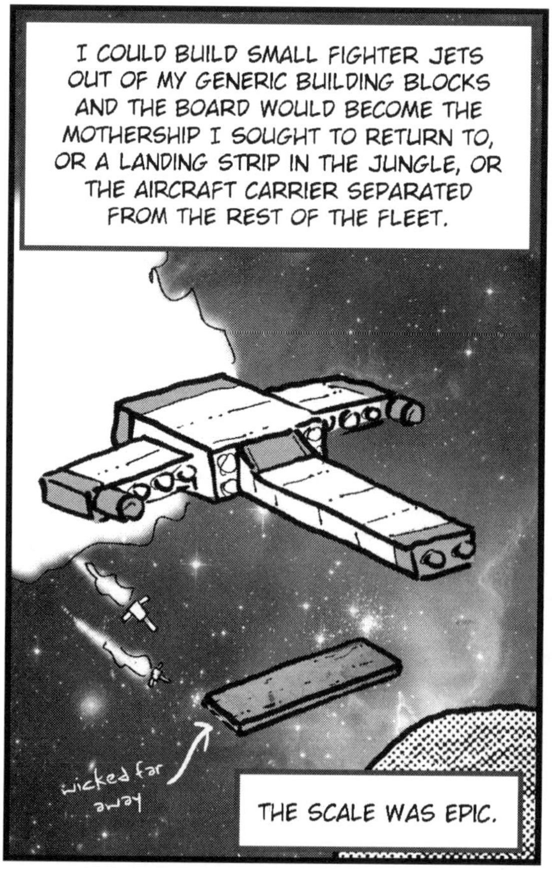
I COULD BUILD SMALL FIGHTER JETS OUT OF MY GENERIC BUILDING BLOCKS AND THE BOARD WOULD BECOME THE MOTHERSHIP I SOUGHT TO RETURN TO, OR A LANDING STRIP IN THE JUNGLE, OR THE AIRCRAFT CARRIER SEPARATED FROM THE REST OF THE FLEET.
wicked far away
THE SCALE WAS EPIC.

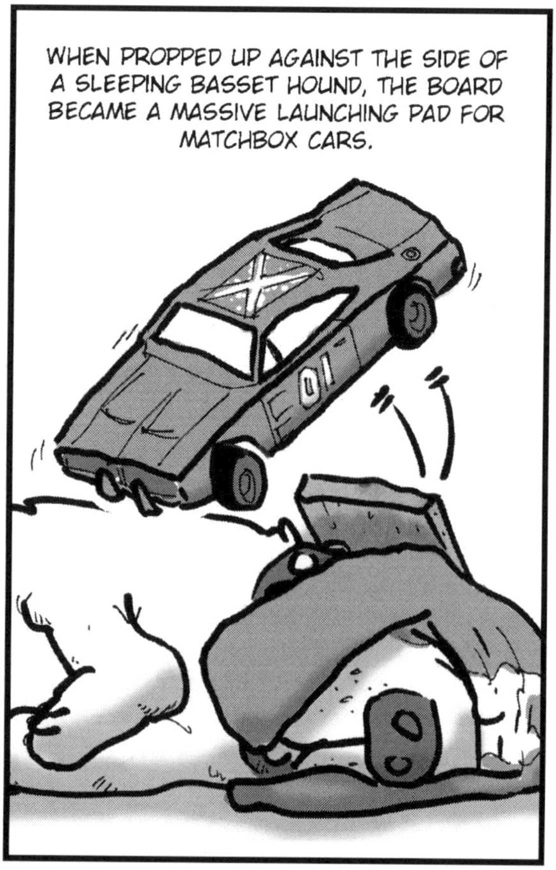
WHEN PROPPED UP AGAINST THE SIDE OF A SLEEPING BASSET HOUND, THE BOARD BECAME A MASSIVE LAUNCHING PAD FOR MATCHBOX CARS.
01

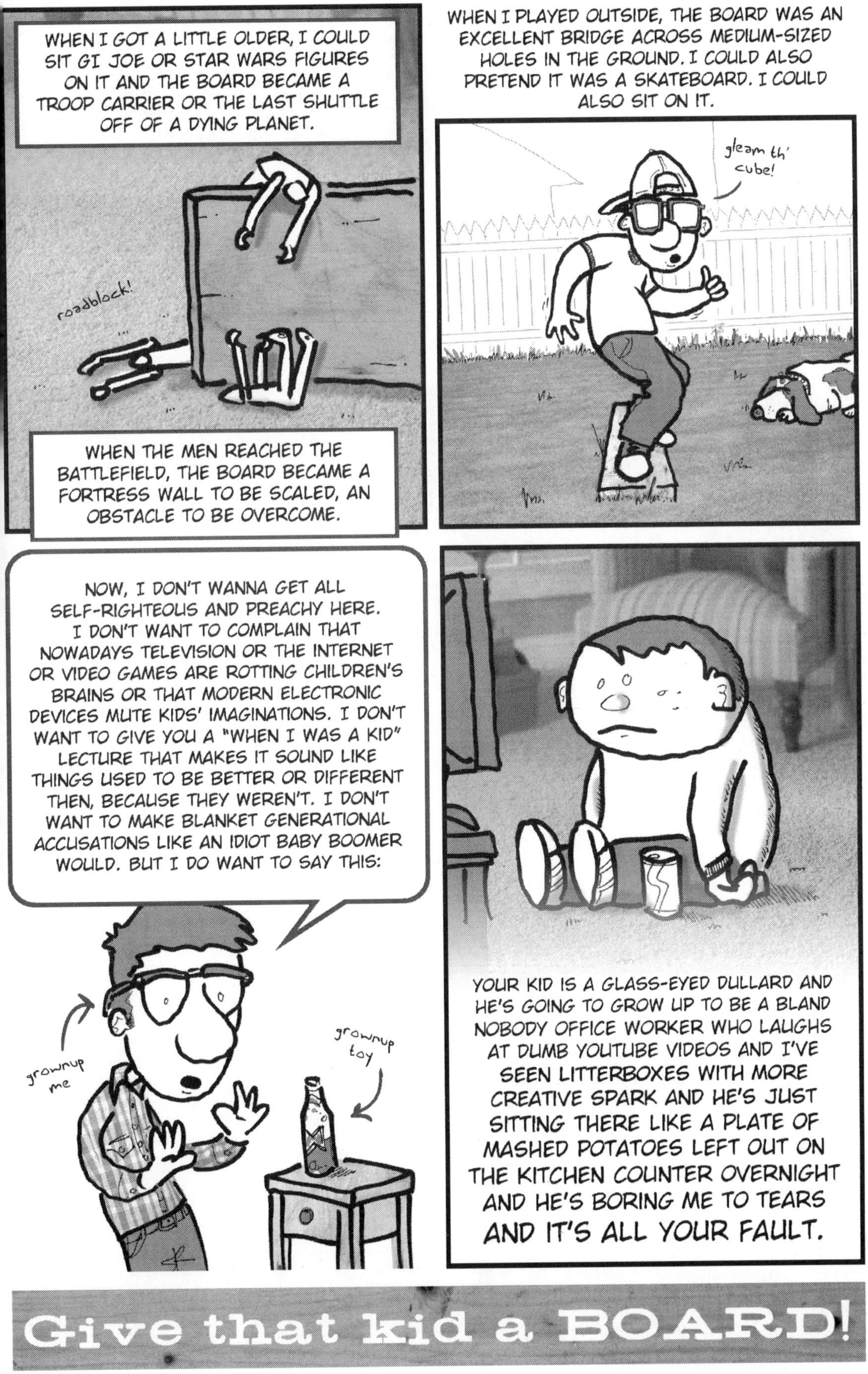
WHEN I GOT A LITTLE OLDER, I COULD SIT GI JOE OR STAR WARS FIGURES ON IT AND THE BOARD BECAME A TROOP CARRIER OR THE LAST SHUTTLE OFF OF A DYING PLANET.
roadblock!
WHEN THE MEN REACHED THE BATTLEFIELD, THE BOARD BECAME A FORTRESS WALL TO BE SCALED, AN OBSTACLE TO BE OVERCOME.
WHEN I PLAYED OUTSIDE, THE BOARD WAS AN EXCELLENT BRIDGE ACROSS MEDIUM-SIZED HOLES IN THE GROUND. I COULD ALSO PRETEND IT WAS A SKATEBOARD. I COULD ALSO SIT ON IT.
gleam th' cube!
NOW, I DON'T WANNA GET ALL SELF-RIGHTEOUS AND PREACHY HERE. I DON'T WANT TO COMPLAIN THAT NOWADAYS TELEVISION OR THE INTERNET OR VIDEO GAMES ARE ROTTING CHILDREN'S BRAINS OR THAT MODERN ELECTRONIC DEVICES MUTE KIDS' IMAGINATIONS. I DON'T WANT TO GIVE YOU A "WHEN I WAS A KID" LECTURE THAT MAKES IT SOUND LIKE THINGS USED TO BE BETTER OR DIFFERENT THEN, BECAUSE THEY WEREN'T. I DON'T WANT TO MAKE BLANKET GENERATIONAL ACCUSATIONS LIKE AN IDIOT BABY BOOMER WOULD. BUT I DO WANT TO SAY THIS:
grownup me
grownup toy
YOUR KID IS A GLASS-EYED DULLARD AND HE'S GOING TO GROW UP TO BE A BLAND NOBODY OFFICE WORKER WHO LAUGHS AT DUMB YOUTUBE VIDEOS AND I'VE SEEN LITTERBOXES WITH MORE CREATIVE SPARK AND HE'S JUST SITTING THERE LIKE A PLATE OF MASHED POTATOES LEFT OUT ON THE KITCHEN COUNTER OVERNIGHT AND HE'S BORING ME TO TEARS AND IT'S ALL YOUR FAULT.
Give that kid a BOARD!

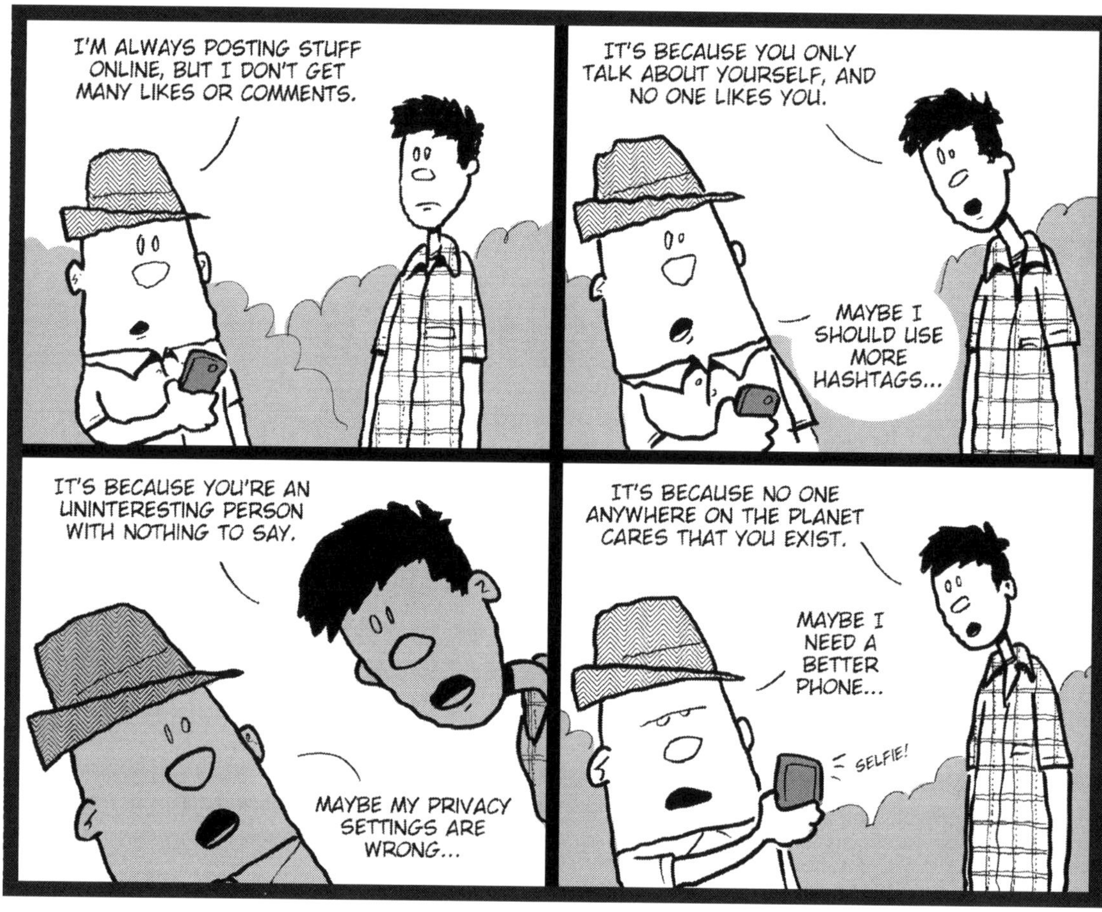
I'M ALWAYS POSTING STUFF ONLINE, BUT I DON'T GET MANY LIKES OR COMMENTS.
IT'S BECAUSE YOU ONLY TALK ABOUT YOURSELF, AND NO ONE LIKES YOU.
MAYBE I SHOULD USE MORE HASHTAGS...
IT'S BECAUSE YOU'RE AN UNINTERESTING PERSON WITH NOTHING TO SAY.
MAYBE MY PRIVACY SETTINGS ARE WRONG...
IT'S BECAUSE NO ONE ANYWHERE ON THE PLANET CARES THAT YOU EXIST.
MAYBE I NEED A BETTER PHONE...
SELFIE!

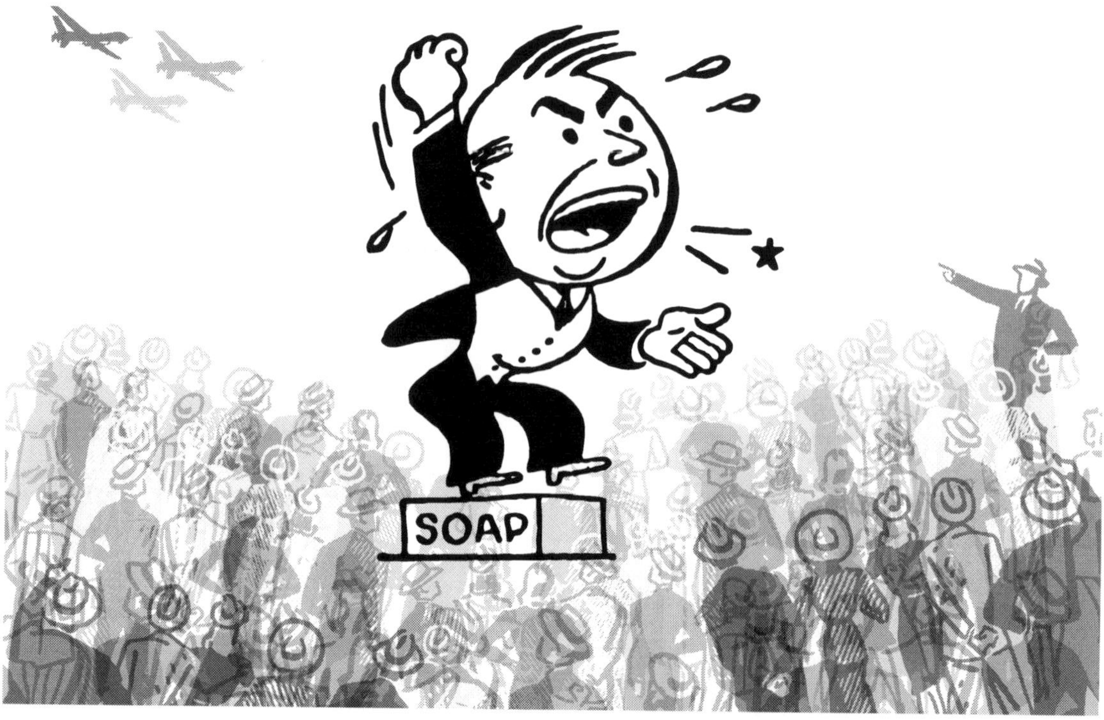
SOAP

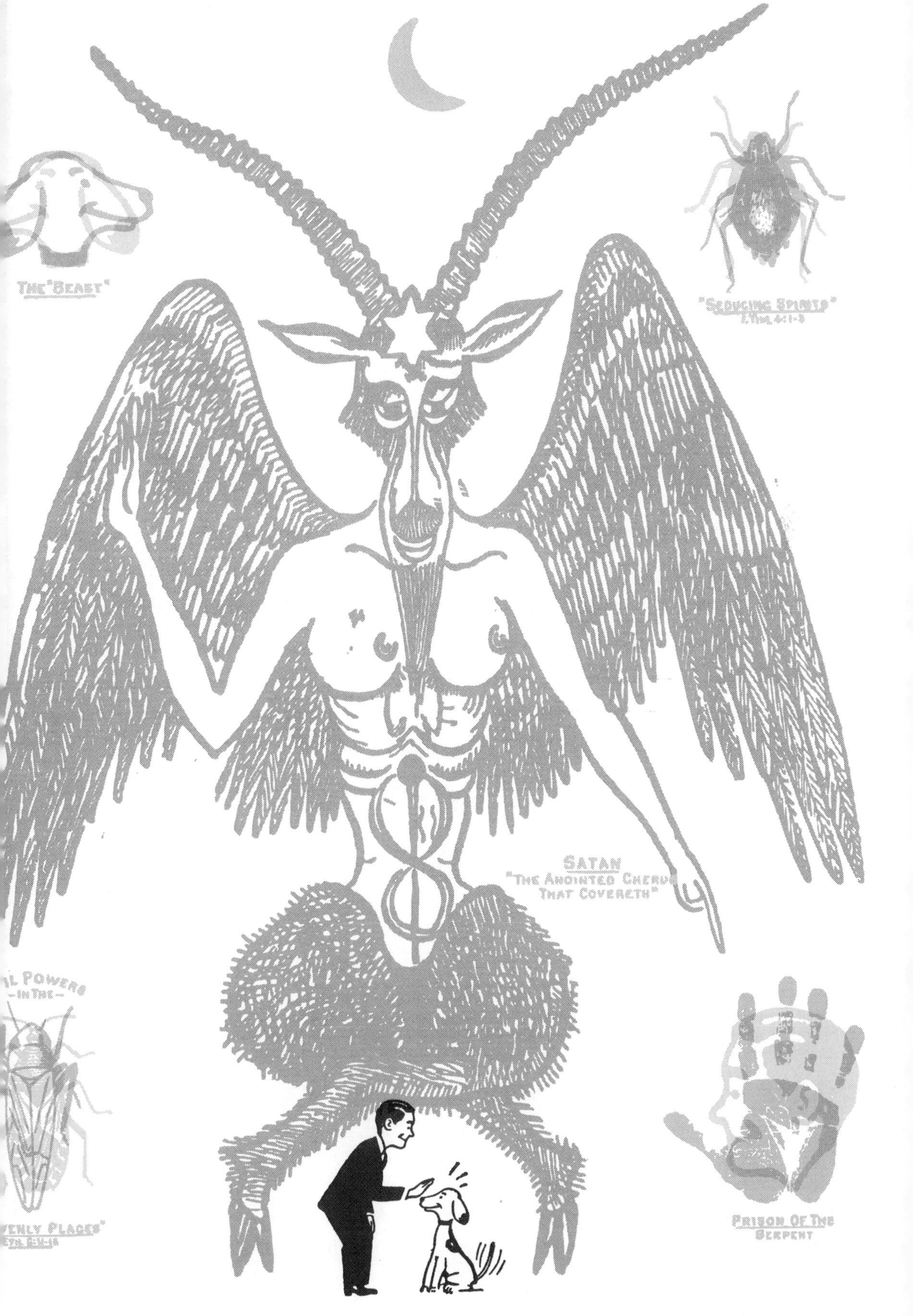

THE "BEAST"
"SEDUCING SPIRITS"
SATAN
"THE ANOINTED CHERUB THAT COVERETH"
PRISON OF THE SERPENT

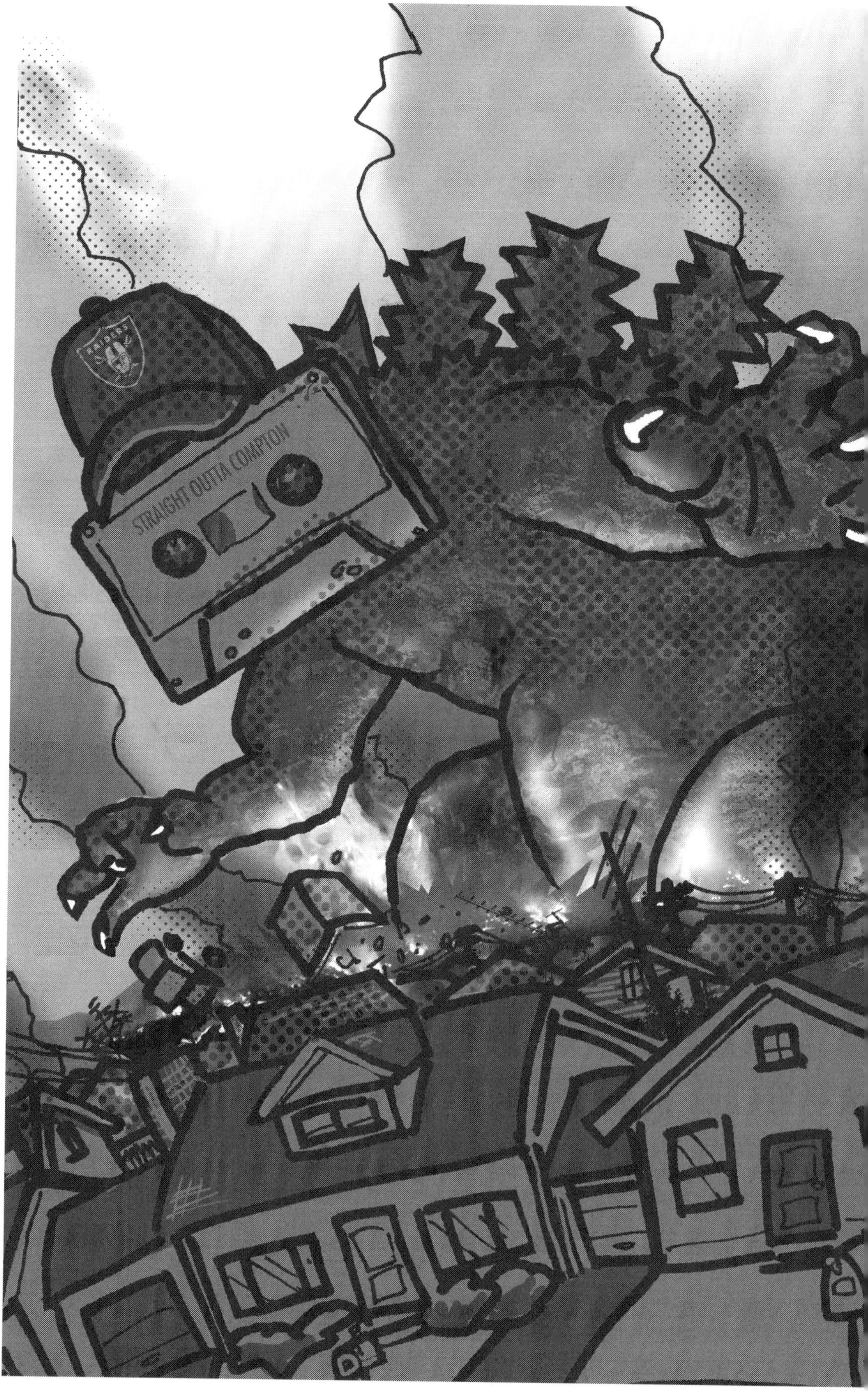
RAIDERS
STRAIGHT OUTTA COMPTON

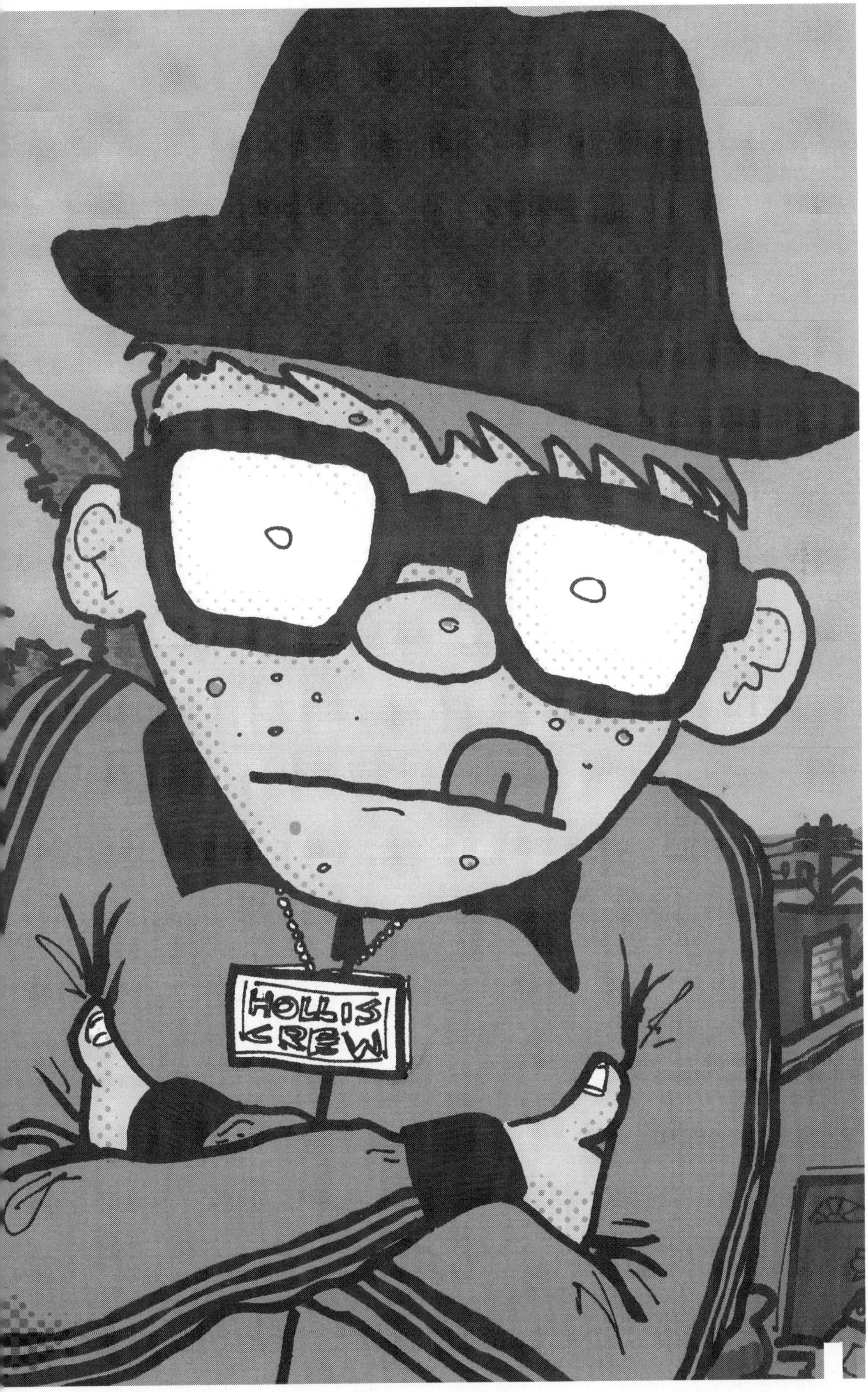
HOLLIS
CREW

pasta pappalardo

A taste of the old country in your very own kitchen! Push some of this between your lips and you'll be saying "mamma mia!" and spitting food everywhere because you're talking with your mouth full.

1 box of some brand of pasta

1 jar of spaghetti sauce that was on sale on the endcap at the supermarket

1 sweet Italian sausage you've left in the fridge for too long, and now sausage panic has set in

Grated cheese you bought because the label looked vaguely "authentic"

1. **Boil** some water in a pot and put the spaghetti in it. Like, a handful, I guess? Cook until bendy.

2. **Throw** the sausage into a frying pan. Don't eat raw meat. Chuck some green pepper and onion in there, too. Is the spaghetti ready yet? Try to not fuck everything up.

3. **Poke** at stuff with a fork so you feel like you're part of the process. Cook the sausage until it's burned. The vegetables will probably still be raw.

4. **Drain** the pasta. If it's still very straight and crunchy, you've fucked up, just like we thought you would. **Order a pizza.**

5. **Mix** everything in with the spaghetti sauce. Add garlic powder until you're sure you've added way too much. Liberally apply store-bought cheese dust. Let it cover everything you see, like a cheese blizzard.

6. **Serve** with red wine in a dirty coffee mug. This will help you blot out your emotions.

SERVES ONE SAD MAN
15 MINUTES

This is a stock photo. Your food will look nothing like this.

Good Morning!

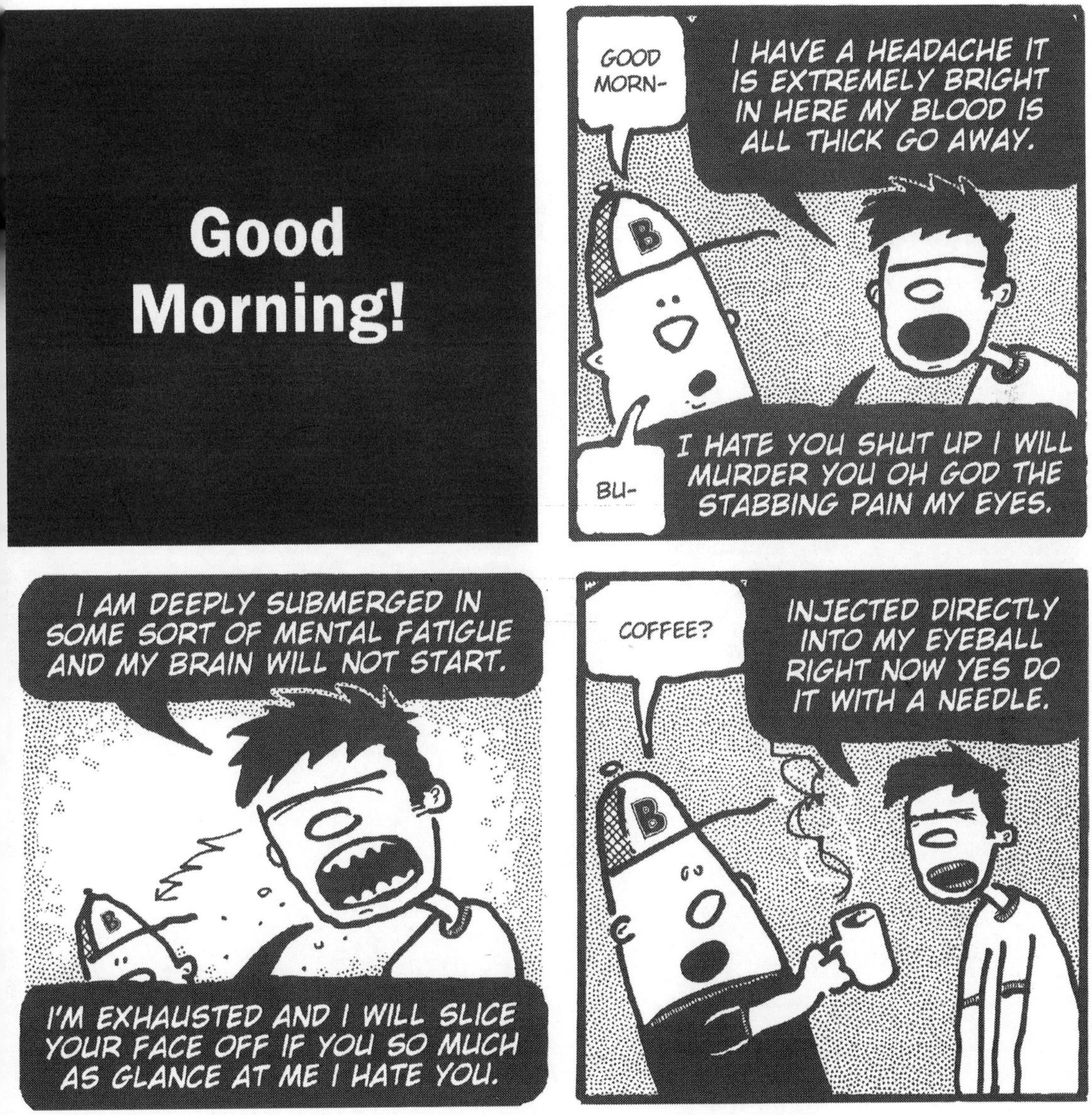
GOOD MORN-
I HAVE A HEADACHE IT IS EXTREMELY BRIGHT IN HERE MY BLOOD IS ALL THICK GO AWAY.
BU-
I HATE YOU SHUT UP I WILL MURDER YOU OH GOD THE STABBING PAIN MY EYES.
I AM DEEPLY SUBMERGED IN SOME SORT OF MENTAL FATIGUE AND MY BRAIN WILL NOT START.
I'M EXHAUSTED AND I WILL SLICE YOUR FACE OFF IF YOU SO MUCH AS GLANCE AT ME I HATE YOU.
COFFEE?
INJECTED DIRECTLY INTO MY EYEBALL RIGHT NOW YES DO IT WITH A NEEDLE.
B

RIME OF THE ANCIENT MARINARA

We barrel into the Main Street Subway laughing, still recovering from a drunken joke I don't remember anymore. Sorry, I don't mean the underground public transportation, I mean the sandwich franchise. Jared, etc. Y'know. Anyway, it's late at night and my buddies launch themselves in two different directions: Dale flops his body into a booth, Joe makes a bee-line for the crapper. We know we won't be seeing him for awhile.

...CAN I HELP YOU, SIR?

I join the line at the sneeze guard, wiping my eyes, dizzy from laughter. There's an old dude with a captain's hat on. I shit you not. I don't drink much socially, which causes me to tell him that I think he has a really super-duper hat. Truly. The little guy eyes me seriously through his thick specs. "Waiting in line like this," he says. "Reminds me of mess hall."

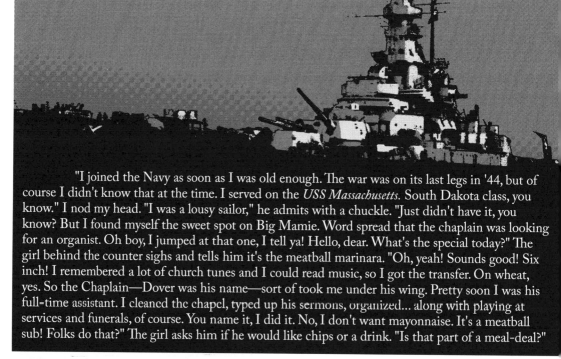

"I joined the Navy as soon as I was old enough. The war was on its last legs in '44, but of course I didn't know that at the time. I served on the *USS Massachusetts*. South Dakota class, you know." I nod my head. "I was a lousy sailor," he admits with a chuckle. "Just didn't have it, you know? But I found myself the sweet spot on Big Mamie. Word spread that the chaplain was looking for an organist. Oh boy, I jumped at that one, I tell ya! Hello, dear. What's the special today?" The girl behind the counter sighs and tells him it's the meatball marinara. "Oh, yeah! Sounds good! Six inch! I remembered a lot of church tunes and I could read music, so I got the transfer. On wheat, yes. So the Chaplain—Dover was his name—sort of took me under his wing. Pretty soon I was his full-time assistant. I cleaned the chapel, typed up his sermons, organized... along with playing at services and funerals, of course. You name it, I did it. No, I don't want mayonnaise. It's a meatball sub! Folks do that?" The girl asks him if he would like chips or a drink. "Is that part of a meal-deal?"

Dale is asleep in his booth. I forget to order and follow the old man to a sticky-clean booth over by the drink machine. "I wish they had Pepsi here instead of Coke," he says. "It's sweeter. Get as old as me and you can't taste anything. I like Pepsi because it's sweeter." He sits down. "So we fought through all sorts of air attacks near Okinawa. This was '45. We hit some choppy weather, passed right through the eye of a 100-knot typhoon. Oh, the crew was a mess. Puke everywhere. The mess, the halls, the bunks. Over half the crew was laid up, everyone was confined belowdecks, and Big Mamie just kept on *rollllllling* off them big waves." He pops the lid off of his cup and chews on an ice cube. "The Chaplain was sick too. Services were canceled for the week."

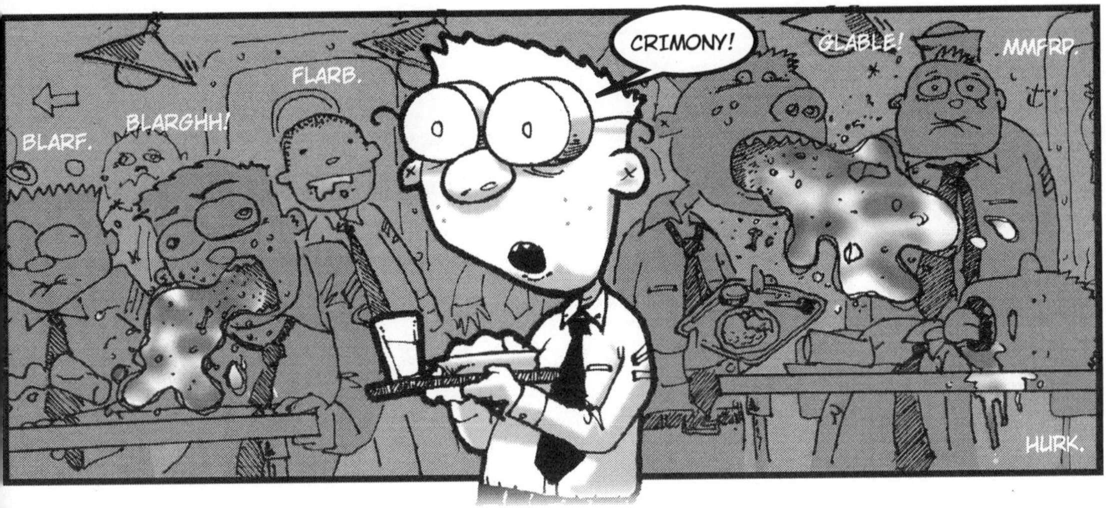
BLARF.
BLARGHH!
FLARB.
CRIMONY!
GLABLE!
MMFRP.
HURK.

"Now me, I was holding myself together pretty well for a kid from Nebraska, but I was almost at the end of my rope with the stench of puke everywhere. So I took my blanket and slept on the chapel floor. The chapel was the quietest, cleanest room on the ship, see? For three or four days I just stayed down there hidden away while we sloshed through that storm. Big Mamie just kept going *up* and *down*. Fixed the bindings on a few hymnals, vacuumed, practiced a little classical on the organ, you know. I went down to the mess hall to get chow each mealtime but couldn't stand to stay long before escaping back to my little paradise. All my buddies were sick in their racks anyway. Everyone was green-faced. Oh, the *smell!*"

"So anyway, I guess it was the fourth day, I run into a buddy of mine during one of my mess hall visits, 'Irish' Jimmy Callahan. I hadn't seen a familiar face in days, you see. So Jimmy says 'You're alive! You're alive!' and I say 'You've gone crazy, Irish!' and then he tells me that I'd been reported overboard! Every hour for two days they'd been calling my name over the ship intercom. But of course I hadn't heard it. The chapel was the only room aboard that didn't have a PA speaker... Because of services, see? Boy, did I get chewed out by the XO! They'd reported me *dead!*" The old man pulls at his meal deal potato chip bag. "Never let the government tell you you're dead, son. The paperwork will kill you."

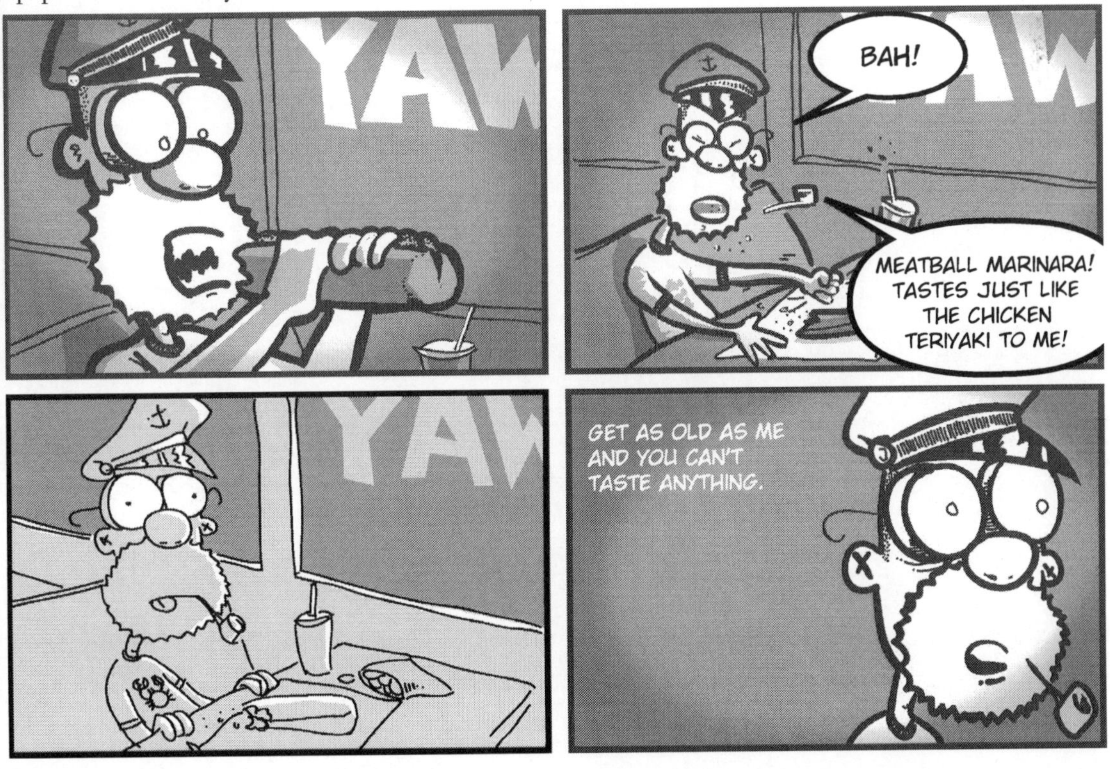
YAW
BAH!
MEATBALL MARINARA! TASTES JUST LIKE THE CHICKEN TERIYAKI TO ME!
YAW
GET AS OLD AS ME AND YOU CAN'T TASTE ANYTHING.

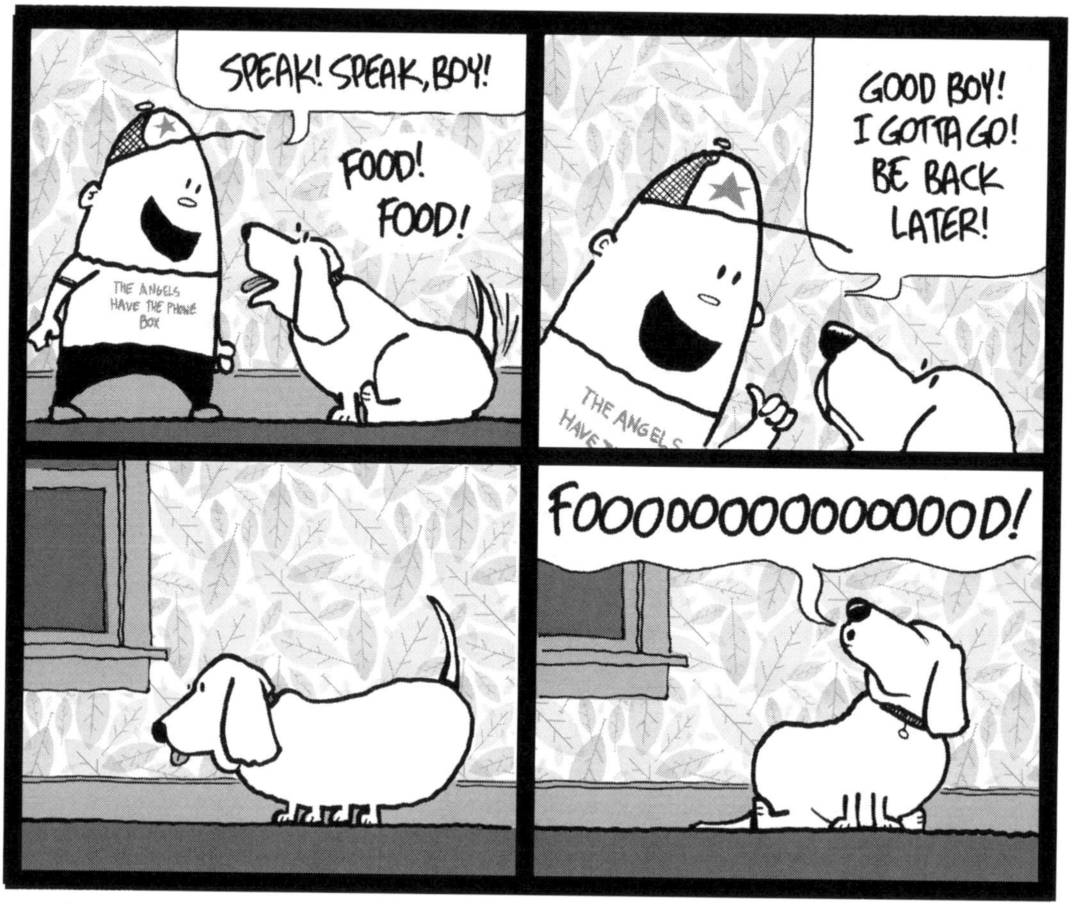
SPEAK! SPEAK, BOY!
FOOD! FOOD!
THE ANGELS HAVE THE PHONE BOX
GOOD BOY! I GOTTA GO! BE BACK LATER!
THE ANGELS HAVE
FOOOOOOOOOOOOOOD!

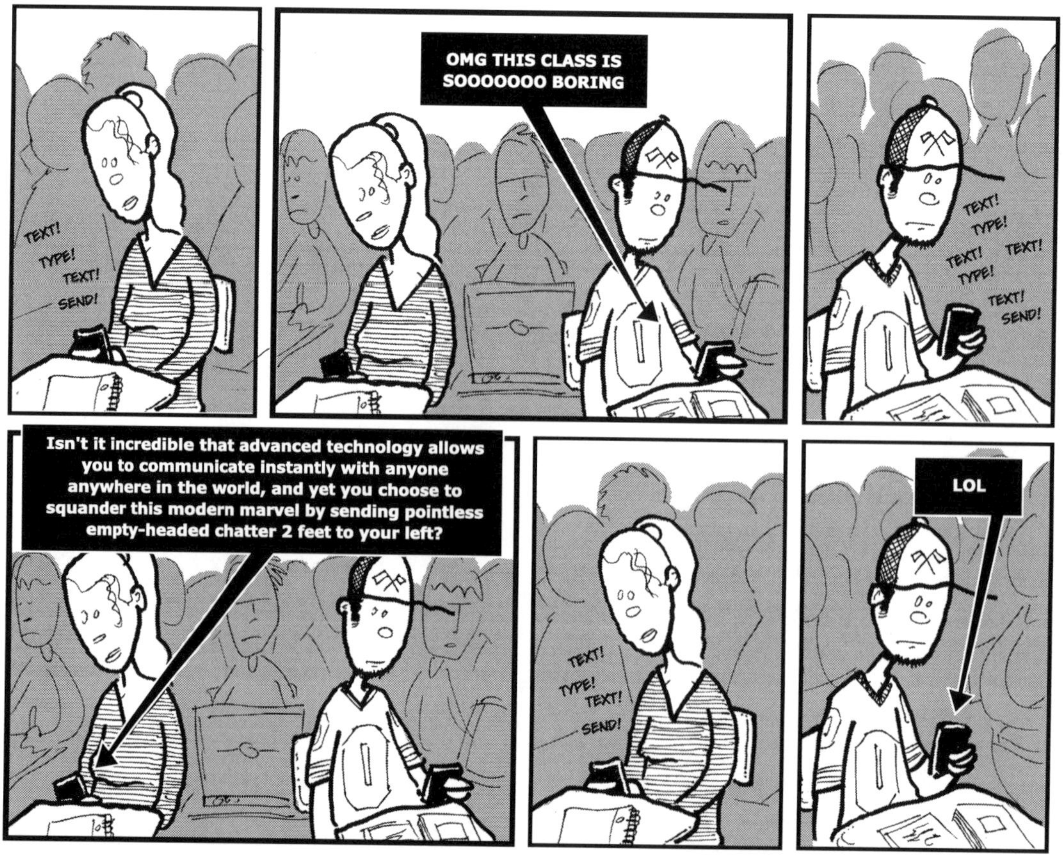
TEXT! TYPE! TEXT! SEND!
OMG THIS CLASS IS SOOOOOOO BORING
TEXT! TYPE! TEXT! TEXT! TYPE! TEXT! SEND!
Isn't it incredible that advanced technology allows you to communicate instantly with anyone anywhere in the world, and yet you choose to squander this modern marvel by sending pointless empty-headed chatter 2 feet to your left?
TEXT! TYPE! TEXT! SEND!
LOL

Travel Mug
I LOVE THIS TRAVEL MUG.
I WANT TO SLEEP WITH THIS TRAVEL MUG UNDER MY PILLOW. I WANT TO CHOP OFF MY HAND AND SURGICALLY MOUNT THIS TRAVEL MUG ONTO THE BLOODY STUMP.
I WANT TO MARRY THIS TRAVEL MUG AND TAKE IT ON AN EXOTIC HONEYMOON.
I WANT TO BE CREMATED AND BURIED IN THIS TRAVEL MUG. I WANT TO SPEND ETERNITY INSIDE THIS TRAVEL MUG.
I THINK YOU'RE A LITTLE TOO EMOTIONALLY ATTACHED TO YOUR CONSUMER GOODS.
I LOVE THIS TRAVEL MUG.

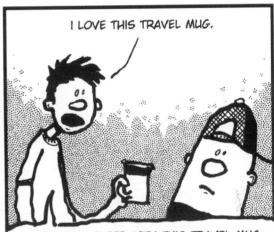

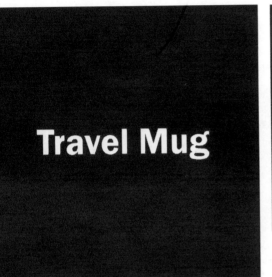

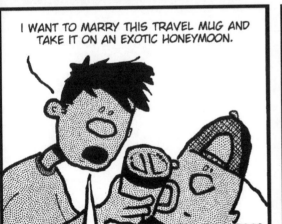

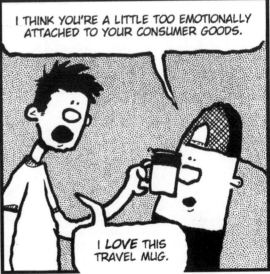

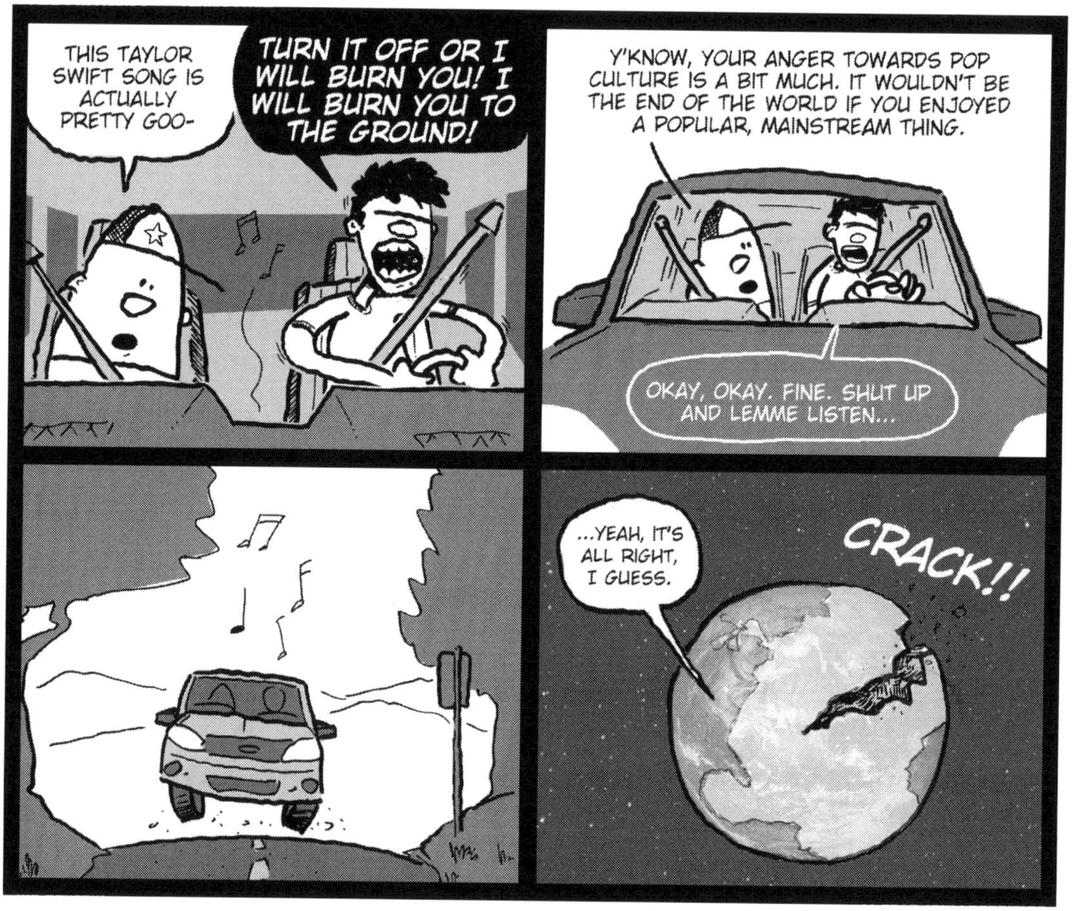
THIS TAYLOR SWIFT SONG IS ACTUALLY PRETTY GOO-
TURN IT OFF OR I WILL BURN YOU! I WILL BURN YOU TO THE GROUND!
Y'KNOW, YOUR ANGER TOWARDS POP CULTURE IS A BIT MUCH. IT WOULDN'T BE THE END OF THE WORLD IF YOU ENJOYED A POPULAR, MAINSTREAM THING.
OKAY, OKAY. FINE. SHUT UP AND LEMME LISTEN...
...YEAH, IT'S ALL RIGHT, I GUESS.
CRACK!!

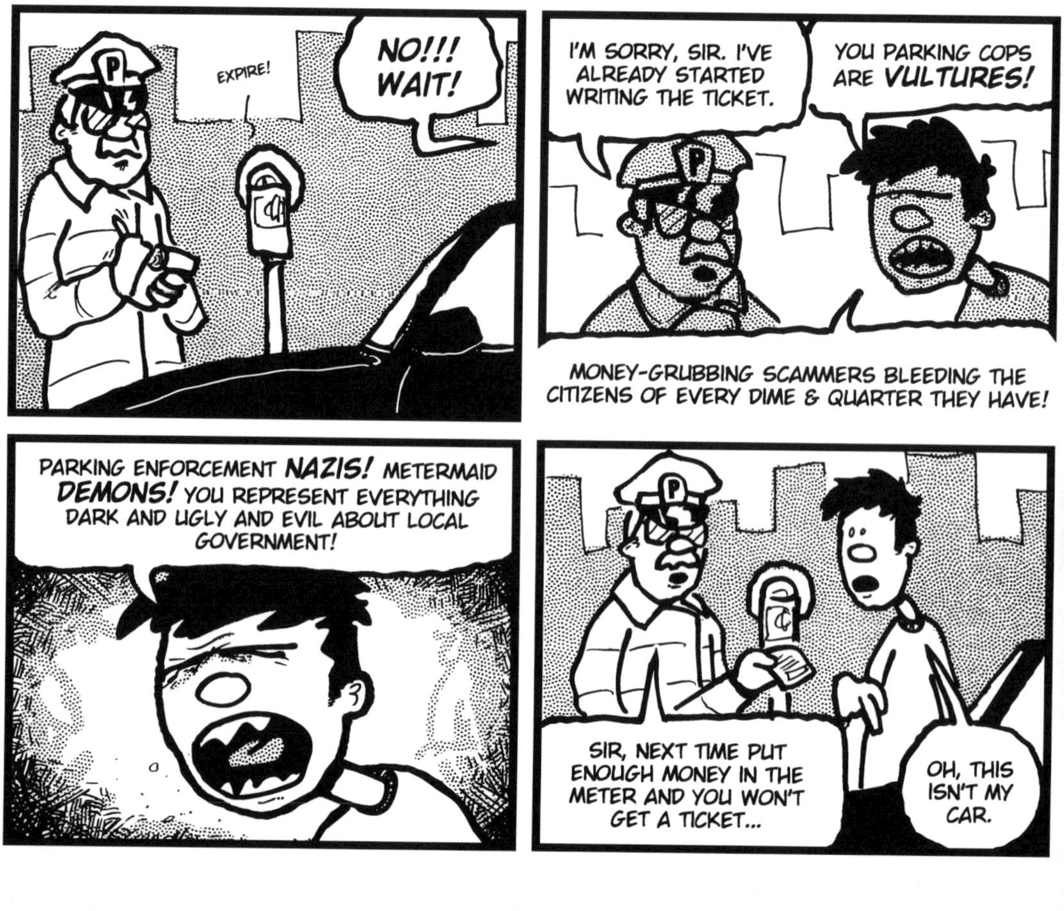
EXPIRE!
NO!!! WAIT!
I'M SORRY, SIR. I'VE ALREADY STARTED WRITING THE TICKET.
YOU PARKING COPS ARE VULTURES!
MONEY-GRUBBING SCAMMERS BLEEDING THE CITIZENS OF EVERY DIME & QUARTER THEY HAVE!
PARKING ENFORCEMENT NAZIS! METERMAID DEMONS! YOU REPRESENT EVERYTHING DARK AND UGLY AND EVIL ABOUT LOCAL GOVERNMENT!
SIR, NEXT TIME PUT ENOUGH MONEY IN THE METER AND YOU WON'T GET A TICKET...
OH, THIS ISN'T MY CAR.

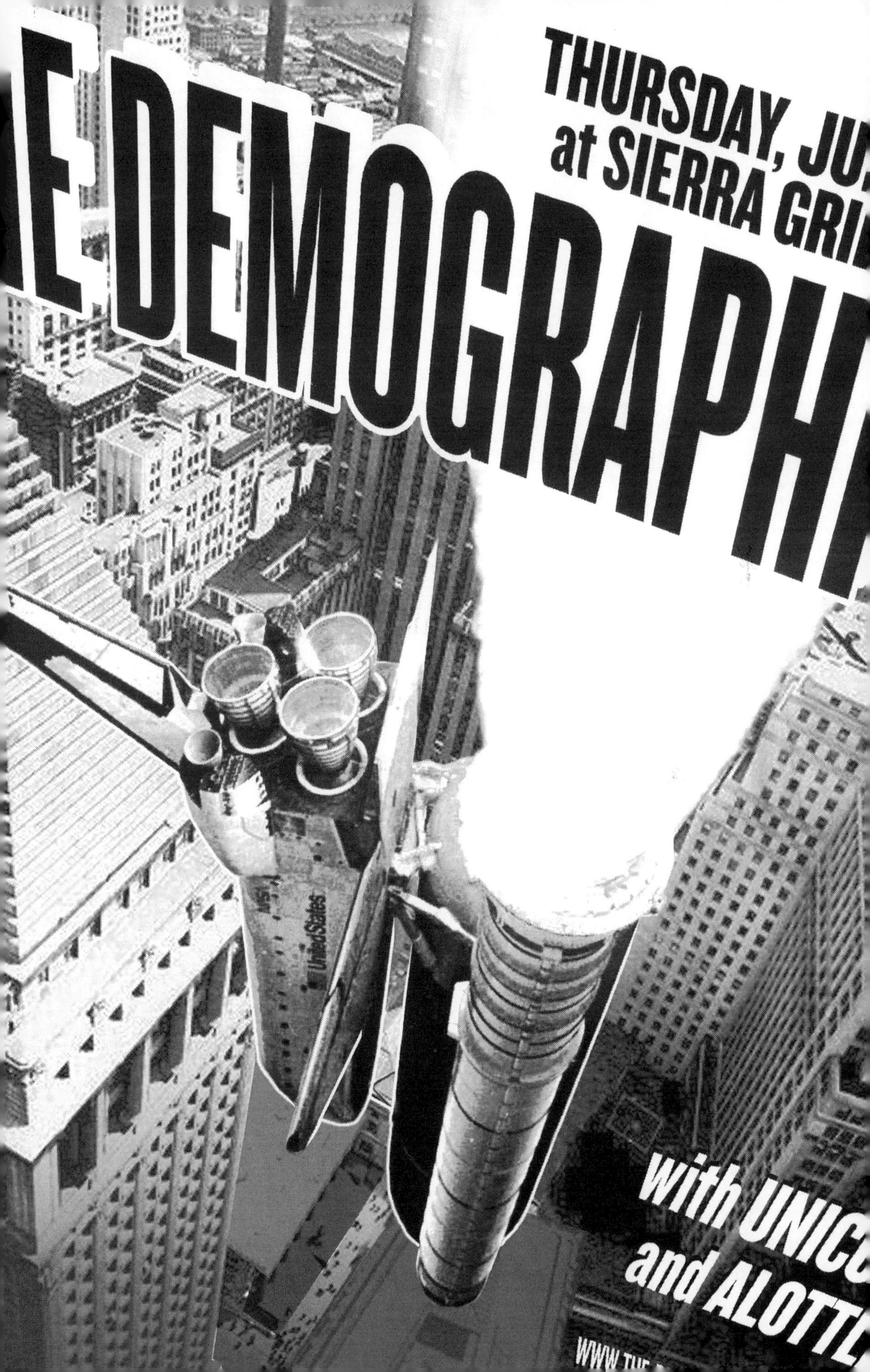

E DEMOGRAPHI
THURSDAY, JU
at SIERRA GRI
United States
with UNIC
and ALOTT
WWW.THE

THE CASH REGISTER TOLLS FOR THEE

It was an average night at the dollar store: the elderly were pocketing ceramic bird figurines while children were buying things with handfuls of pennies. Unknown brand names lined the shelves. The blank audio cassettes, hair scrunchies, and Virgin Mary nightlights were selling briskly. I answered customer inquiries such as "How much is this?" and "Is this a dollar?" and "How much would two of these cost?"

This was southern New Hampshire, the early 1990s, and I worked at All For a Dollar. I pushed buttons on a cash register, I stocked shelves, I cleaned. It was a low-pressure work environment, and I was one of the better employees. My minimal investment of effort somehow made me an outstanding worker in the eyes of my superiors, and I was promoted to Assistant Manager (I wanted a name tag that said ASS MAN but I was told that this was not going to happen). For a 20-year-old cartoonist looking to avoid responsibility and get a paycheck, this job provided a lovely place to sit.

I was slouched behind the counter one night, drawing a comic and listening to the mall's Tape Loop Of Hits play over and over again. The Tape Loop Of Hits emanated from a speaker somewhere above the bootleg "Co-ed Naked" t-shirt kiosk outside my store's entrance. You could gauge the length of your shift by how many times you'd heard the instrumental version of The Cranberries' 1993 hit "Linger."

An angry-looking mom led her crying son into the store by his wrist. They'd been in shopping a little while earlier, and I sensed my night was about to get annoying. She strode up to my register. "What do you have to say?" she demanded.

I froze. Had she witnessed me and my part-timer cutting open glow sticks and splattering the toxic stuff on the ceiling ("It looks like stars!")? Had she seen me taking Ramen Noodles off the front end cap for my lunch? Could she see I was drawing a comic about annoying All For a Dollar customers? I panicked. The boy looked up at his mother and made a blubbering noise. Ahh, she was talking to him. Good good good.

"I'm sorry," the little boy sobbed at the floor. I smiled my vacuous retail worker smile, because I didn't understand or care about what was going on.

"What did you do?" the mother asked in a disappointed voice.

He held a small toy truck out to me with his free hand. "I took it," he said to me, bursting into fresh tears.

I held my empty smile. I still didn't really care. The dollar store bled merchandise every day. Shoplifting was built into the business plan. I looked at the boy and said "Oh yeah?" I looked at his mother with my blank, dumb smile. She didn't smile back.

"And what do *you* say?" she said to me. To *me!* What did *I* do? I was baffled. I looked down at the wet-faced child and reality hit me like a ton of Virgin Mary nightlights: *This kid was afraid of me.* This wretched woman had recruited me in the effort to discipline her beastly snot-factory. Without my consent, she had appointed me the representative of AUTHORITY. I had been shanghaied. My carefree days of youthful irresponsibility came crashing to a halt. With just a few words, she had transformed me into the one thing I most despised: I had become THE MAN.

I held out my hand and accepted a toy that probably had a wholesale price of twelve cents. I dropped my retail smile and spoke to the boy in as serious a voice as I could muster. I said the only thing I could think of. I said, "Stealing is bad." He cried even more. Gross booger bubble.

"We're *very* sorry," the mother said to me. "Aren't we," she scowled at her son. He made a gurgling mucus-y sound of anguish and she led him out of the store. I stood at the counter, dumbfounded, contemplating my new role in the world, the Mantle of Responsibility weighing heavily upon my shoulders. A man approached me from the back of the store. His hand held a spatula; his eyes held a question.

"It's a dollar," I said.

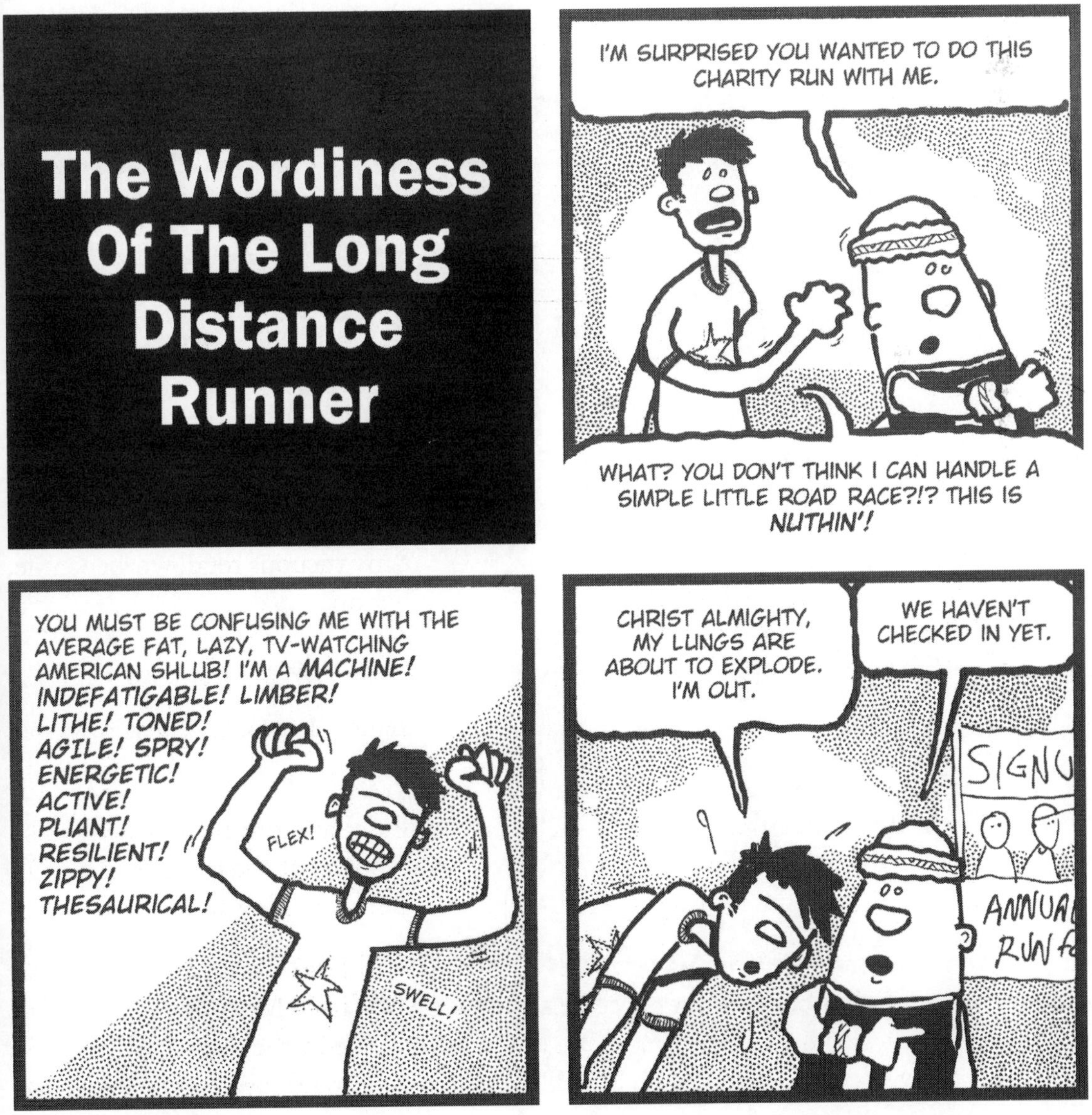

The Wordiness Of The Long Distance Runner
I'M SURPRISED YOU WANTED TO DO THIS CHARITY RUN WITH ME.
WHAT? YOU DON'T THINK I CAN HANDLE A SIMPLE LITTLE ROAD RACE?!? THIS IS NUTHIN'!
YOU MUST BE CONFUSING ME WITH THE AVERAGE FAT, LAZY, TV-WATCHING AMERICAN SHLUB! I'M A MACHINE! INDEFATIGABLE! LIMBER! LITHE! TONED! AGILE! SPRY! ENERGETIC! ACTIVE! PLIANT! RESILIENT! ZIPPY! THESAURICAL!
FLEX!
SWELL!
CHRIST ALMIGHTY, MY LUNGS ARE ABOUT TO EXPLODE. I'M OUT.
WE HAVEN'T CHECKED IN YET.
SIGNU
ANNUA
RUN f

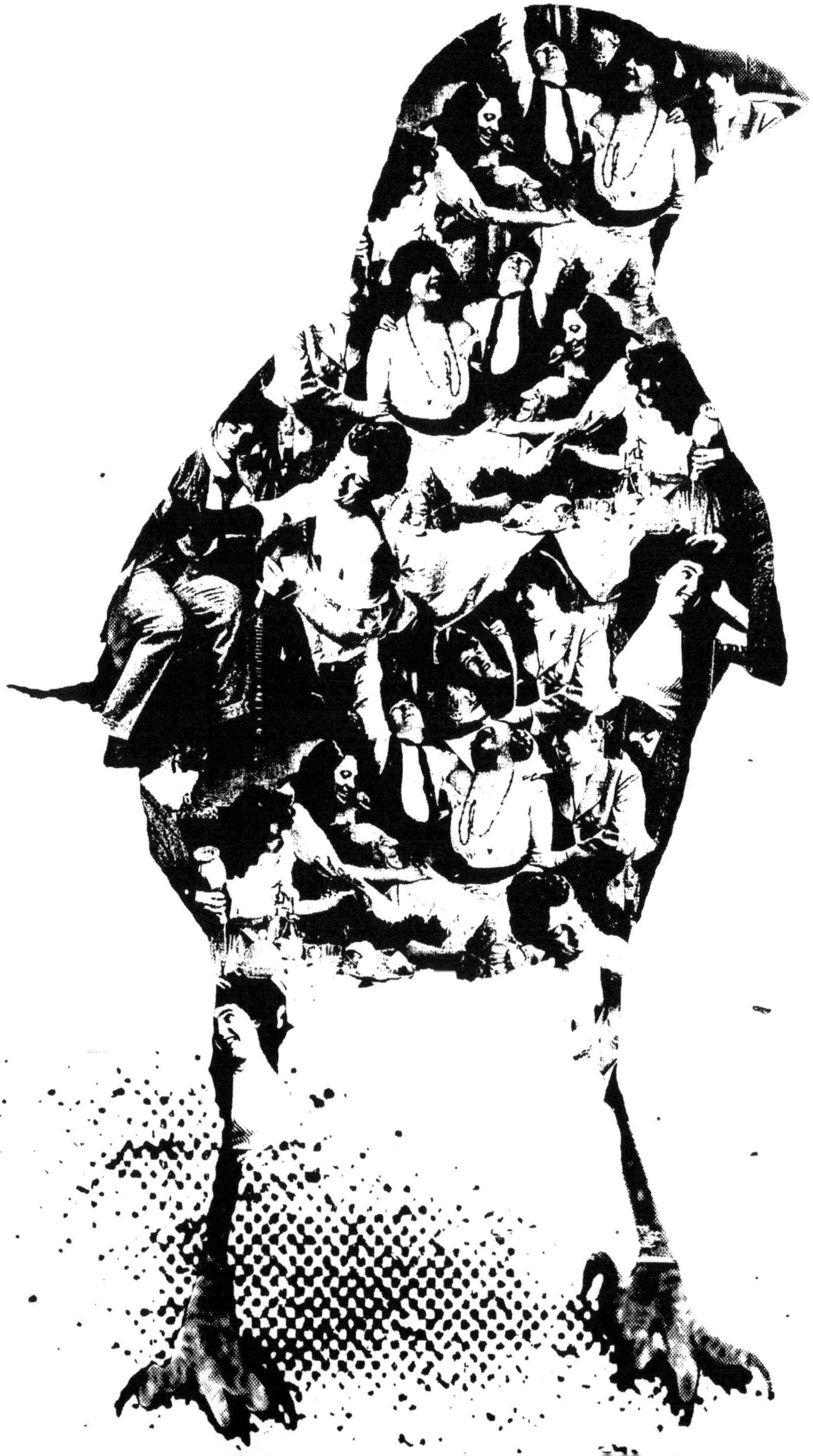

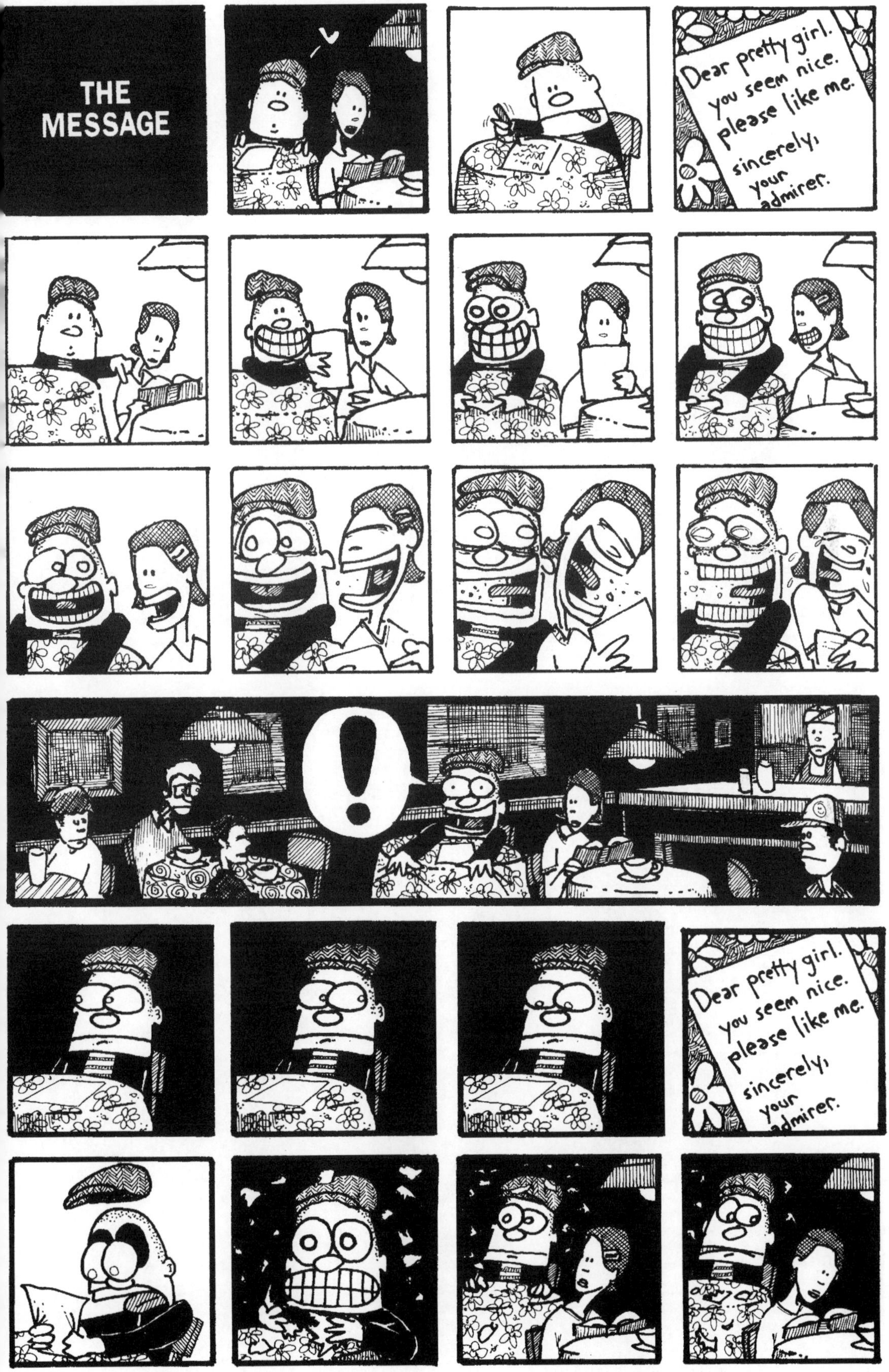
THE MESSAGE
Dear pretty girl.
you seem nice.
please like me.
sincerely,
your
admirer.
!
Dear pretty girl.
you seem nice.
please like me.
sincerely,
your
admirer.

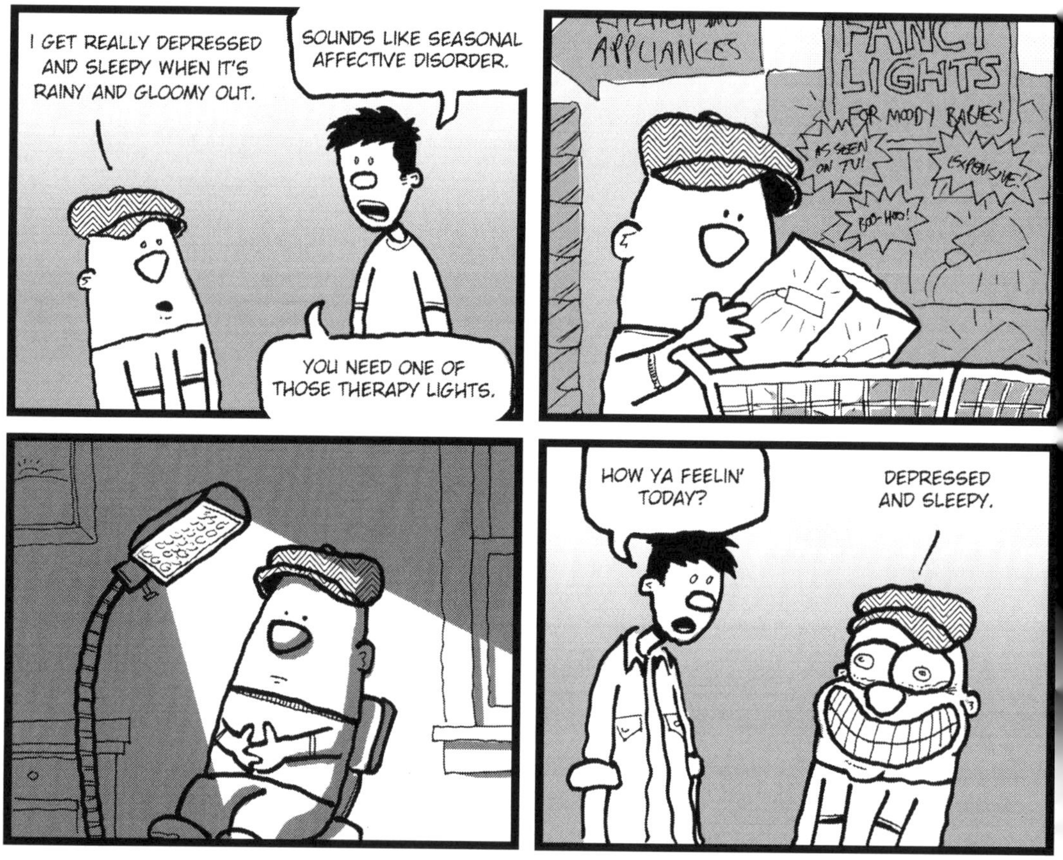
I GET REALLY DEPRESSED AND SLEEPY WHEN IT'S RAINY AND GLOOMY OUT.
SOUNDS LIKE SEASONAL AFFECTIVE DISORDER.
YOU NEED ONE OF THOSE THERAPY LIGHTS.
APPLIANCES
FANCY LIGHTS
FOR MOODY BABIES!
AS SEEN ON TV!
EXPENSIVE!
BOO-HOO!
HOW YA FEELIN' TODAY?
DEPRESSED AND SLEEPY.

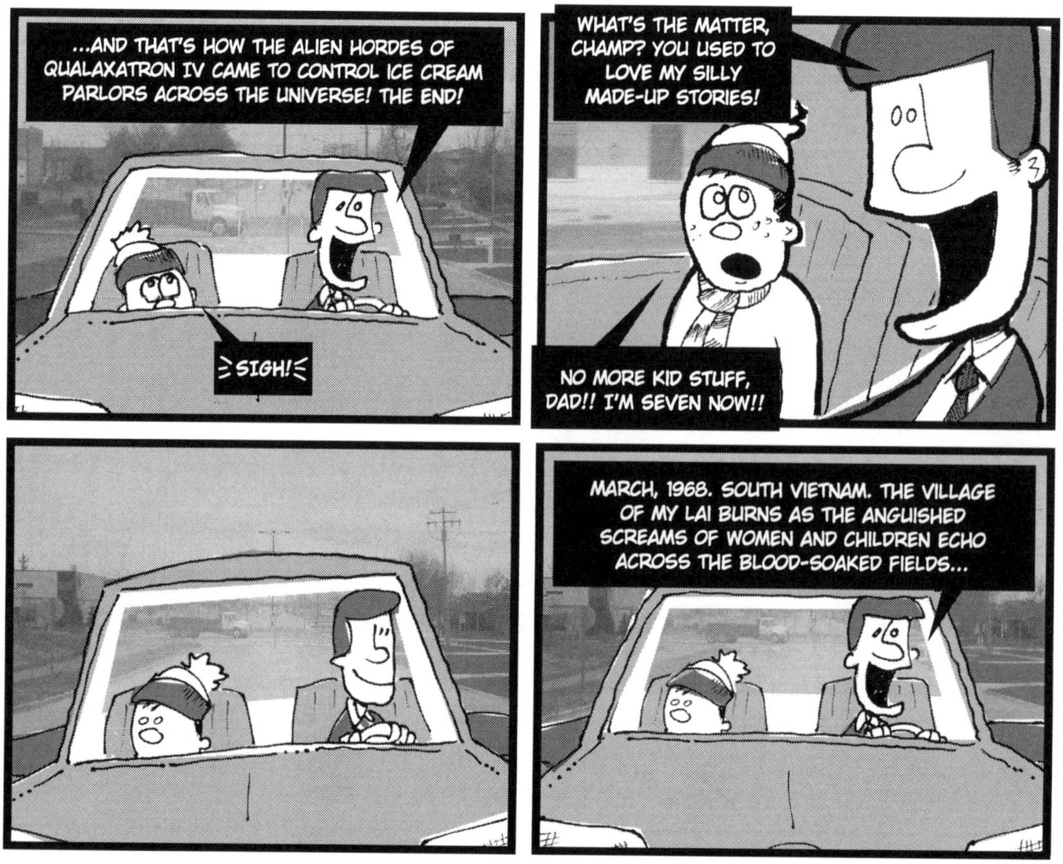
...AND THAT'S HOW THE ALIEN HORDES OF QUALAXATRON IV CAME TO CONTROL ICE CREAM PARLORS ACROSS THE UNIVERSE! THE END!
SIGH!
WHAT'S THE MATTER, CHAMP? YOU USED TO LOVE MY SILLY MADE-UP STORIES!
NO MORE KID STUFF, DAD!! I'M SEVEN NOW!!
MARCH, 1968. SOUTH VIETNAM. THE VILLAGE OF MY LAI BURNS AS THE ANGUISHED SCREAMS OF WOMEN AND CHILDREN ECHO ACROSS THE BLOOD-SOAKED FIELDS...

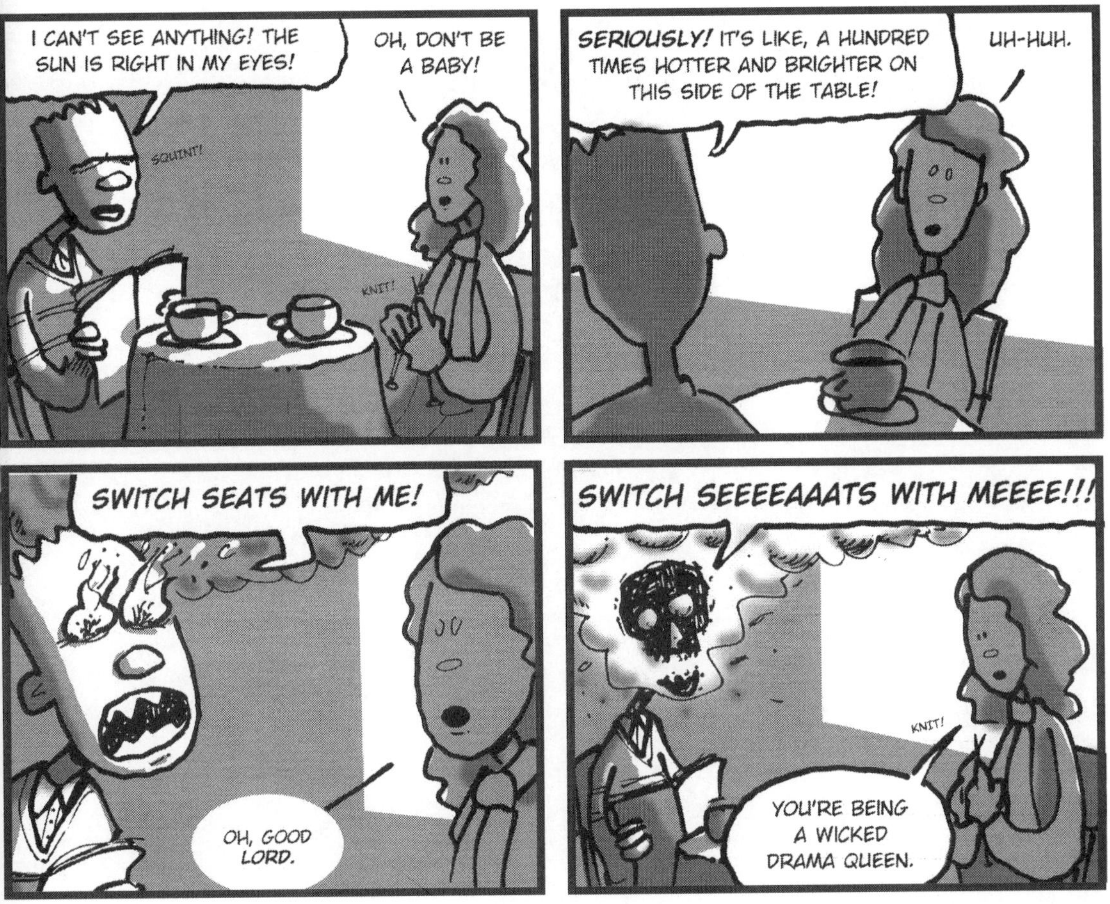
I CAN'T SEE ANYTHING! THE SUN IS RIGHT IN MY EYES!
SQUINT!
OH, DON'T BE A BABY!
KNIT!
SERIOUSLY! IT'S LIKE, A HUNDRED TIMES HOTTER AND BRIGHTER ON THIS SIDE OF THE TABLE!
UH-HUH.
SWITCH SEATS WITH ME!
OH, GOOD LORD.
SWITCH SEEEEAAATS WITH MEEEE!!!
KNIT!
YOU'RE BEING A WICKED DRAMA QUEEN.

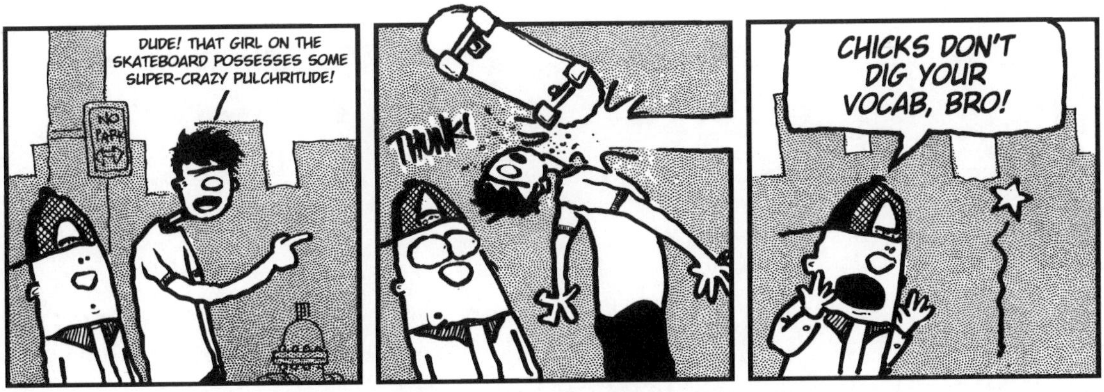
DUDE! THAT GIRL ON THE SKATEBOARD POSSESSES SOME SUPER-CRAZY PULCHRITUDE!
NO PARK
THUNK!
CHICKS DON'T DIG YOUR VOCAB, BRO!

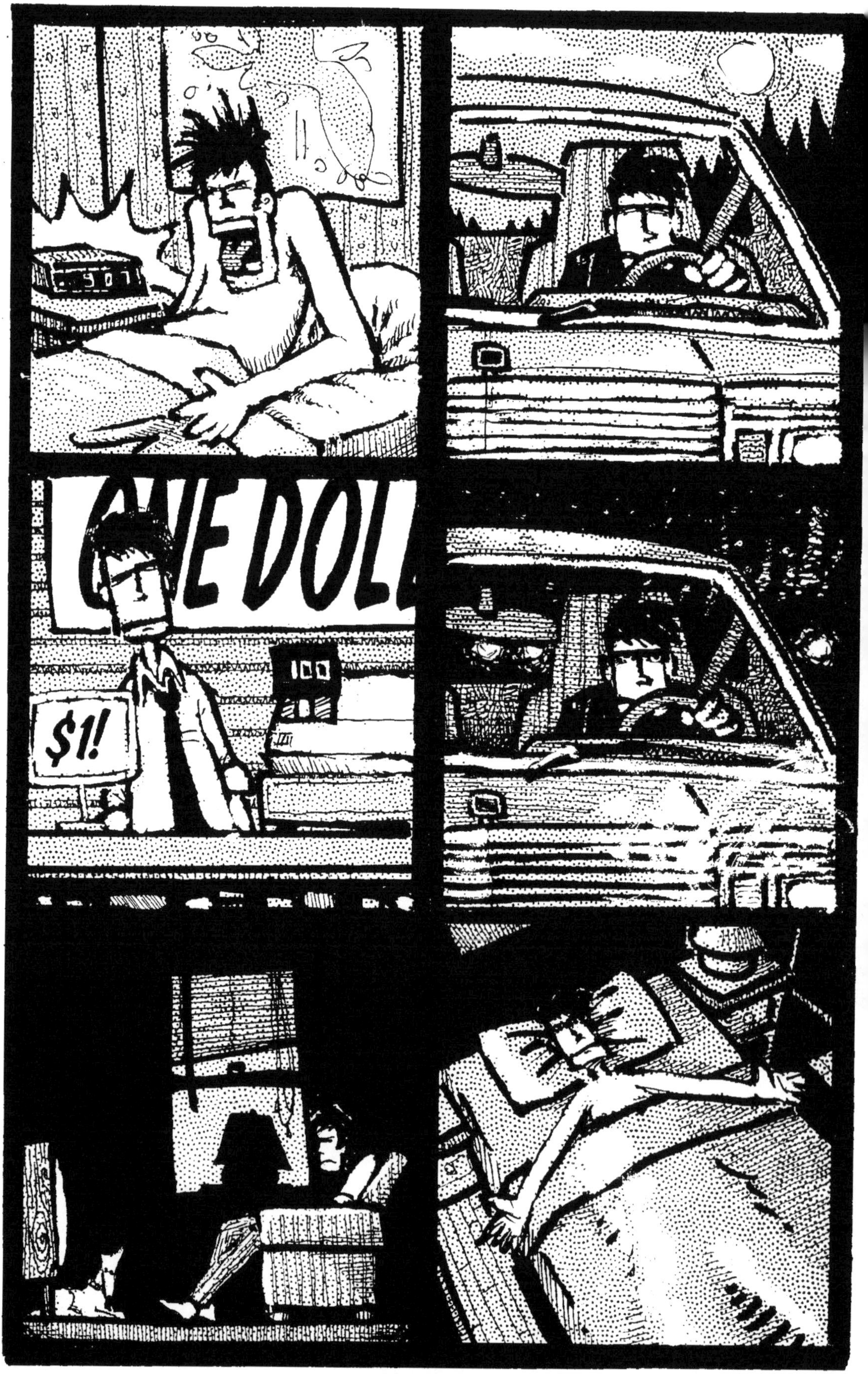
$1!

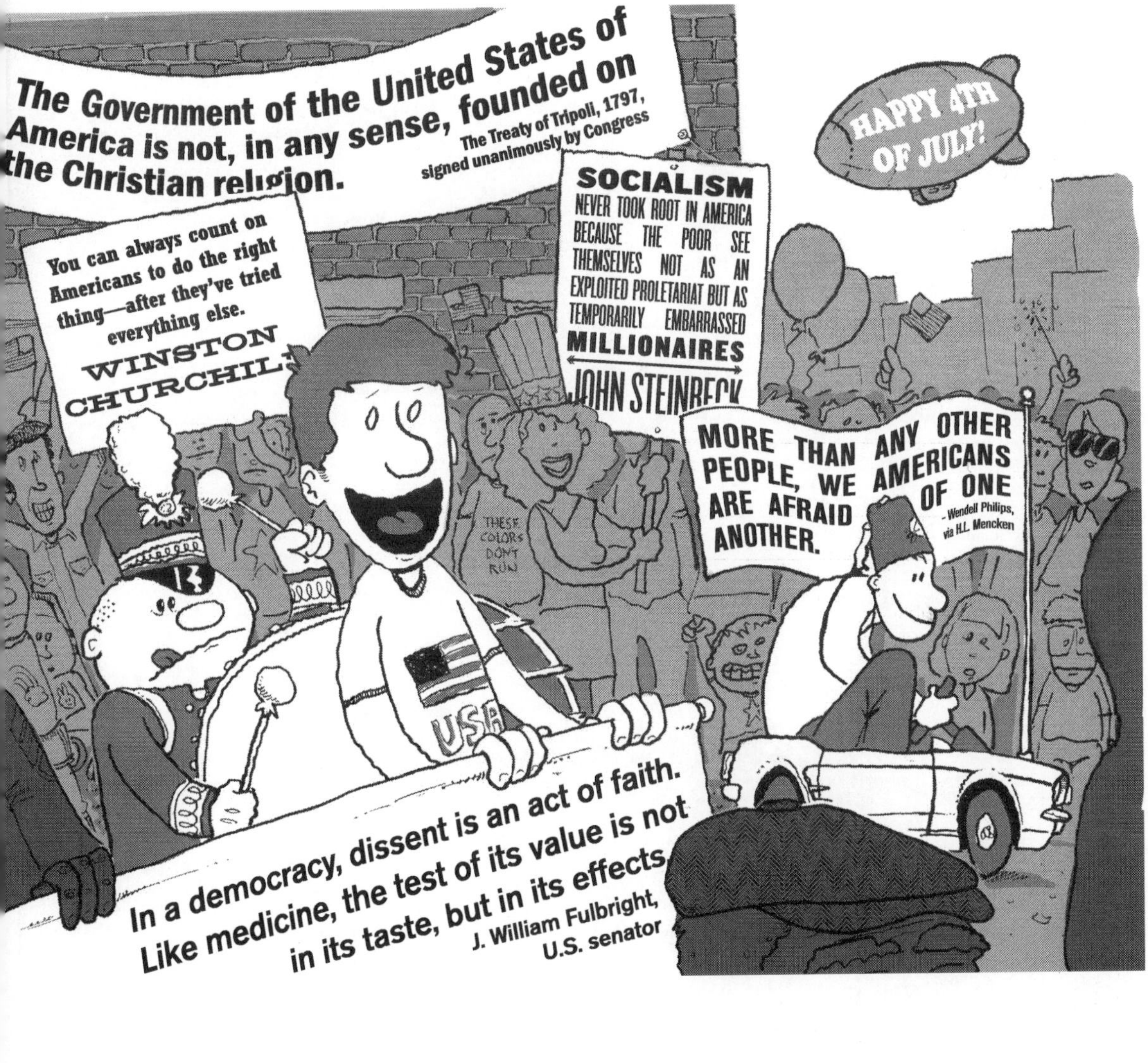
The Government of the United States of America is not, in any sense, founded on the Christian religion.
The Treaty of Tripoli, 1797, signed unanimously by Congress
You can always count on Americans to do the right thing—after they've tried everything else.
WINSTON CHURCHILL
SOCIALISM NEVER TOOK ROOT IN AMERICA BECAUSE THE POOR SEE THEMSELVES NOT AS AN EXPLOITED PROLETARIAT BUT AS TEMPORARILY EMBARRASSED MILLIONAIRES
JOHN STEINBECK
HAPPY 4TH OF JULY!
THESE COLORS DON'T RUN
USA
MORE THAN ANY OTHER PEOPLE, WE AMERICANS ARE AFRAID OF ONE ANOTHER.
- Wendell Philips, via H.L. Mencken
In a democracy, dissent is an act of faith. Like medicine, the test of its value is not in its taste, but in its effects.
J. William Fulbright, U.S. senator

OH, NO!

The man-sized cat isn't feeling well! Let's color him better!

<u>COLOR KEY:</u> A. Orange B. Blue C. Every crayon you own.

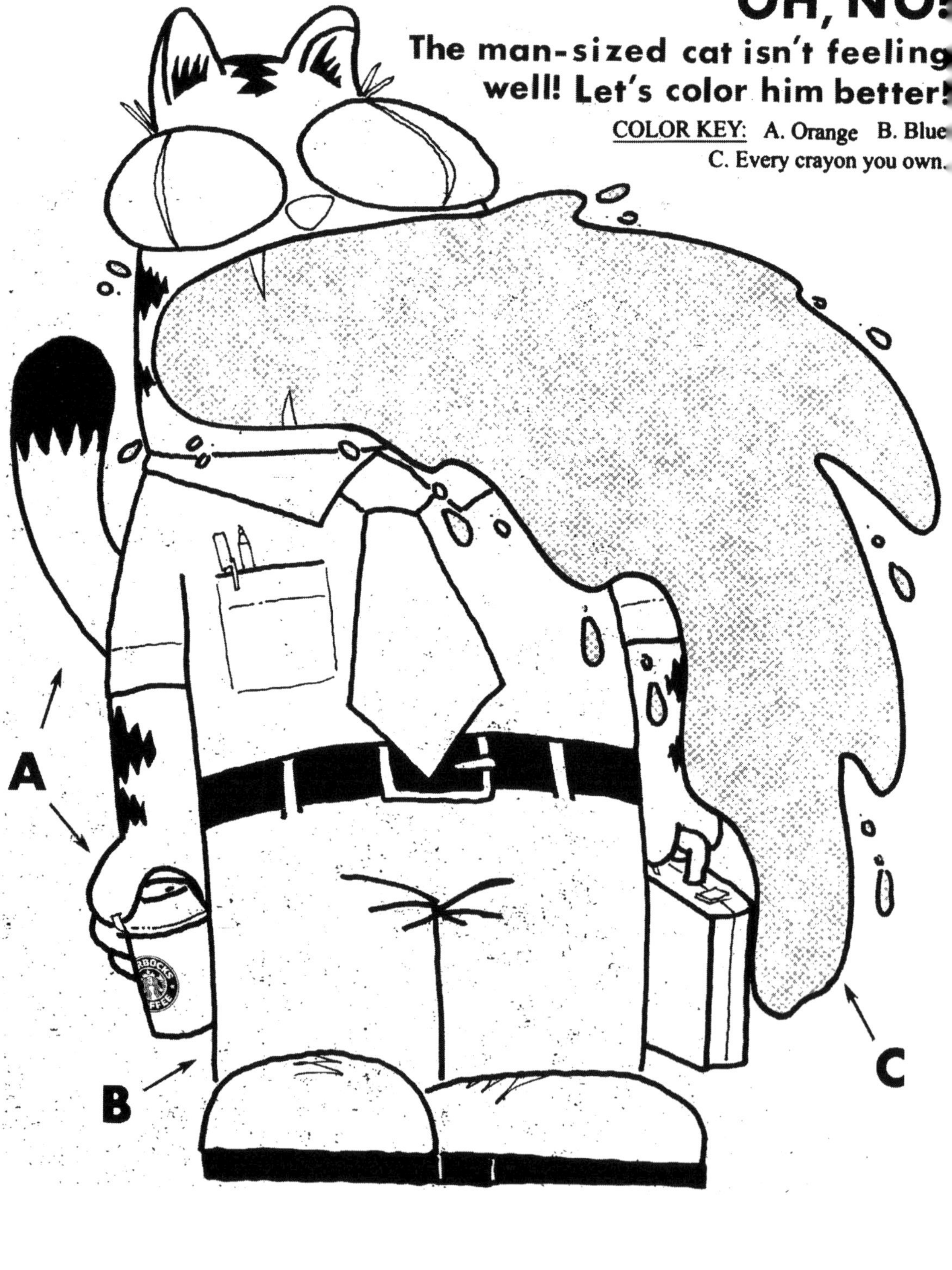
A
B
C

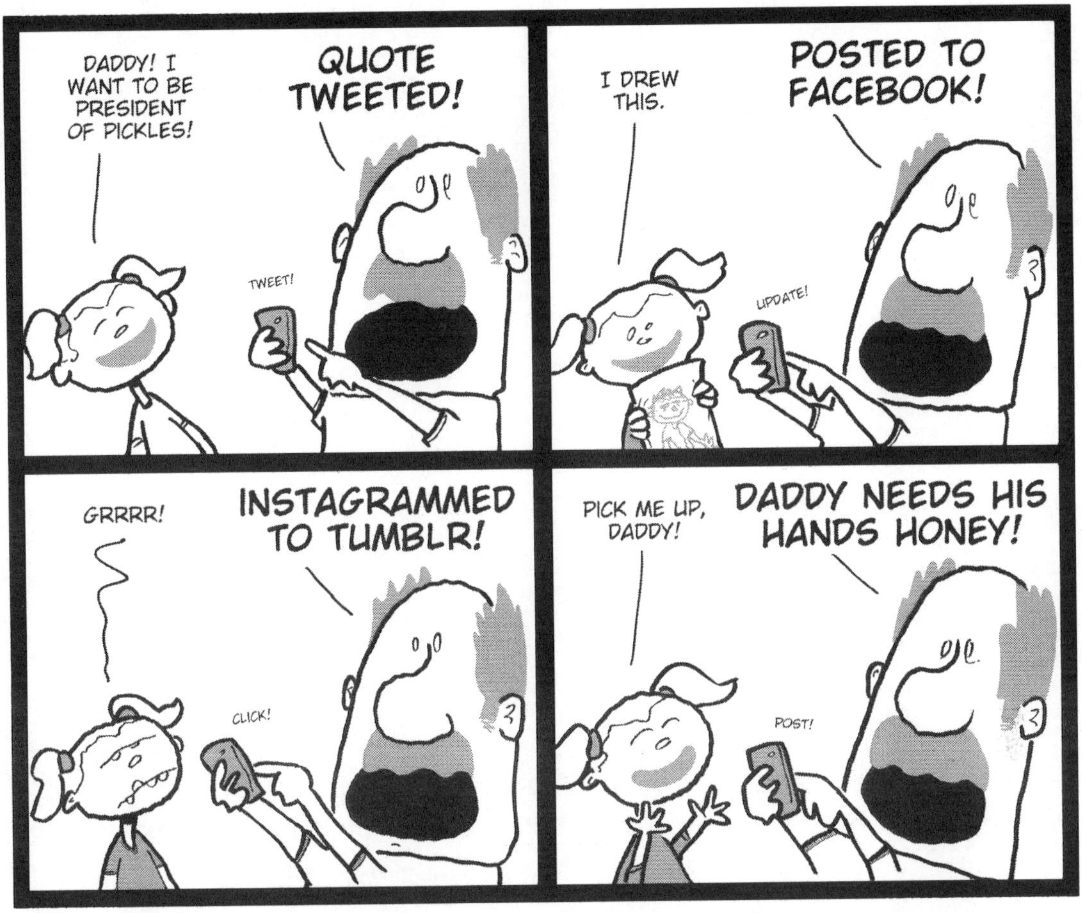
DADDY! I WANT TO BE PRESIDENT OF PICKLES!
QUOTE TWEETED!
TWEET!
I DREW THIS.
POSTED TO FACEBOOK!
UPDATE!
GRRRR!
INSTAGRAMMED TO TUMBLR!
CLICK!
PICK ME UP, DADDY!
DADDY NEEDS HIS HANDS HONEY!
POST!

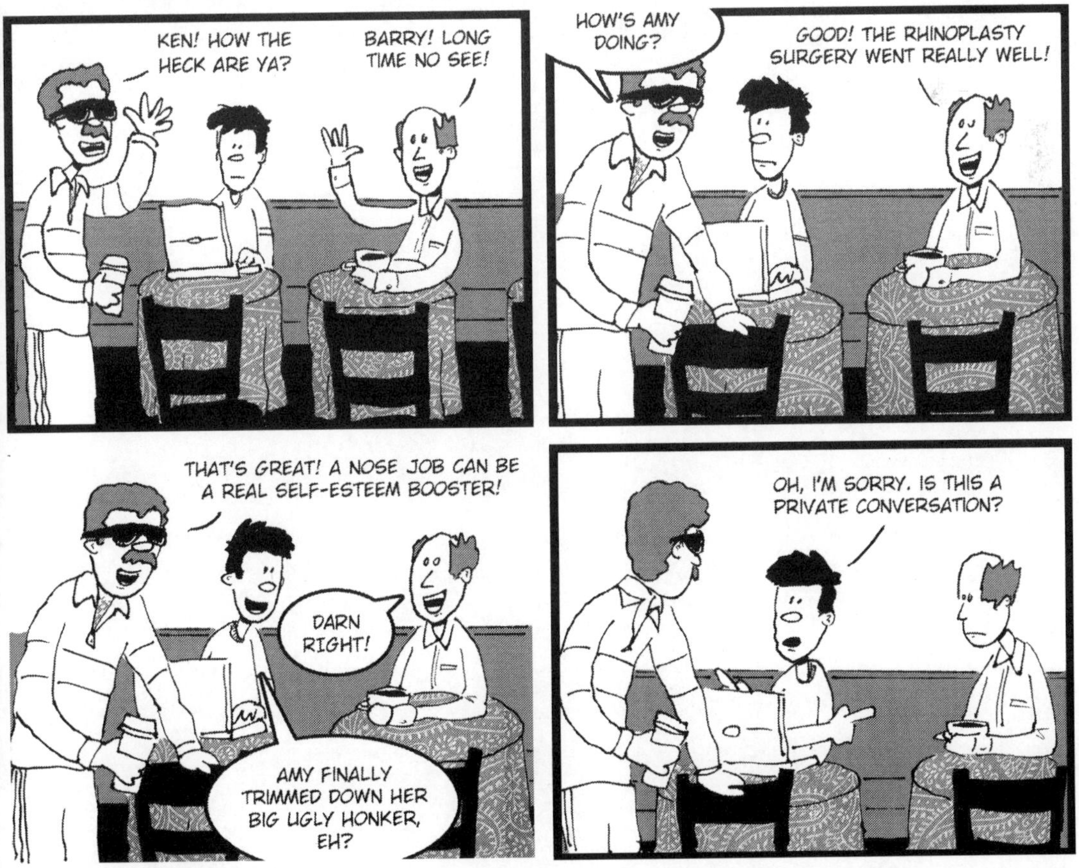
KEN! HOW THE HECK ARE YA?
BARRY! LONG TIME NO SEE!
HOW'S AMY DOING?
GOOD! THE RHINOPLASTY SURGERY WENT REALLY WELL!
THAT'S GREAT! A NOSE JOB CAN BE A REAL SELF-ESTEEM BOOSTER!
DARN RIGHT!
AMY FINALLY TRIMMED DOWN HER BIG UGLY HONKER, EH?
OH, I'M SORRY. IS THIS A PRIVATE CONVERSATION?

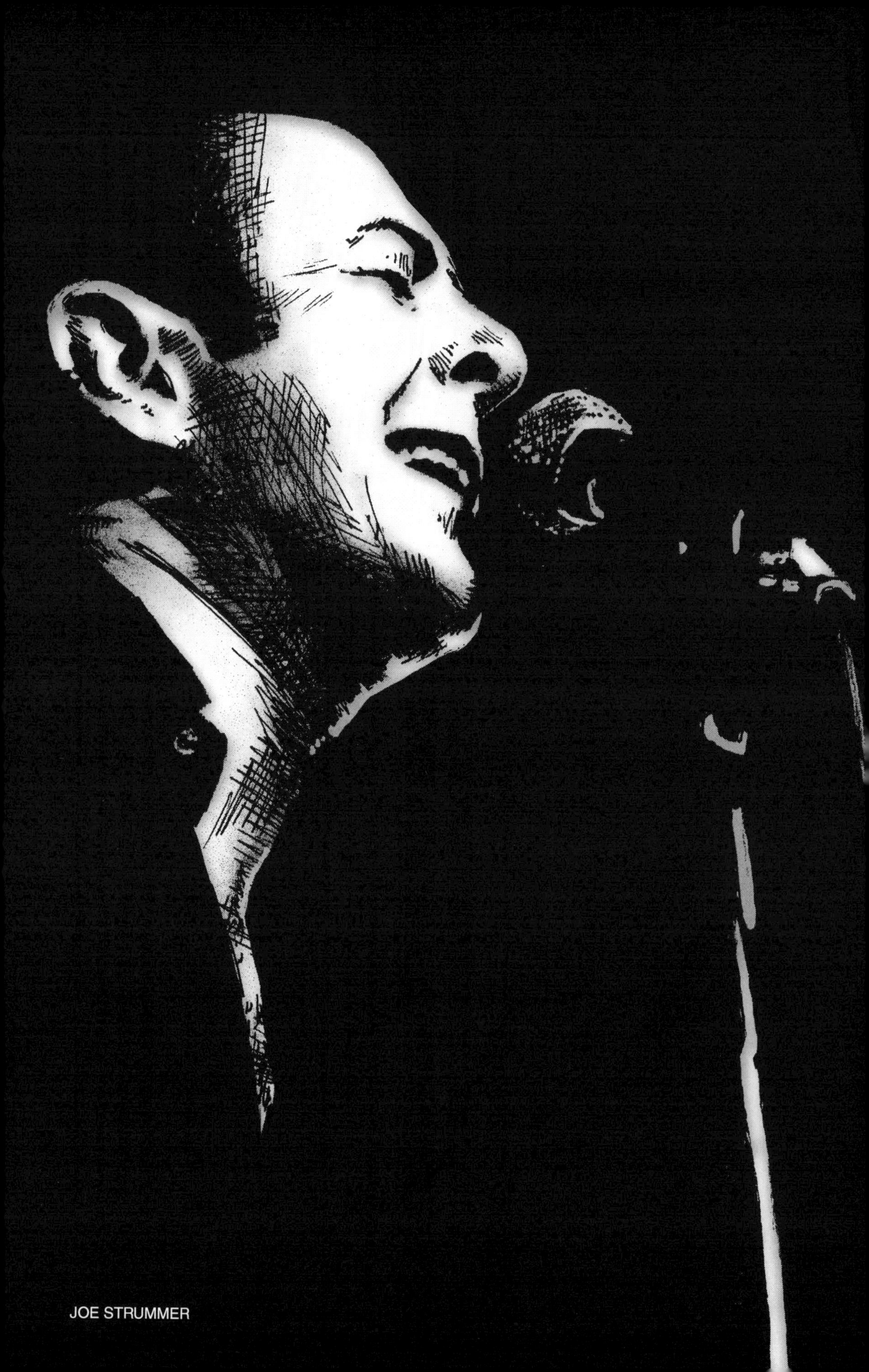

JOE STRUMMER

SAY, HOW'S THE WATER?
COLD!
HOW COLD IS IT?
I JUST CHECKED MY TESTICLES FOR LUMPS BY MOVING MY TONGUE AROUND.

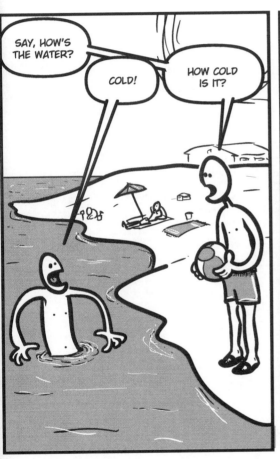

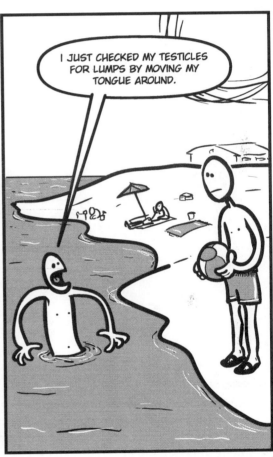

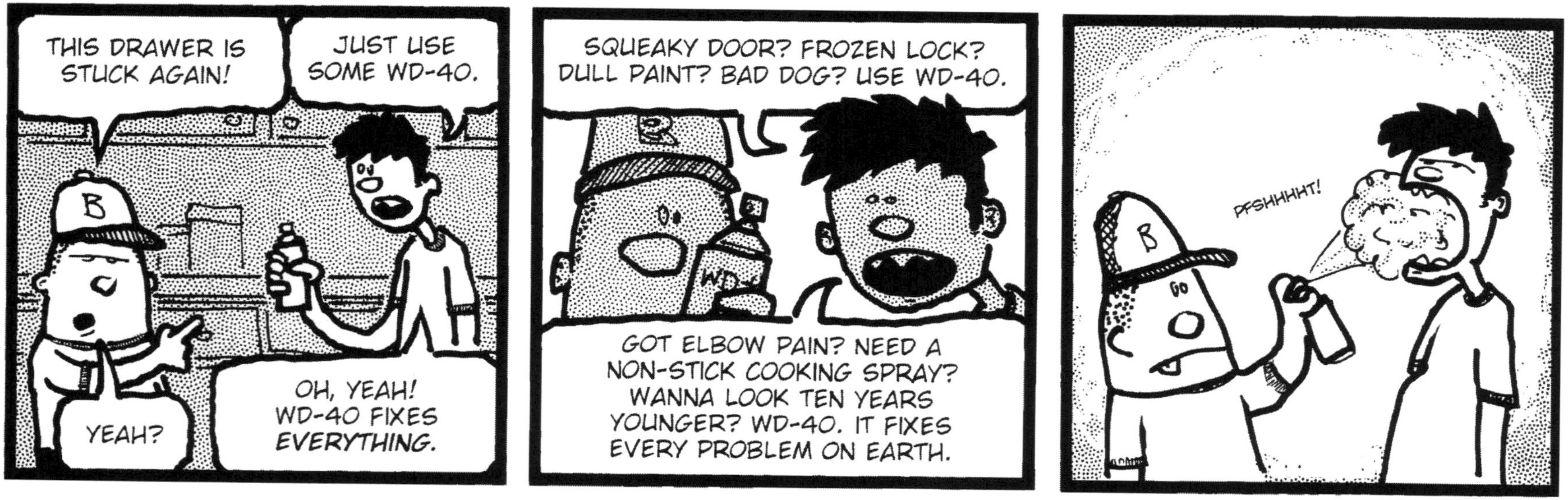
THIS DRAWER IS STUCK AGAIN!
JUST USE SOME WD-40.
YEAH?
OH, YEAH! WD-40 FIXES EVERYTHING.
SQUEAKY DOOR? FROZEN LOCK? DULL PAINT? BAD DOG? USE WD-40.
GOT ELBOW PAIN? NEED A NON-STICK COOKING SPRAY? WANNA LOOK TEN YEARS YOUNGER? WD-40. IT FIXES EVERY PROBLEM ON EARTH.
PFSHHHHT!

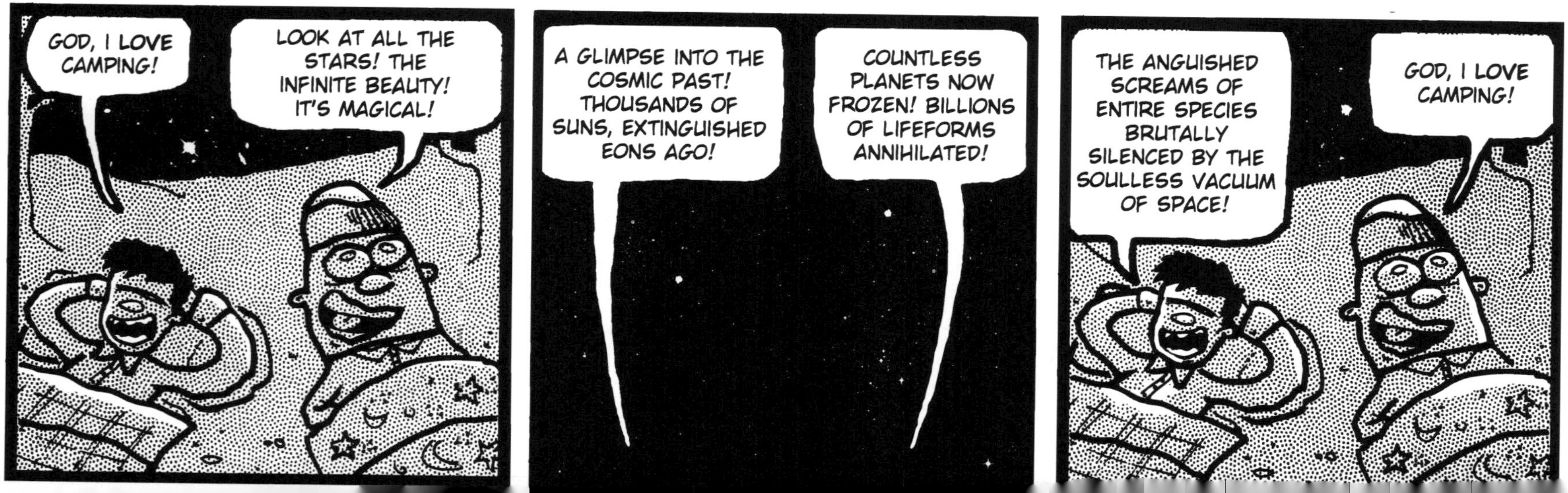
GOD, I LOVE CAMPING!
LOOK AT ALL THE STARS! THE INFINITE BEAUTY! IT'S MAGICAL!
A GLIMPSE INTO THE COSMIC PAST! THOUSANDS OF SUNS, EXTINGUISHED EONS AGO!
COUNTLESS PLANETS NOW FROZEN! BILLIONS OF LIFEFORMS ANNIHILATED!
THE ANGUISHED SCREAMS OF ENTIRE SPECIES BRUTALLY SILENCED BY THE SOULLESS VACUUM OF SPACE!
GOD, I LOVE CAMPING!

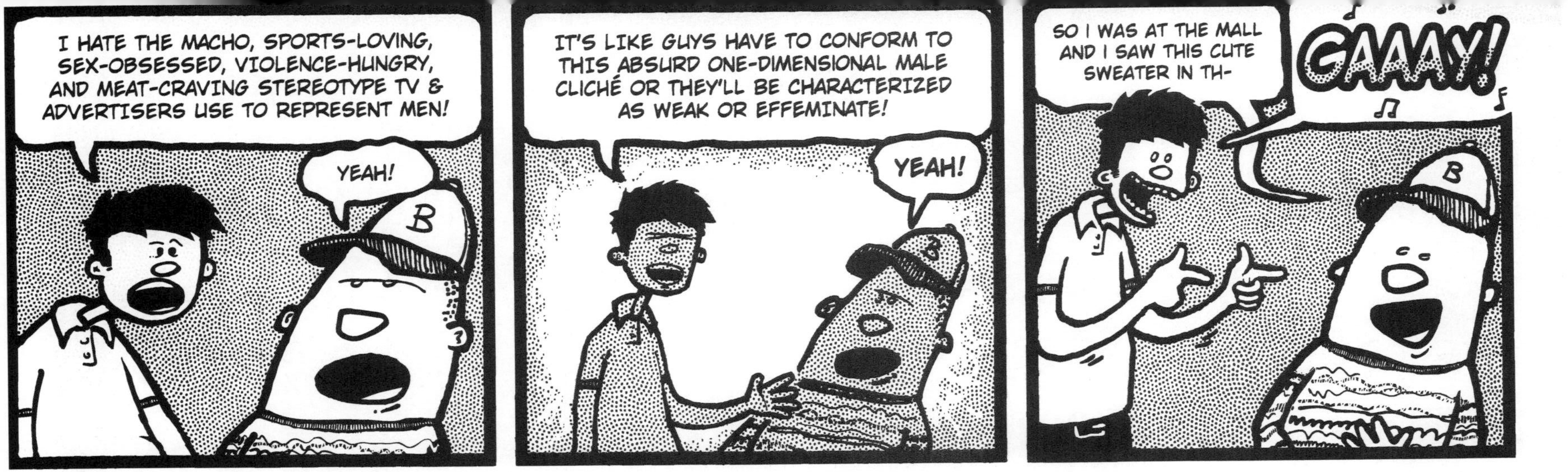
I HATE THE MACHO, SPORTS-LOVING, SEX-OBSESSED, VIOLENCE-HUNGRY, AND MEAT-CRAVING STEREOTYPE TV & ADVERTISERS USE TO REPRESENT MEN!
YEAH!
IT'S LIKE GUYS HAVE TO CONFORM TO THIS ABSURD ONE-DIMENSIONAL MALE CLICHÉ OR THEY'LL BE CHARACTERIZED AS WEAK OR EFFEMINATE!
YEAH!
SO I WAS AT THE MALL AND I SAW THIS CUTE SWEATER IN TH-
GAAAY!

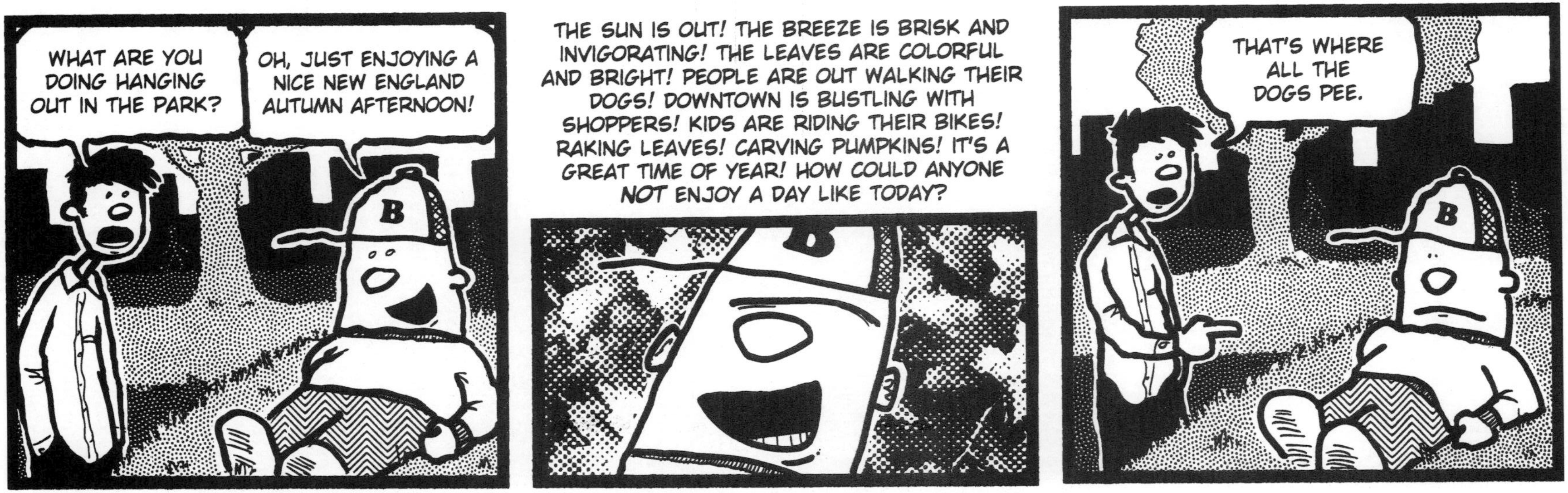
WHAT ARE YOU DOING HANGING OUT IN THE PARK?
OH, JUST ENJOYING A NICE NEW ENGLAND AUTUMN AFTERNOON!
THE SUN IS OUT! THE BREEZE IS BRISK AND INVIGORATING! THE LEAVES ARE COLORFUL AND BRIGHT! PEOPLE ARE OUT WALKING THEIR DOGS! DOWNTOWN IS BUSTLING WITH SHOPPERS! KIDS ARE RIDING THEIR BIKES! RAKING LEAVES! CARVING PUMPKINS! IT'S A GREAT TIME OF YEAR! HOW COULD ANYONE *NOT* ENJOY A DAY LIKE TODAY?
THAT'S WHERE ALL THE DOGS PEE.

UHF

It was the summer of '81 and Eddie couldn't hit a dog's ass with a fistful of TV Guides. He spent long stifling nights on his porch, coaxing clear signal from his portable black and white Japanese television set. Had particular trouble getting channel 32 from out Waterville way. Horizontal lines, verticals not holding, frequencies fighting frequencies on the inside of the little Shibaura's picture tube. He crawled around behind the tray table the TV rested on, the screwdriver slipping out of his sweaty palm as he tweaked back panel adjustment screws he didn't fully comprehend, cursing the limitations of the set's built-in telescoping antenna. He'da given his left you know what for one of those rooftop Yagis but it just wasn't in the cards.

Always fiddling, he reshaped the rabbit ears, taped on coat hangers, wrapped it all in tin foil, even tried to incorporate the aluminum flag pole mounted on the side of the porch, but nothing took. Finally ended up hooking 'er to the water pipes in the house with a spool of speaker wire. Still didn't satisfy him. Eddie wanted crisp. Eddie wanted sharp. Eddie wanted clarity. He learned that if he held the UHF knob between 32 and 31, the picture marginally improved. He would hold it and hold it and hold it until he had to slap away a mosquito. When he let go things went hinky.

He had simmered at first, soon came to a boil, finally phoned up the station's main office and scalded them for their part in the conspiracy to send him weak signal. The roundish, perfectly pleasant middle-aged receptionist, Miss Berube (privately nicknamed "Doughnut" by Stan Meeks, the station's sole cameraman), informed Eddie that his request to have the TV32 transmitter pointed directly at his house was a request the station could not honor. Some five, ten minutes of hinky-knob ranting later she was left with no alternative but to hang up on him, deeming his proposal to have his television set hardwired directly to the TV station via A Real Long Wire to be overreaching and unrealistic. Mind you, that's some thirty-five-odd miles as the crow flies, never mind the logistics on how to get it over Cullyard's Creek, or across the railroad tracks. Eddie slammed the phone back on the cradle and wished and hoped and prayed that everyone who worked at TV32 would die in front of their mothershitting children and Satan himself would impale their mothershitting faces on the red hot stalagmites of Hell by jumping up and down repeatedly on the back of their heads with his evil hooves. Especially Doughnut, whom he referred to in his head as "That 32 Whore."

Eddie drew hard lines on his wrists with the jagged edge of a soup can lid during "The White Shadow," right before the boys began singing in the locker room showers. His body temperature had dropped considerably by Dick Harvey's 6:00 TV32 weekend weather update, and his skin had become downright cool by the time the end credits of "The Rat Patrol" filled the static-infested screen. His sweat evaporated and the mosquitoes paid him no mind. Summer spun out its plot on the little Shibaura as the oppressive humidity of "Barney Miller" pressed down on Cumberland County.

FAKE ADVERTISEMENT

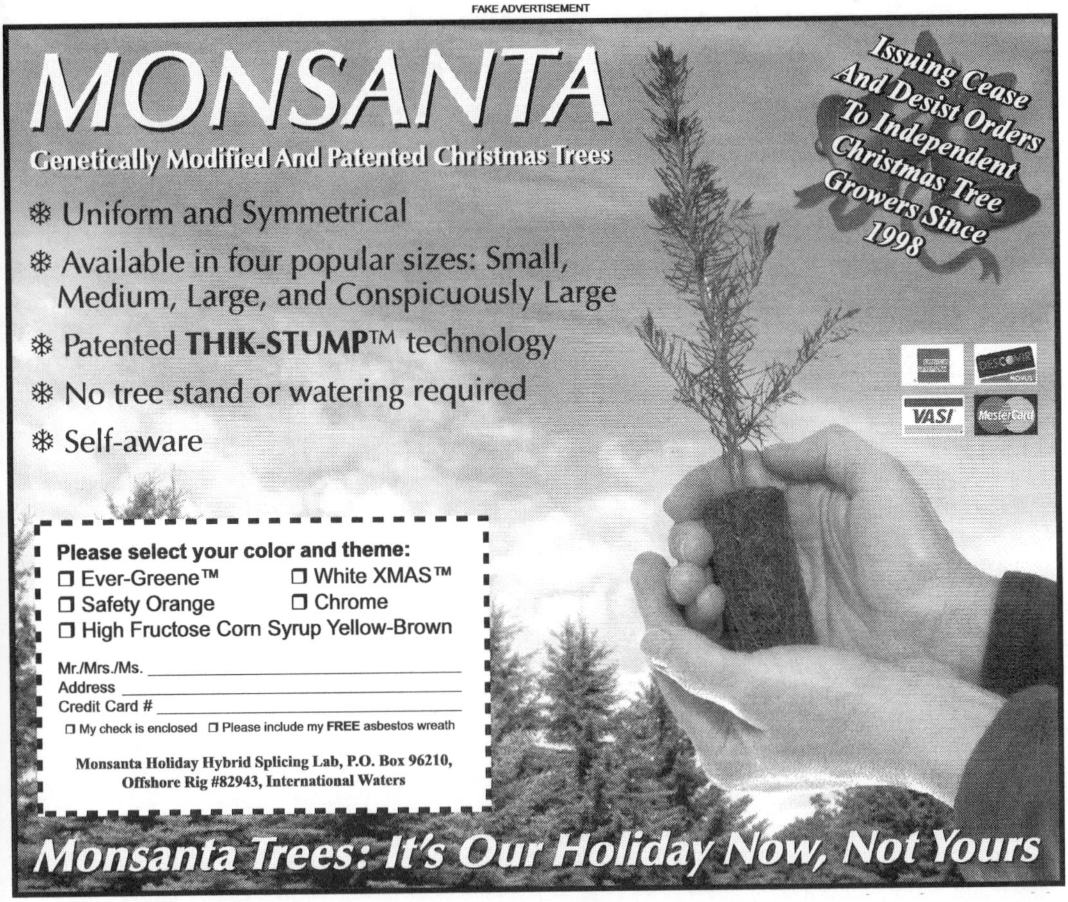
MONSANTA
Genetically Modified And Patented Christmas Trees
❄ Uniform and Symmetrical
❄ Available in four popular sizes: Small, Medium, Large, and Conspicuously Large
❄ Patented THIK-STUMP™ technology
❄ No tree stand or watering required
❄ Self-aware
Issuing Cease And Desist Orders To Independent Christmas Tree Growers Since 1998
VASI
MesterCard
Please select your color and theme:
❒ Ever-Greene™
❒ White XMAS™
❒ Safety Orange
❒ Chrome
❒ High Fructose Corn Syrup Yellow-Brown
Mr./Mrs./Ms. ____
Address ____
Credit Card # ____
❒ My check is enclosed ❒ Please include my FREE asbestos wreath
Monsanta Holiday Hybrid Splicing Lab, P.O. Box 96210, Offshore Rig #82943, International Waters
Monsanta Trees: It's Our Holiday Now, Not Yours

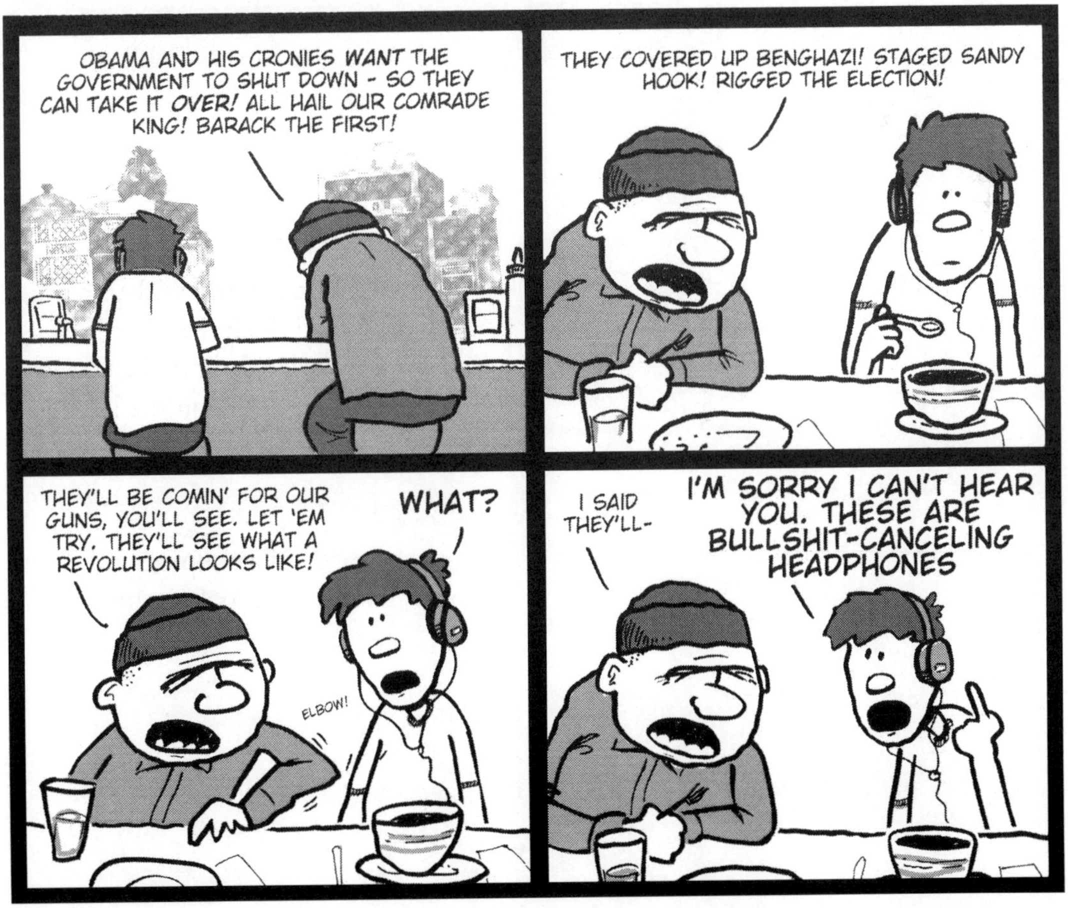
OBAMA AND HIS CRONIES WANT THE GOVERNMENT TO SHUT DOWN - SO THEY CAN TAKE IT OVER! ALL HAIL OUR COMRADE KING! BARACK THE FIRST!
THEY COVERED UP BENGHAZI! STAGED SANDY HOOK! RIGGED THE ELECTION!
THEY'LL BE COMIN' FOR OUR GUNS, YOU'LL SEE. LET 'EM TRY. THEY'LL SEE WHAT A REVOLUTION LOOKS LIKE!
WHAT?
ELBOW!
I SAID THEY'LL-
I'M SORRY I CAN'T HEAR YOU. THESE ARE BULLSHIT-CANCELING HEADPHONES

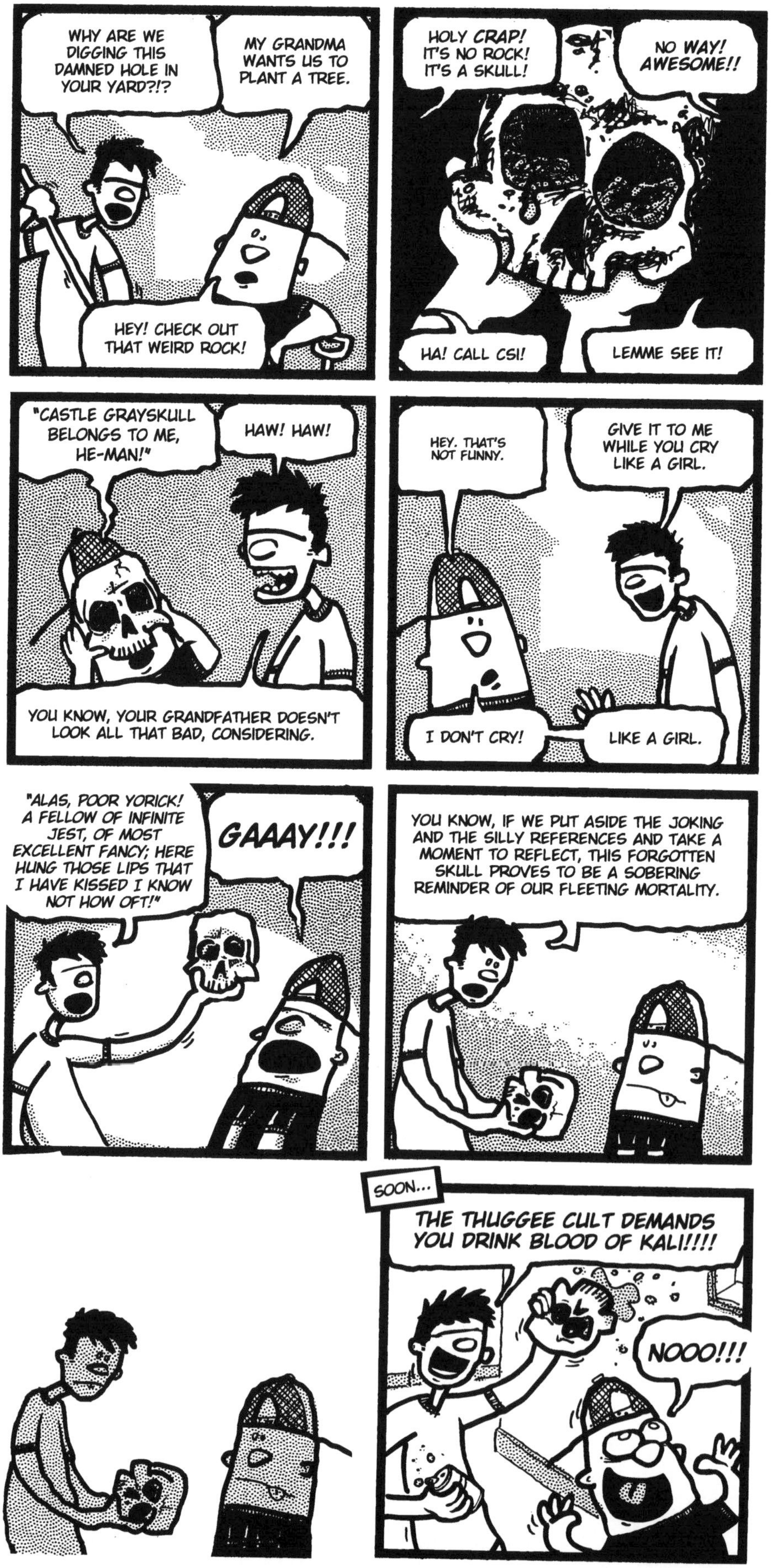
WHY ARE WE DIGGING THIS DAMNED HOLE IN YOUR YARD?!?
MY GRANDMA WANTS US TO PLANT A TREE.
HEY! CHECK OUT THAT WEIRD ROCK!
HOLY CRAP! IT'S NO ROCK! IT'S A SKULL!
NO WAY! AWESOME!!
HA! CALL CSI!
LEMME SEE IT!
"CASTLE GRAYSKULL BELONGS TO ME, HE-MAN!"
HAW! HAW!
YOU KNOW, YOUR GRANDFATHER DOESN'T LOOK ALL THAT BAD, CONSIDERING.
HEY. THAT'S NOT FUNNY.
GIVE IT TO ME WHILE YOU CRY LIKE A GIRL.
I DON'T CRY!
LIKE A GIRL.
"ALAS, POOR YORICK! A FELLOW OF INFINITE JEST, OF MOST EXCELLENT FANCY; HERE HUNG THOSE LIPS THAT I HAVE KISSED I KNOW NOT HOW OFT!"
GAAAY!!!
YOU KNOW, IF WE PUT ASIDE THE JOKING AND THE SILLY REFERENCES AND TAKE A MOMENT TO REFLECT, THIS FORGOTTEN SKULL PROVES TO BE A SOBERING REMINDER OF OUR FLEETING MORTALITY.
SOON...
THE THUGGEE CULT DEMANDS YOU DRINK BLOOD OF KALI!!!!
NOOO!!!

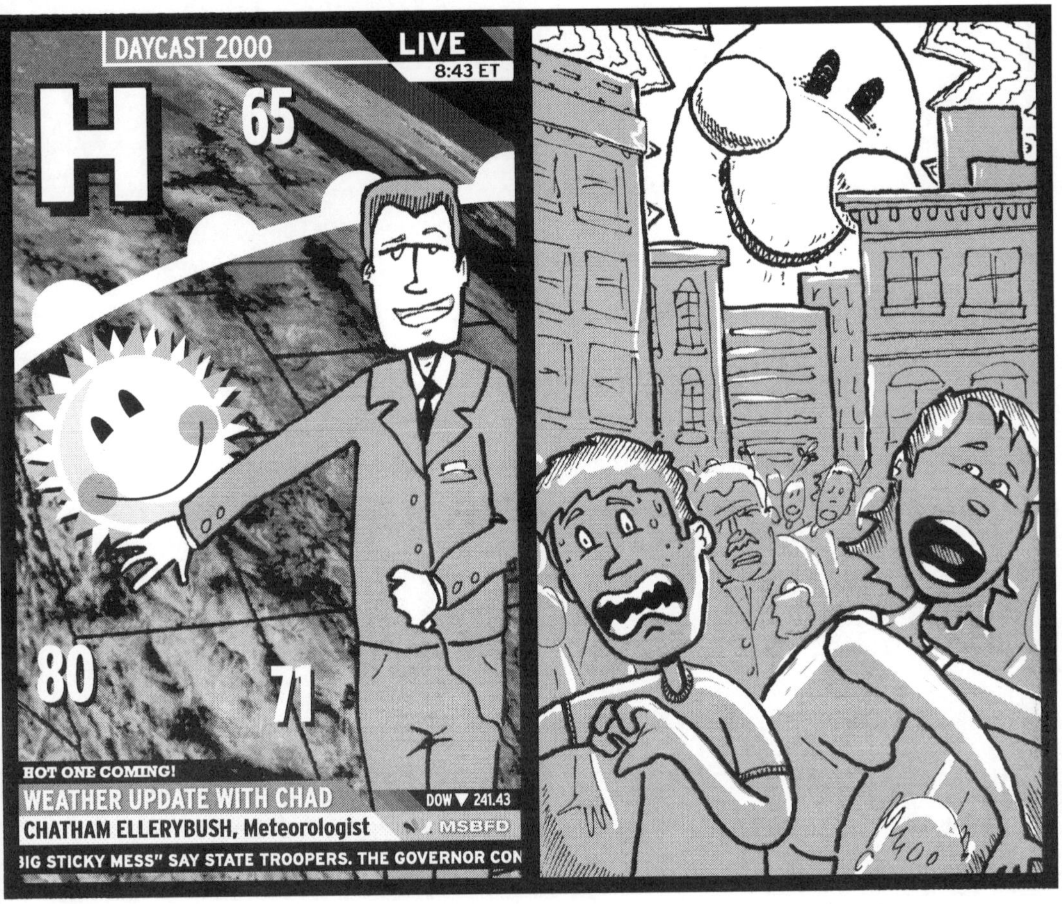
DAYCAST 2000
LIVE
8:43 ET
H
65
80
71
HOT ONE COMING!
WEATHER UPDATE WITH CHAD
DOW ▼ 241.43
CHATHAM ELLERYBUSH, Meteorologist
MSBFD
BIG STICKY MESS" SAY STATE TROOPERS. THE GOVERNOR CON

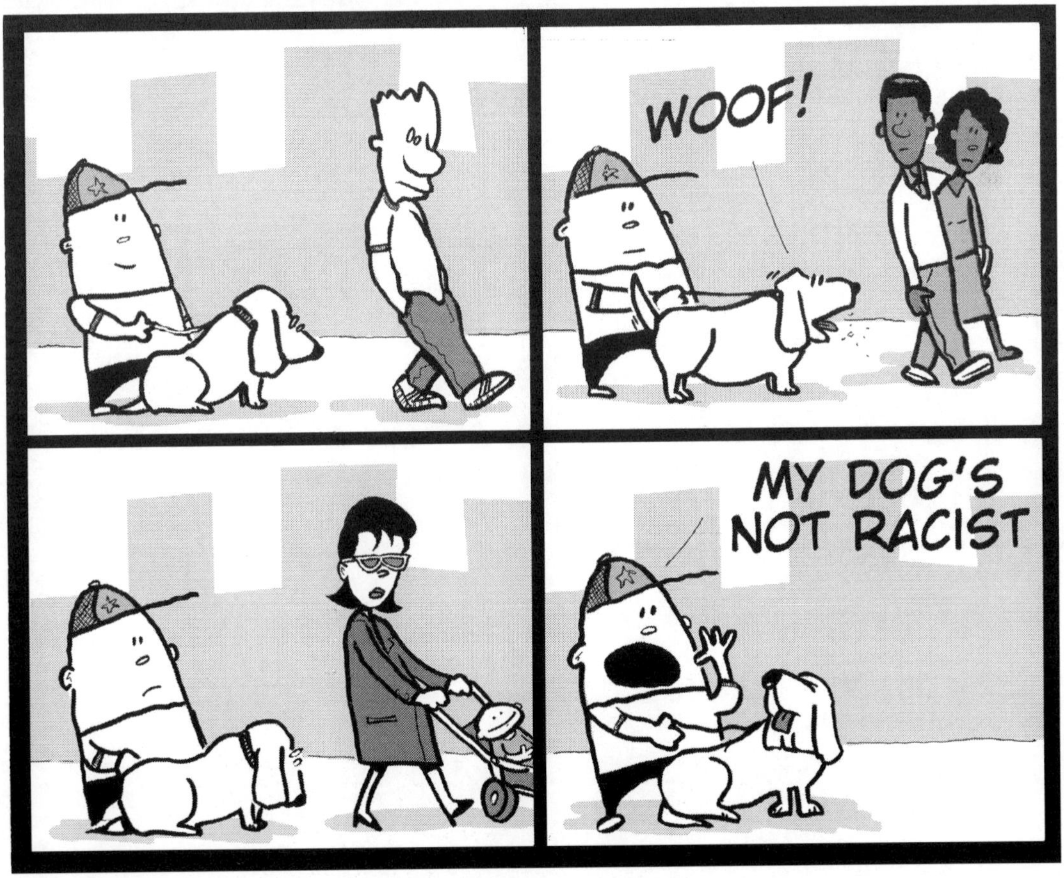
WOOF!
MY DOG'S NOT RACIST

Environmentally Friendly

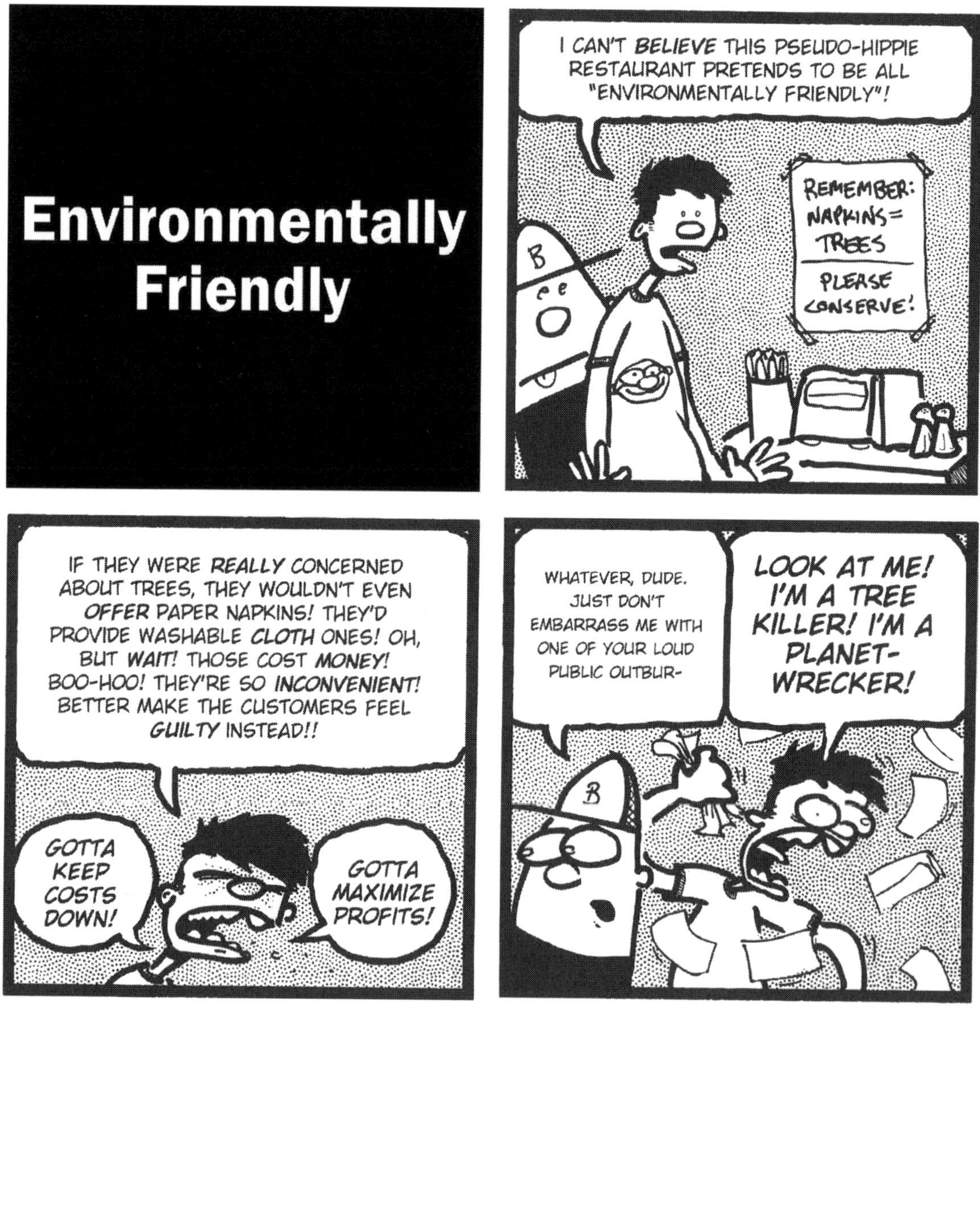
I CAN'T BELIEVE THIS PSEUDO-HIPPIE RESTAURANT PRETENDS TO BE ALL "ENVIRONMENTALLY FRIENDLY"!
REMEMBER: NAPKINS = TREES
PLEASE CONSERVE!
IF THEY WERE REALLY CONCERNED ABOUT TREES, THEY WOULDN'T EVEN OFFER PAPER NAPKINS! THEY'D PROVIDE WASHABLE CLOTH ONES! OH, BUT WAIT! THOSE COST MONEY! BOO-HOO! THEY'RE SO INCONVENIENT! BETTER MAKE THE CUSTOMERS FEEL GUILTY INSTEAD!!
GOTTA KEEP COSTS DOWN!
GOTTA MAXIMIZE PROFITS!
WHATEVER, DUDE. JUST DON'T EMBARRASS ME WITH ONE OF YOUR LOUD PUBLIC OUTBUR-
LOOK AT ME! I'M A TREE KILLER! I'M A PLANET-WRECKER!

Laundromat Paranoia

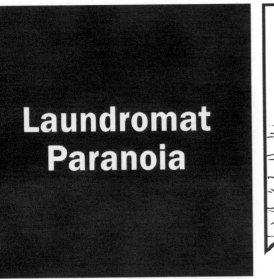

I HAVE THIS PARANOID LAUNDROMAT FEAR THAT I'M GOING TO TAKE MY CLOTHES OUT OF THE DRYER AND SOMEONE WILL ACCUSE ME OF STEALING THEM AND I WON'T BE ABLE TO PROVE THEY'RE MINE. DUMB, RIGHT?

SUPER-DUMB.

FOLD!

HEY, KID! GET YOUR HANDS OFF OF MY CLOTHES!!!

HE'S JOKING WE'RE FRIENDS

LISTEN: In 1928, Walt Disney released "Steamboat Willie." This short film has been on the cusp of entering the public domain several times (in 1956, 1976, and 1998), but never has. Many claim the delay is due to the aggressive congressional lobbying for copyright extension by the Walt Disney Company.

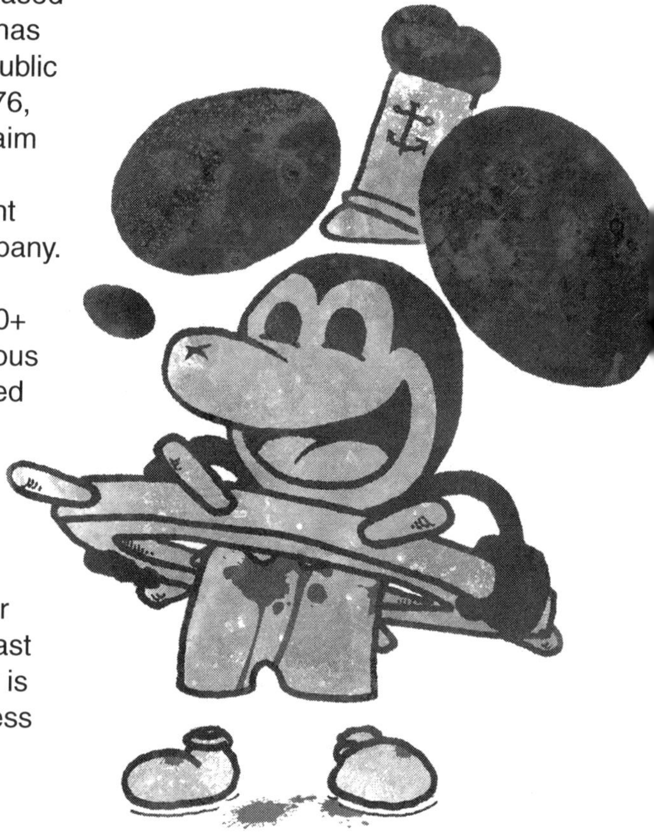

BUT: Over the course of the last 80+ years, Disney has released numerous films and merchandise lines adapted from public domain stories, fairy tales, and fables, earning them billions in profits.

MORAL: A corporation is allowed to co-opt our culture, repackage our storytelling heritage, and sell our past back to us. But a corporation's past is sacrosanct. Don't touch it. Don't mess with it...

...that would be *stealing*.

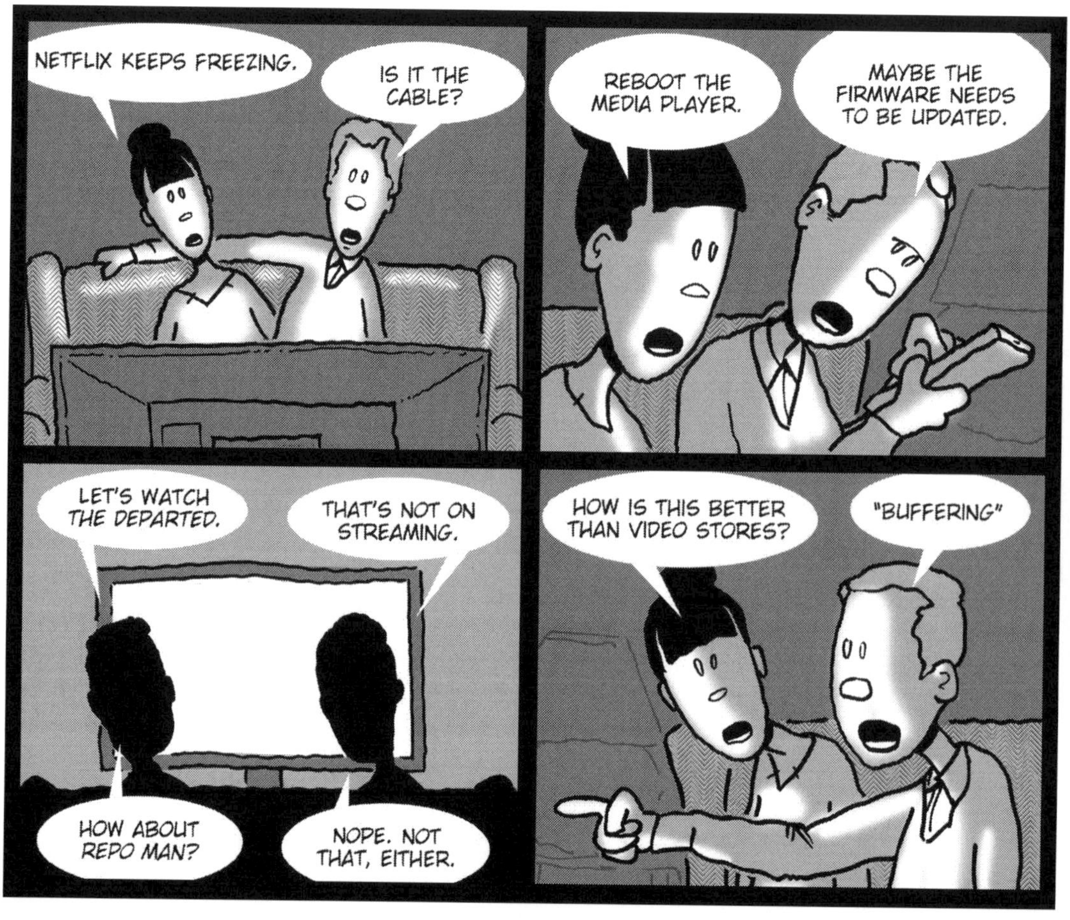
NETFLIX KEEPS FREEZING.
IS IT THE CABLE?
REBOOT THE MEDIA PLAYER.
MAYBE THE FIRMWARE NEEDS TO BE UPDATED.
LET'S WATCH THE DEPARTED.
THAT'S NOT ON STREAMING.
HOW ABOUT REPO MAN?
NOPE. NOT THAT, EITHER.
HOW IS THIS BETTER THAN VIDEO STORES?
"BUFFERING"

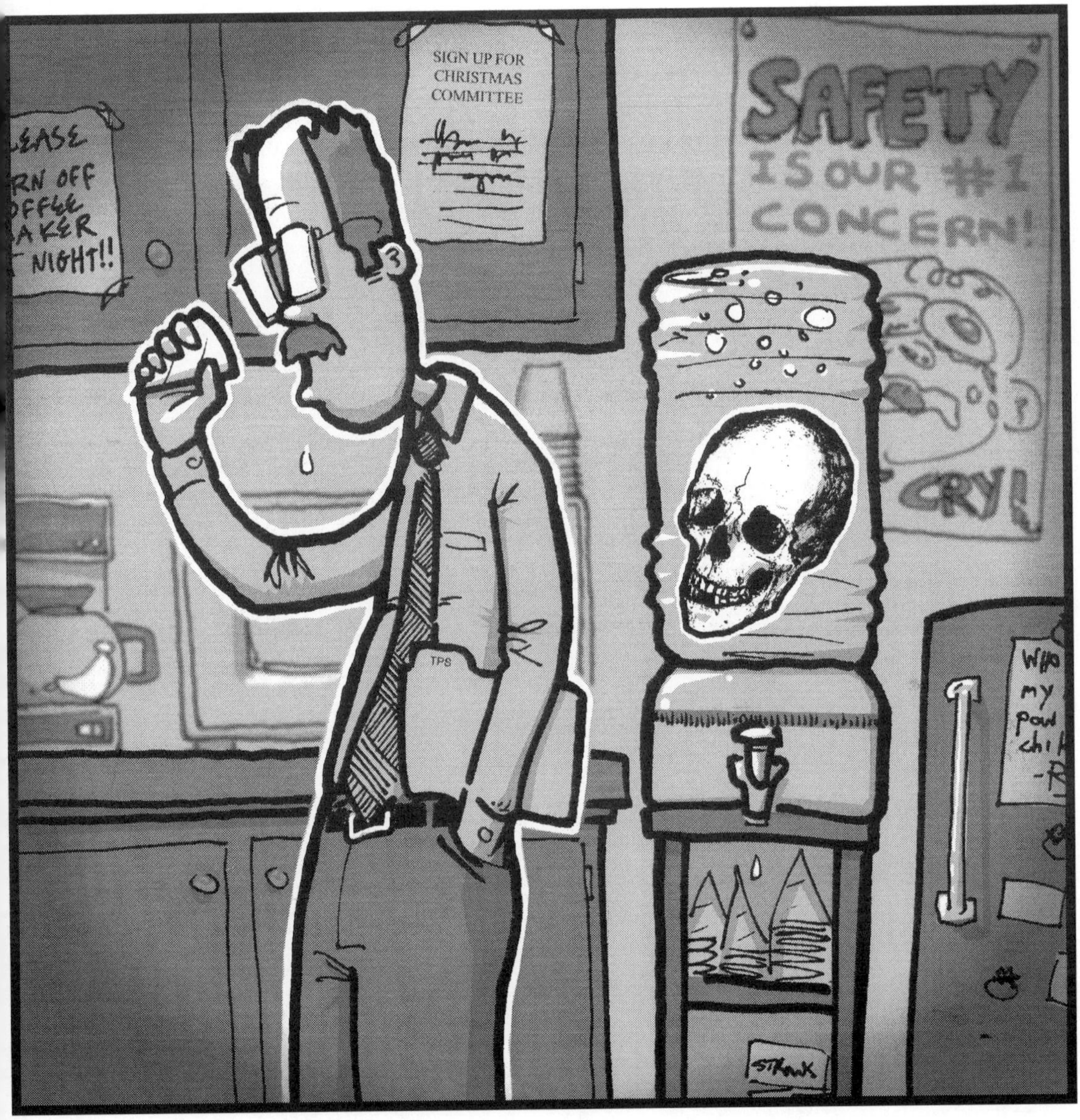

SIGN UP FOR CHRISTMAS COMMITTEE
SAFETY IS OUR #1 CONCERN!
TPS

AN EVENING WITH

BIG BUSINESS, PORN, ALTAMONT & SURP

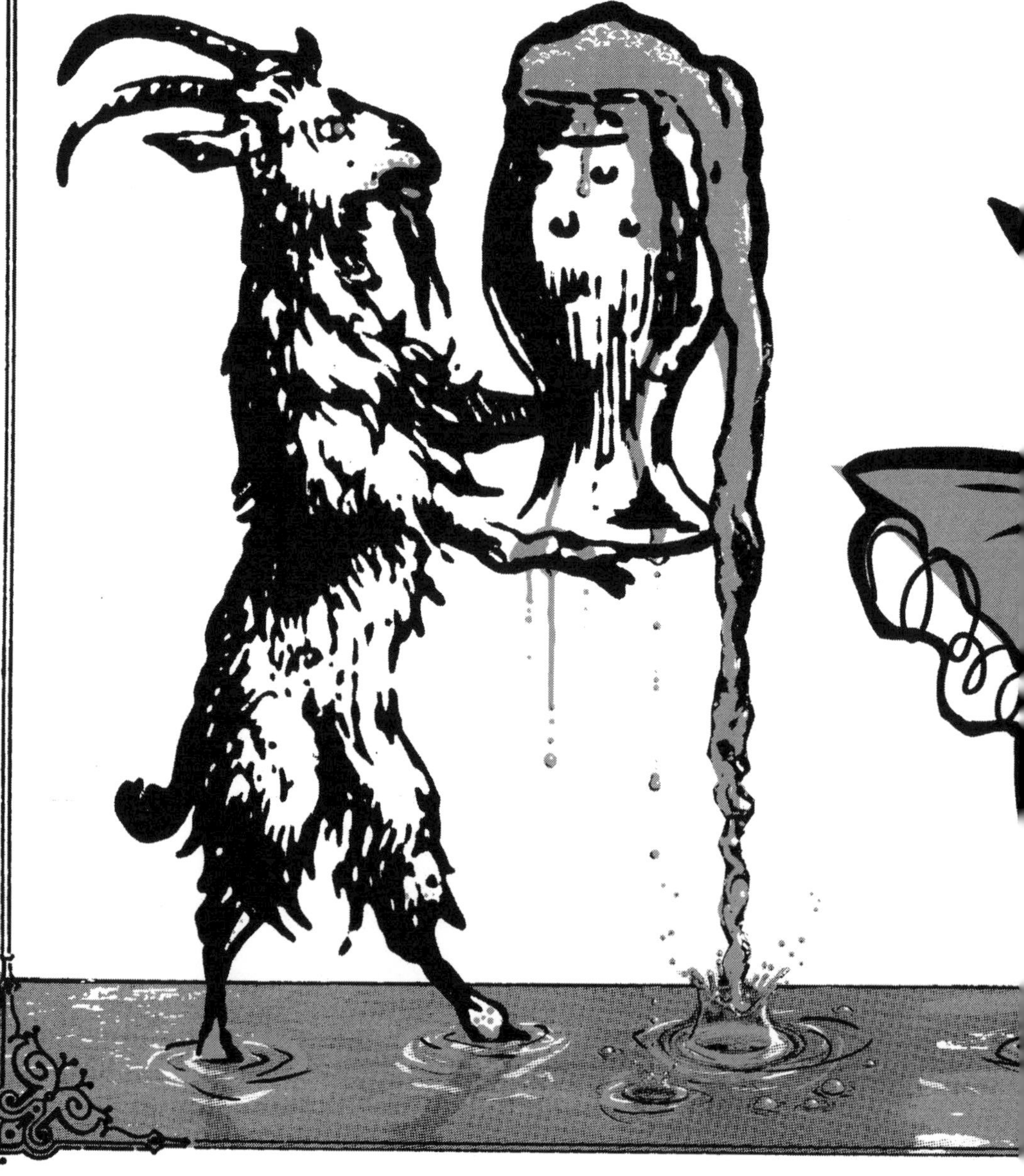

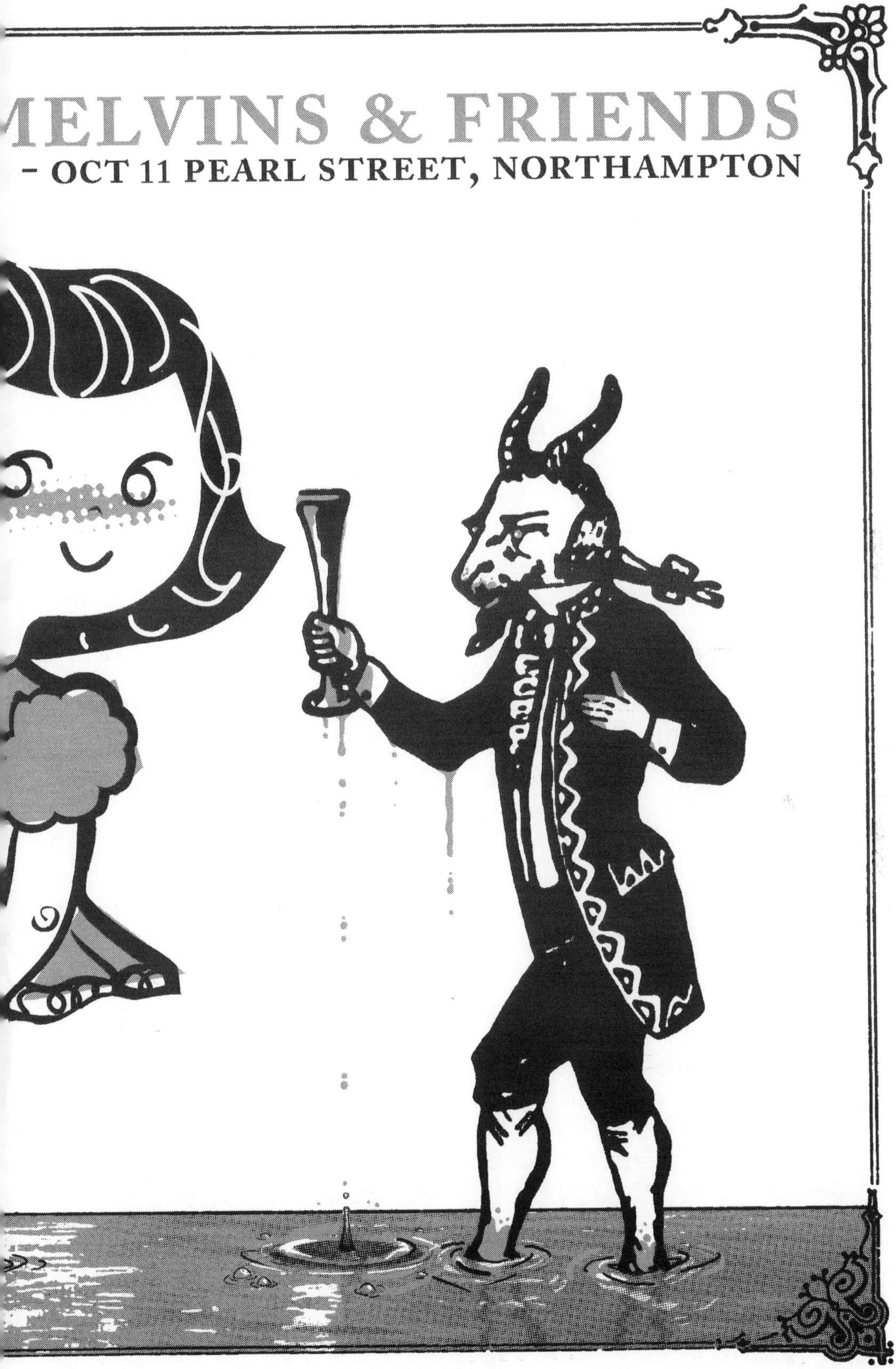
MELVINS & FRIENDS
– OCT 11 PEARL STREET, NORTHAMPTON

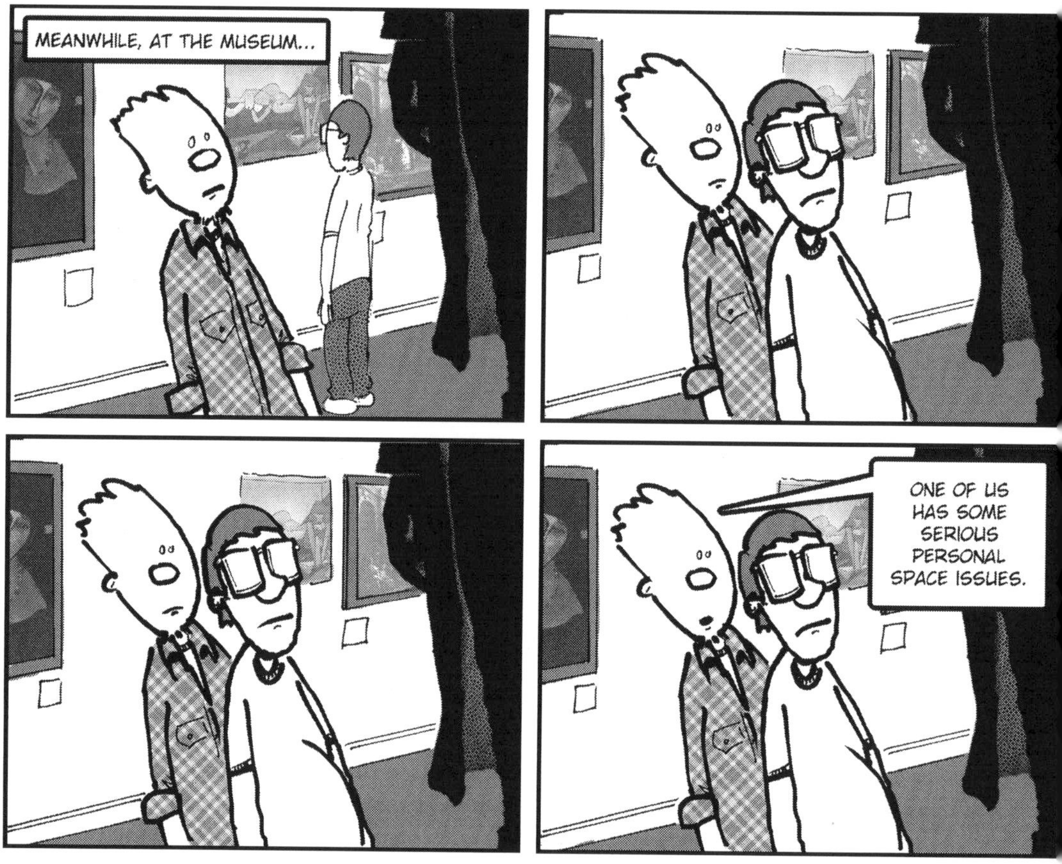
MEANWHILE, AT THE MUSEUM...
ONE OF US HAS SOME SERIOUS PERSONAL SPACE ISSUES.

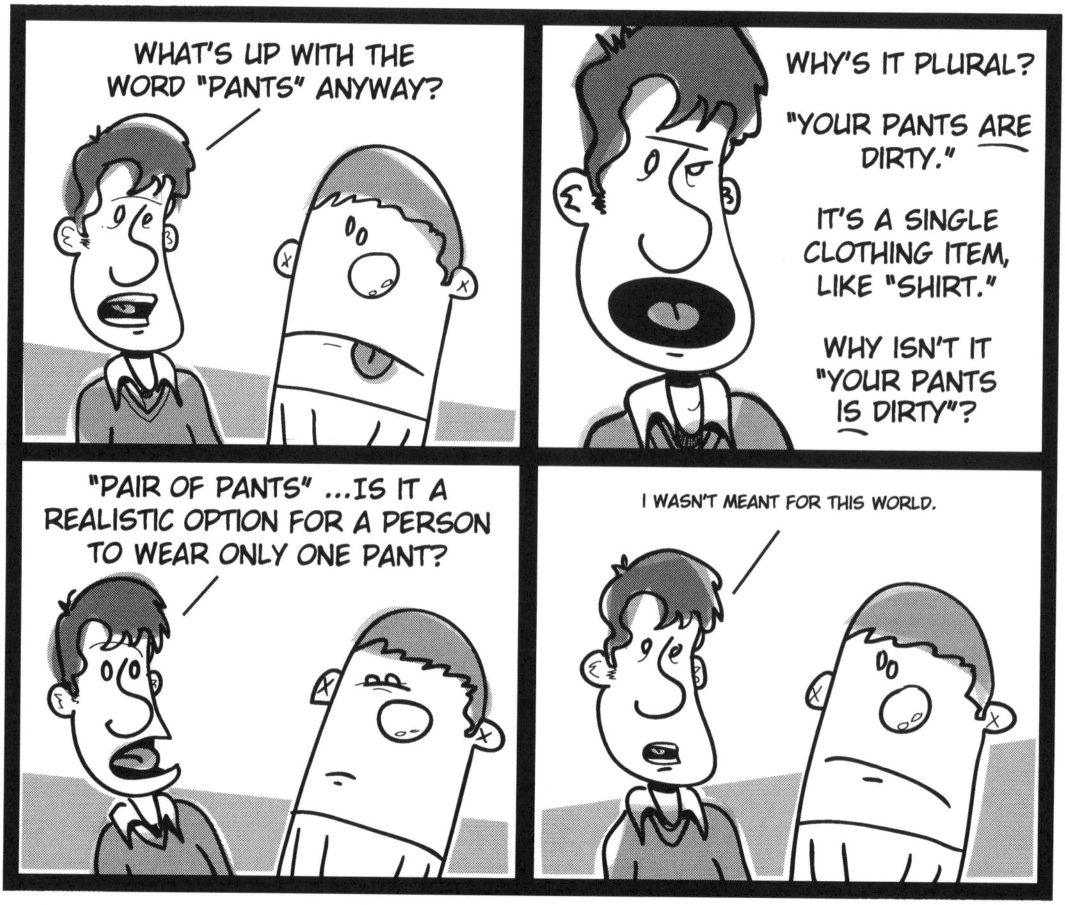
WHAT'S UP WITH THE WORD "PANTS" ANYWAY?
WHY'S IT PLURAL?
"YOUR PANTS ARE DIRTY."
IT'S A SINGLE CLOTHING ITEM, LIKE "SHIRT."
WHY ISN'T IT "YOUR PANTS IS DIRTY"?
"PAIR OF PANTS" ...IS IT A REALISTIC OPTION FOR A PERSON TO WEAR ONLY ONE PANT?
I WASN'T MEANT FOR THIS WORLD.

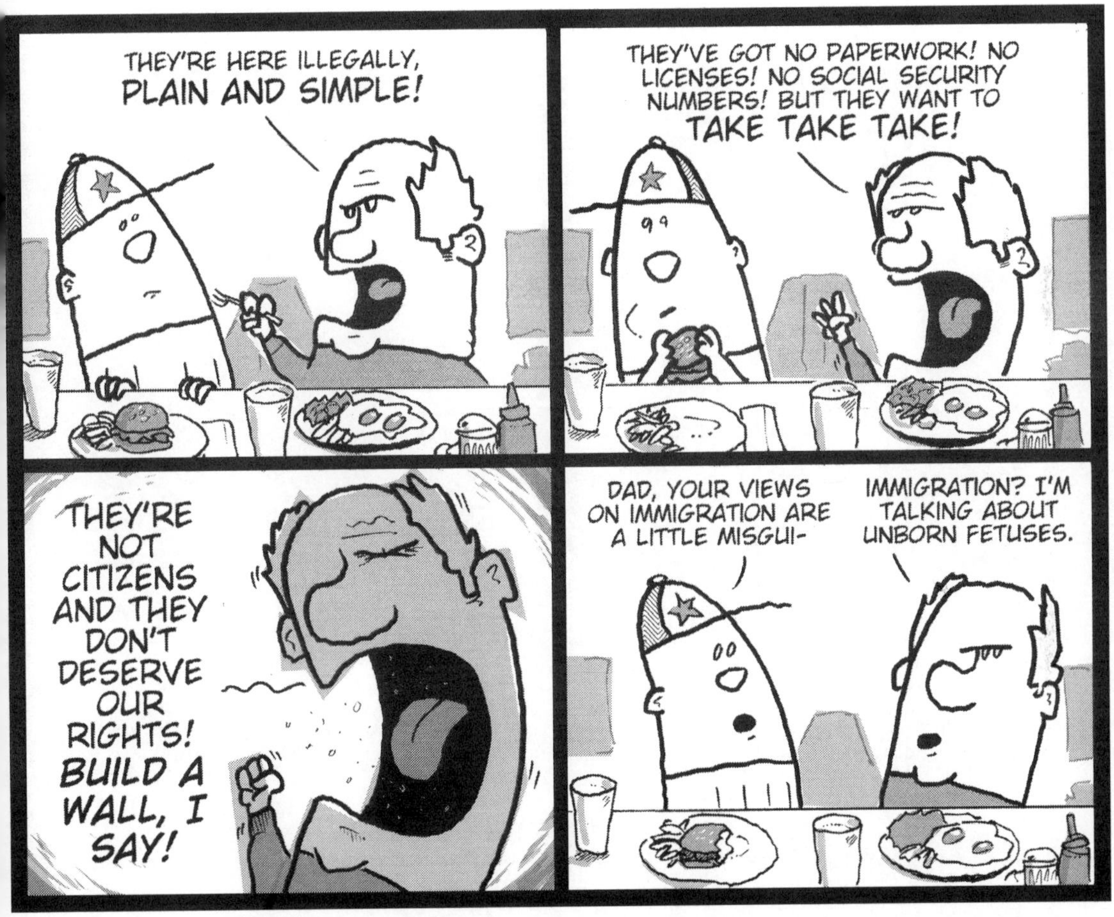
THEY'RE HERE ILLEGALLY, PLAIN AND SIMPLE!
THEY'VE GOT NO PAPERWORK! NO LICENSES! NO SOCIAL SECURITY NUMBERS! BUT THEY WANT TO TAKE TAKE TAKE!
THEY'RE NOT CITIZENS AND THEY DON'T DESERVE OUR RIGHTS! BUILD A WALL, I SAY!
DAD, YOUR VIEWS ON IMMIGRATION ARE A LITTLE MISGUI-
IMMIGRATION? I'M TALKING ABOUT UNBORN FETUSES.

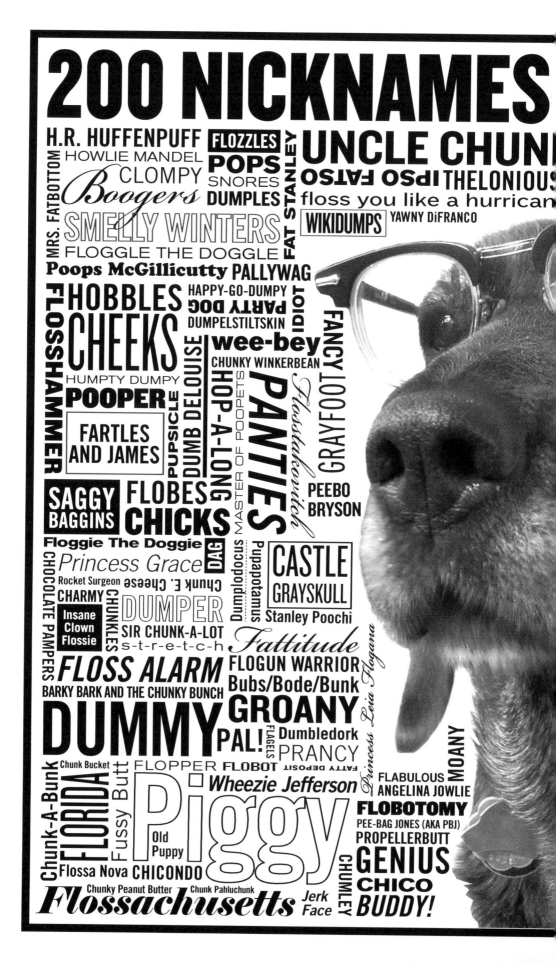

200 NICKNAMES

H.R. HUFFENPUFF
HOWLIE MANDEL
MRS. FATBOTTOM
CLOMPY
Boogers
SMELLY WINTERS
FLOGGLE THE DOGGLE
Poops McGillicutty PALLYWAG

FLOZZLES
POPS
SNORES
DUMPLES
WIKIDUMPS

FAT STANLEY
UNCLE CHUN
IPSO FATSO THELONIOUS
floss you like a hurrican
YAWNY DiFRANCO

FLOSSHAMMER
HOBBLES
CHEEKS
HUMPTY DUMPY
POOPER
FARTLES AND JAMES
SAGGY BAGGINS
FLOBES
CHICKS
Floggie The Doggie
Princess Grace
Rocket Surgeon
CHOCOLATE PAMPERS
CHARMY
Insane Clown Flossie
CHUNKLES
DUMPER
SIR CHUNK-A-LOT
s-t-r-e-t-c-h
FLOSS ALARM
BARKY BARK AND THE CHUNKY BUNCH
DUMMY
PAL!

HAPPY-GO-DUMPY
PARTY DOG
DUMPELSTILTSKIN
wee-bey
CHUNKY WINKERBEAN
HOP-A-LONG
DUMB DELOUISE
PUPSICLE
Flosstafcovitch
PANTIES
MASTER OF POOPETS
DAG
Dumplodocus
Pupapotamus
Chunk E. Cheese
Fattitude
FLOGUN WARRIOR
Bubs/Bode/Bunk
GROANY
FLAGELS
Dumbledork
PRANCY
FATTY DEPOSIT

IDIOT
FANCY
GRAYFOOT
PEEBO BRYSON
CASTLE GRAYSKULL
Stanley Poochi
Princess Leia Flogana

Chunk-A-Bunk
Chunk Bucket
FLORIDA
Fussy Butt
FLOPPER
FLOBOT
Old Puppy
Wheezie Jefferson
Piggy
Flossa Nova CHICONDO
Flossachusetts
Chunky Peanut Butter
Chunk Pahluchunk
Jerk Face
CHUMLEY

MOANY
FLABULOUS
ANGELINA JOWLIE
FLOBOTOMY
PEE-BAG JONES (AKA PBJ)
PROPELLERBUTT
GENIUS
CHICO
BUDDY!

MY DOG FLOSSIE

DREWS
OW
SURE-FLO
SOFT SERVE
FATTY TUNA
FATSY CLINE
FLOBERT
FARTS
MR. PEE-BODY
MR. SNIFFERS
MRS. CHICKEN
THE CHICKEN
MR. WRINKLES
MR. FLOJANGLES
FLOSSOPHER
FLO-BEE
FLOFLO
FLOSS
FLORENCE
SNIFFERONI
FLO-NASE
SNIFFY
FLOOZIE
FLOSSTRADAMUS
FLOGGLE
FLOPPIE
HOUND DOGGY
FLO-JAMS CHUCKLES PUPPY MONTGOMERY
FLORENCE THE PLORENCE
FLAURENCIA
MISS FLO
mayor fartlesby of fartelsburg
FATTY
PONTIAC
SNOOPY
PUPALARDO
CHICKEN LEG
ARTHUR FLOSSARELLI
snuffles
PUP
FATBURGER
FLO
STUPID
CHUNKY A
FATTYBIRD
SKIPPY
FLOMAX
FATNESS
FLOSSER
DUMPY
FLOSSIE AND JETSAM
PICKLES
SNEEZY
DOGALOGALA
LASER-WOLF
ASHTON POOCHER
BUNCHY
FLO-NOZZLE
Florence Of Arabia
WHEEZLES
DENTAL FLOSS
CLARENCE
WHIZZY-WIG
POLICE FLOSSIFER
gray baby
SONIC DEATH FLOSSIE
GOOPY
DUD (DOG +BUD)
Her Royal Sighness
PUDDING
CHUNKY HOMIE STYLE
BLUBBO BAGGINS
RIGHTEOUS PORKCHOP
GROANY BALONEY
MY POOR MEATBALL
CHUMMY STINKBUCKETS
POKEY
BRAWNCHO BLUBBY
BEFLONCÉ
PLUMPY
CHUNK CHANGE
Flosseraptor
CHARLIE
chuckalicious
RHUBARB
PUPPET
OLD BABY
HOMEDOGGY
TURD FACTORY
KICKSTAND
HOGGYDOGGY JOKEFENOKEE
CLOWNBAG CLUMPY
FLOSSOPHY MAJOR
FLUPPY
CHUNKAGE
PUPPLE DUPPLE
CHAMPION
FLASH

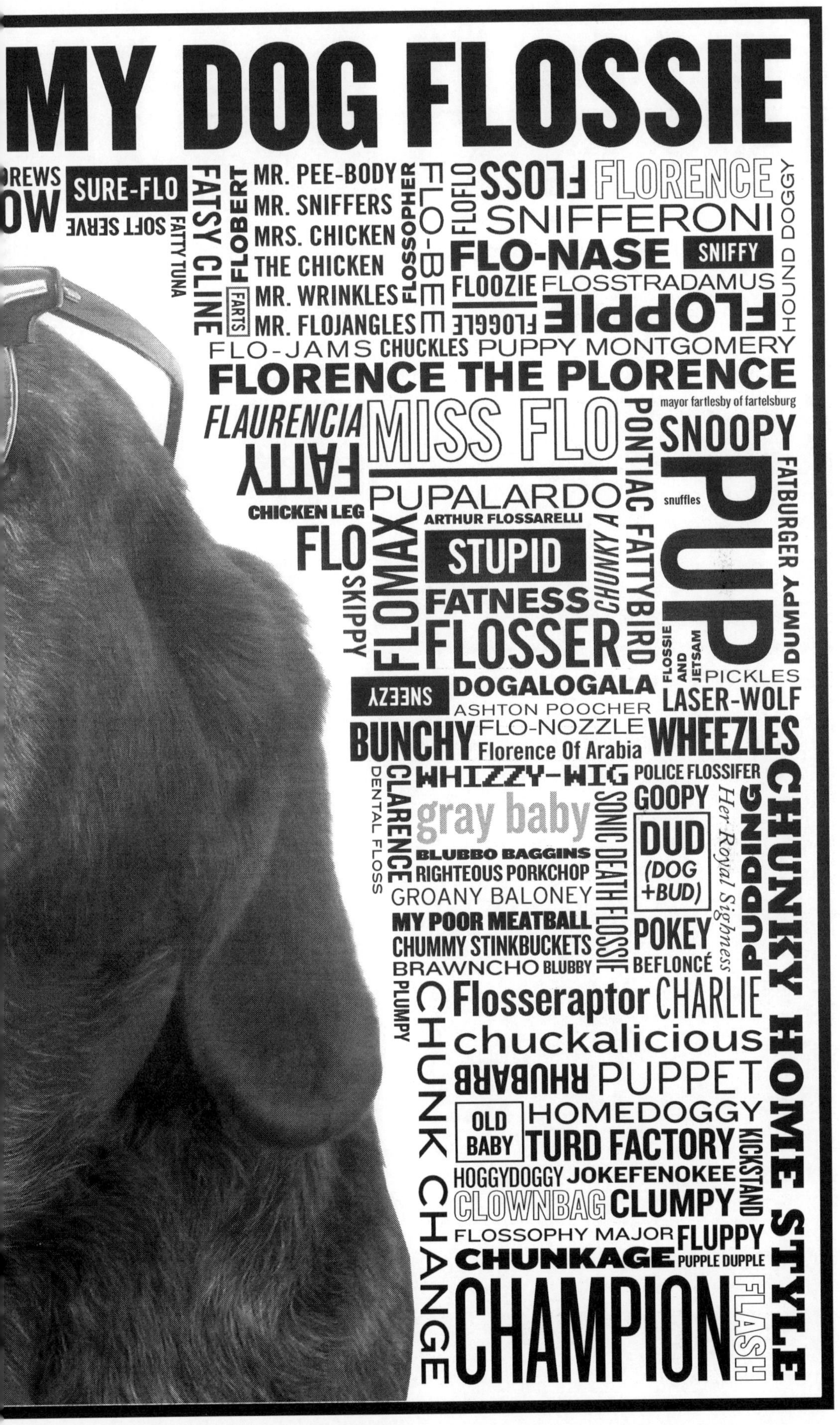

Cartooning Vs. Technology

Cartooning is, to me, an art form of simplification. The artist uses a minimal amount of lines to communicate characters and place to a reader. Mouths are often oddly-shaped black holes. Cartoon evolution does away with lips, body hair, elbows. Eyebrows are reduced to lines. Eyes become dots. A background might be a line indicating where the floor and wall meet. Maybe a squiggle of distant trees, or a cloud. Maybe just a flat field of color.

Cartooning is also about communicating an idea in the briefest terms possible. It is a shorthand form of storytelling. If you're making a comic strip, and that joke takes place in a restaurant and the setting is important to the joke or narrative, you damn well better explain that as quickly as possible in the first frame so you can get on with what you've got to say. In short, in gag cartooning things need to be made *apparent*.

In many ways, technology—especially consumer-driven technology—has been striving for the same thing as cartoonists for years now. Simpler, smaller, more streamlined. Minimalist. Removing as much of the object as possible, leaving only the key components (in technology's case, the interface, the screen). Steve Jobs led the way for elegant and simple device design, and it's a beautiful thing. But a cartoonist might reach a point where representing something in a super-simplified style when the object itself is already super-simplified becomes increasingly difficult. Let's take a look at a few examples:

Drawing a person talking on a telephone once looked like this...

WHY HELLO THERE EUNICE HOW IS YOUR COW?

With the miniaturization of electronics, now talking on the phone looks like this:

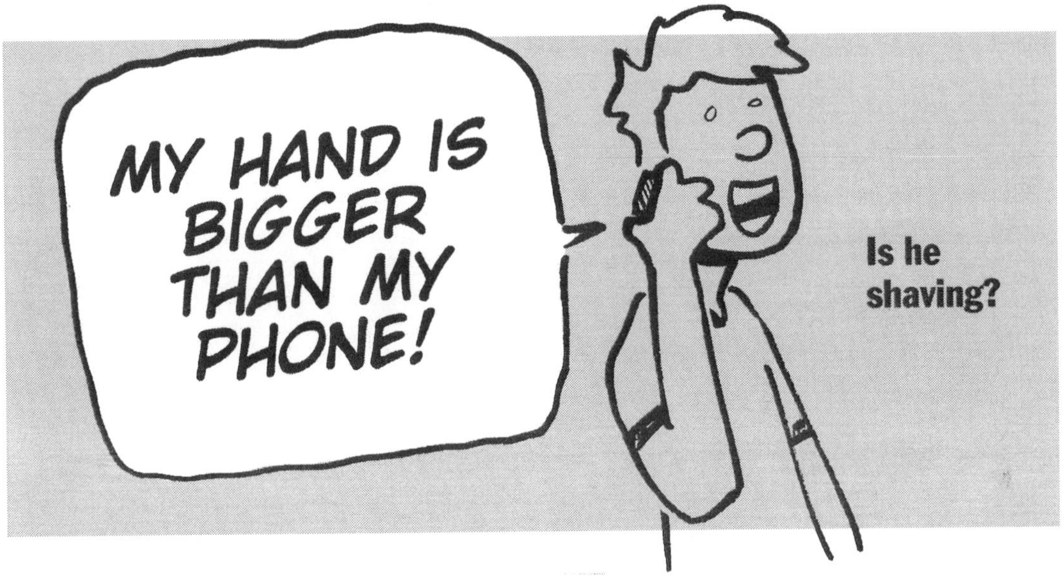
MY HAND IS BIGGER THAN MY PHONE!
Is he shaving?

Or even worse… The dreaded Bluetooth:

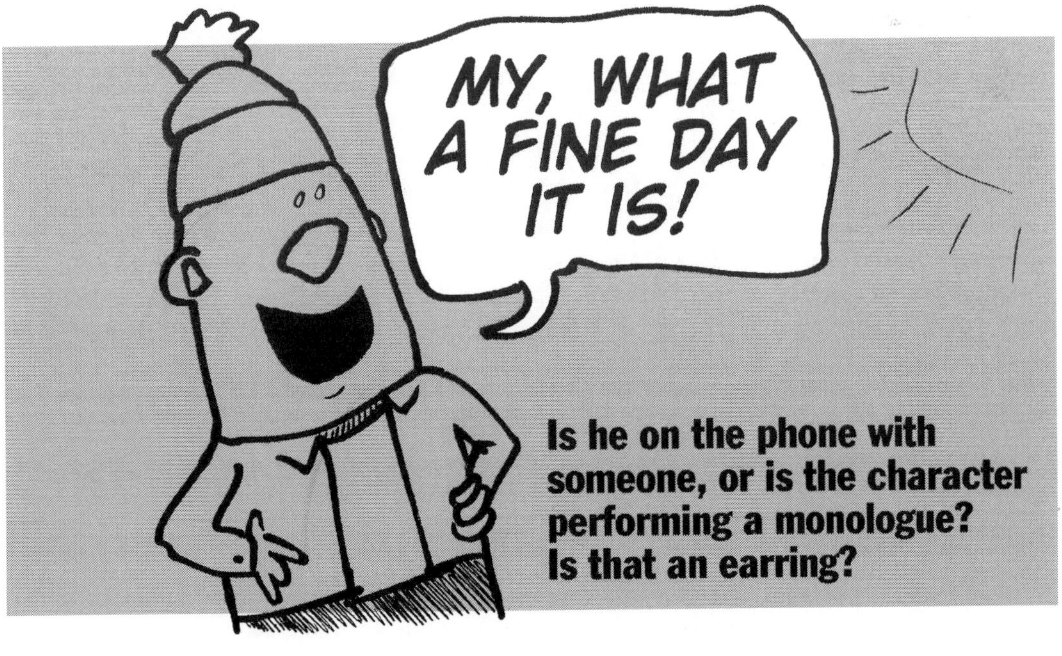
MY, WHAT A FINE DAY IT IS!
Is he on the phone with someone, or is the character performing a monologue? Is that an earring?

And then there's the changing technology of how people get their news. Newspaper jokes used to look like this...

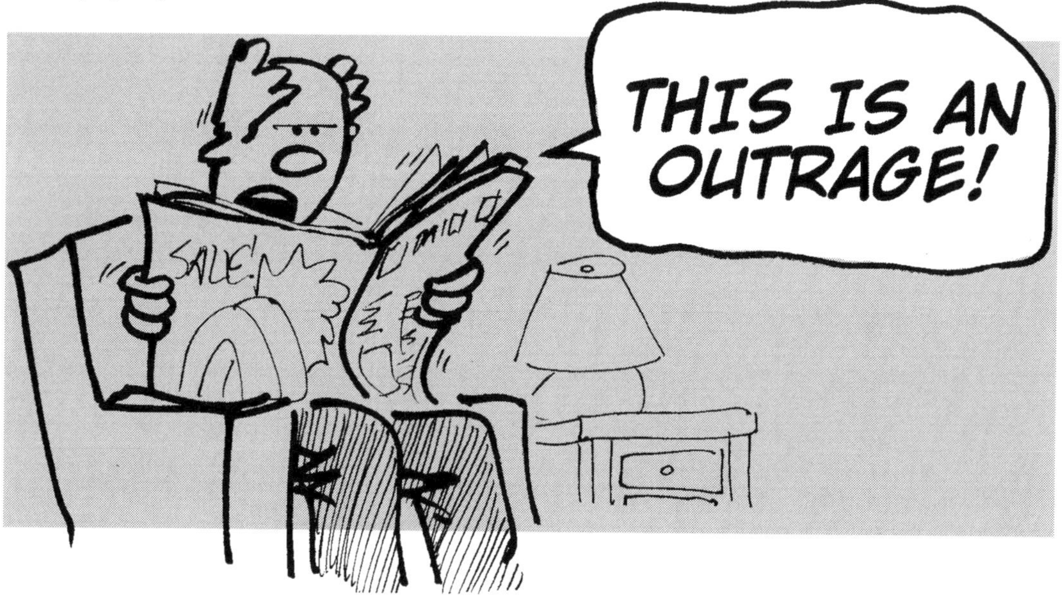
THIS IS AN OUTRAGE!
SALE!

<disdain> Ewww, gross! What is this? 2006?? </disdain>

But how do you quickly and succinctly communicate to the reader that a person is reading an iPad or an e-reader?

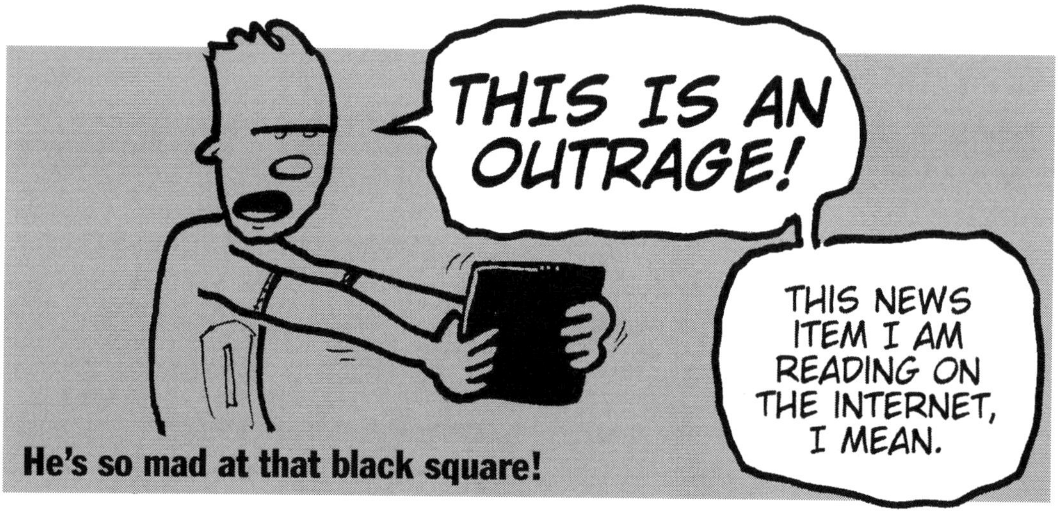
THIS IS AN OUTRAGE!
THIS NEWS ITEM I AM READING ON THE INTERNET, I MEAN.
He's so mad at that black square!

And let's not forget that the rise of discreet earbuds – not introduced but certainly popularized by the iPod – makes drawing a person listening to music a less cut-and-dry endeavor. It causes the cartoonist to fall back on outdated tropes like floating music notes surrounding the listener's head. (Which I personally never liked because they are unclear communicators. The character could be 1. Listening to music via headphones, 2. listening to music being broadcast to the room they're in, or 3. humming. I also never liked them because they don't hint at music genre, which in any other medium would be a huge part of the scene). At least back in The Good Old Days™ headphones were huge stupid-looking easily-identifiable headgear.

THEN:

He's listening to music. ⬅

NOW:

He might be a Secret Service agent. ⬅

The miniaturization and simplification of interface has hit all corners of consumer electronics, and cartoonists have had to adapt as best they can. Some machines have disappeared altogether: I myself, as an under-40 old fogey, sincerely miss answering machine jokes. The voice-speaking-into-an-empty-room (or a voice speaking to a person screening their calls) is essentially an obsolete joke set-up. Voice mail—an auto-forward to a remote hard drive of compressed WAV files—has killed it. And don't even get me started on the rich comedic vein of "don't forget to rewind the VHS tape before you return it to the video store" jokes that have passed from this earthly realm! Or "I forgot to wind my watch" gag setups! Or writing "BOOBS" on a calculator! Wait, I'm drifting off-topic...

Let's not forget the still-central piece of American consumer hardware: The TV. For generations, cartoonists have drawn their own private versions of The Fat American Dimwit slouched in front of a huge, room-dominating television set. Sturdy furniture! The grandeur! The poor reception! You could put a thirty pound VCR on top of it! It made mechanical noises when you changed the channel!

← It's wood paneled!

But alas...

Now TVs look like this...

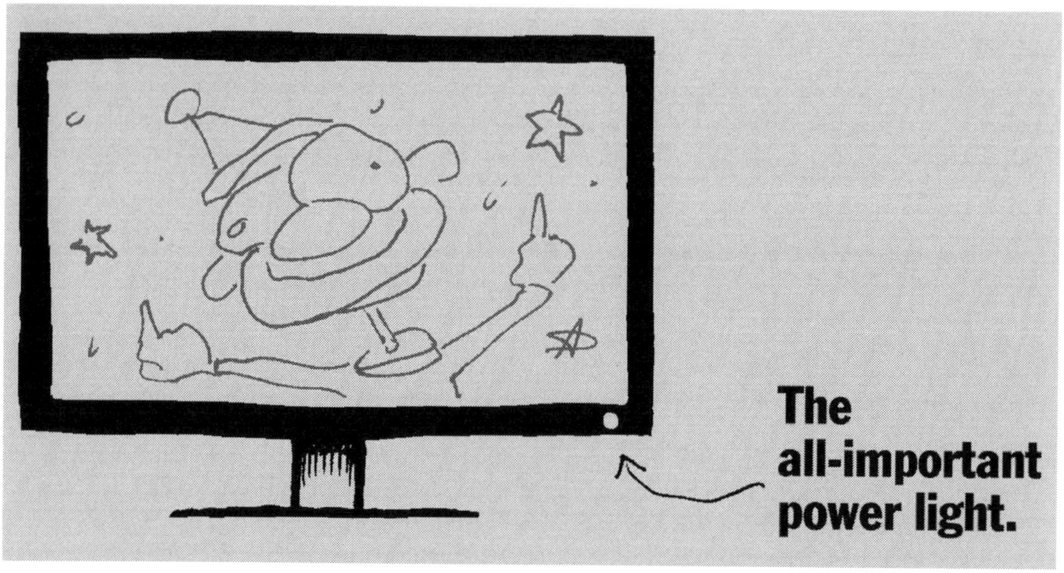
The all-important power light.

Why is the power light so important? Because otherwise it's just a black rectangle. Or, even worse, a TV might be a wall-mounted black rectangle:

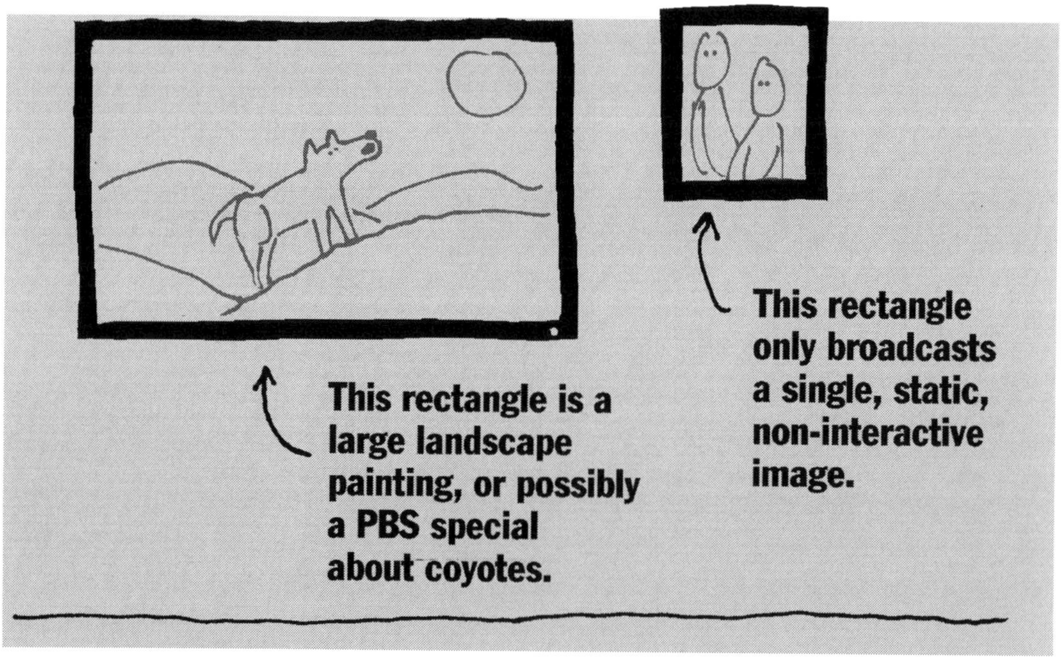
This rectangle is a large landscape painting, or possibly a PBS special about coyotes.
This rectangle only broadcasts a single, static, non-interactive image.

TVs, smartphones, computers… they've all been reduced to screens with thin little edges (or nothing at all). The only way to distinguish them visually is the size of them. A drawing of a smartphone sitting on a table might be confused with a widescreen tablet computer. There might be no way to tell which is which unless there's a coffee cup or a hand next to it to provide scale.

Perhaps one of the biggest challenges facing sequential artists (and really, all illustrators, photographers, movie makers, and visual storytellers) who want to portray what life is like in this wonderful modern age we exist in is this:

People interacting with multi-purpose electronic devices aren't *doing* anything.

I could be watching a YouTube video or using GPS or playing Angry Birds, but this word balloon lets you know that I'm actually texting someone. Or maybe I'm reading a text from someone else. It sort of depends on whether you think my thumbs are moving or not.

And by *doing*, I mean they're not doing anything particularly *visual*. They are sitting or standing, moving their eyes, maybe tapping the screen, maybe swiping. They might be doing something crucially important to the narrative of the story you're trying to tell, or the joke you're trying to set up, but in appearance they're just... standin' there. It forces the storyteller to drop a big dialogue hint to clue the reader in, like:

"Hi! I was just calling to leave you a message..."
or
"This Bluetooth headset is so comfortable I barely notice it!"
or maybe
"My, this is a wonderful video I am viewing on my portable media playback device!"

As interfaces with technology continue to become smaller, thinner, less obtrusive, less noticeable, and less identifiable, creative artists will need to continue to adapt and improve their visual communication skills. Some day soon even the small electronic devices will disappear, and the tyranny of the black rectangle will come to an end, leaving visual storytellers in an even more challenging environment: A world of people laughing, talking, and staring off into the middle distance as their neural implants amuse, entertain, and sell them things.

That'll look exciting.

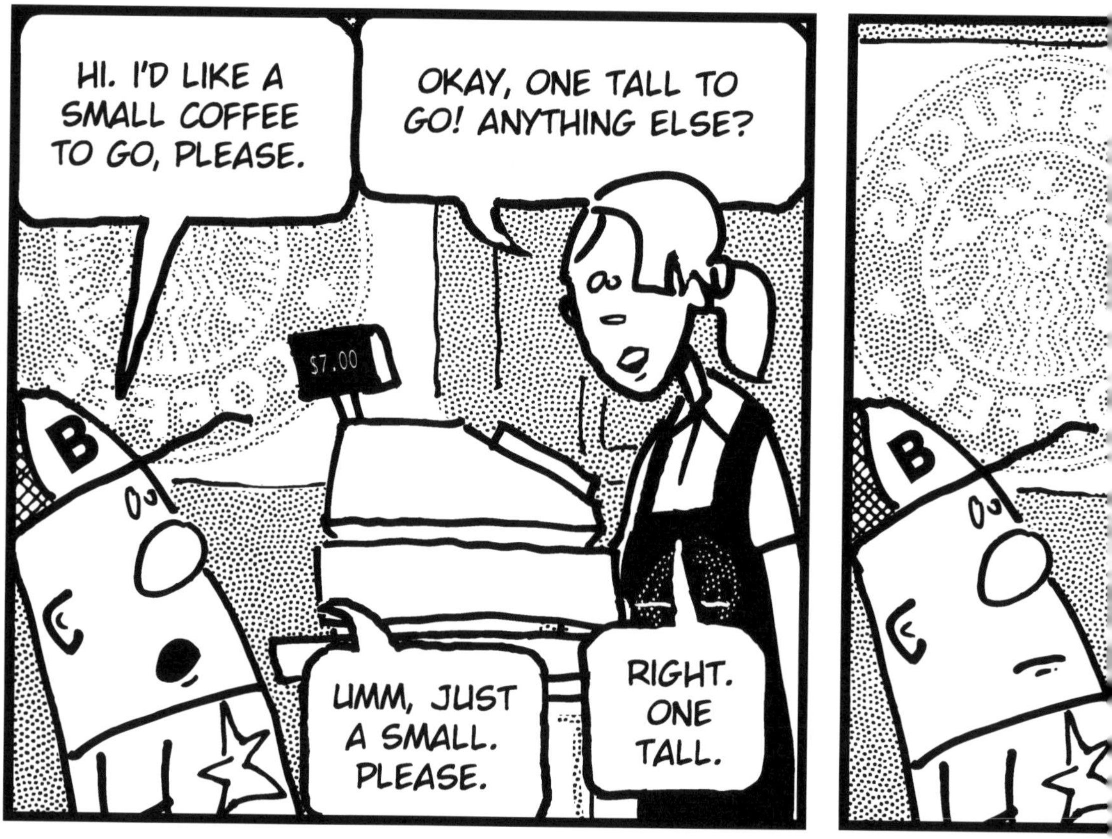
HI. I'D LIKE A SMALL COFFEE TO GO, PLEASE.
OKAY, ONE TALL TO GO! ANYTHING ELSE?
$7.00
UMM, JUST A SMALL. PLEASE.
RIGHT. ONE TALL.

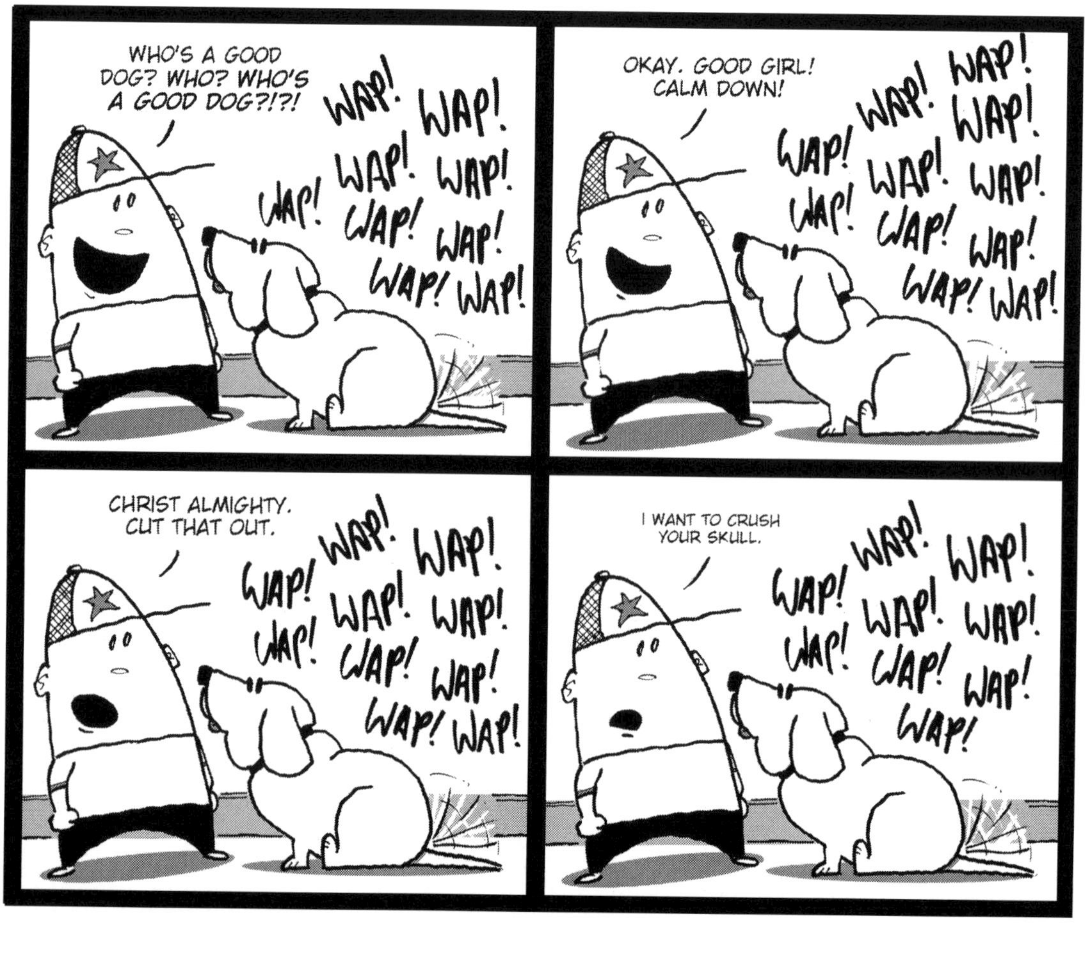
WHO'S A GOOD DOG? WHO? WHO'S A GOOD DOG?!?!
WAP! WAP! WAP! WAP! WAP! WAP! WAP! WAP! WAP!
OKAY. GOOD GIRL! CALM DOWN!
WAP! WAP! WAP! WAP! WAP! WAP! WAP! WAP! WAP! WAP! WAP!
CHRIST ALMIGHTY. CUT THAT OUT.
WAP! WAP! WAP! WAP! WAP! WAP! WAP! WAP! WAP! WAP!
I WANT TO CRUSH YOUR SKULL.
WAP! WAP! WAP! WAP! WAP! WAP! WAP! WAP! WAP!

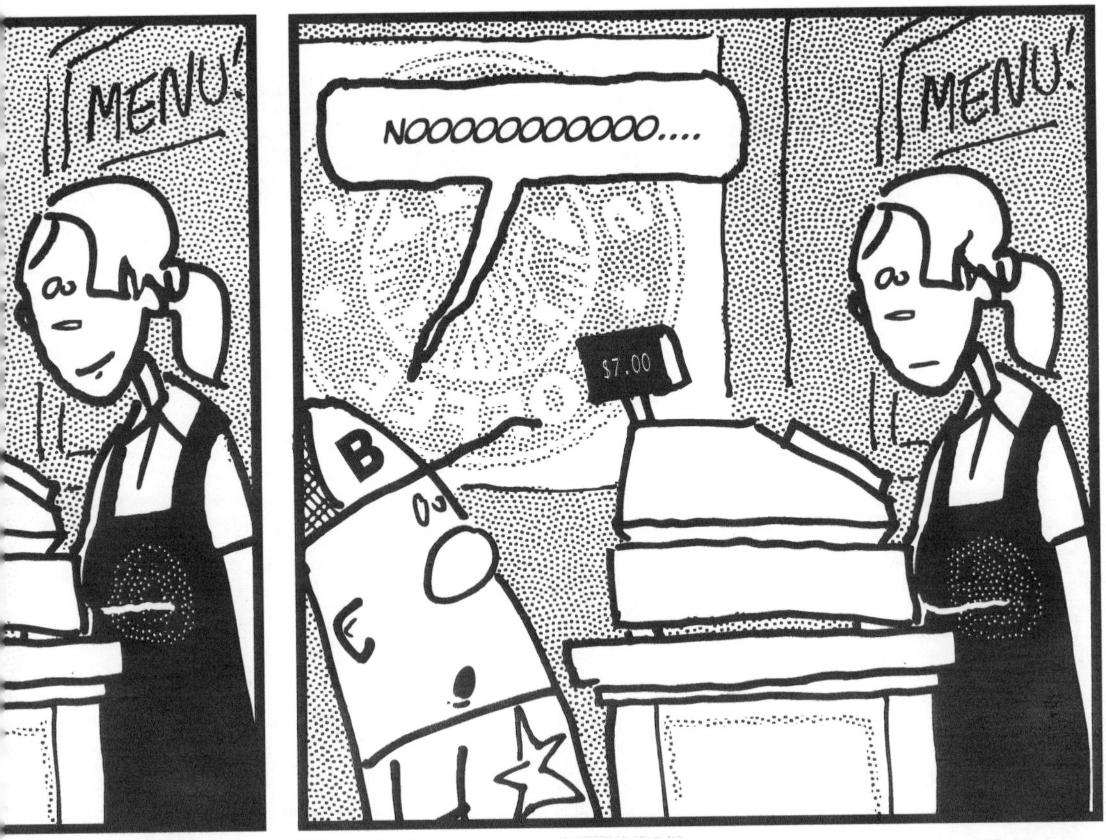
MENU!
NOOOOOOOOOOO....
$7.00
MENU!

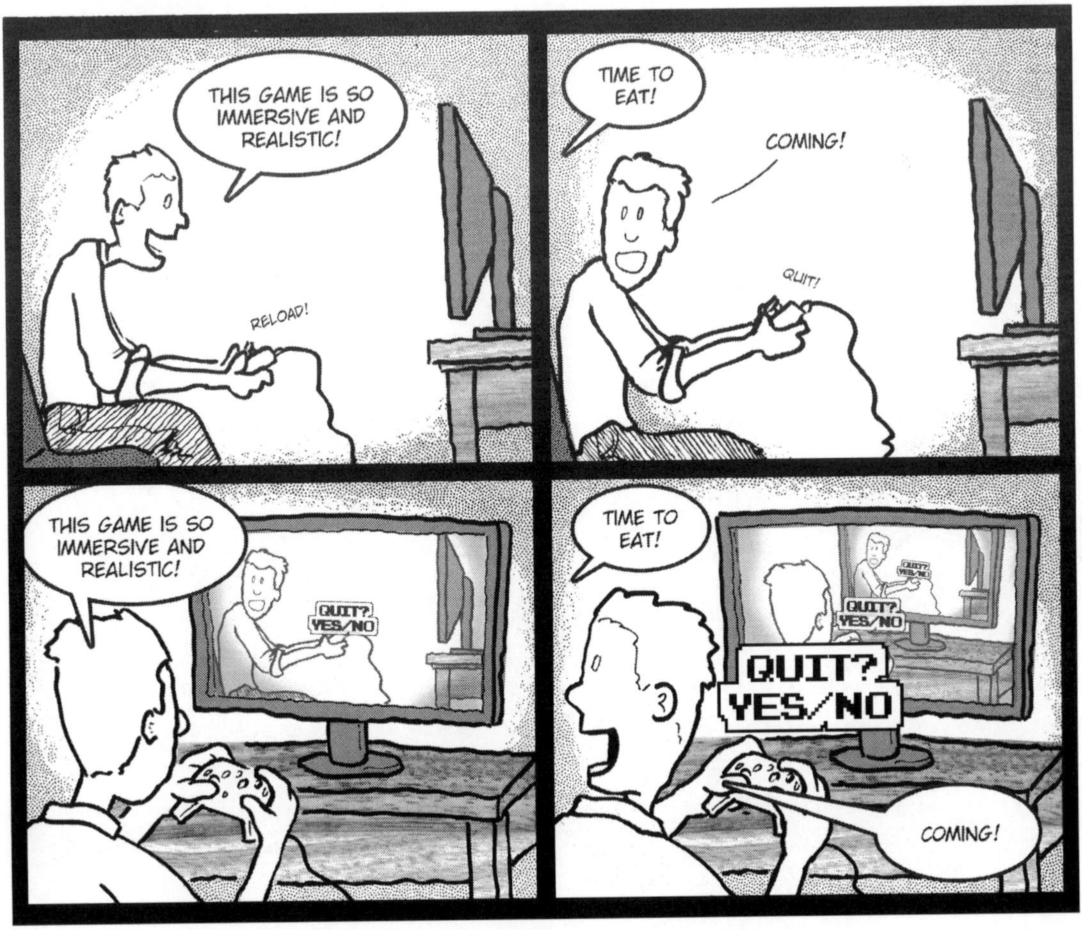
THIS GAME IS SO IMMERSIVE AND REALISTIC!
RELOAD!
TIME TO EAT!
COMING!
QUIT!
THIS GAME IS SO IMMERSIVE AND REALISTIC!
QUIT? YES/NO
TIME TO EAT!
QUIT? YES/NO
QUIT? YES/NO
QUIT? YES/NO
COMING!

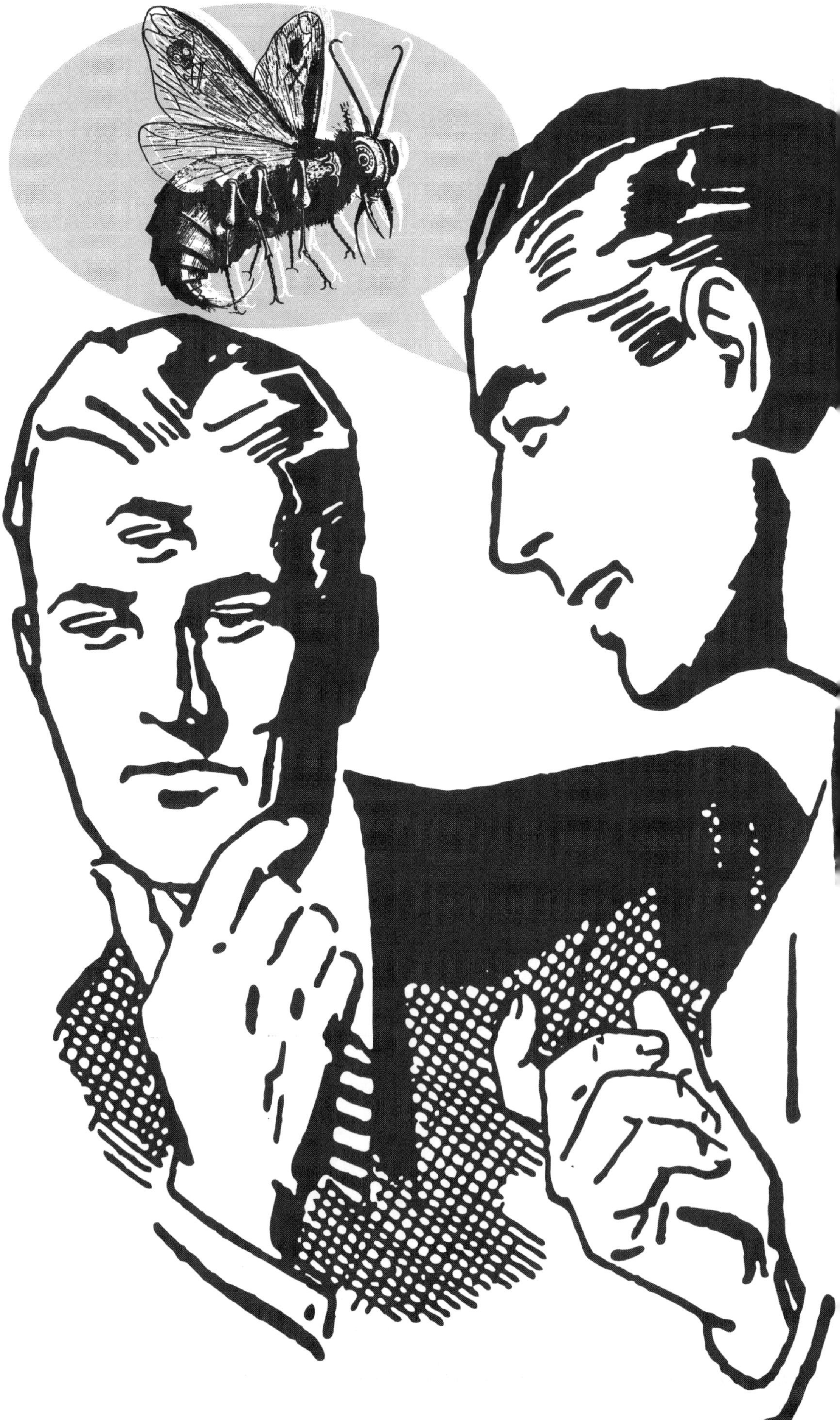

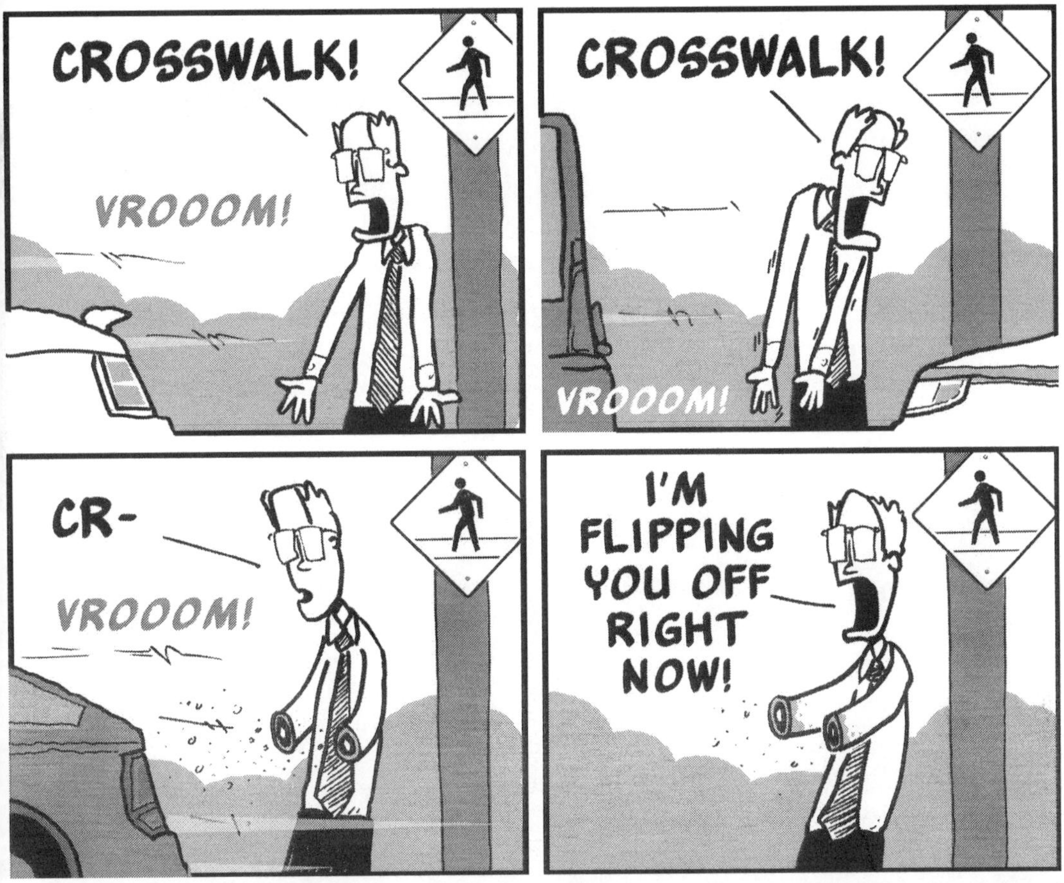
CROSSWALK!
VROOOM!
CROSSWALK!
VROOOM!
CR-
VROOOM!
I'M FLIPPING YOU OFF RIGHT NOW!

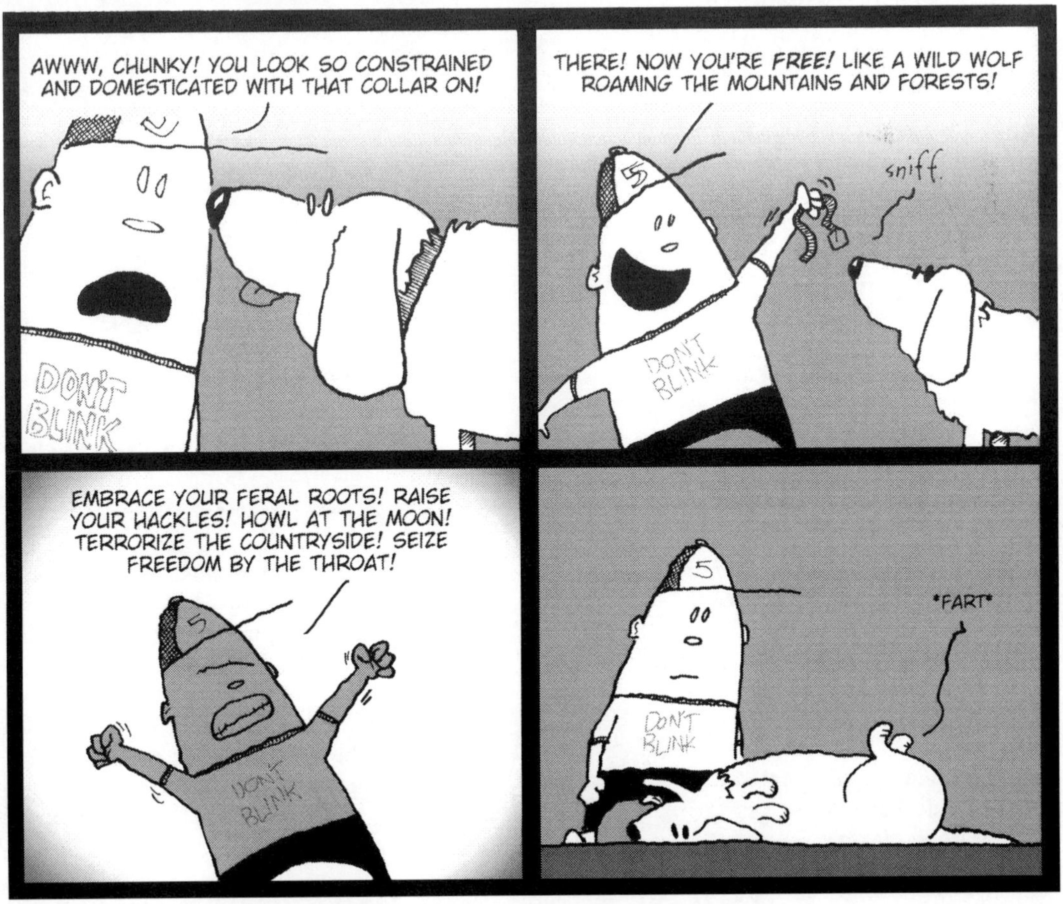
AWWW, CHUNKY! YOU LOOK SO CONSTRAINED AND DOMESTICATED WITH THAT COLLAR ON!
DON'T BLINK
THERE! NOW YOU'RE FREE! LIKE A WILD WOLF ROAMING THE MOUNTAINS AND FORESTS!
sniff.
DON'T BLINK
EMBRACE YOUR FERAL ROOTS! RAISE YOUR HACKLES! HOWL AT THE MOON! TERRORIZE THE COUNTRYSIDE! SEIZE FREEDOM BY THE THROAT!
DON'T BLINK
FART
DON'T BLINK

HOLLYWOOD BLOCKBUSTER FRANCHISE REBOOT 2.0

I used to be the type of person who would get indignant and huffy when Hollywood would deem it necessary to remake a classic film. I would whine about the original film's integrity being compromised. It is art, I would reason, and some art should not be trifled with. Well, I was wrong. Honestly, who cares?

Let's take, for instance, the 1998 remake of "Psycho" (Now, since no one actually bothered watching it, we can't be *positive* it sucked, but let's just *assume*). Myopic film nerds were up in arms when this project was announced, decrying this blasphemy against Hitchcock. But here we are, well over a decade later, and has it in any way, shape, or form hurt the reputation or stature of the original? No, of course not. Did it give crybaby movie writers something to wring their carpal-tunneled hands about? Oh, yes.

Don't get me wrong, the notion of movie-remaking is wholly commercial, sometimes crass, and generally misguided. But despite someone somewhere making or losing money on the remake, the original remains intact. If nothing else, remakes usually revive an interest in the original, and at least the old-school fans get a nicely restored re-release out of it. So let the money-makers try to make their money.

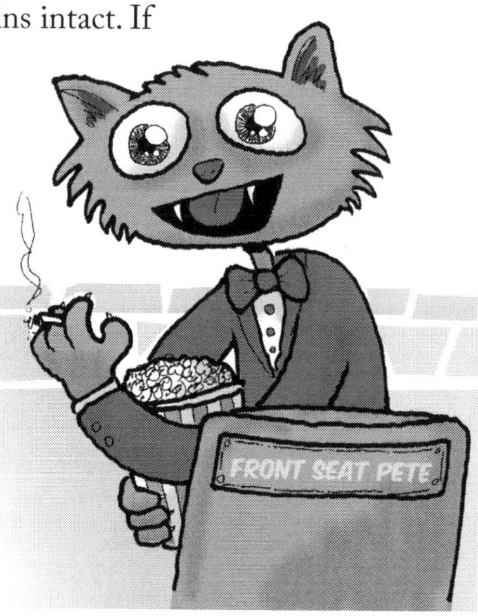
FRONT SEAT PETE

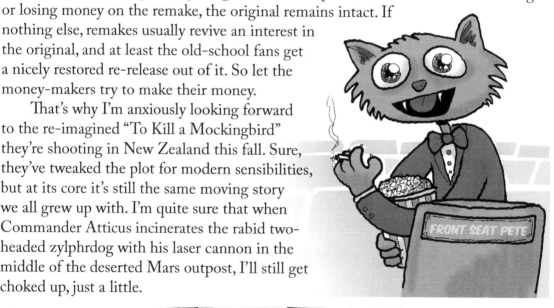

That's why I'm anxiously looking forward to the re-imagined "To Kill a Mockingbird" they're shooting in New Zealand this fall. Sure, they've tweaked the plot for modern sensibilities, but at its core it's still the same moving story we all grew up with. I'm quite sure that when Commander Atticus incinerates the rabid two-headed zylphrdog with his laser cannon in the middle of the deserted Mars outpost, I'll still get choked up, just a little.

When I Was A Teenager

When I was a headbanger,

I didn't know the difference between Dusty Springfield and Buffalo Springfield,

or the difference between Richie Havens and Ritchie Valens.

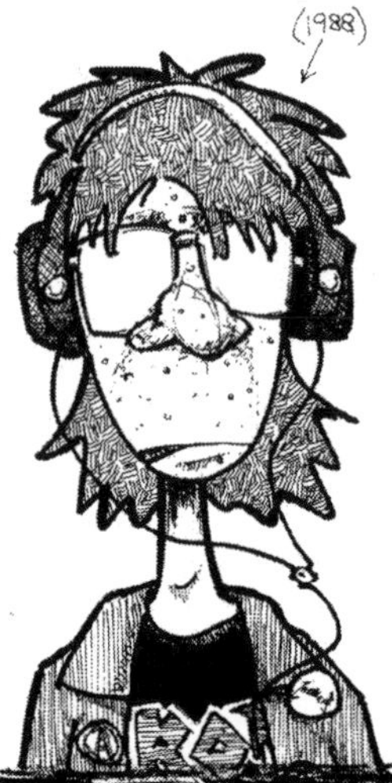
(1988)

I thought Boz Scaggs was a band and Jethro Tull was a guy.

I didn't know the difference between Van Morrison, Jim Morrison, and Morrissey.

I thought Maceo Parker was an Irish guy named "Macy."

But I knew that Clive Burr and Paul Di-Anno were part of the original lineup of Iron Maiden, and that Bruce Dickinson used to be in Samson.

FAKE ADVERTISEMENT

Feeling Tired? Depressed? Disconnected? Alone?
TAKE control of YOUR OWN LIFE
What causes depression? Maybe your noggin chemicals are all effed up. Maybe no one likes you because you're such a major downer. Maybe you're a defective human being. Who can really say?
We can.
We're Phlaxxo-Kinderfresser, a subsidiary of Uni-Chem Pharmaceuticals, and we're here to help.
Introducing ENDITOL.
ENDiTOL
ENDiTOL
DO IT for your friends DO IT for your family DO IT for yourself
The most common side effects of ENDITOL include: Postmortem dissolution, reincarnation, second thoughts, blurred visions of a bright otherworldly light, a cessation of vital functions, and in a few rare cases, may contribute to a subdued yet palpable sense of relief from loved ones. Less commonly, sensitivity to life may briefly occur. ENDITOL kind of protects against sexually transmitted diseases, in sort of a roundabout way. Ask your mortician if Enditol is right for you. Phlaxxo-Kinderfresser is a part of the Uni-Chem Pharmaceuticals Global Products family.

"You may want to seriously consider an apology to the entire community for the recklessness of your satire."

"On any day, this ad would be in horrible taste..."

"How deprived of morals must one be to present suicide as entertainment."

"Be aware that you've offended this reader, and I rather hope others, too."

"I had to read the ad several times to realize that it was a parody."

"I've tried to kill myself 3 times times, and I think it's funny. Loosen up, yo."

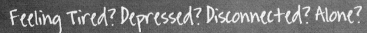

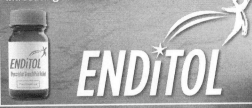

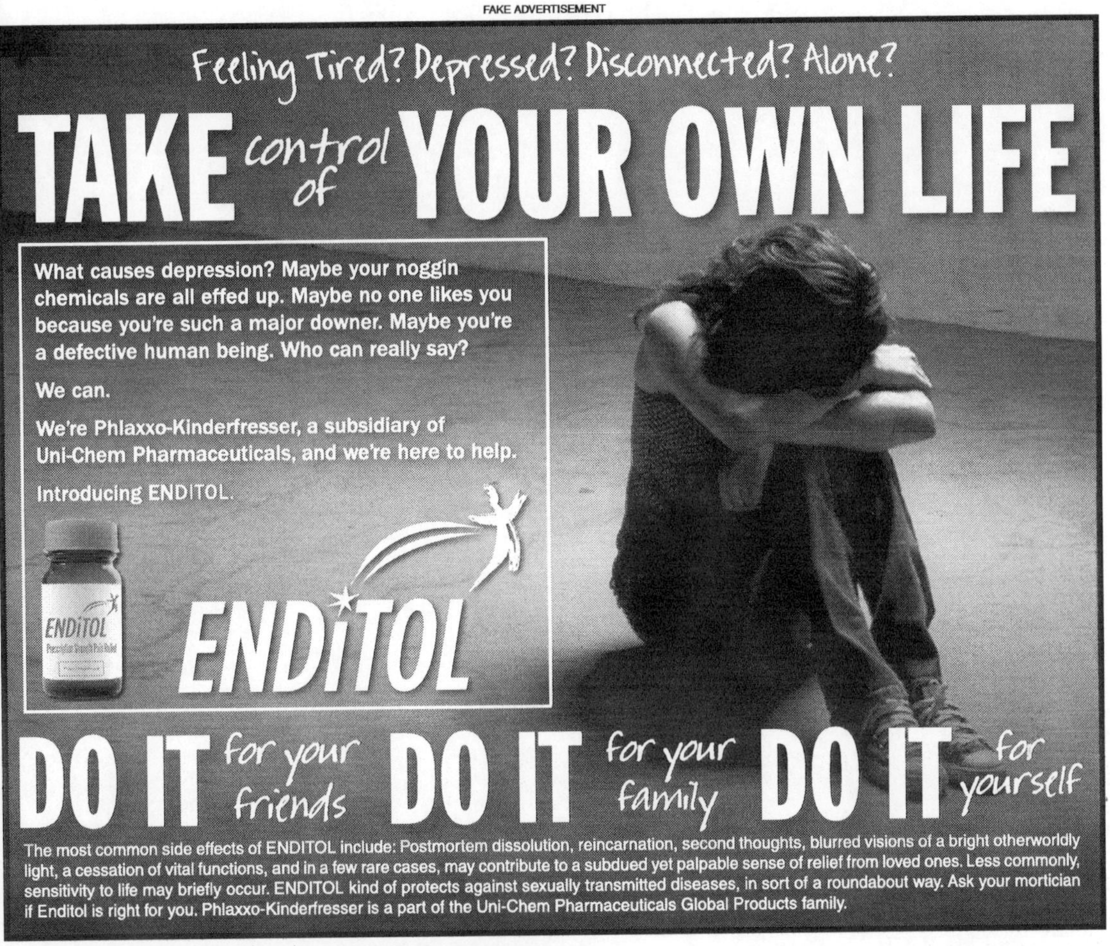

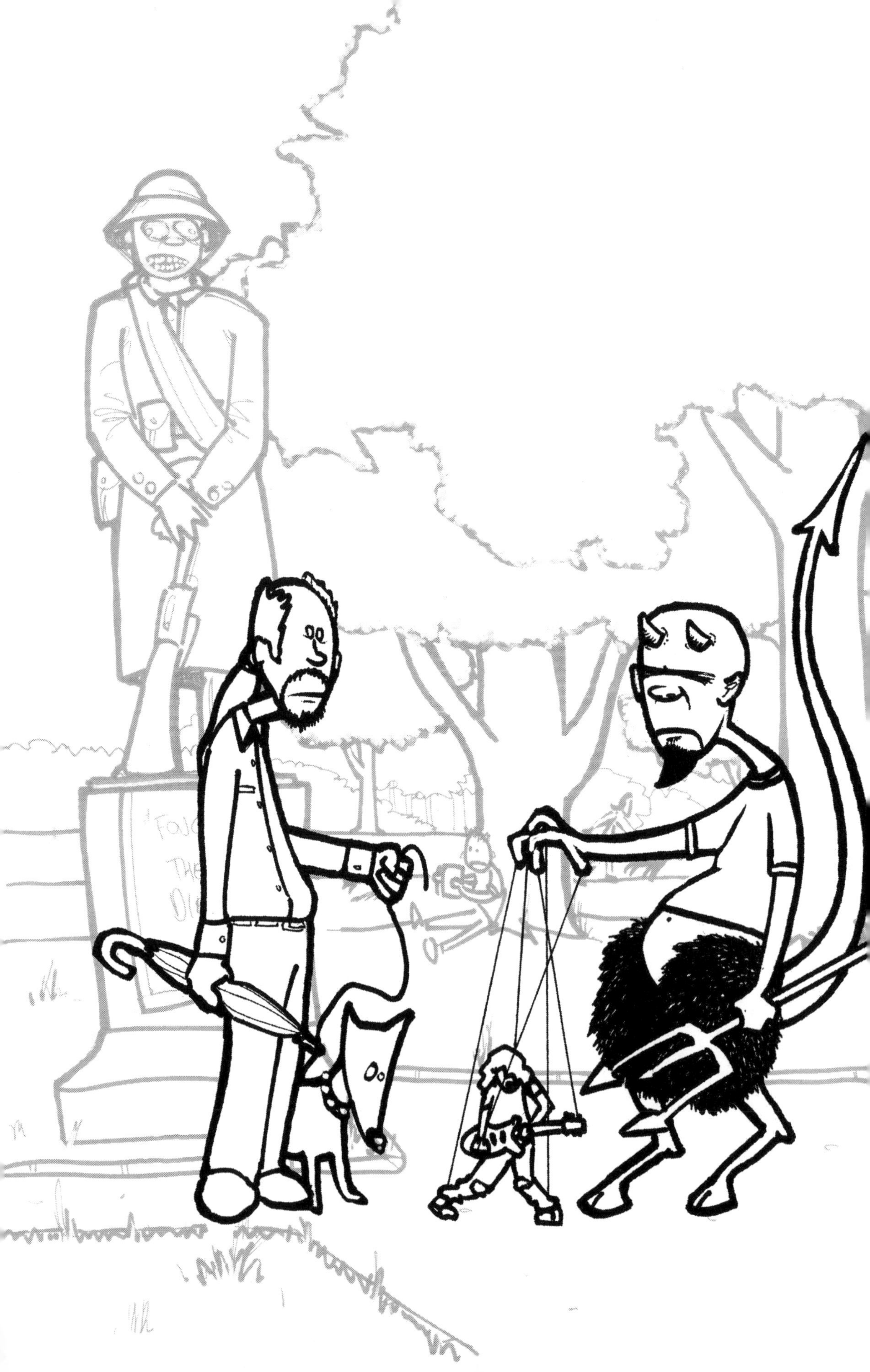

The Word Problem

...WELL, I'VE BEEN GOING OVER YOUR TEST, AND FRANKLY, I FIND YOUR USE OF THE WORD "NIGGARDLY" TO BE RATHER... UNNECESSARY.

OH, **OK!** **HERE** WE GO! IT'S **NOT** A RACIAL SLUR! IT HAS **NO** ETYMOLOGICAL BASIS REGARDING RACE, IT JUST **SOUNDS** SIMILAR TO A TERRIBLE WORD! SO NOW YOU'RE GONNA GET ALL UPTIGHT AND "POLITICALLY CORRECT" ABOUT IT! BRING ON THE CENSORSHIP!

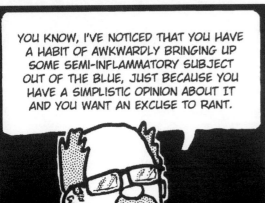

YOU KNOW, I'VE NOTICED THAT YOU HAVE A HABIT OF AWKWARDLY BRINGING UP SOME SEMI-INFLAMMATORY SUBJECT OUT OF THE BLUE, JUST BECAUSE YOU HAVE A SIMPLISTIC OPINION ABOUT IT AND YOU WANT AN EXCUSE TO RANT.

I DON'T DO THAT!

THIS IS AN ALGEBRA TEST.

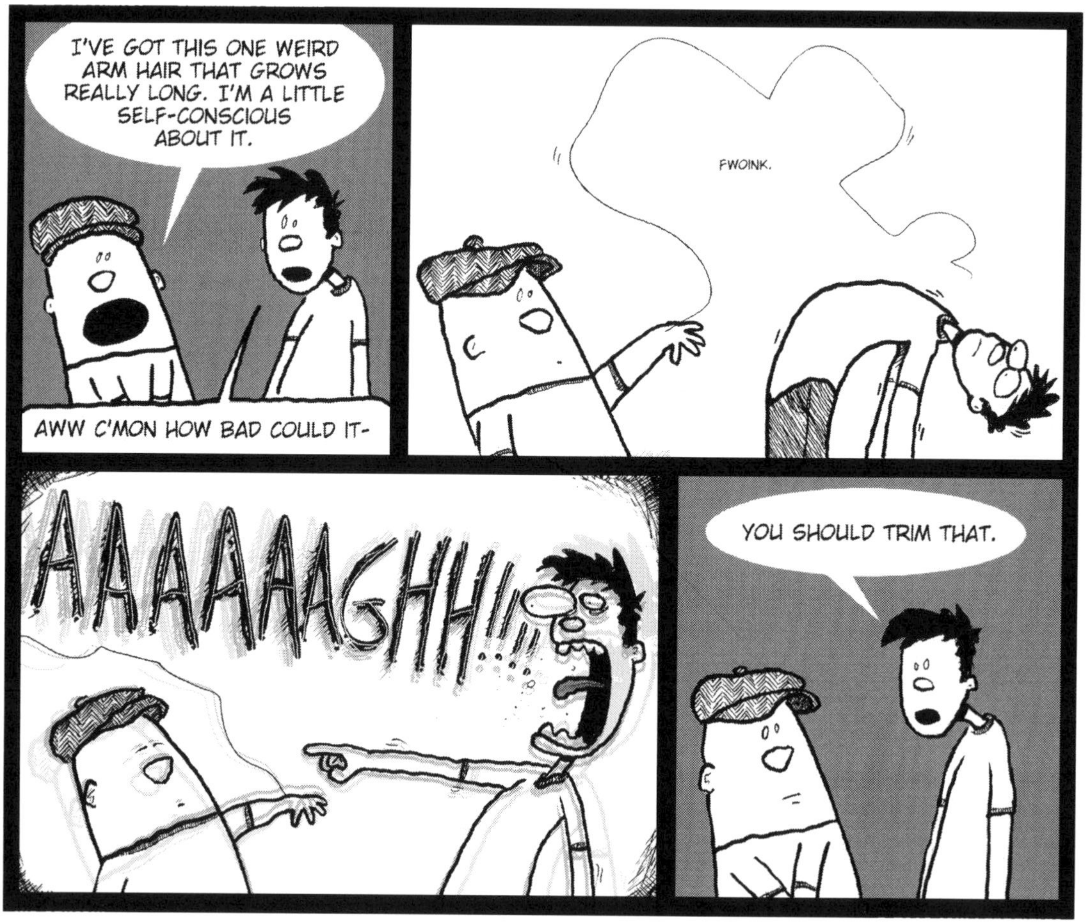
I'VE GOT THIS ONE WEIRD ARM HAIR THAT GROWS REALLY LONG. I'M A LITTLE SELF-CONSCIOUS ABOUT IT.
AWW C'MON HOW BAD COULD IT-
FWOINK.
AAAAAAGHH!!!!
YOU SHOULD TRIM THAT.

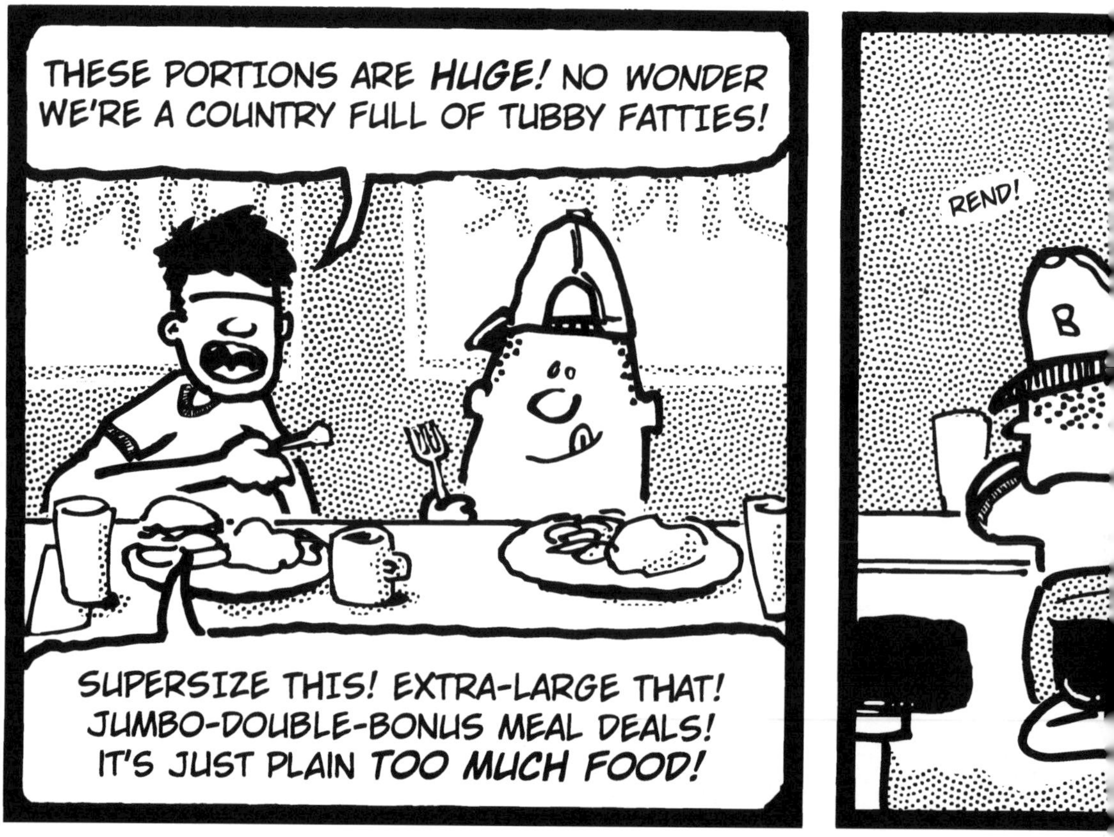
THESE PORTIONS ARE HUGE! NO WONDER WE'RE A COUNTRY FULL OF TUBBY FATTIES!
SUPERSIZE THIS! EXTRA-LARGE THAT! JUMBO-DOUBLE-BONUS MEAL DEALS! IT'S JUST PLAIN TOO MUCH FOOD!
REND!
B

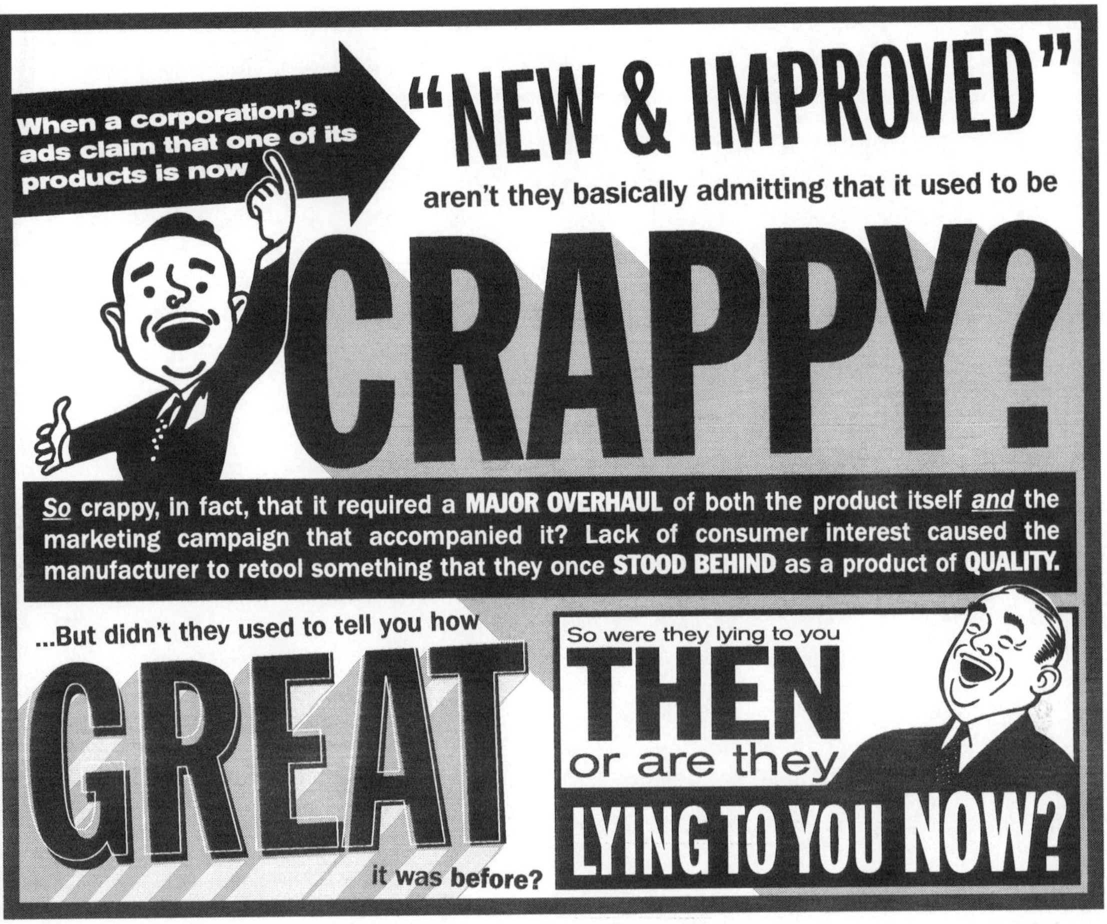
When a corporation's ads claim that one of its products is now
"NEW & IMPROVED"
aren't they basically admitting that it used to be
CRAPPY?
So crappy, in fact, that it required a MAJOR OVERHAUL of both the product itself and the marketing campaign that accompanied it? Lack of consumer interest caused the manufacturer to retool something that they once STOOD BEHIND as a product of QUALITY.
...But didn't they used to tell you how
GREAT
it was before?
So were they lying to you
THEN
or are they
LYING TO YOU NOW?

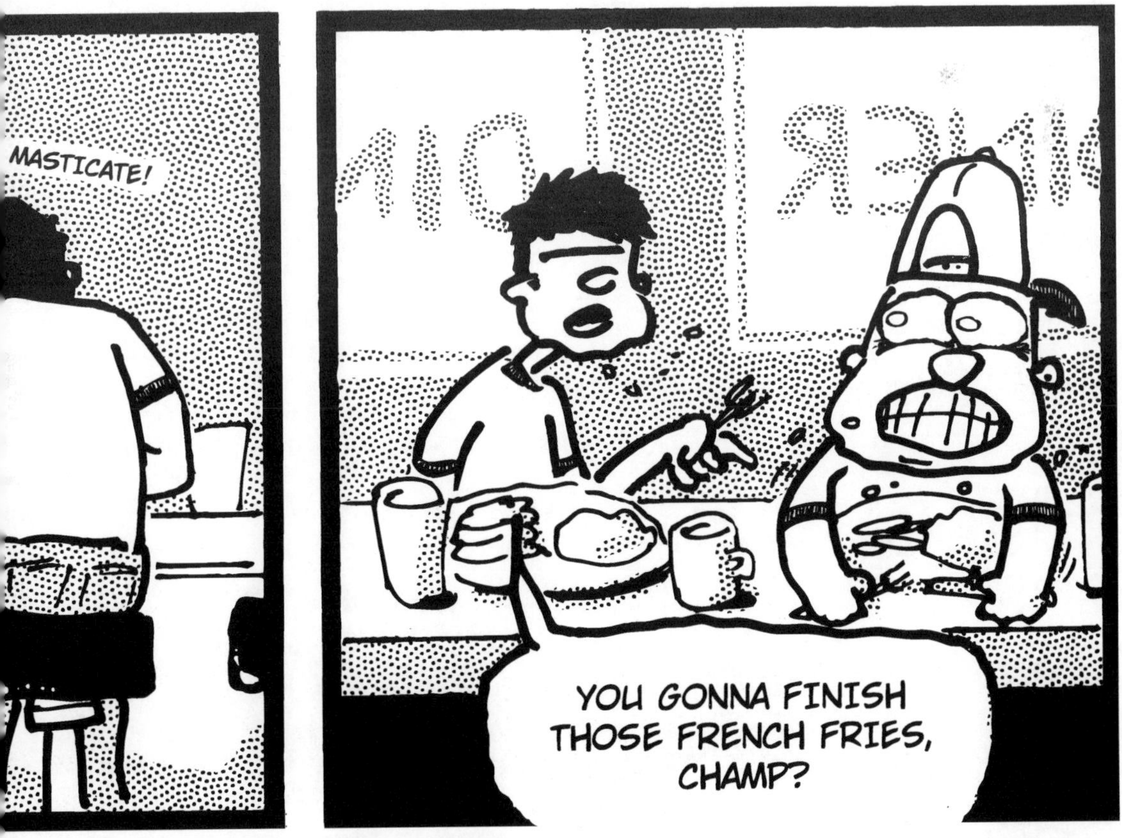
MASTICATE!
YOU GONNA FINISH THOSE FRENCH FRIES, CHAMP?

the wordpuncher

Etymologizing Wordcabulary and Slanguage and Stuff

Words. I *love* words. I love learning big fancy new words and then forgetting what they mean and then pretending that I have always known what they mean. It is mellifluously awesome. I realize that sometimes language can be a little overwhelming, so I'm here to help you, the inept reader, navigate these treacherous waters. Let's take a look at some oft-confused words you should try working into your "vocab", because right now you sound like "a halfwit."

CAREEN — To lean, sway or tip to one side
CAREER — To move forward at full speed
CAROM — To strike an object and rebound
CAROL — To strike an object with terrible singing
EXAMPLE: *"I careered down the course in my coupe, careened into a corner and caromed into a crowd of Christmas carolers."*

CLIQUE — An exclusive group of people
CLAQUE — A hired group of clapping sycophants
CLINIQUE — A group of sycophants with really nice skin
CLOQUE — A classy way to spell "cloak"
CALQUE — An expression introduced into one language by translating it from another.
EXAMPLE: *"I do not know if 'calque' is a calque."*
CLUQUE — The sound a French chicken makes

LITERATE — Able to read and write
ALITERATE — One who doesn't feel like reading or writing words starting with the letter 'A'
ALLITERATE — One who only wants to read or write words starting with the letter 'A'
ILLITERATE — Able to read fresh rhymes and fly lyrics
PRELITERATE — Able to read things before they are written

BON MOT — A French phrase meaning 'clever or witty remark'
BON SCOTT — An Australian phrase meaning 'sleep on your side'

EXTRICATE — To remove oneself from a situation
COLLIQUATE — To change from solid to liquid EXAMPLE: *"Pardon me, Good Lady. I must hastily extricate myself from this fancy dinner party because my poops are colliquating."*

COLLISION — When two moving objects strike each other
ALLISION — When a moving object strikes a stationary object
ELISION — When a word starts losin' letters
ELUSION — The act of escapin' or evadin'
ALISON — An Elvis Costello song
ALLUSION — A casual reference to an Elvis Costello song

USAGE: Drunk drivers have *collisions* with innocent people. When you drag them out of their wrecked cars and start whaling on them, your fist and their dumb faces are *allisioning*. Now, pretend that drunk jackass is someone named *Alison*, or Elvis Costello. "Your aim is true, my ass!" you shout angrily. A bystander calls 911. It all adds up to a funky situation. This is an *allusion* to a Public Enemy song, but the reference *eludes* the majority of my older readers, but probably not Elvis Costello, because he is a hip dude, but he probably isn't reading this. And neither is science fiction writer Harlan *Ellison*. Wait, what?

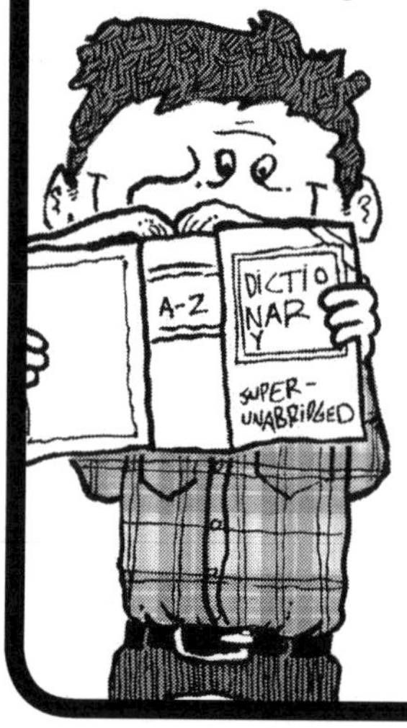

A-Z
DICTIONARY
SUPER-UNABRIDGED

fig. A: THE LEARNED SCHOLAR

the wordpuncher pop quiz!

Which of the following sentences is structured correctest?

1. "My friend Doug forwarded me a hilarious link to a cat video."
2. "My friend Doug forwarded me a link to a hilarious cat video."
3. "Doug isn't my friend anymore because he forwarded me idiotic crap."

ANSWER: D

KAKISTOCRACY — A form of government in which the worst people are in power (Greek root: "kaka")
DEMOCRACY — A form of government you record on a 4-track in your poorly soundproofed garage
THEOCRACY — A political theory designed by Gordon Gartrell
OCHLOCRACY — A non-Ozzy Black Sabbath album
GYNECOCRACY — A political movement led by Tom Collins
VODKOCRACY — A political system from Black Russia in which one person seizes Absolut power
CHINESE DEMOCRACY — A system of rule in which one person seizes power and then ruins everything
MARTYROCRACY — When the president makes you feel guilty for not visiting more often
MERITOCRACY — The theory of skilled and educated people holding positions of power. I know! It's *hilarious!*
OGLIARCHY — A country run by an unattractive monarch
MONARCHY — The preferred Jamaican form of government
GOLDENARCHY — A burger kingdom's greatest threat
NOAHSARCHY — Each participating group elects two representatives: one male, one female
ANARCHY — The anti-establishment political theory (ironically, it's the only one with a decent logo)

Which One Should I Use?!?

1. THEY'RE	"They are"
2. THEIR	Belonging to thems
3. THAYER	One who thays
4. THEI'RE	Probably a *Star Trek* character or something

...And So Forth!

A quick guide to referencing groups.

Use "etc." to end a list of THINGS.
Use "et al." to end a list of PEOPLE.
Use "et tu" to end a list of ASSASSINS.

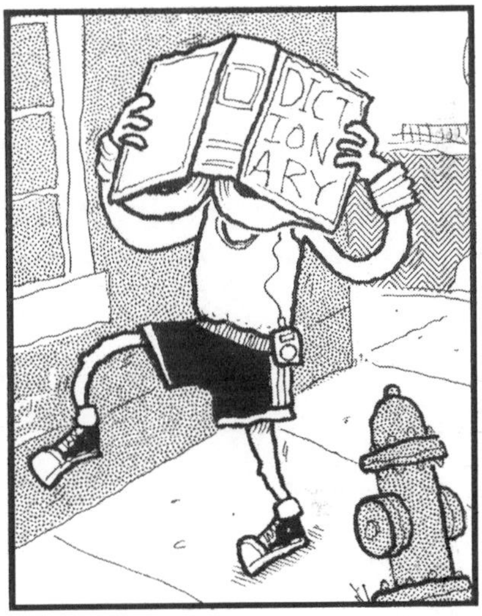
DICT ION ARY

fig. B: LEXERCISING

Here Are Some More Vocabularys

BOUQUETS — How people with silly fake French accents pronounce "bookcase"
BILDUNGSROMAN — A novel about a Roman building, from construction to demolition
CRAZINESS — Short for "crazy business"
GNAT — Past tense of "knit"
KILT — Past tense of "kill" *(Scottish)*
MALICIOUS — A delicious militia
MOT JUSTE — The exactly appropriate snooty French thing to say. SEE ALSO: *Baguette*
NUTSY — A zany member of the slapstick Nutsy Party
PROLIX — Extended to an unnecessary or tedious length and long and wordy and really really really really really drawn out and dragged out to an annoying degree and like, super verbose and stuff
PUISSANT — Is, surprisingly, not a dirty word
RAISIN — A statement made by a sassy Southern belle in justification of a belief or action. EXAMPLE: *"I do declayuh I need no raisin to attend yoah cotillion."*
SHELLFISH — Devoted to or caring only for oneshelf; consherned primarily with one'sh own welfare, regardlesh of othersh.
SUPPLIES — How a person faking a terribly offensive Chinese accent says "surprise"
SYCOPHANT — An elephant who never forgets to compliment you
VACATION — The opposite of a vocation

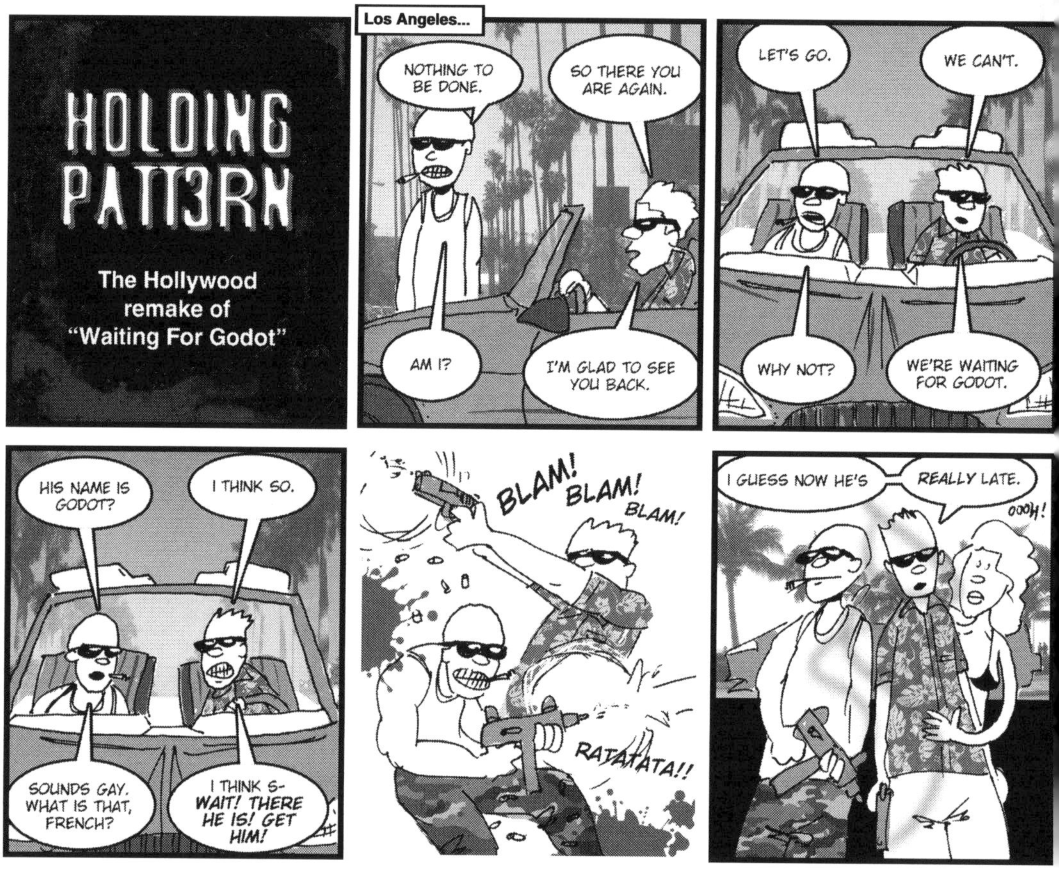
HOLDING PATT3RN
The Hollywood remake of "Waiting For Godot"
Los Angeles...
NOTHING TO BE DONE.
SO THERE YOU ARE AGAIN.
AM I?
I'M GLAD TO SEE YOU BACK.
LET'S GO.
WE CAN'T.
WHY NOT?
WE'RE WAITING FOR GODOT.
HIS NAME IS GODOT?
I THINK SO.
SOUNDS GAY. WHAT IS THAT, FRENCH?
I THINK S- WAIT! THERE HE IS! GET HIM!
BLAM! BLAM! BLAM!
RATATATA!!
I GUESS NOW HE'S
REALLY LATE.
OOOH!

Pets That Can Talk?!?

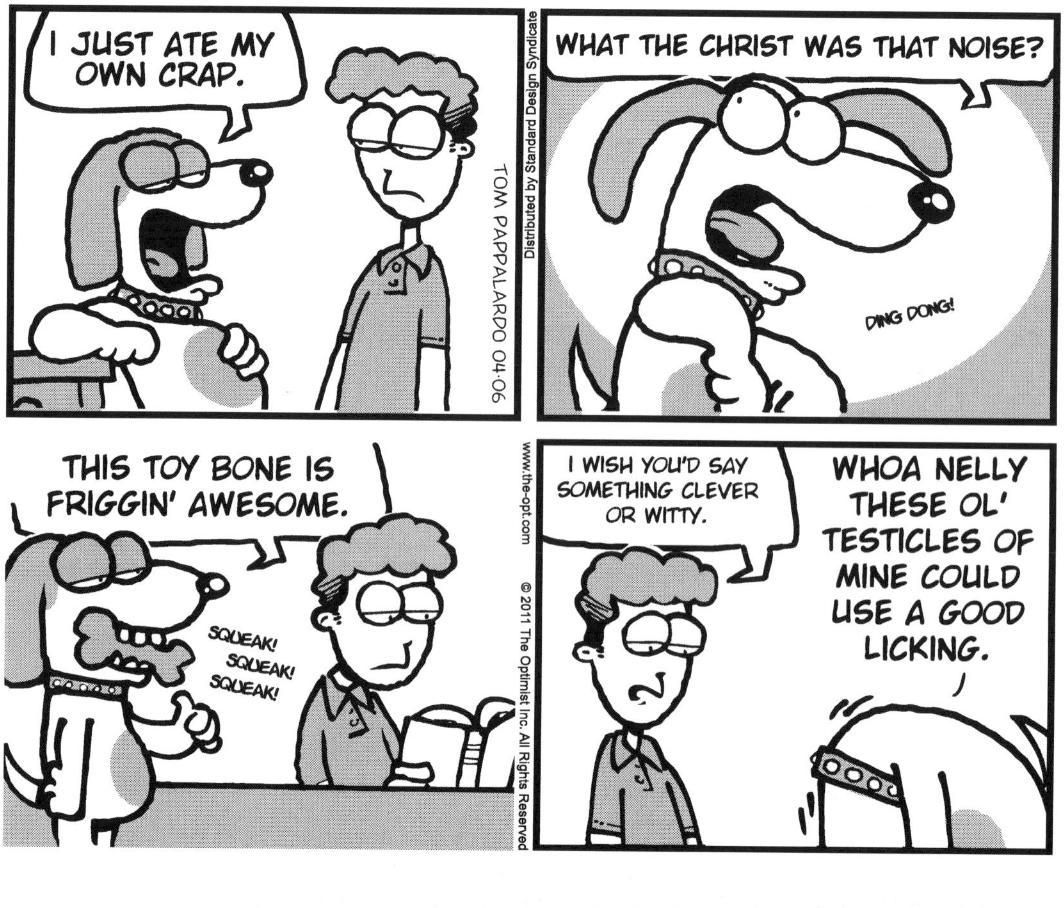
I JUST ATE MY OWN CRAP.
TOM PAPPALARDO 04-06
Distributed by Standard Design Syndicate
WHAT THE CHRIST WAS THAT NOISE?
DING DONG!
THIS TOY BONE IS FRIGGIN' AWESOME.
SQUEAK! SQUEAK! SQUEAK!
www.the-opt.com © 2011 The Optimist Inc. All Rights Reserved
I WISH YOU'D SAY SOMETHING CLEVER OR WITTY.
WHOA NELLY THESE OL' TESTICLES OF MINE COULD USE A GOOD LICKING.

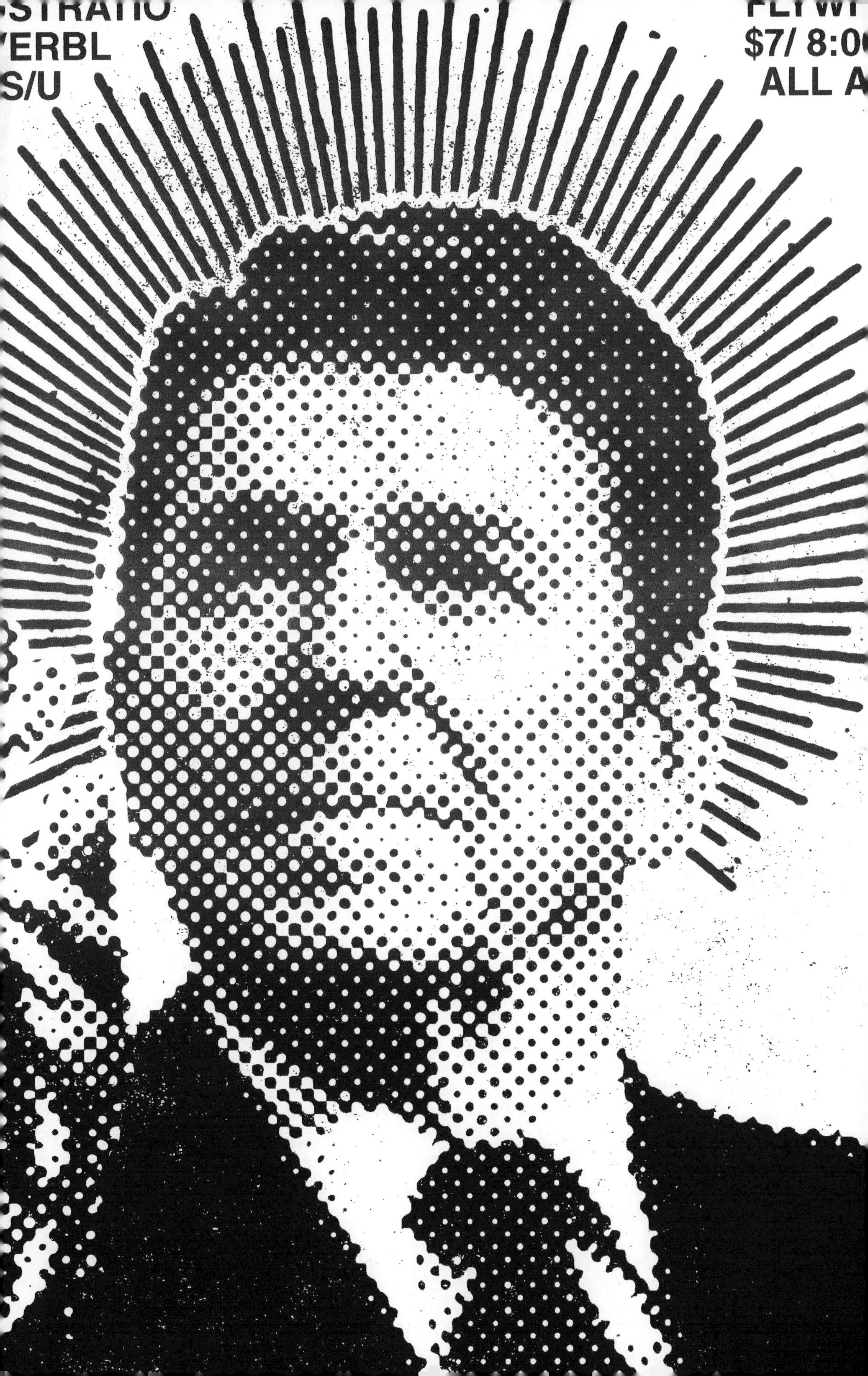

VERBL
S/U
$7/ 8:0
ALL A

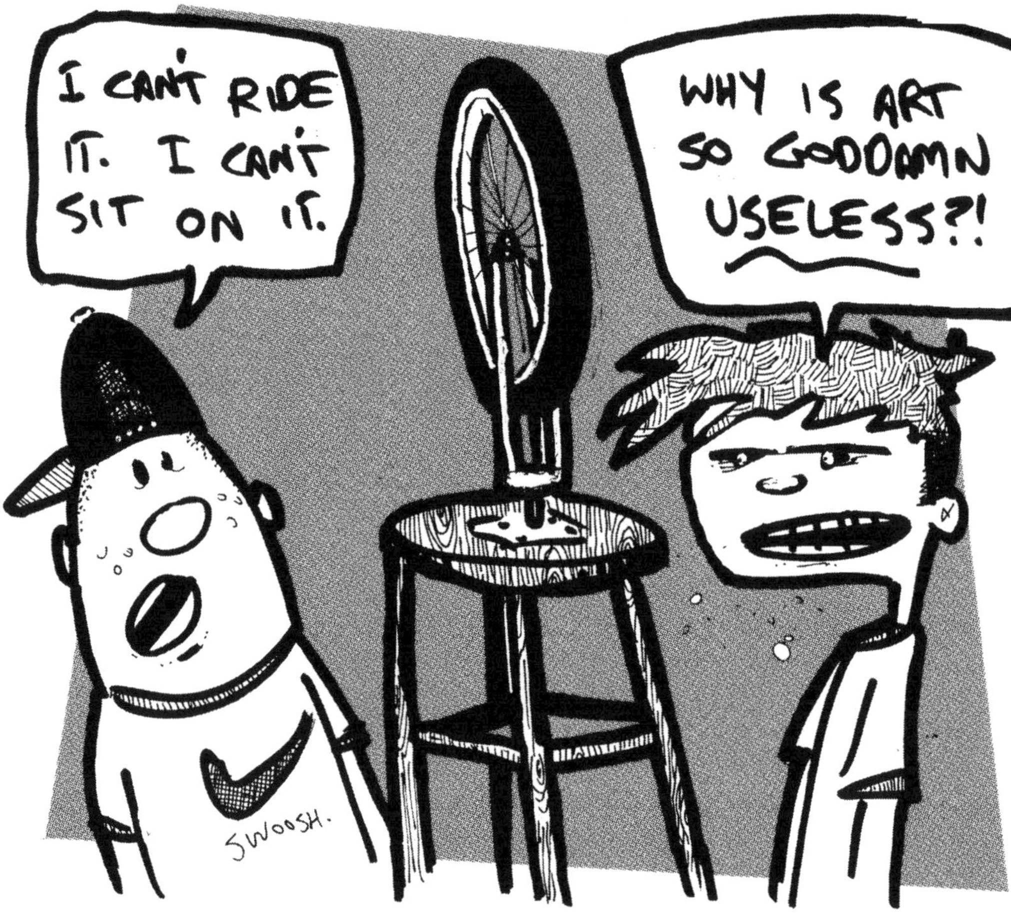
I CAN'T RIDE IT. I CAN'T SIT ON IT.
WHY IS ART SO GODDAMN USELESS?!
SWOOSH.

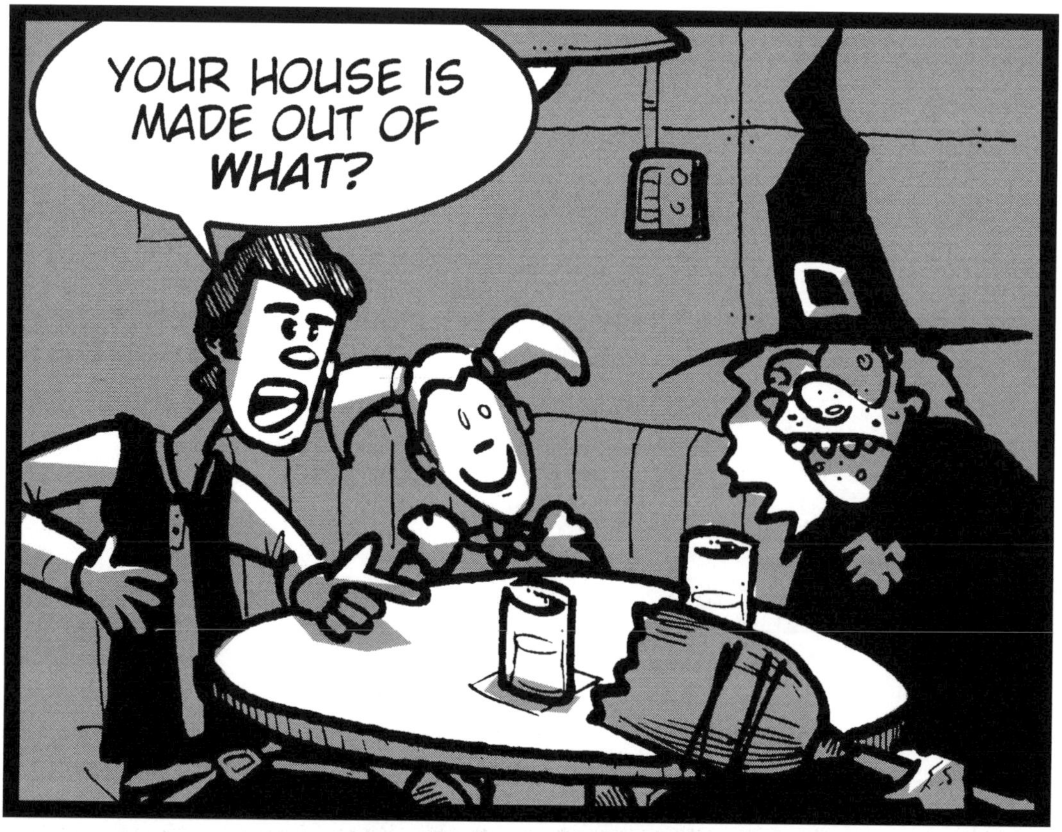
YOUR HOUSE IS MADE OUT OF WHAT?

Han Solo and Gretel

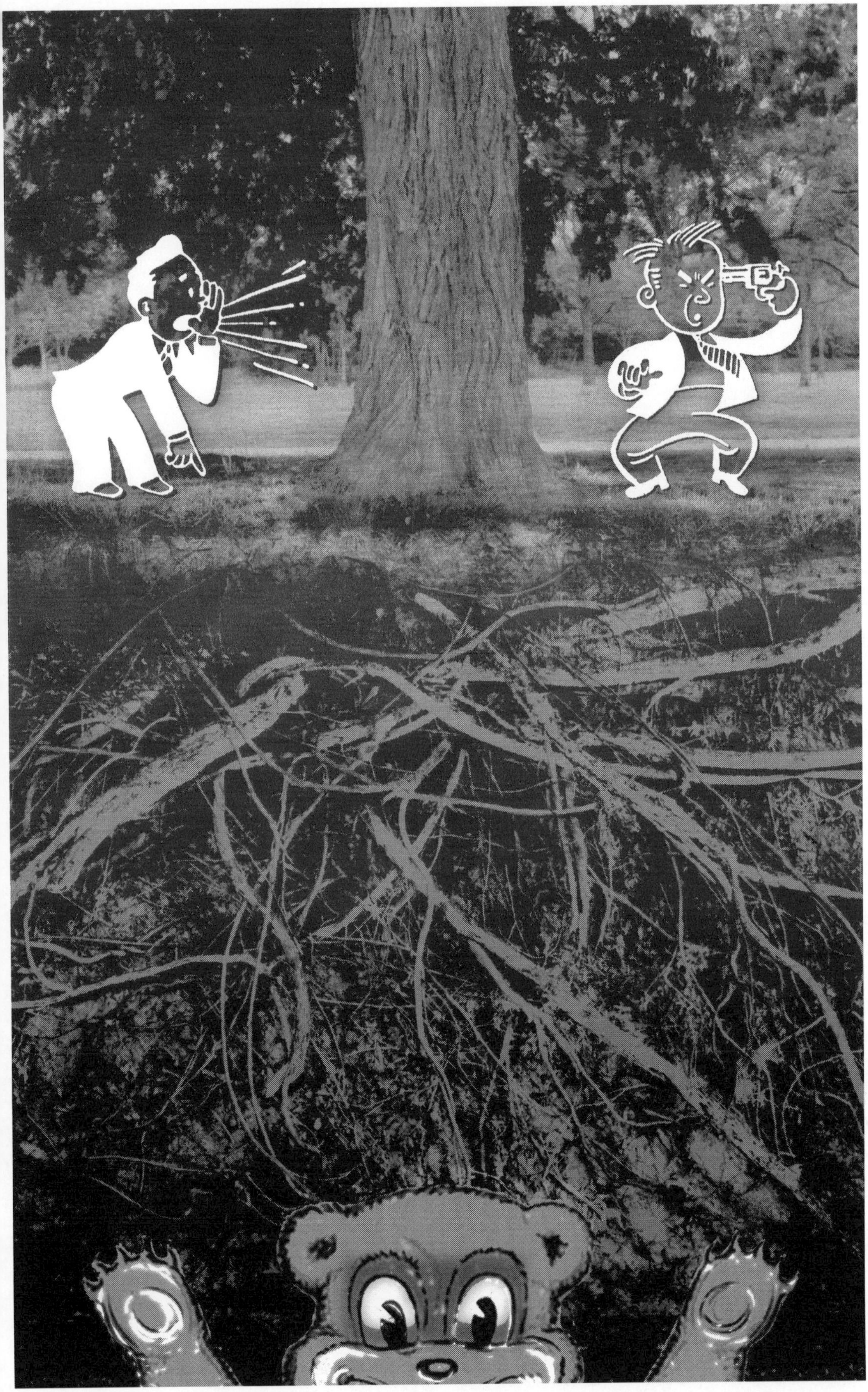

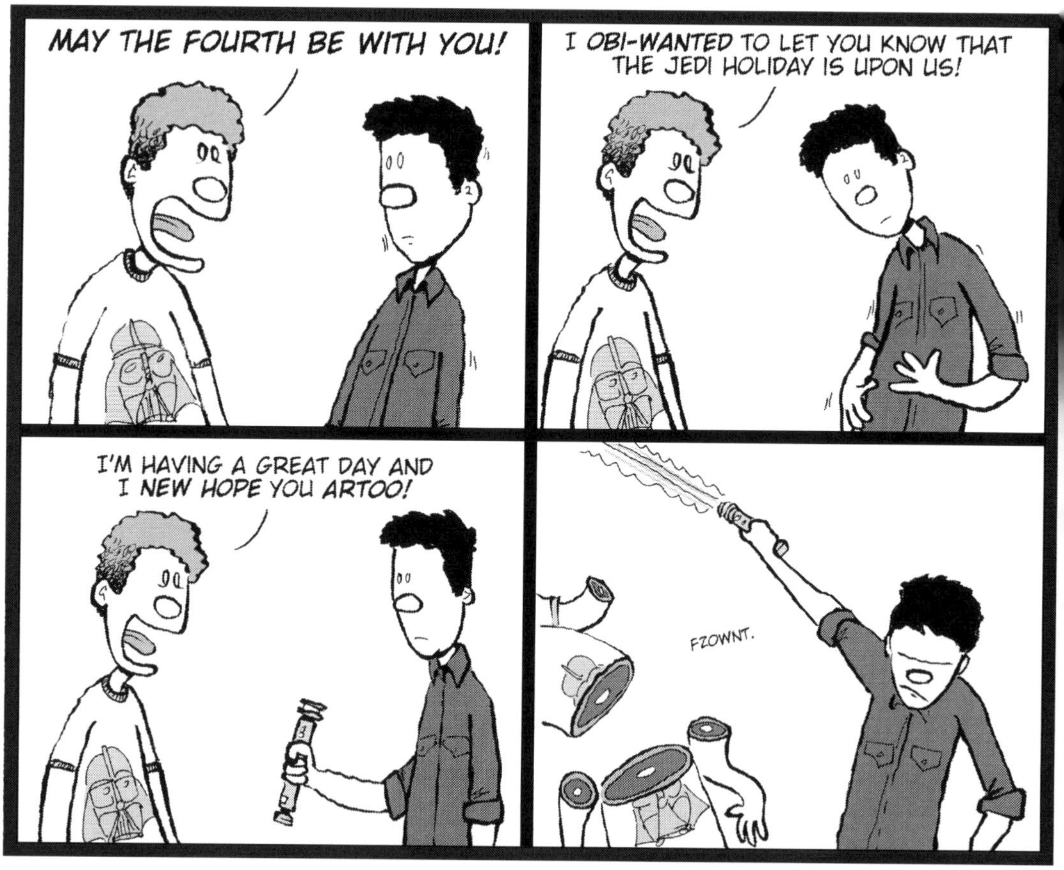
MAY THE FOURTH BE WITH YOU!
I OBI-WANTED TO LET YOU KNOW THAT THE JEDI HOLIDAY IS UPON US!
I'M HAVING A GREAT DAY AND I NEW HOPE YOU ARTOO!
FZOWNT.

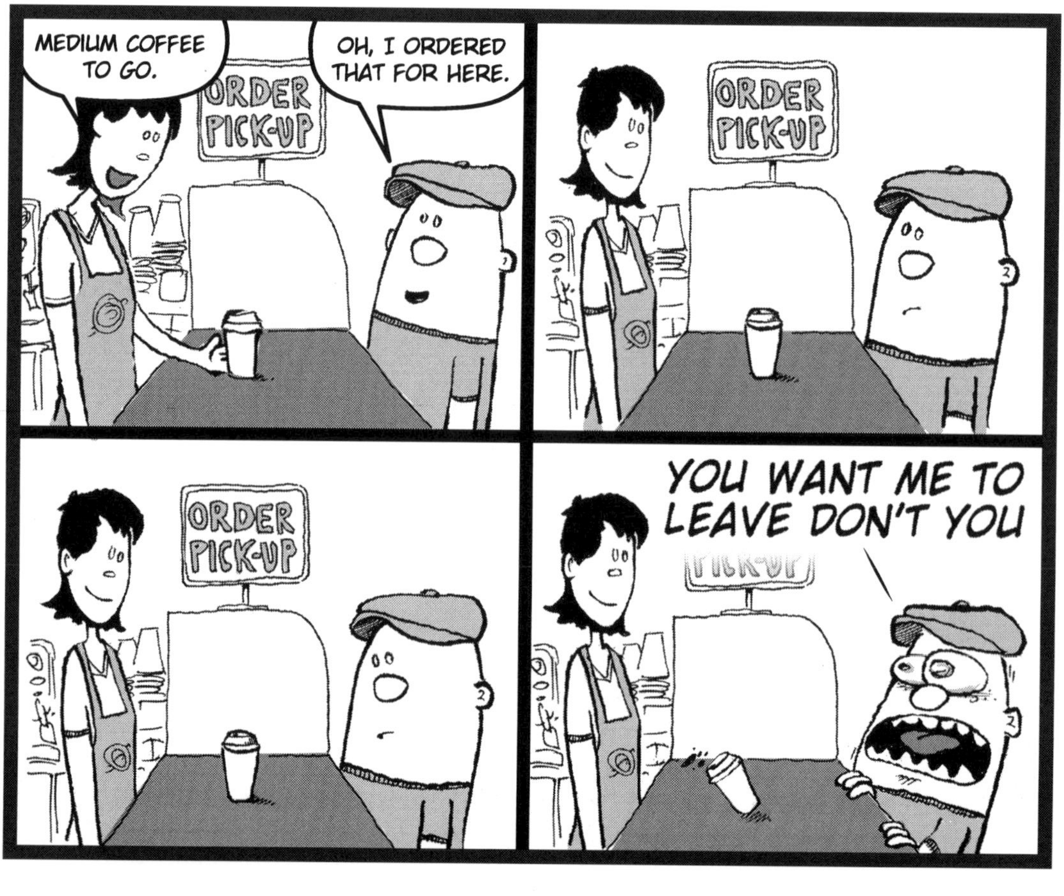
MEDIUM COFFEE TO GO.
OH, I ORDERED THAT FOR HERE.
ORDER PICK-UP
ORDER PICK-UP
ORDER PICK-UP
YOU WANT ME TO LEAVE DON'T YOU

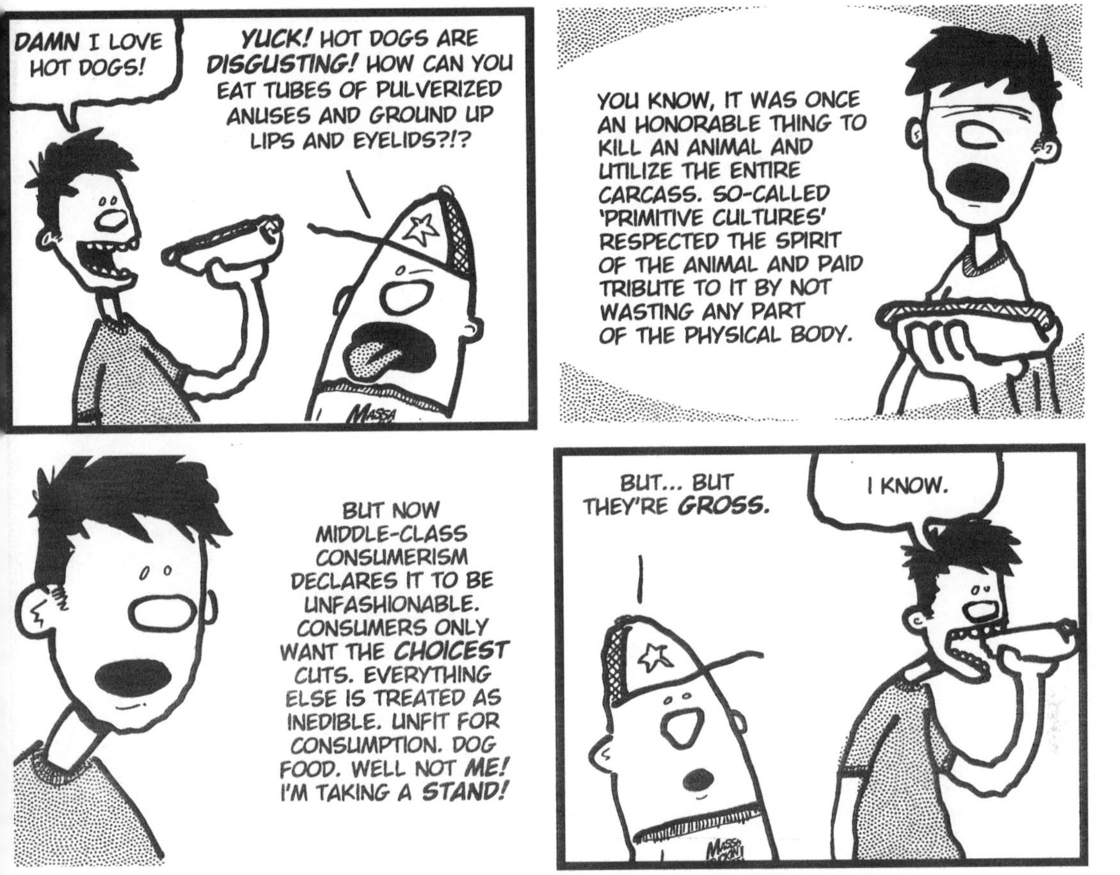
DAMN I LOVE HOT DOGS!
YUCK! HOT DOGS ARE DISGUSTING! HOW CAN YOU EAT TUBES OF PULVERIZED ANUSES AND GROUND UP LIPS AND EYELIDS?!?
YOU KNOW, IT WAS ONCE AN HONORABLE THING TO KILL AN ANIMAL AND UTILIZE THE ENTIRE CARCASS. SO-CALLED 'PRIMITIVE CULTURES' RESPECTED THE SPIRIT OF THE ANIMAL AND PAID TRIBUTE TO IT BY NOT WASTING ANY PART OF THE PHYSICAL BODY.
BUT NOW MIDDLE-CLASS CONSUMERISM DECLARES IT TO BE UNFASHIONABLE. CONSUMERS ONLY WANT THE CHOICEST CUTS. EVERYTHING ELSE IS TREATED AS INEDIBLE. UNFIT FOR CONSUMPTION. DOG FOOD. WELL NOT ME! I'M TAKING A STAND!
BUT... BUT THEY'RE GROSS.
I KNOW.

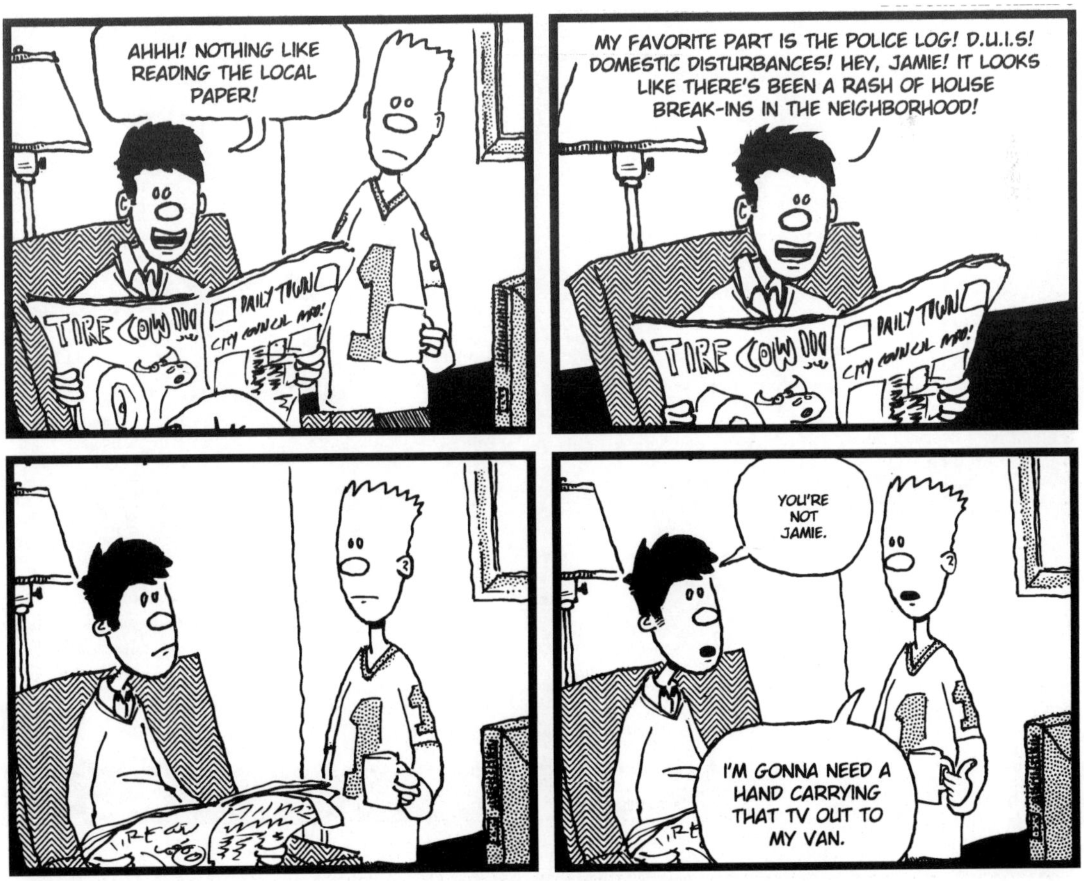
AHHH! NOTHING LIKE READING THE LOCAL PAPER!
MY FAVORITE PART IS THE POLICE LOG! D.U.I.S! DOMESTIC DISTURBANCES! HEY, JAMIE! IT LOOKS LIKE THERE'S BEEN A RASH OF HOUSE BREAK-INS IN THE NEIGHBORHOOD!
YOU'RE NOT JAMIE.
I'M GONNA NEED A HAND CARRYING THAT TV OUT TO MY VAN.

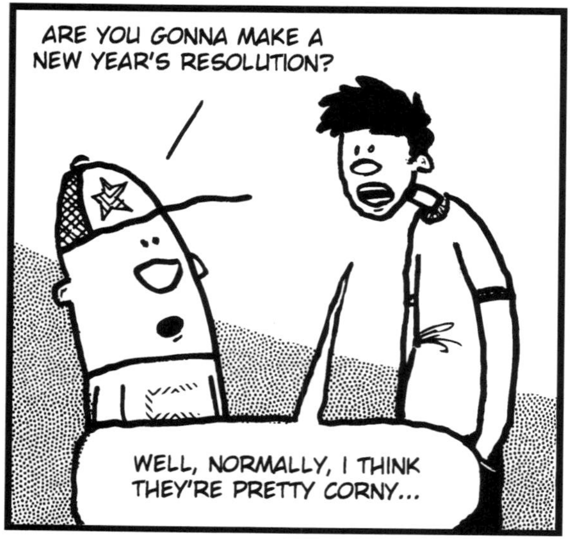
ARE YOU GONNA MAKE A NEW YEAR'S RESOLUTION?
WELL, NORMALLY, I THINK THEY'RE PRETTY CORNY...

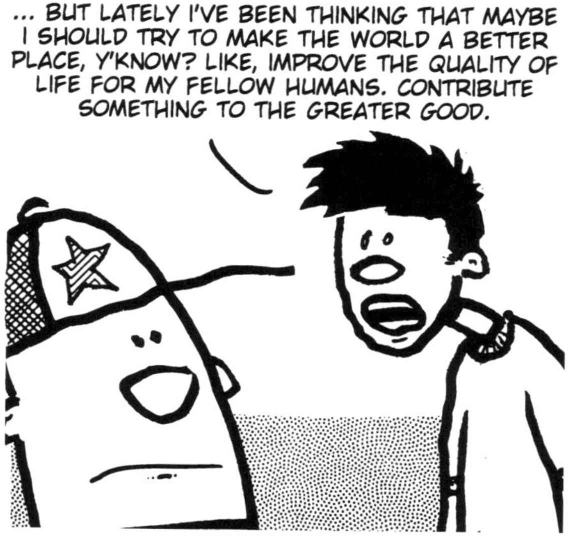
... BUT LATELY I'VE BEEN THINKING THAT MAYBE I SHOULD TRY TO MAKE THE WORLD A BETTER PLACE, Y'KNOW? LIKE, IMPROVE THE QUALITY OF LIFE FOR MY FELLOW HUMANS. CONTRIBUTE SOMETHING TO THE GREATER GOOD.

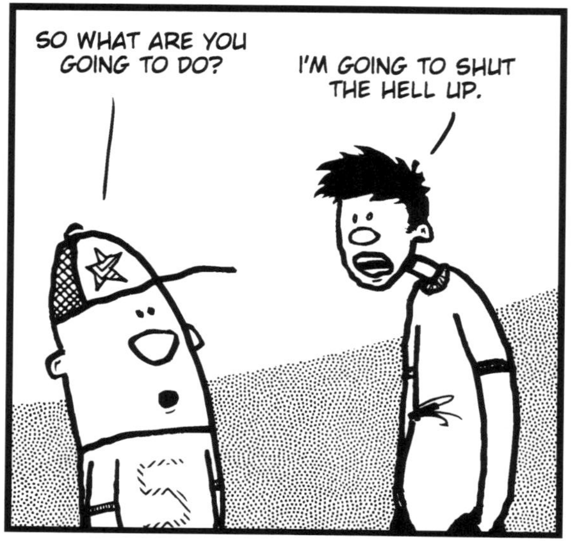
SO WHAT ARE YOU GOING TO DO?
I'M GOING TO SHUT THE HELL UP.

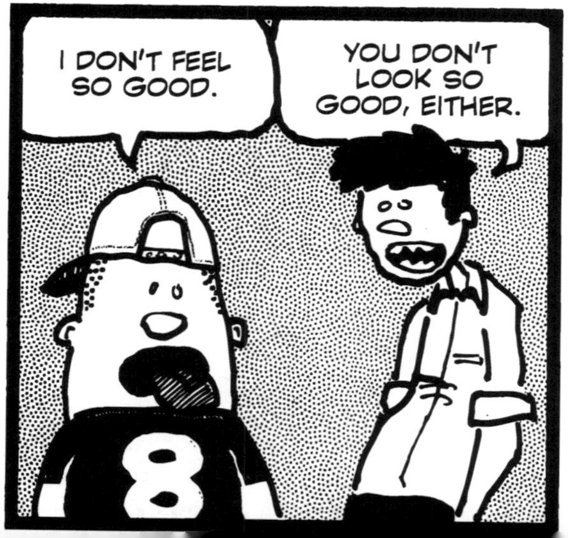
I DON'T FEEL SO GOOD.
YOU DON'T LOOK SO GOOD, EITHER.

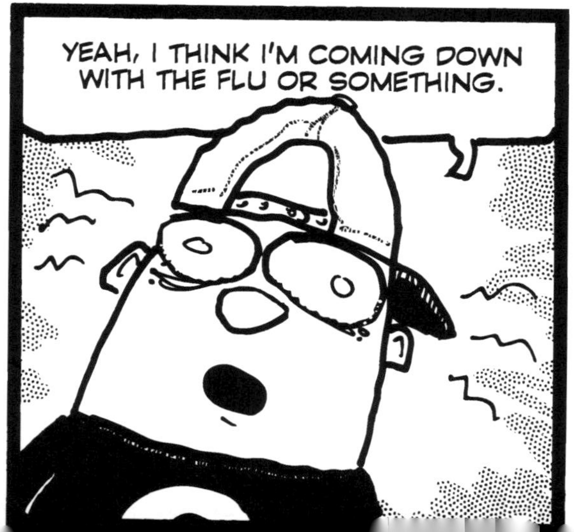
YEAH, I THINK I'M COMING DOWN WITH THE FLU OR SOMETHING.

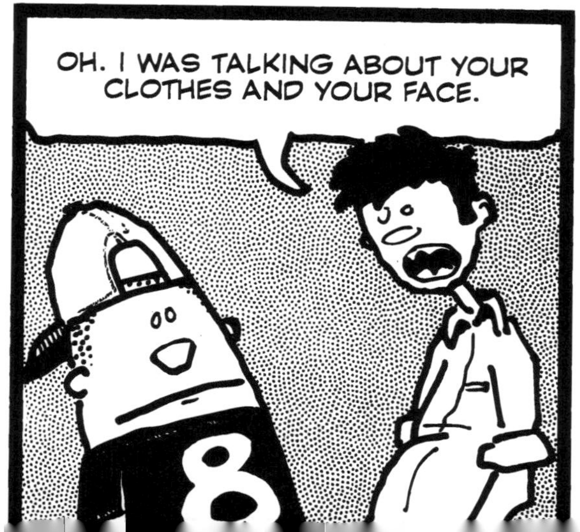
OH. I WAS TALKING ABOUT YOUR CLOTHES AND YOUR FACE.

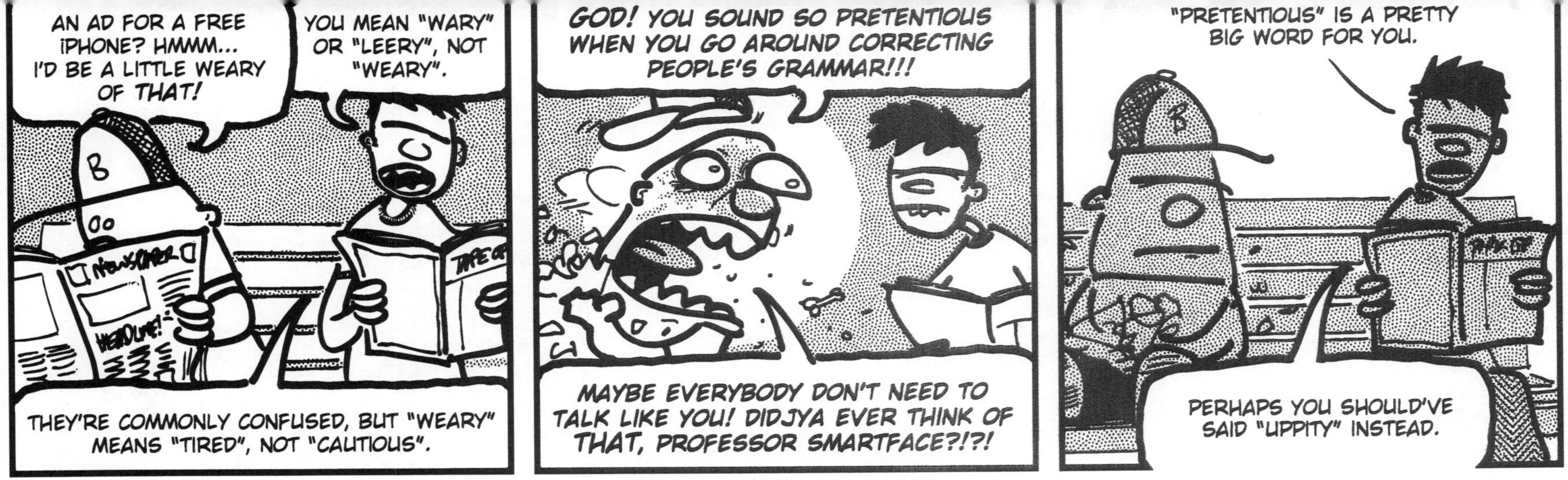
AN AD FOR A FREE iPHONE? HMMM... I'D BE A LITTLE WEARY OF THAT!
YOU MEAN "WARY" OR "LEERY", NOT "WEARY".
THEY'RE COMMONLY CONFUSED, BUT "WEARY" MEANS "TIRED", NOT "CAUTIOUS".
GOD! YOU SOUND SO PRETENTIOUS WHEN YOU GO AROUND CORRECTING PEOPLE'S GRAMMAR!!!
MAYBE EVERYBODY DON'T NEED TO TALK LIKE YOU! DIDJYA EVER THINK OF THAT, PROFESSOR SMARTFACE?!?!
"PRETENTIOUS" IS A PRETTY BIG WORD FOR YOU.
PERHAPS YOU SHOULD'VE SAID "UPPITY" INSTEAD.

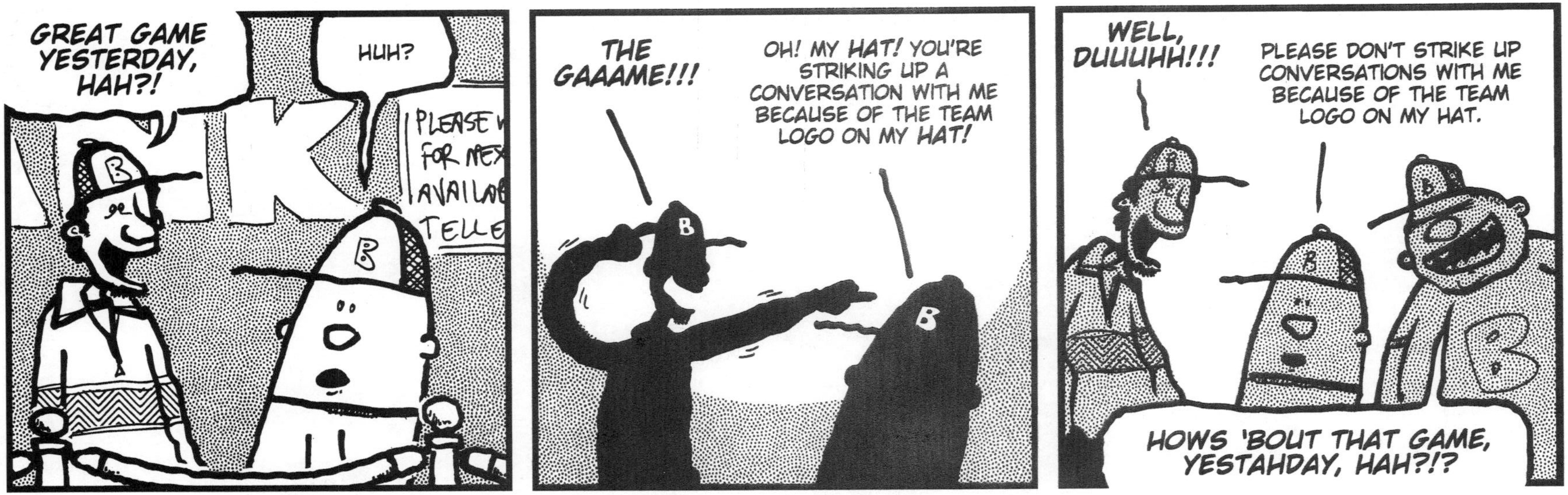
GREAT GAME YESTERDAY, HAH?!
HUH?
THE GAAAME!!!
OH! MY HAT! YOU'RE STRIKING UP A CONVERSATION WITH ME BECAUSE OF THE TEAM LOGO ON MY HAT!
WELL, DUUUHH!!!
PLEASE DON'T STRIKE UP CONVERSATIONS WITH ME BECAUSE OF THE TEAM LOGO ON MY HAT.
HOWS 'BOUT THAT GAME, YESTAHDAY, HAH?!?

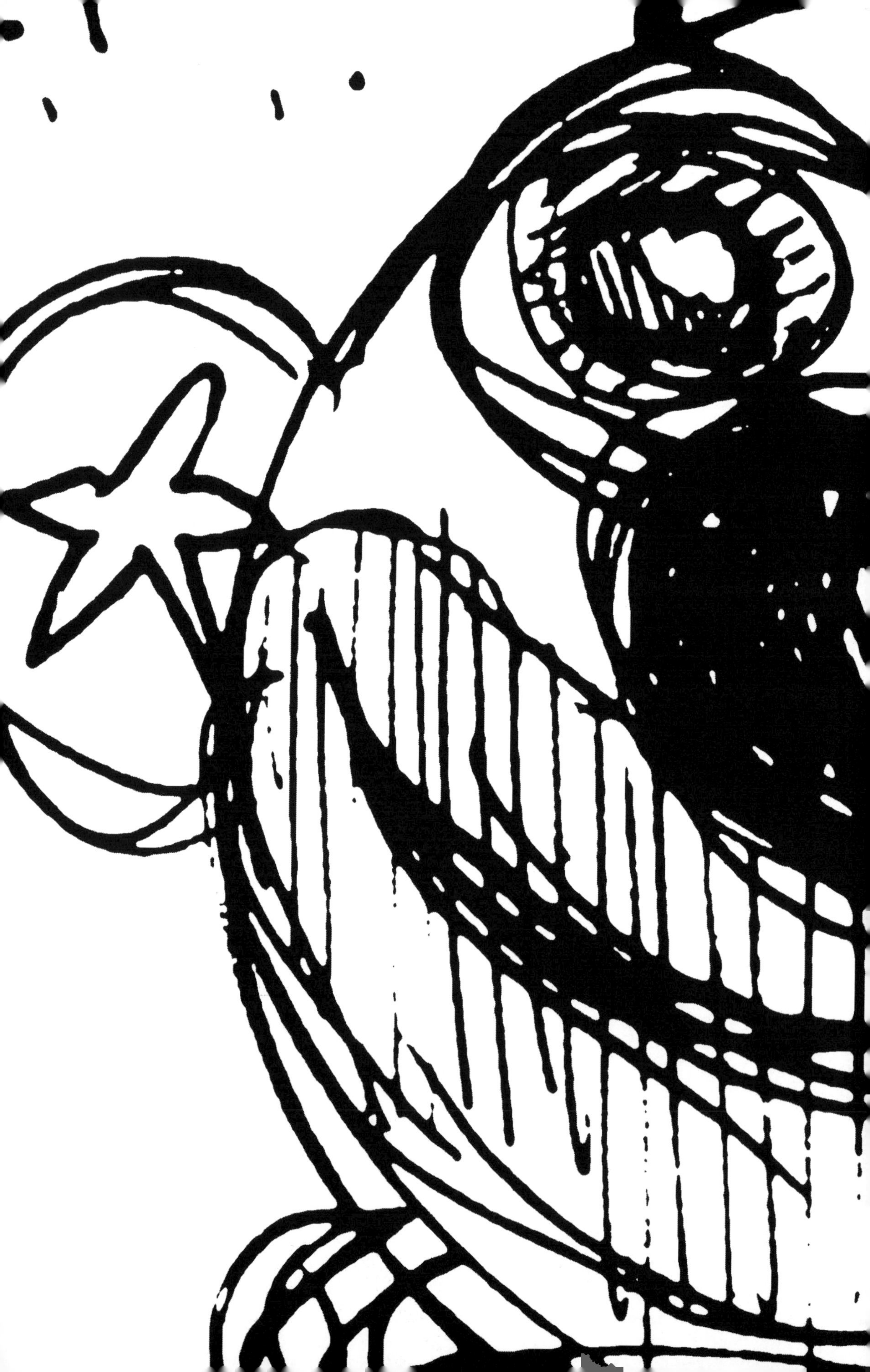

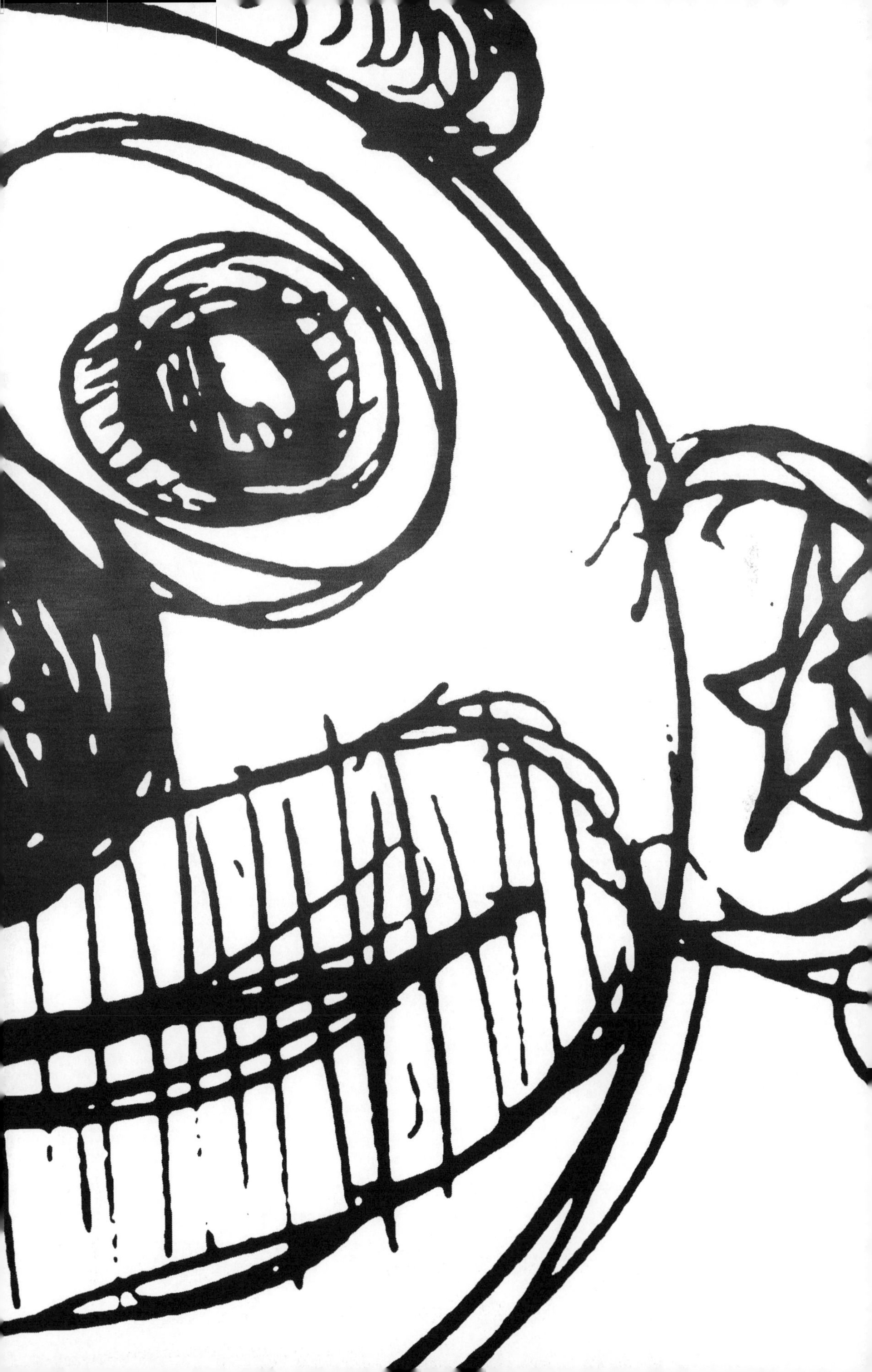

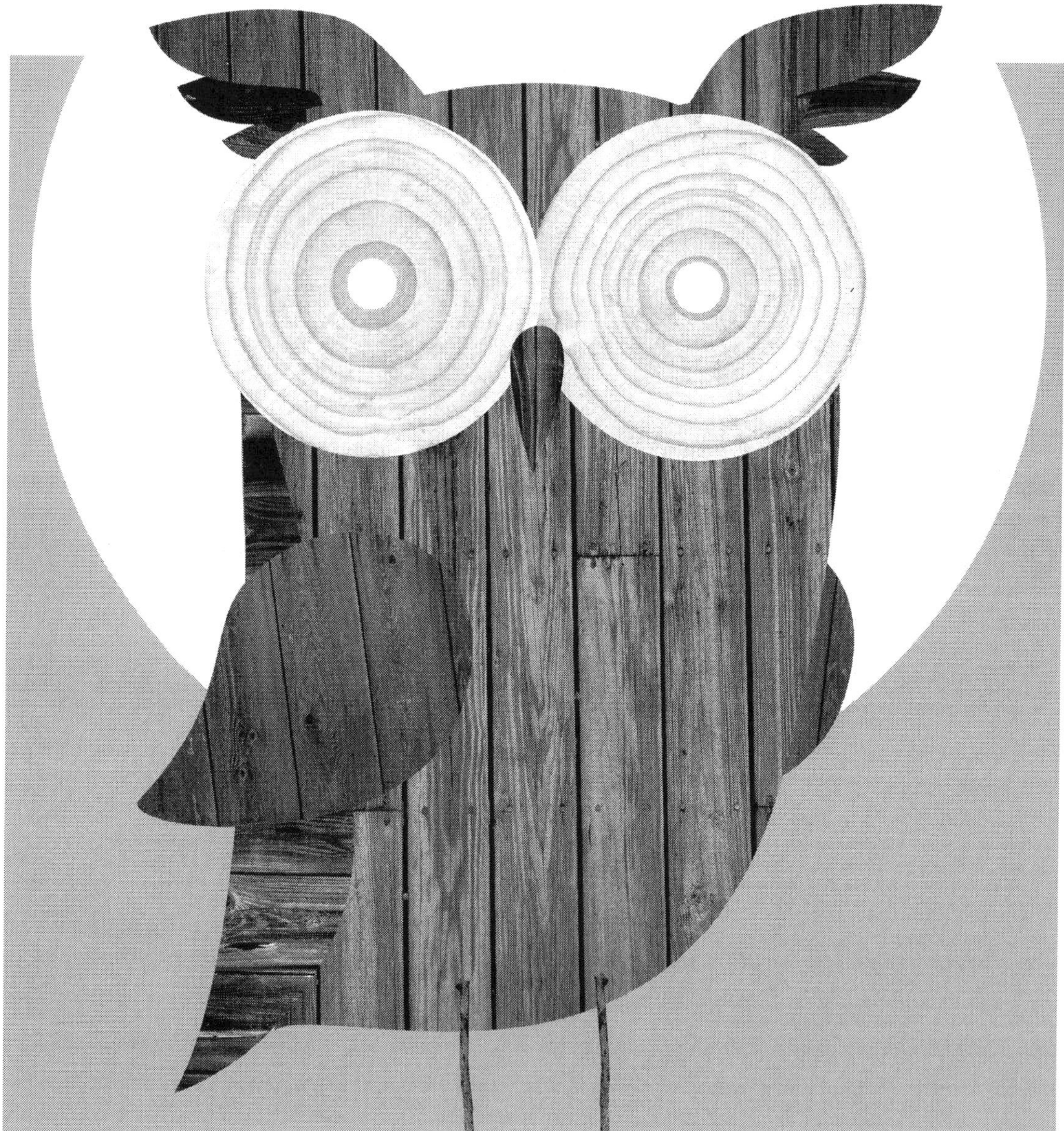

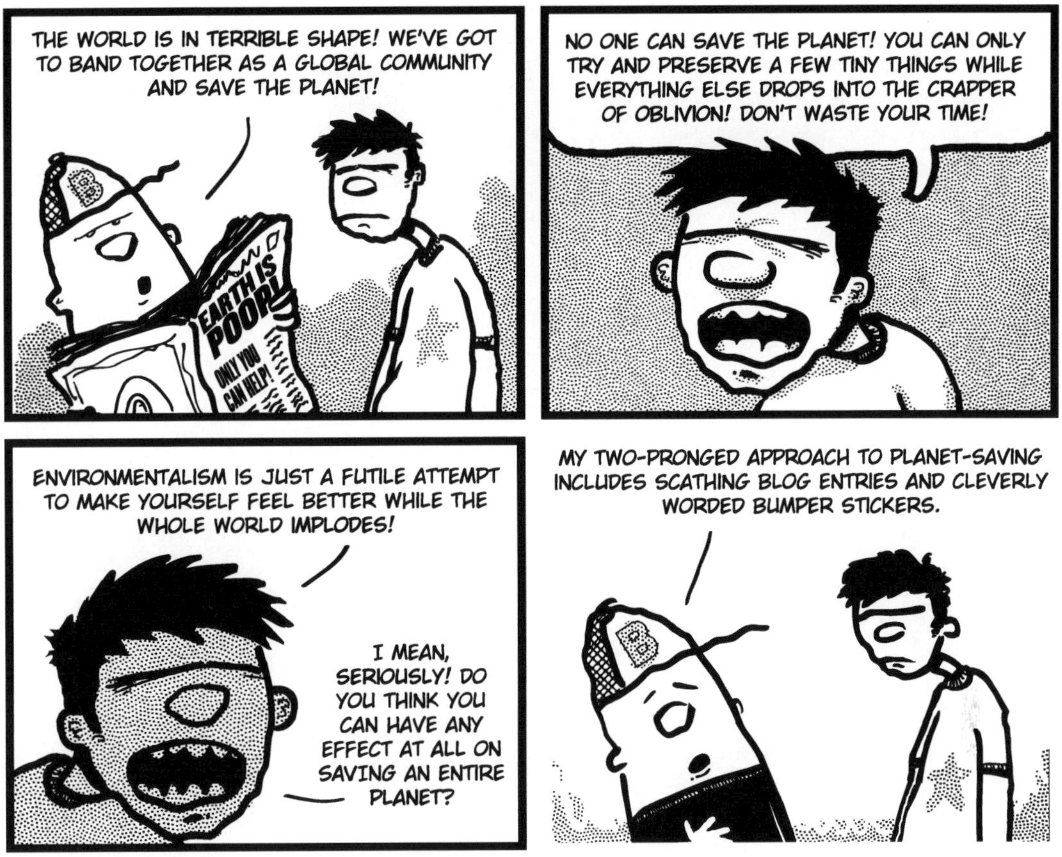
THE WORLD IS IN TERRIBLE SHAPE! WE'VE GOT TO BAND TOGETHER AS A GLOBAL COMMUNITY AND SAVE THE PLANET!
EARTH IS POOP!
ONLY YOU CAN HELP!
NO ONE CAN SAVE THE PLANET! YOU CAN ONLY TRY AND PRESERVE A FEW TINY THINGS WHILE EVERYTHING ELSE DROPS INTO THE CRAPPER OF OBLIVION! DON'T WASTE YOUR TIME!
ENVIRONMENTALISM IS JUST A FUTILE ATTEMPT TO MAKE YOURSELF FEEL BETTER WHILE THE WHOLE WORLD IMPLODES!
I MEAN, SERIOUSLY! DO YOU THINK YOU CAN HAVE ANY EFFECT AT ALL ON SAVING AN ENTIRE PLANET?
MY TWO-PRONGED APPROACH TO PLANET-SAVING INCLUDES SCATHING BLOG ENTRIES AND CLEVERLY WORDED BUMPER STICKERS.

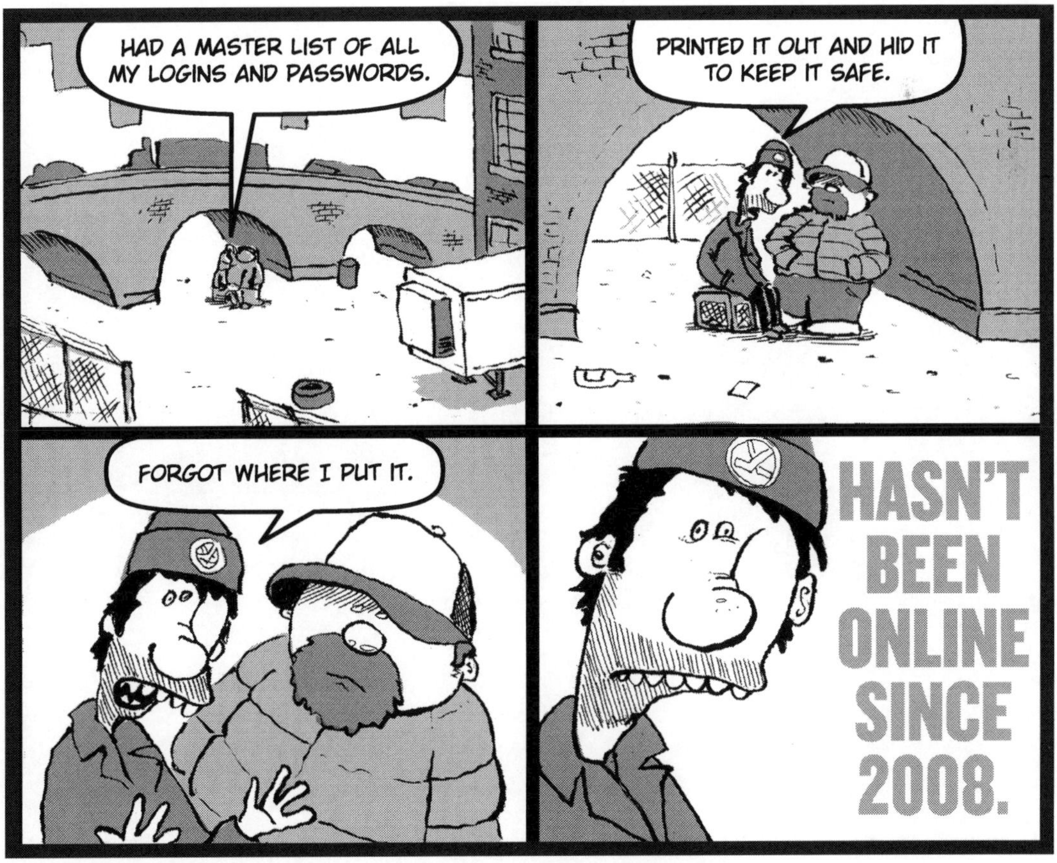
HAD A MASTER LIST OF ALL MY LOGINS AND PASSWORDS.
PRINTED IT OUT AND HID IT TO KEEP IT SAFE.
FORGOT WHERE I PUT IT.
HASN'T BEEN ONLINE SINCE 2008.

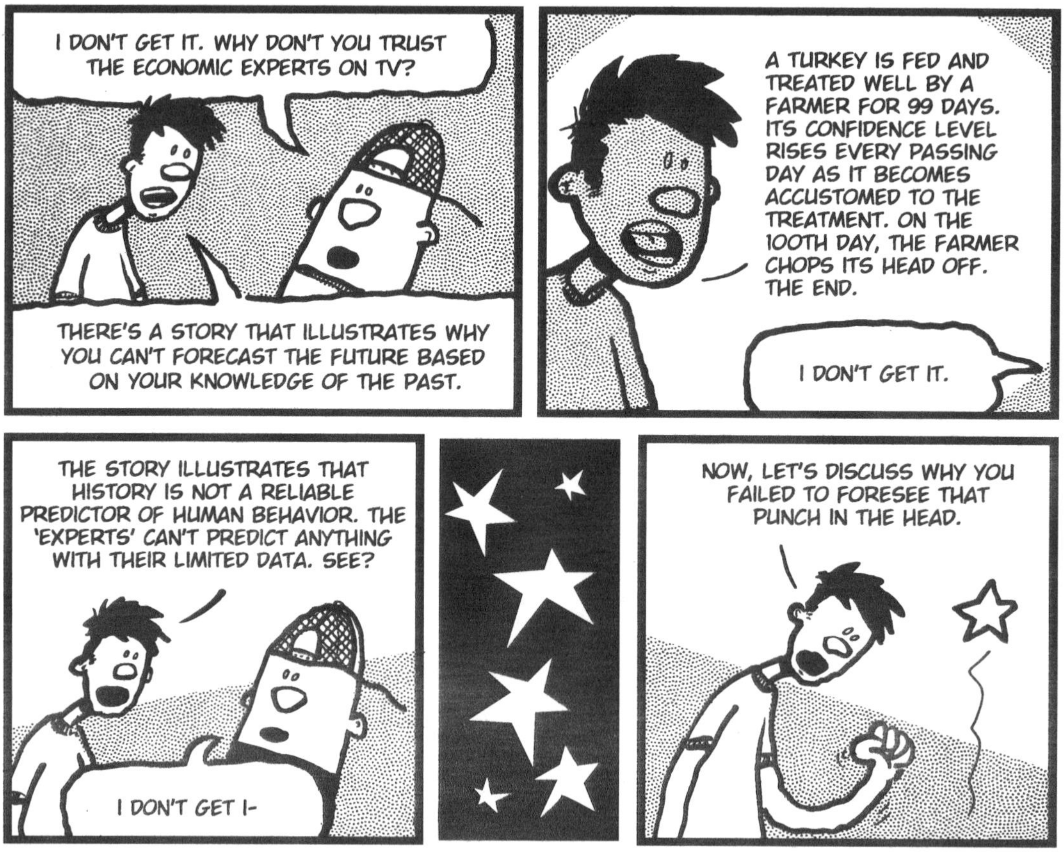
I DON'T GET IT. WHY DON'T YOU TRUST THE ECONOMIC EXPERTS ON TV?
THERE'S A STORY THAT ILLUSTRATES WHY YOU CAN'T FORECAST THE FUTURE BASED ON YOUR KNOWLEDGE OF THE PAST.
A TURKEY IS FED AND TREATED WELL BY A FARMER FOR 99 DAYS. ITS CONFIDENCE LEVEL RISES EVERY PASSING DAY AS IT BECOMES ACCUSTOMED TO THE TREATMENT. ON THE 100TH DAY, THE FARMER CHOPS ITS HEAD OFF. THE END.
I DON'T GET IT.
THE STORY ILLUSTRATES THAT HISTORY IS NOT A RELIABLE PREDICTOR OF HUMAN BEHAVIOR. THE 'EXPERTS' CAN'T PREDICT ANYTHING WITH THEIR LIMITED DATA. SEE?
I DON'T GET I-
NOW, LET'S DISCUSS WHY YOU FAILED TO FORESEE THAT PUNCH IN THE HEAD.

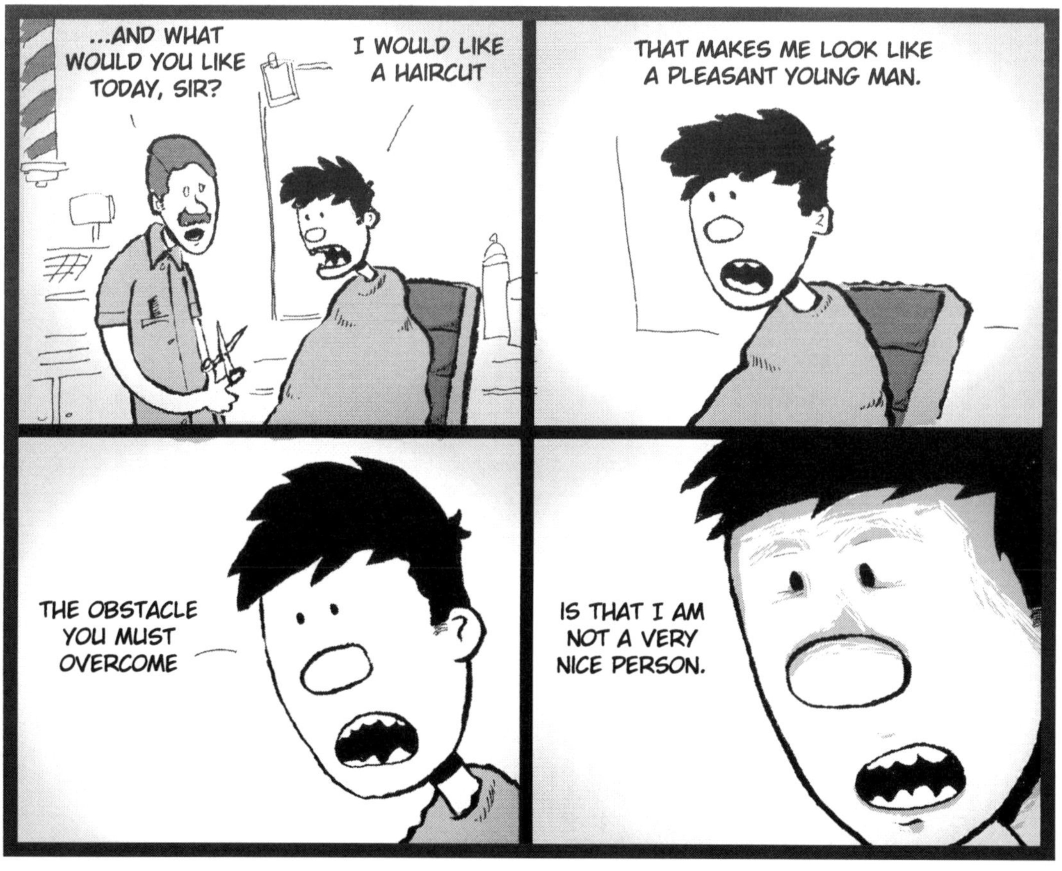
...AND WHAT WOULD YOU LIKE TODAY, SIR?
I WOULD LIKE A HAIRCUT
THAT MAKES ME LOOK LIKE A PLEASANT YOUNG MAN.
THE OBSTACLE YOU MUST OVERCOME
IS THAT I AM NOT A VERY NICE PERSON.

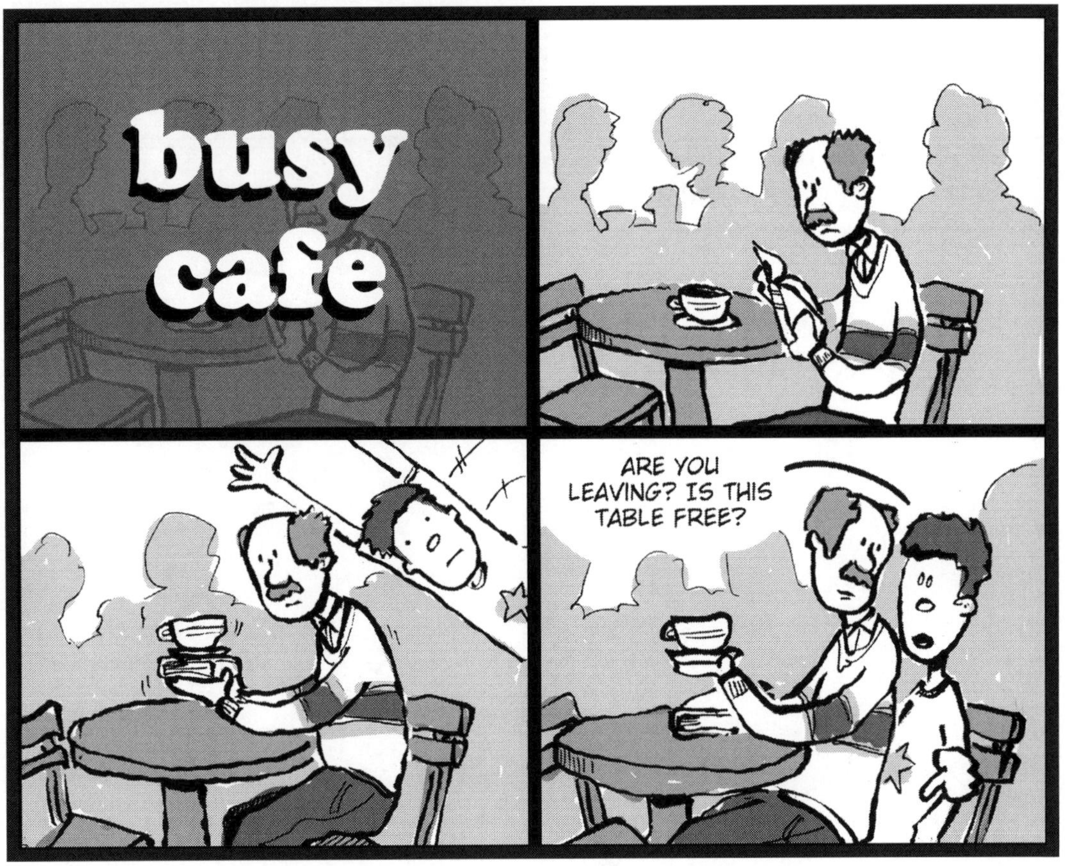
busy cafe
ARE YOU LEAVING? IS THIS TABLE FREE?

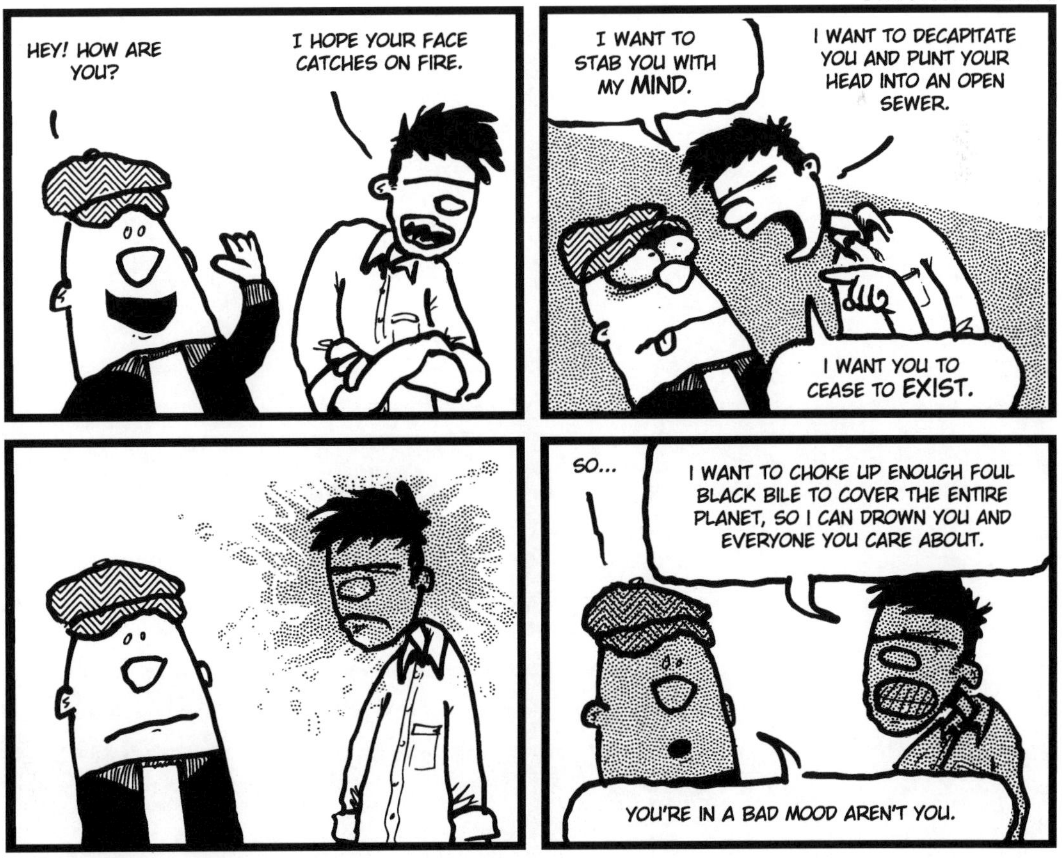
HEY! HOW ARE YOU?
I HOPE YOUR FACE CATCHES ON FIRE.
I WANT TO STAB YOU WITH MY MIND.
I WANT TO DECAPITATE YOU AND PUNT YOUR HEAD INTO AN OPEN SEWER.
I WANT YOU TO CEASE TO EXIST.
SO...
I WANT TO CHOKE UP ENOUGH FOUL BLACK BILE TO COVER THE ENTIRE PLANET, SO I CAN DROWN YOU AND EVERYONE YOU CARE ABOUT.
YOU'RE IN A BAD MOOD AREN'T YOU.

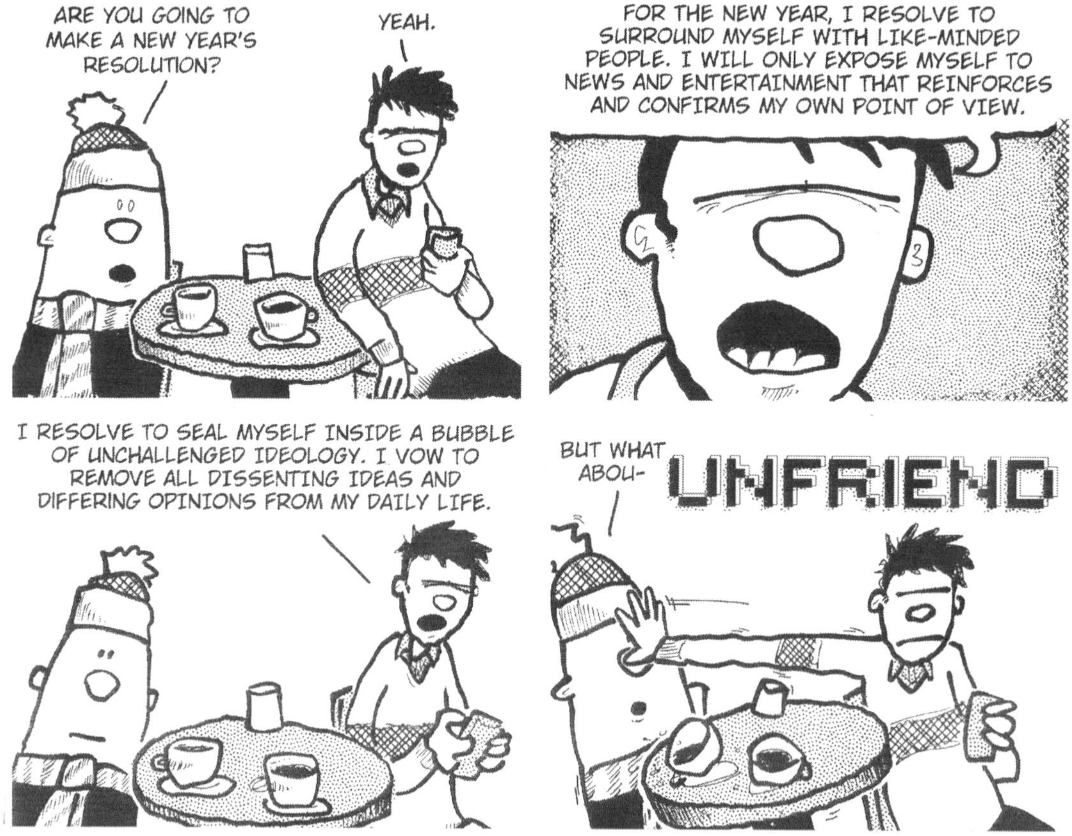
ARE YOU GOING TO MAKE A NEW YEAR'S RESOLUTION?
YEAH.
FOR THE NEW YEAR, I RESOLVE TO SURROUND MYSELF WITH LIKE-MINDED PEOPLE. I WILL ONLY EXPOSE MYSELF TO NEWS AND ENTERTAINMENT THAT REINFORCES AND CONFIRMS MY OWN POINT OF VIEW.
I RESOLVE TO SEAL MYSELF INSIDE A BUBBLE OF UNCHALLENGED IDEOLOGY. I VOW TO REMOVE ALL DISSENTING IDEAS AND DIFFERING OPINIONS FROM MY DAILY LIFE.
BUT WHAT ABOU-
UNFRIEND

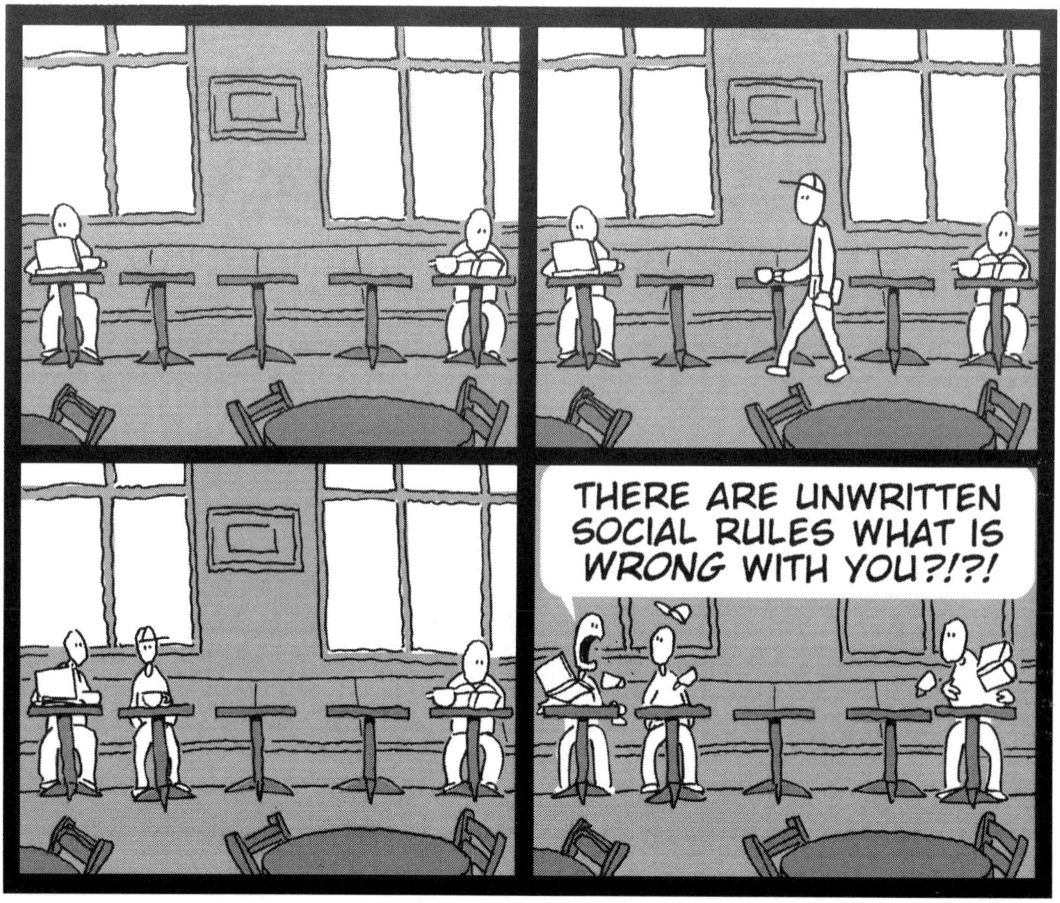
THERE ARE UNWRITTEN SOCIAL RULES WHAT IS WRONG WITH YOU?!?!

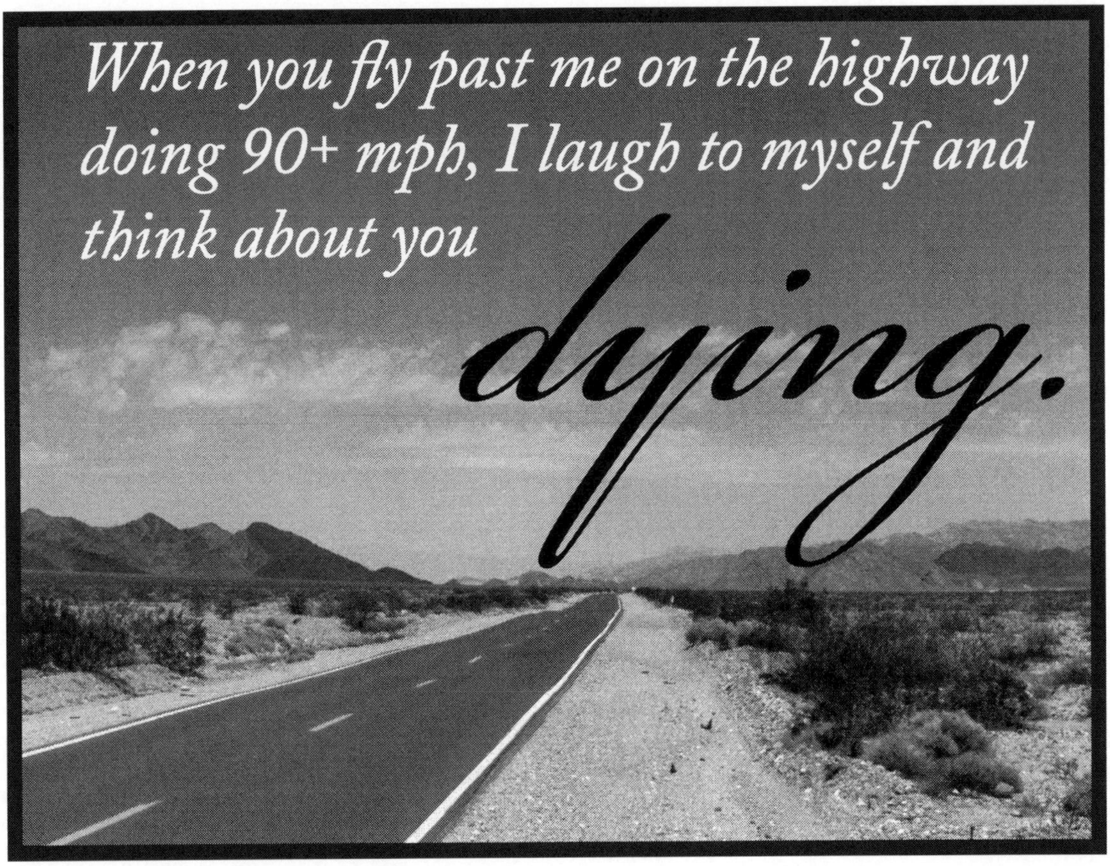
When you fly past me on the highway doing 90+ mph, I laugh to myself and think about you
dying.

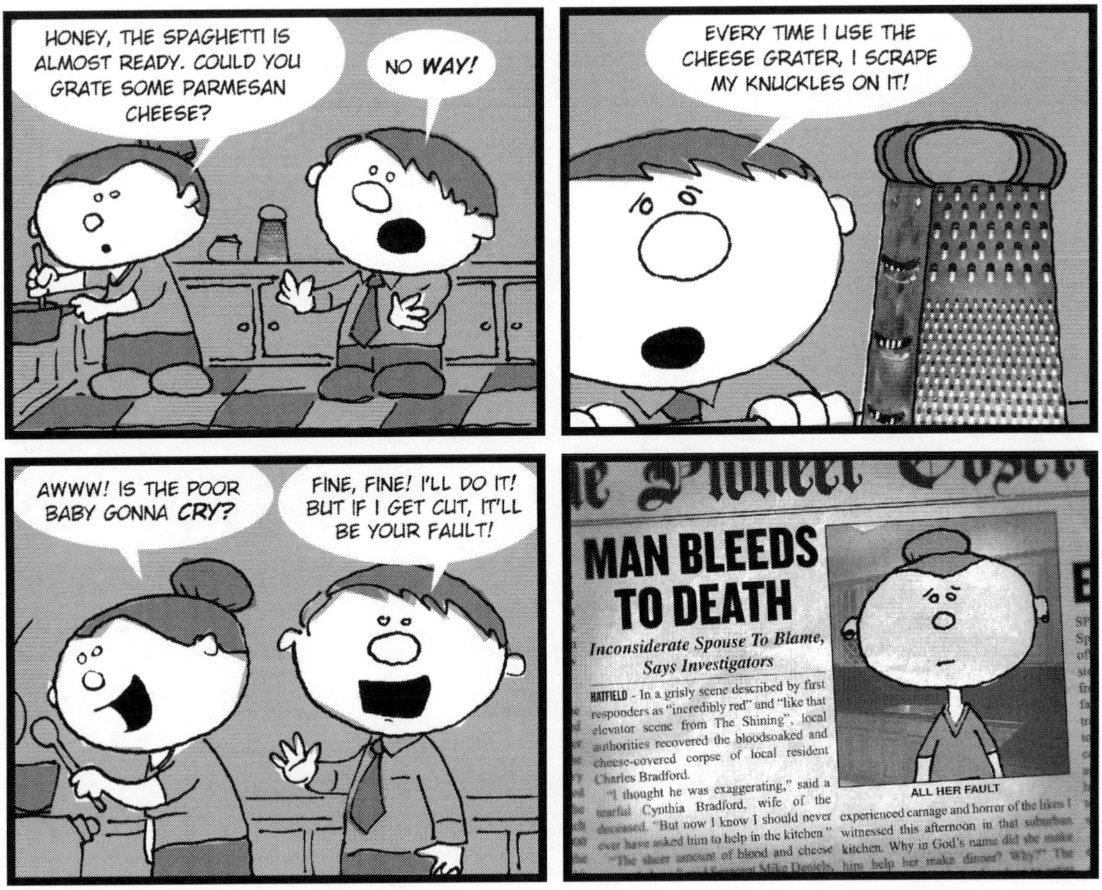
HONEY, THE SPAGHETTI IS ALMOST READY. COULD YOU GRATE SOME PARMESAN CHEESE?
NO WAY!
EVERY TIME I USE THE CHEESE GRATER, I SCRAPE MY KNUCKLES ON IT!
AWWW! IS THE POOR BABY GONNA CRY?
FINE, FINE! I'LL DO IT! BUT IF I GET CUT, IT'LL BE YOUR FAULT!
MAN BLEEDS TO DEATH
Inconsiderate Spouse To Blame, Says Investigators
HATFIELD - In a grisly scene described by first responders as "incredibly red" and "like that elevator scene from The Shining", local authorities recovered the bloodsoaked and cheese-covered corpse of local resident Charles Bradford.
"I thought he was exaggerating," said a tearful Cynthia Bradford, wife of the deceased. "But now I know I should never ever have asked him to help in the kitchen."
ALL HER FAULT
experienced carnage and horror of the likes I witnessed this afternoon in that suburban kitchen. Why in God's name did she make him help her make dinner? Why?"

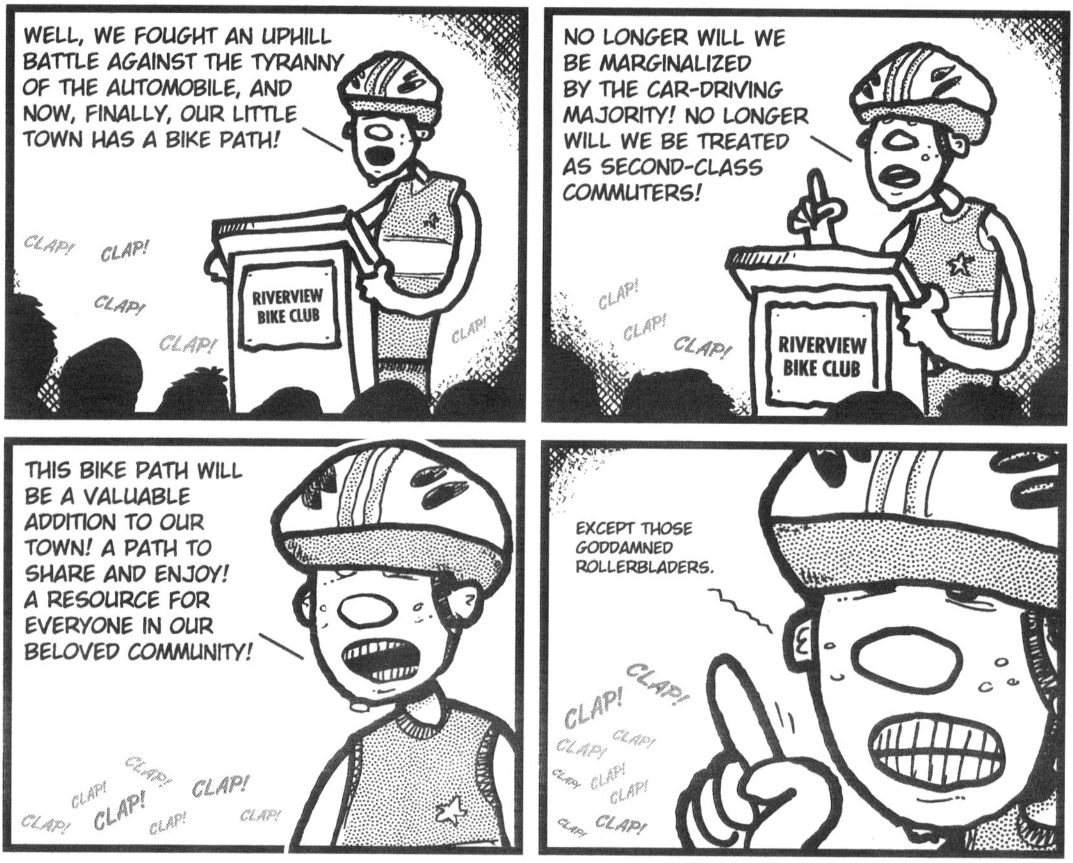
WELL, WE FOUGHT AN UPHILL BATTLE AGAINST THE TYRANNY OF THE AUTOMOBILE, AND NOW, FINALLY, OUR LITTLE TOWN HAS A BIKE PATH!
CLAP! CLAP! CLAP! CLAP! CLAP!
RIVERVIEW BIKE CLUB
NO LONGER WILL WE BE MARGINALIZED BY THE CAR-DRIVING MAJORITY! NO LONGER WILL WE BE TREATED AS SECOND-CLASS COMMUTERS!
CLAP! CLAP! CLAP!
RIVERVIEW BIKE CLUB
THIS BIKE PATH WILL BE A VALUABLE ADDITION TO OUR TOWN! A PATH TO SHARE AND ENJOY! A RESOURCE FOR EVERYONE IN OUR BELOVED COMMUNITY!
CLAP! CLAP! CLAP! CLAP! CLAP! CLAP! CLAP!
EXCEPT THOSE GODDAMNED ROLLERBLADERS.
CLAP! CLAP! CLAP! CLAP! CLAP! CLAP! CLAP!

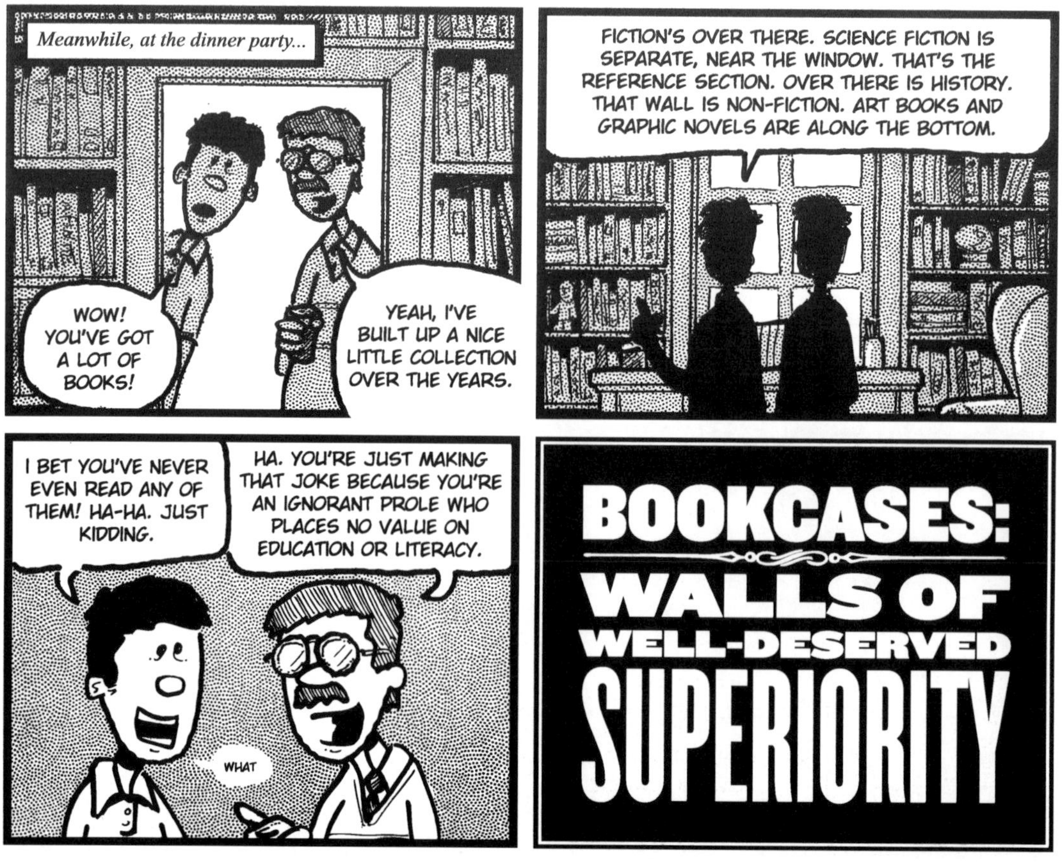
Meanwhile, at the dinner party...
WOW! YOU'VE GOT A LOT OF BOOKS!
YEAH, I'VE BUILT UP A NICE LITTLE COLLECTION OVER THE YEARS.
FICTION'S OVER THERE. SCIENCE FICTION IS SEPARATE, NEAR THE WINDOW. THAT'S THE REFERENCE SECTION. OVER THERE IS HISTORY. THAT WALL IS NON-FICTION. ART BOOKS AND GRAPHIC NOVELS ARE ALONG THE BOTTOM.
I BET YOU'VE NEVER EVEN READ ANY OF THEM! HA-HA. JUST KIDDING.
HA. YOU'RE JUST MAKING THAT JOKE BECAUSE YOU'RE AN IGNORANT PROLE WHO PLACES NO VALUE ON EDUCATION OR LITERACY.
WHAT
BOOKCASES:
WALLS OF WELL-DESERVED SUPERIORITY

USELESS FACTS

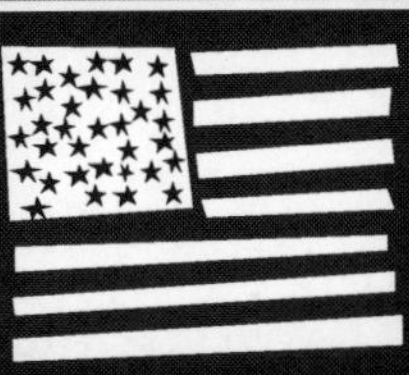

The Pledge of Allegiance was created by a magazine as a marketing promotion to sell American flags.

In 2008, the Little Tikes Company sold 457,000 Cozy Coupes, making it the highest selling car of the year.

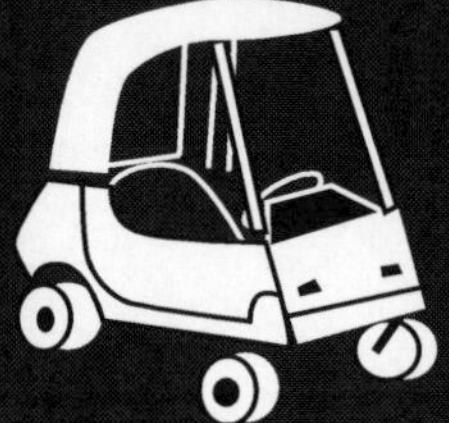

@#&!$

The **purlicue** is the space between your thumb and forefinger. A **plectrum** is a guitar pick. A **grawlix** is the cartooning symbol for cussing.

North Americans are so fat that the continent holds **more than 33%** of the world population's body weight, despite being home to **less than 10%** of the planet's people.

OVER $21 TRILLION

has been squirreled away in offshore tax-havens by **90,000** super-rich tax-cheats.

The British spelling of this word *(squirrelled)* is the longest one syllable standard English word. (11 letters)

Spuds MacKenzie's real name was Honey Tree Evil Eye.

The Apollo 11 Guidance Computer had 2K of memory and a 1-MHz processor, roughly equivalent to an Atari 2600.

George R. R. Martin writes in Wordstar on a DOS computer.

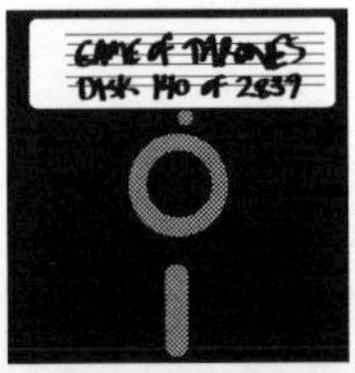
GAME of THRONES
DISK 140 of 2837

The circumference of the Earth is **24,901** miles.

1983 Chevy Corvettes and 1964 Ford Mustangs don't technically exist.

Blues great Bessie Smith was buried in an unmarked grave for thirty-three years, until Janis Joplin paid for a gravestone in 1970.

Nirvana's *In Utero* and Morphine's *Cure For Pain* were both released on the same day.

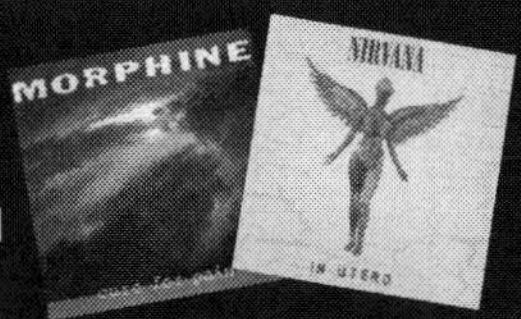
MORPHINE
NIRVANA
IN UTERO

The same dude that founded **Atari, Inc.** founded **Chuck E. Cheese**, and the same dude that created **Wonder Woman** invented the **lie detector.**

A Czech study claims that dogs poop along the north-south axis of the Earth's magnetic field.

Your sinuses produce about two cups of mucus each day. You swallow most of it.

Michael J. Fox's middle name is Andrew.

Dropping your R's is called a "non-rhotic accent"

You can type the word **typewriter** using only the the top row of keys on your keyboard.

Geraldo Rivera was, for a short period of time, Kurt Vonnegut's son-in-law.

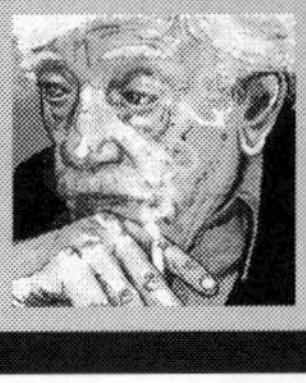

Those stringy bits on bananas are called **PHLOEM BUNDLES**

Y'KNOW, IT'S A LITTLE-KNOWN FACT THAT ALL PARKING METERS ACCEPT PENNIES.
I DIDN'T KNOW THAT!
OH, YEAH. IT'S EVERY CITY'S DIRTY LITTLE SECRET. IT'S IN THE CONSTITUTION. "LEGAL TENDER FOR ALL DEBTS." ALL THAT.
CRAM!
FORCE!
I DIDN'T KNOW THAT!
THIS METER'S JAMMED OR SOMETHING! WHY DOES THIS ALWAYS HAPPEN TO ME?! WHY ARE MY TAX DOLLARS WASTED ON THIS JUNK?!?
YOU DON'T PAY TA-
BROKEN METER MEANS YOU PARK FOR FREE. THAT IS A FACT.
I DIDN'T KNOW THAT!

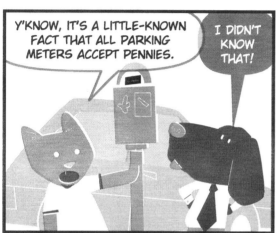

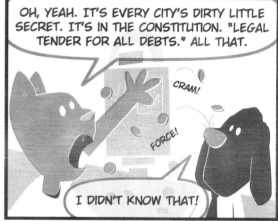

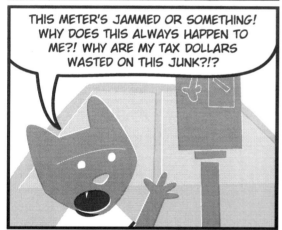

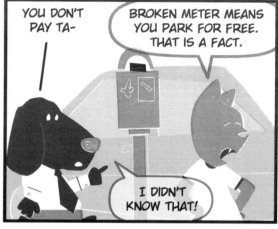

SAY, I COULD GO FOR A COFFEE.
COFFEE. BLACK. TO GO.
TEA, PLEASE.
MMM, GOOD.
BOY, I NEEDED THAT.
YOU DON'T REALIZE HOW CLOSE I CAME TO KILLING YOU.

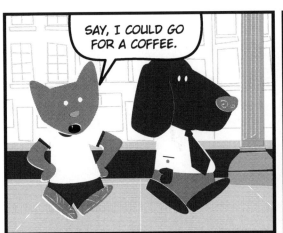

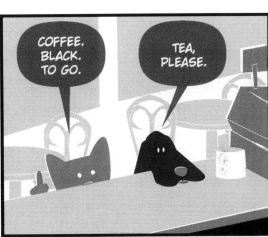

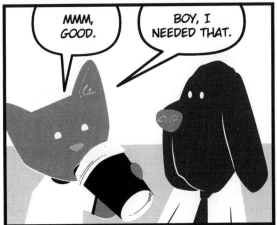

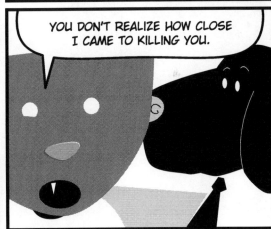

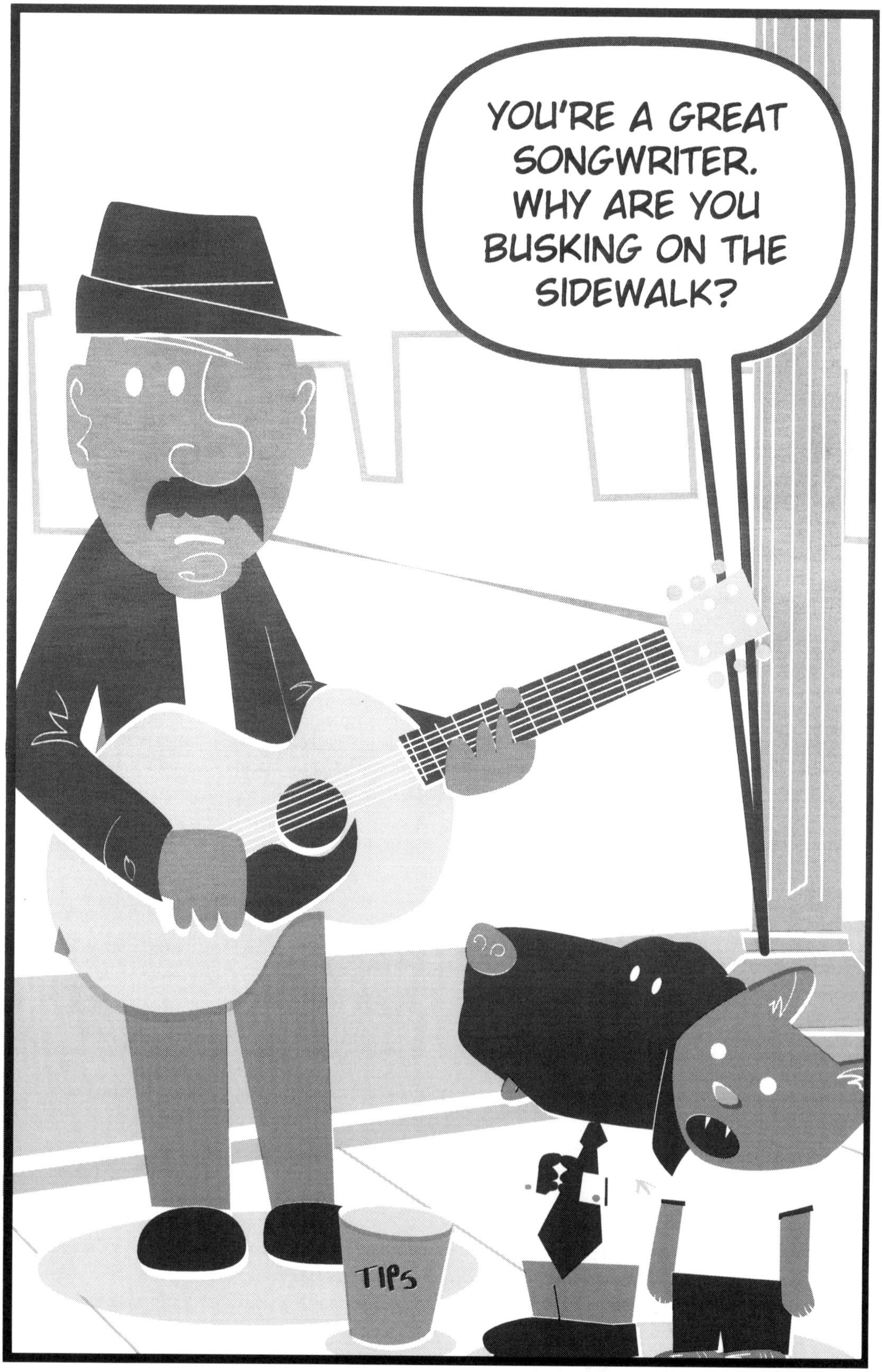
YOU'RE A GREAT SONGWRITER. WHY ARE YOU BUSKING ON THE SIDEWALK?
TIPS

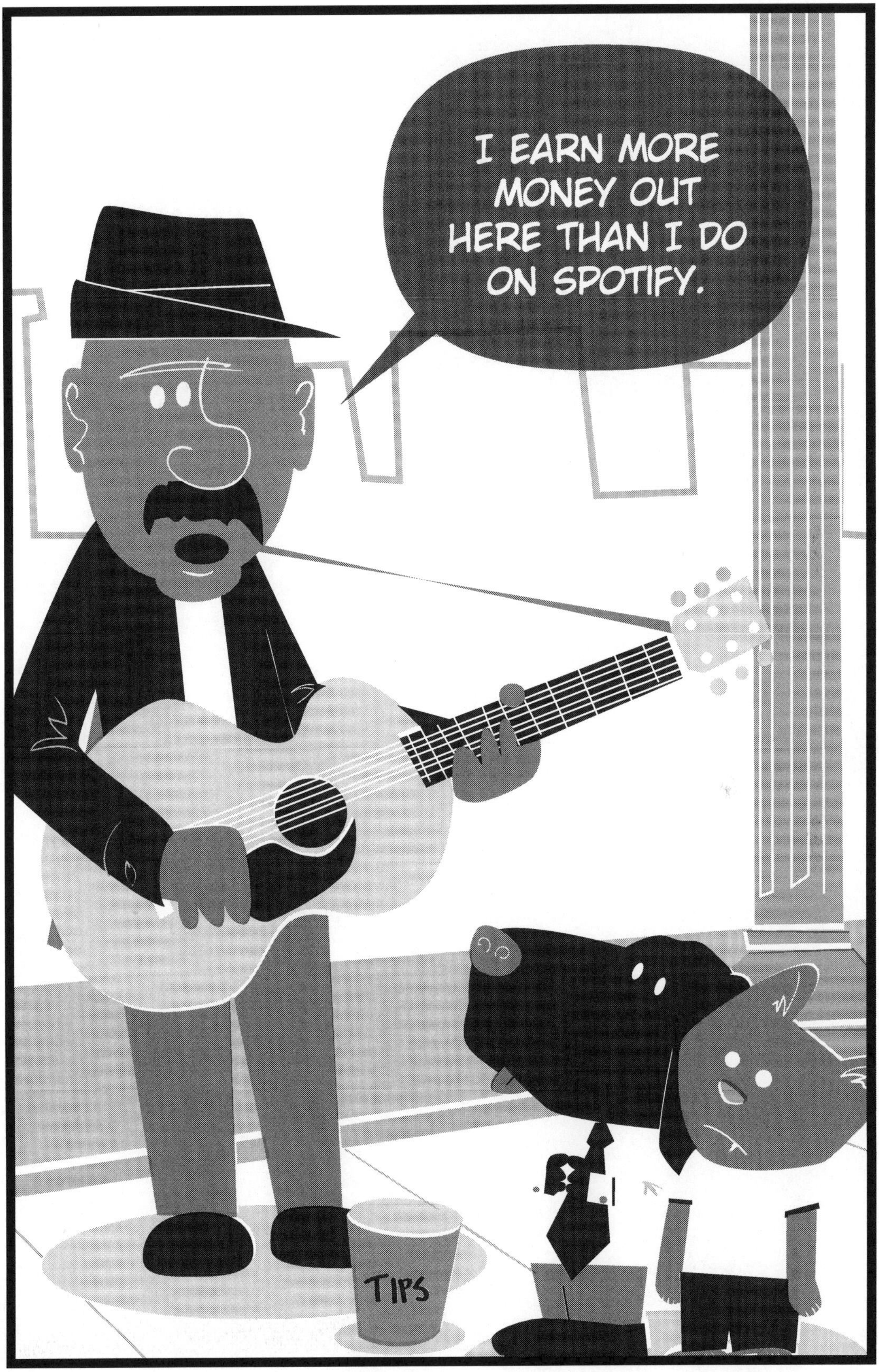
I EARN MORE MONEY OUT HERE THAN I DO ON SPOTIFY.
TIPS

WOULD YOU MIND WATCHING MY STUFF WHILE I GO TO THE RESTROOM?
SURE.
HI. WOULD YOU MIND WATCHING HIM WATCH MY STUFF WHILE I GO TO THE RESTROOM?
UH... OKAY.
HEY. WOULD YOU MIND WATCHING HER WATCH HIM WATCH MY STUFF WHILE I GO TO THE RESTROOM?
HAH?
Coffeehouse Trust

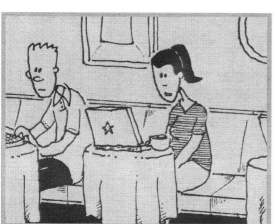

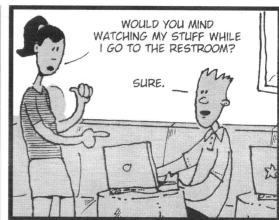

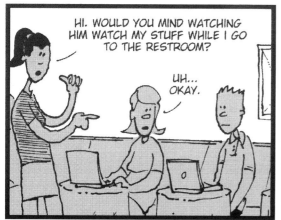

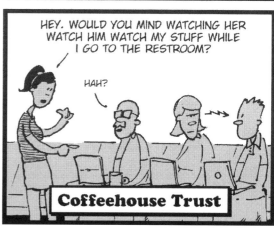

nana

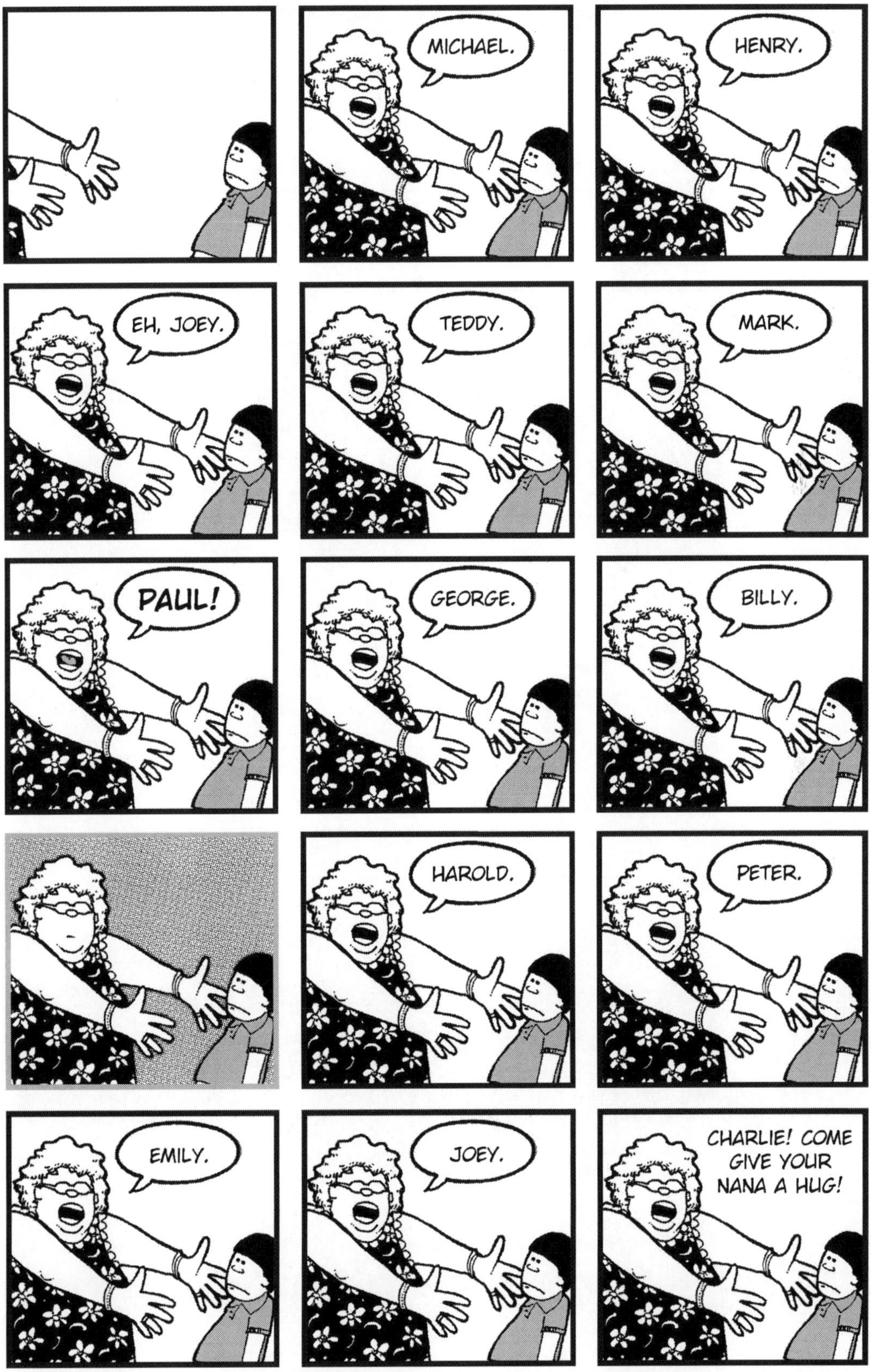
MICHAEL.
HENRY.
EH, JOEY.
TEDDY.
MARK.
PAUL!
GEORGE.
BILLY.
HAROLD.
PETER.
EMILY.
JOEY.
CHARLIE! COME GIVE YOUR NANA A HUG!

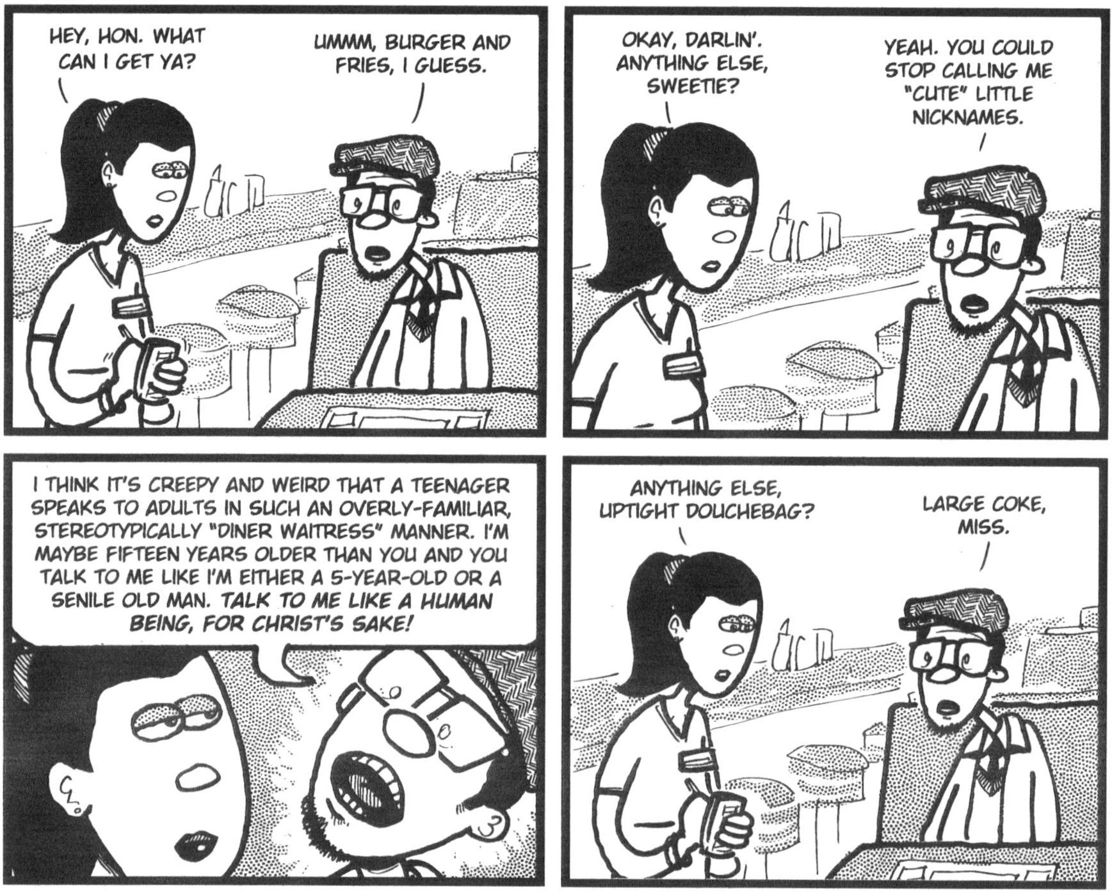
HEY, HON. WHAT CAN I GET YA?
UMMM, BURGER AND FRIES, I GUESS.
OKAY, DARLIN'. ANYTHING ELSE, SWEETIE?
YEAH. YOU COULD STOP CALLING ME "CUTE" LITTLE NICKNAMES.
I THINK IT'S CREEPY AND WEIRD THAT A TEENAGER SPEAKS TO ADULTS IN SUCH AN OVERLY-FAMILIAR, STEREOTYPICALLY "DINER WAITRESS" MANNER. I'M MAYBE FIFTEEN YEARS OLDER THAN YOU AND YOU TALK TO ME LIKE I'M EITHER A 5-YEAR-OLD OR A SENILE OLD MAN. TALK TO ME LIKE A HUMAN BEING, FOR CHRIST'S SAKE!
ANYTHING ELSE, UPTIGHT DOUCHEBAG?
LARGE COKE, MISS.

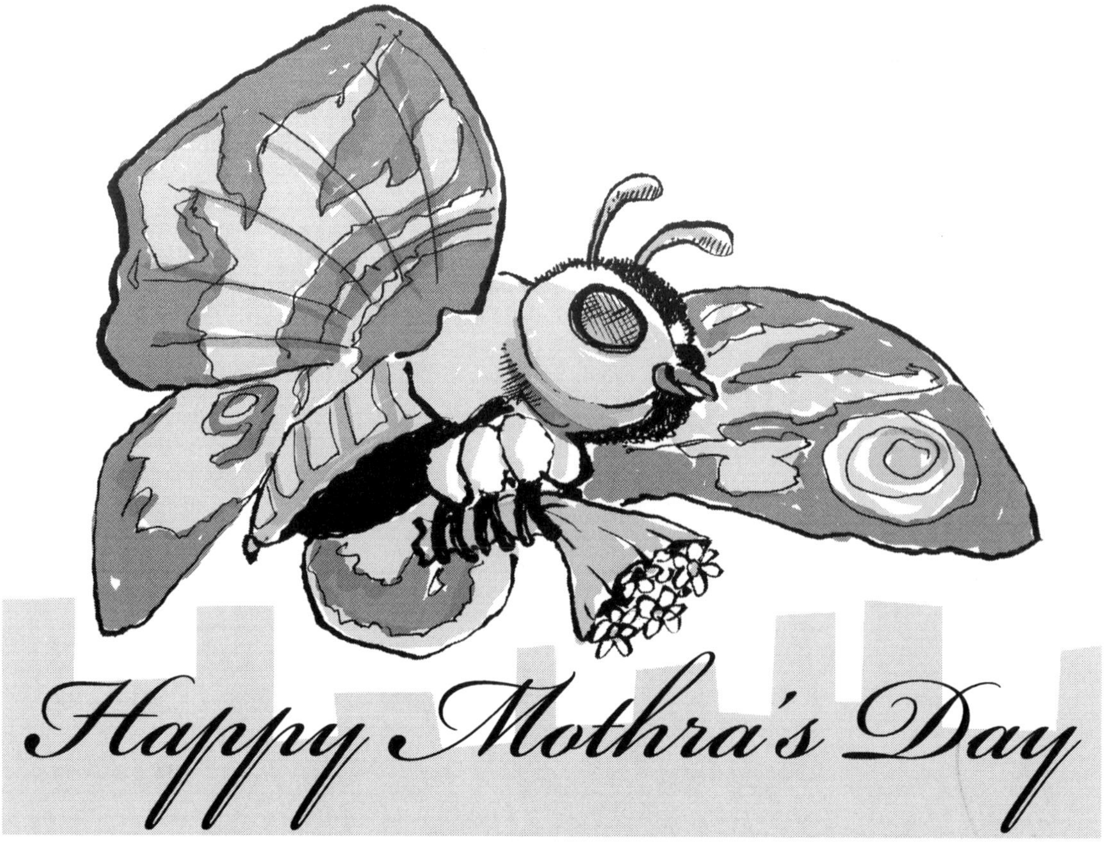
Happy Mothra's Day

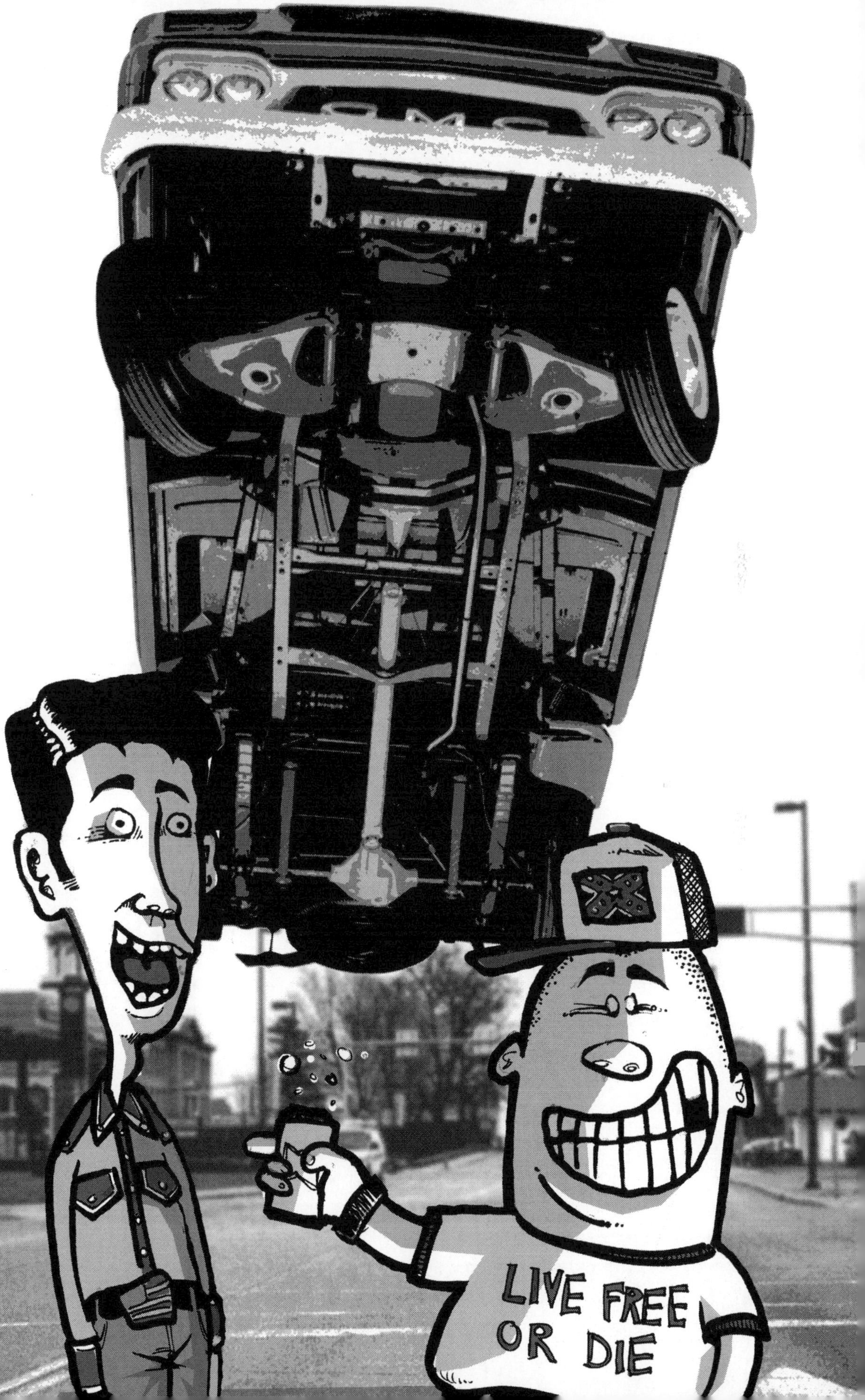
LIVE FREE
OR DIE

FORGETTING

I have a bad memory. My high school friends will tell me stories about myself from our teenage years, and I enjoy them as if they are about someone else. When I go to a restaurant I've been to many times before, I will forget what I like or dislike on the menu. Sometimes when I'm watching TV, I'll start flipping around the channels during a commercial break, and I'll forget what show I was watching (admittedly, this might not be my memory's fault—I watch some pretty forgettable crap). Ever get in the shower and wash your hair twice? Ever forget what street you parked your car on? Ever forget when your father died? I had to Google it. It was 2002.

I'm especially bad with names. If you're a casual acquaintance of mine, and I run into you downtown, there is an 89% chance that while I am nodding and smiling at you during our conversation, I will have no idea what your name is. If you are a man, and I greet you with a variation of "Hey, dude," then I have no idea what your name is. If you're a woman and I greet you with a friendly "Hey, there," then I have no idea what your name is. Please "pepper" a few hints into the conversation as subtly as possible. A couple of suggestions:

"Hey, Tom, have I ever shown you my driver's license?"

or maybe

"Hello, Tom. Do you remember my name?"

Also please note that while you're talking to me and I'm busy trying to recall your name, I'm not listening to what you're saying, because I'm busy trying to recall your name. Which makes it a hundred times more likely that I won't recall what you said later, because I didn't hear it in the first place. Also note that I am not paying attention to what I'm saying, either, which explains why I say so many stupid things.

I'm also bad with numbers. I was a huge *LOST* fan, but I never knew what that notorious sequence of digits were. I know it started with an 18, and possibly had a 42 in it. I still keep my phone number written down in my trusty notebook in case anyone asks me for it. License plate? No way. Social security number? Sometimes. Those extra digits they added to my zip code a quarter of a century ago? Noooo. You know the old carpenter's adage 'measure twice and cut once'? Well, I measure thrice, and as an extra measure, I write it down. I still mess up the cut, but that's because I'm a terrible carpenter. Can't blame the ol' memory for everything.

I've forgotten so much of my years on this planet—events, conversations, entire human beings—it makes me assume that what I do remember must be worth remembering. And yet I've retained memories of so much useless crap—Fido Dido t-shirts, episodes of "Beans Baxter," the paperback novelization of *Top Gun* I bought at the supermarket when I was thirteen… Surely, these things are worthy of forgetting, right? Darren McGavin in *Firebird Twenty-Fifteen AD*? The time I backed my grandmother's car into a guardrail—twice? A Luke Skywalker action figure I lost in a rock wall in Littleton, Massachusetts? Why are these things squatting on my precious mental real estate when I can barely recall my first three or four girlfriends? Why do I remember a kid with really dry hands from first grade, but I forget what I had for dinner two nights ago?

My memory is selective, randomly discerning, and a mystery to me. I forget his name. I forget her birthday. I forget if I already mentioned the thing about showering. Time drifts by, phone calls are not returned, emails remain unwritten.

Do I not remember things because they're unimportant to me? Is it a bona fide medical condition? Am I just a mentally lazy person? Is it getting worse? Do I have too much RAM and not enough hard drive? Did the preceding sentence come out sounding sorta dirty? Don't know that, either. But I do know this: I might forget you someday—your name and face and everything about you—but I need *you* to remember *me*. What I've liked and who I've loved and where I've lived and what I've done. In case I forget, and need a reminder.

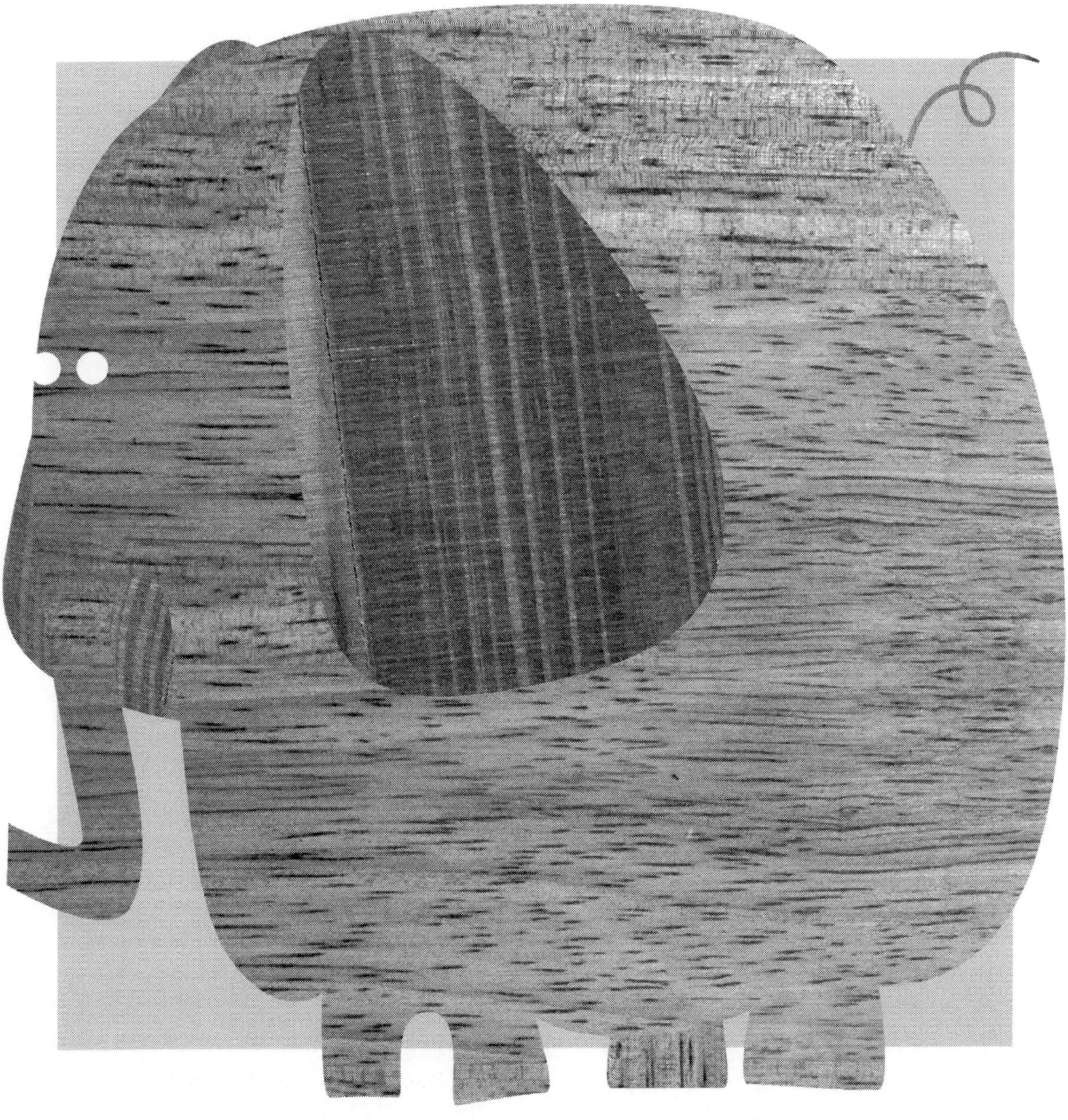

SPACE MISSI

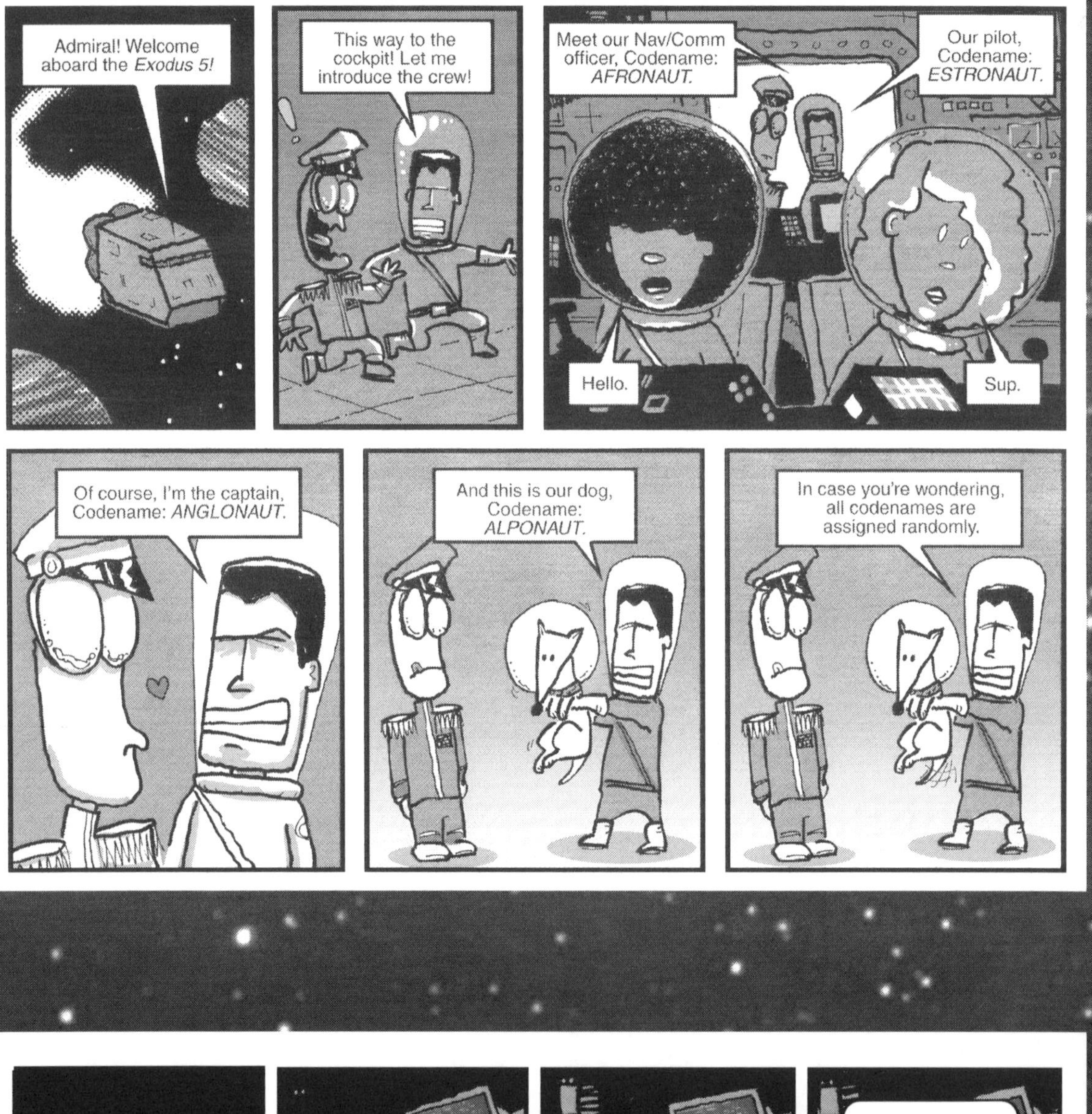
Admiral! Welcome aboard the *Exodus 5!*
This way to the cockpit! Let me introduce the crew!
Meet our Nav/Comm officer, Codename: *AFRONAUT.*
Our pilot, Codename: *ESTRONAUT.*
Hello.
Sup.
Of course, I'm the captain, Codename: *ANGLONAUT.*
And this is our dog, Codename: *ALPONAUT.*
In case you're wondering, all codenames are assigned randomly.

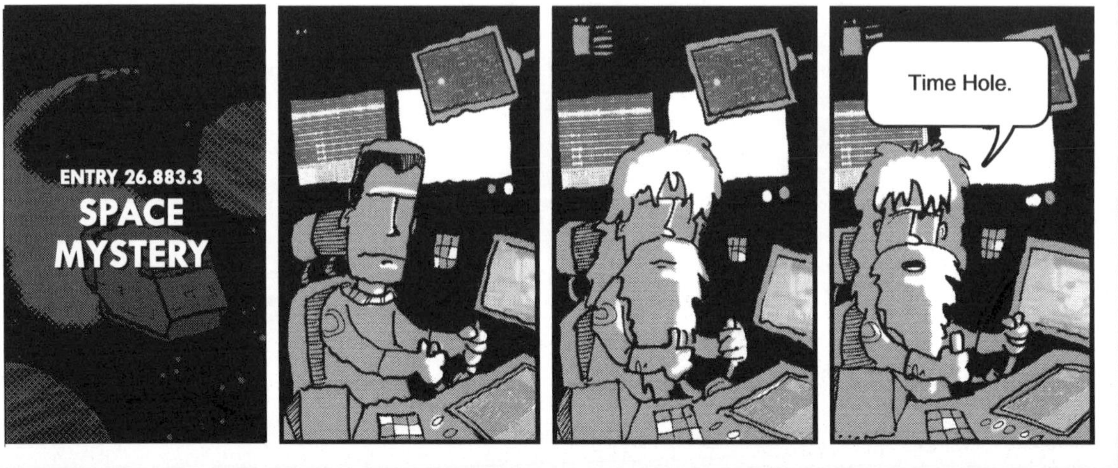
ENTRY 26.883.3
SPACE MYSTERY
Time Hole.

CREW: 3025

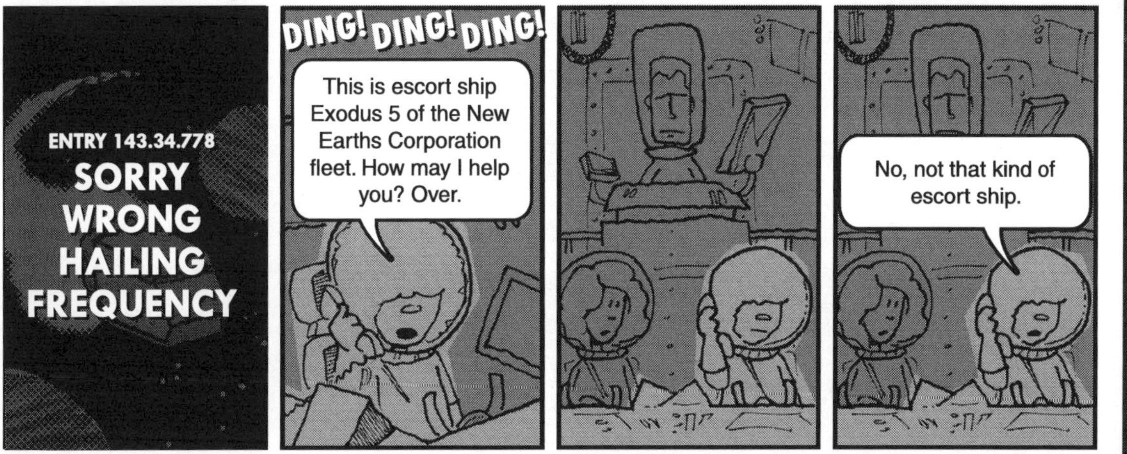
ENTRY 143.34.778
SORRY WRONG HAILING FREQUENCY
DING! DING! DING!
This is escort ship Exodus 5 of the New Earths Corporation fleet. How may I help you? Over.
No, not that kind of escort ship.

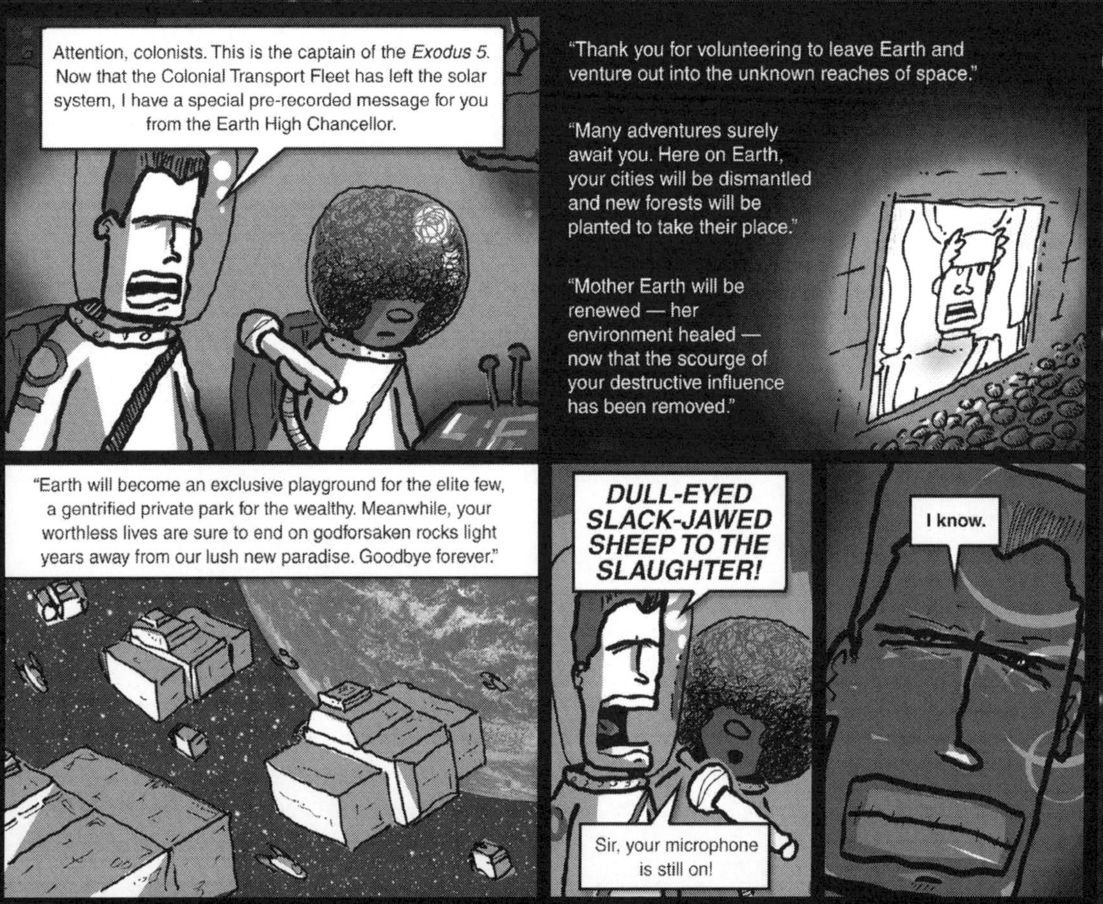
Attention, colonists. This is the captain of the *Exodus 5*. Now that the Colonial Transport Fleet has left the solar system, I have a special pre-recorded message for you from the Earth High Chancellor.
"Thank you for volunteering to leave Earth and venture out into the unknown reaches of space."
"Many adventures surely await you. Here on Earth, your cities will be dismantled and new forests will be planted to take their place."
"Mother Earth will be renewed — her environment healed — now that the scourge of your destructive influence has been removed."
"Earth will become an exclusive playground for the elite few, a gentrified private park for the wealthy. Meanwhile, your worthless lives are sure to end on godforsaken rocks light years away from our lush new paradise. Goodbye forever."
DULL-EYED SLACK-JAWED SHEEP TO THE SLAUGHTER!
Sir, your microphone is still on!
I know.

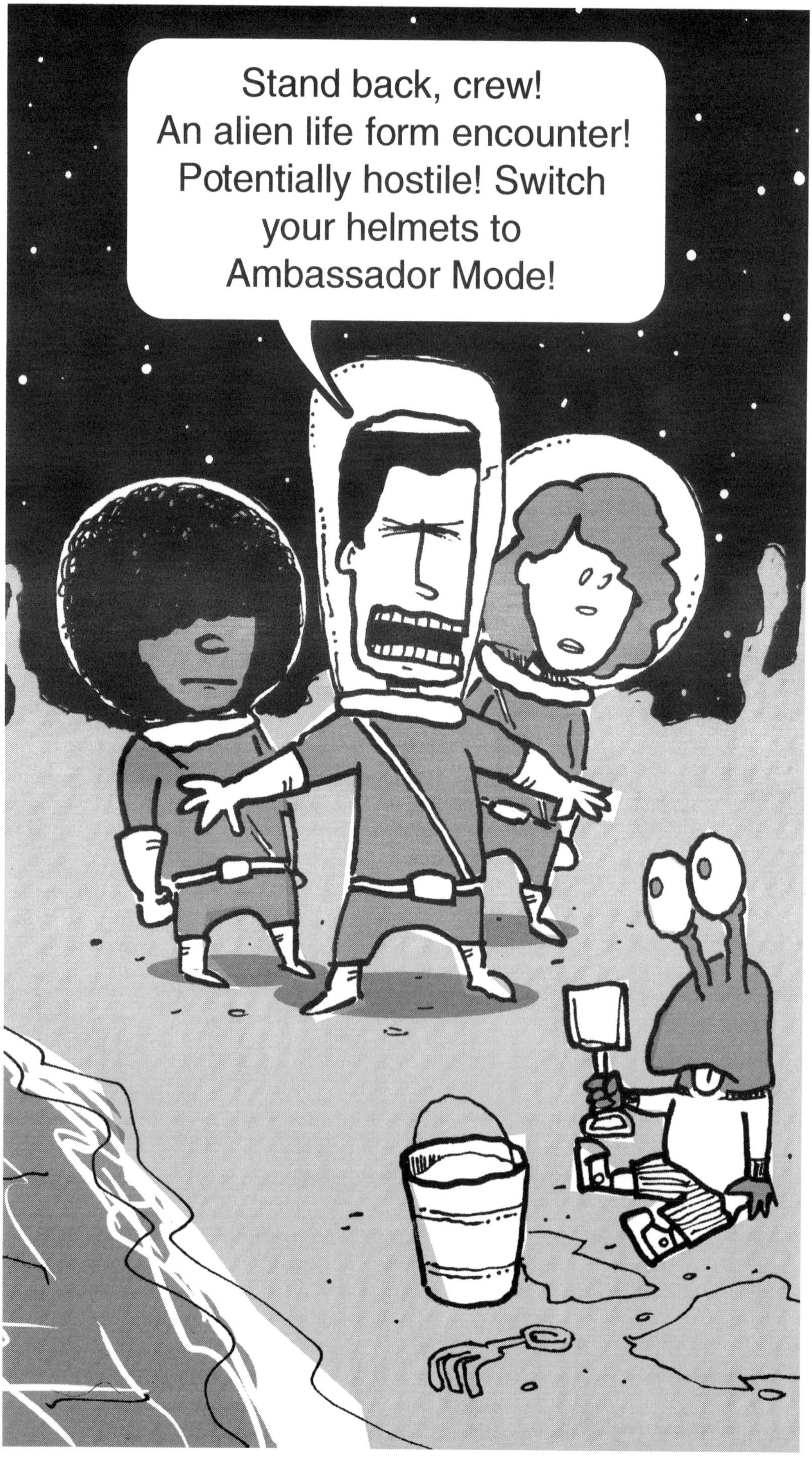
Stand back, crew! An alien life form encounter! Potentially hostile! Switch your helmets to Ambassador Mode!

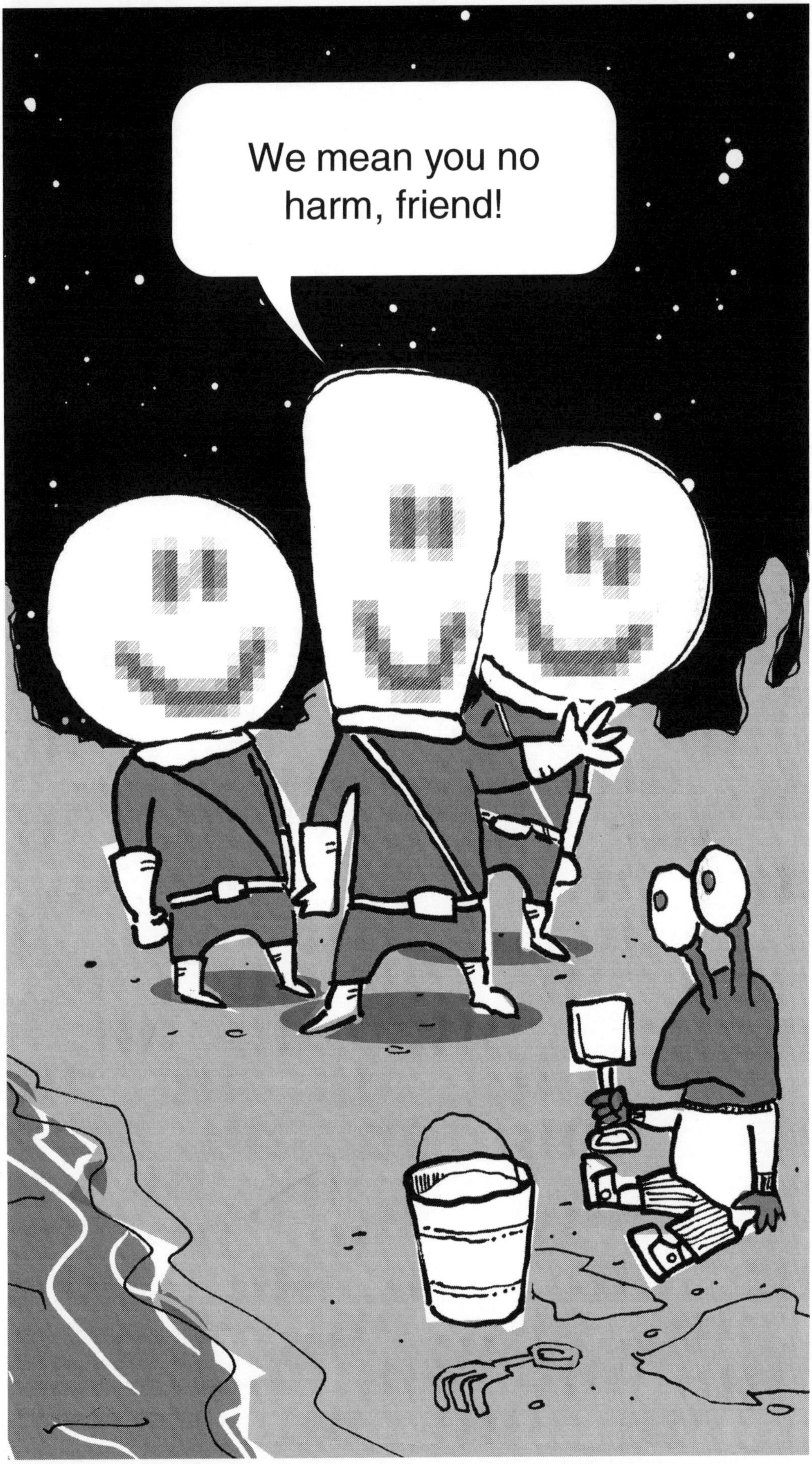
We mean you no harm, friend!

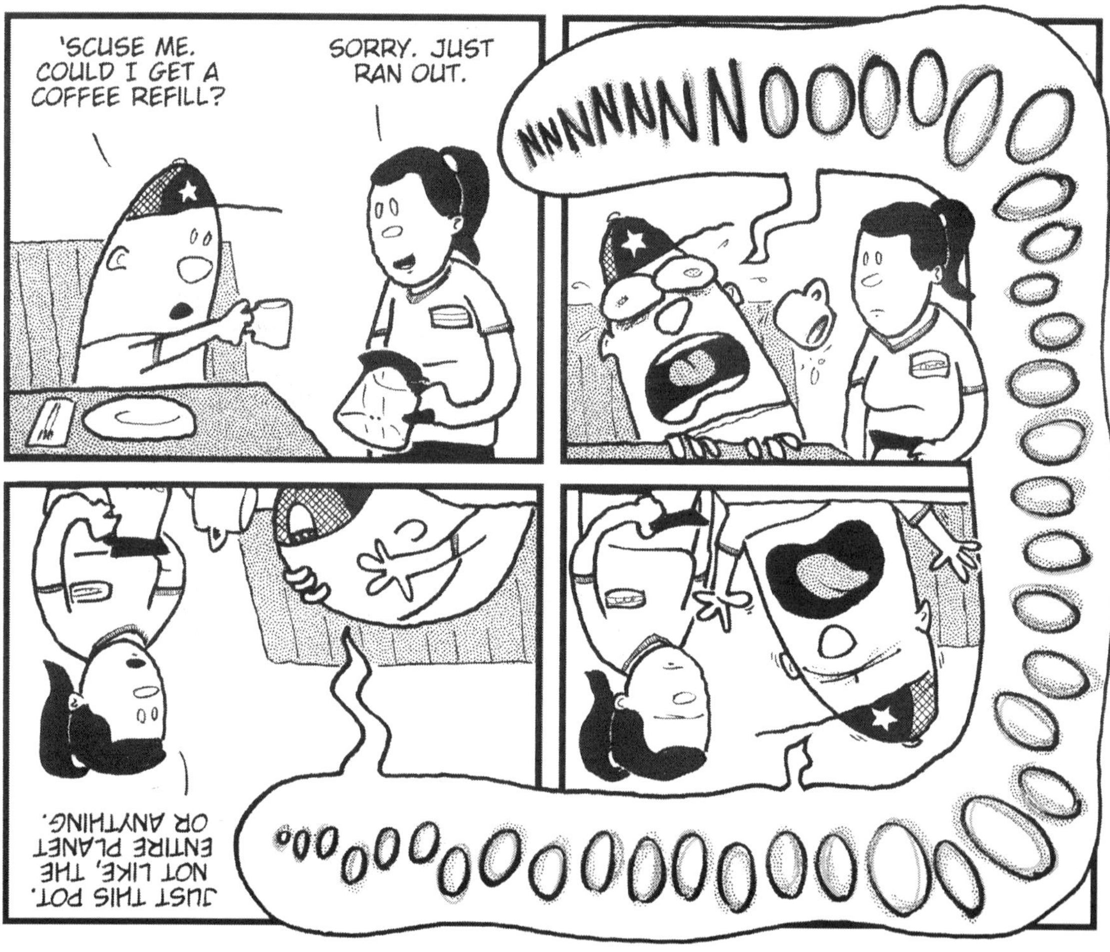
'SCUSE ME. COULD I GET A COFFEE REFILL?
SORRY. JUST RAN OUT.
NNNNNNNOOOOOOOOOOOOOOOOOOOOOOOOOOOOOOOOOOOOOOOOOO
JUST THIS POT. NOT LIKE, THE ENTIRE PLANET OR ANYTHING.

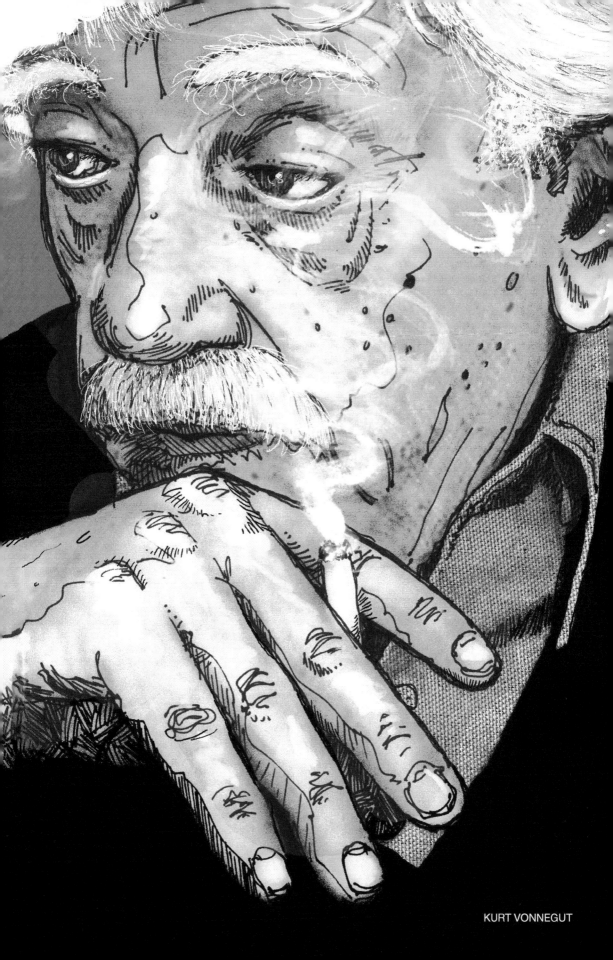

KURT VONNEGUT

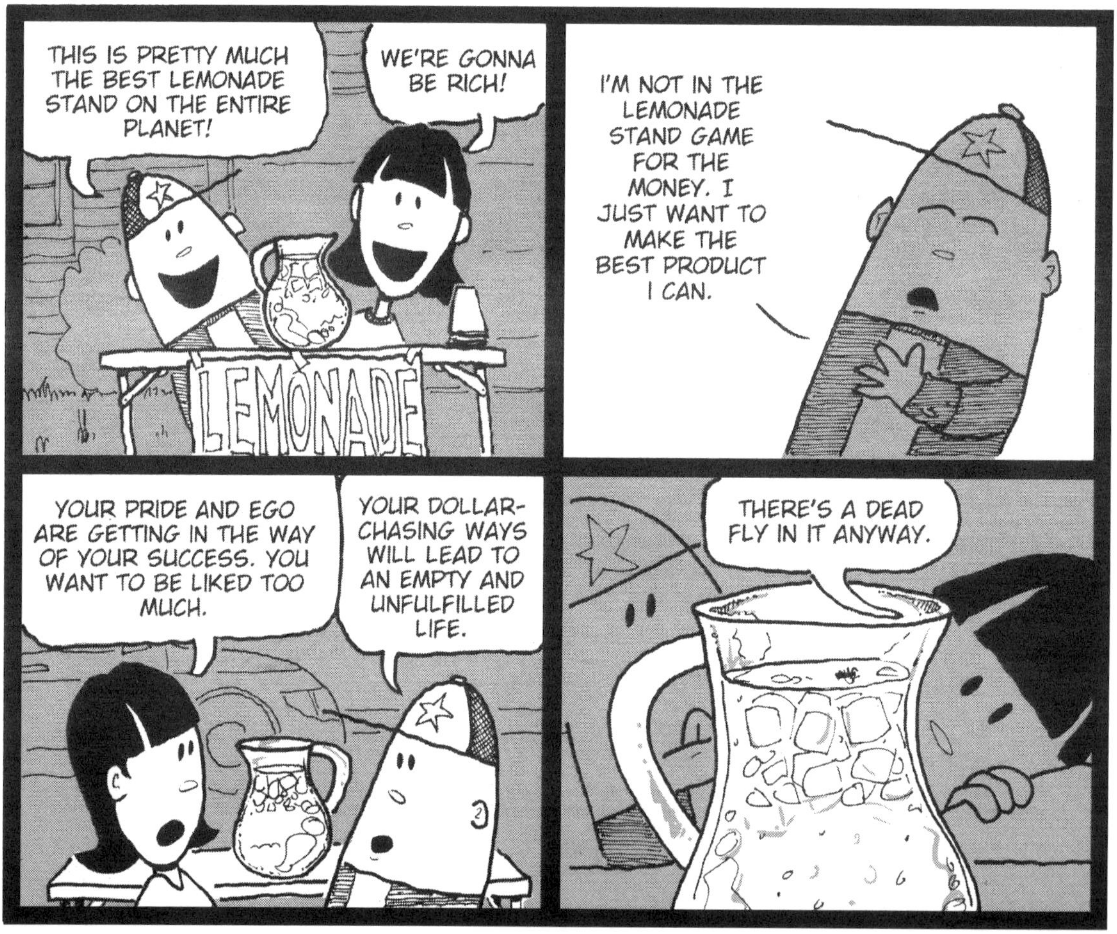
THIS IS PRETTY MUCH THE BEST LEMONADE STAND ON THE ENTIRE PLANET!
WE'RE GONNA BE RICH!
LEMONADE
I'M NOT IN THE LEMONADE STAND GAME FOR THE MONEY. I JUST WANT TO MAKE THE BEST PRODUCT I CAN.
YOUR PRIDE AND EGO ARE GETTING IN THE WAY OF YOUR SUCCESS. YOU WANT TO BE LIKED TOO MUCH.
YOUR DOLLAR-CHASING WAYS WILL LEAD TO AN EMPTY AND UNFULFILLED LIFE.
THERE'S A DEAD FLY IN IT ANYWAY.

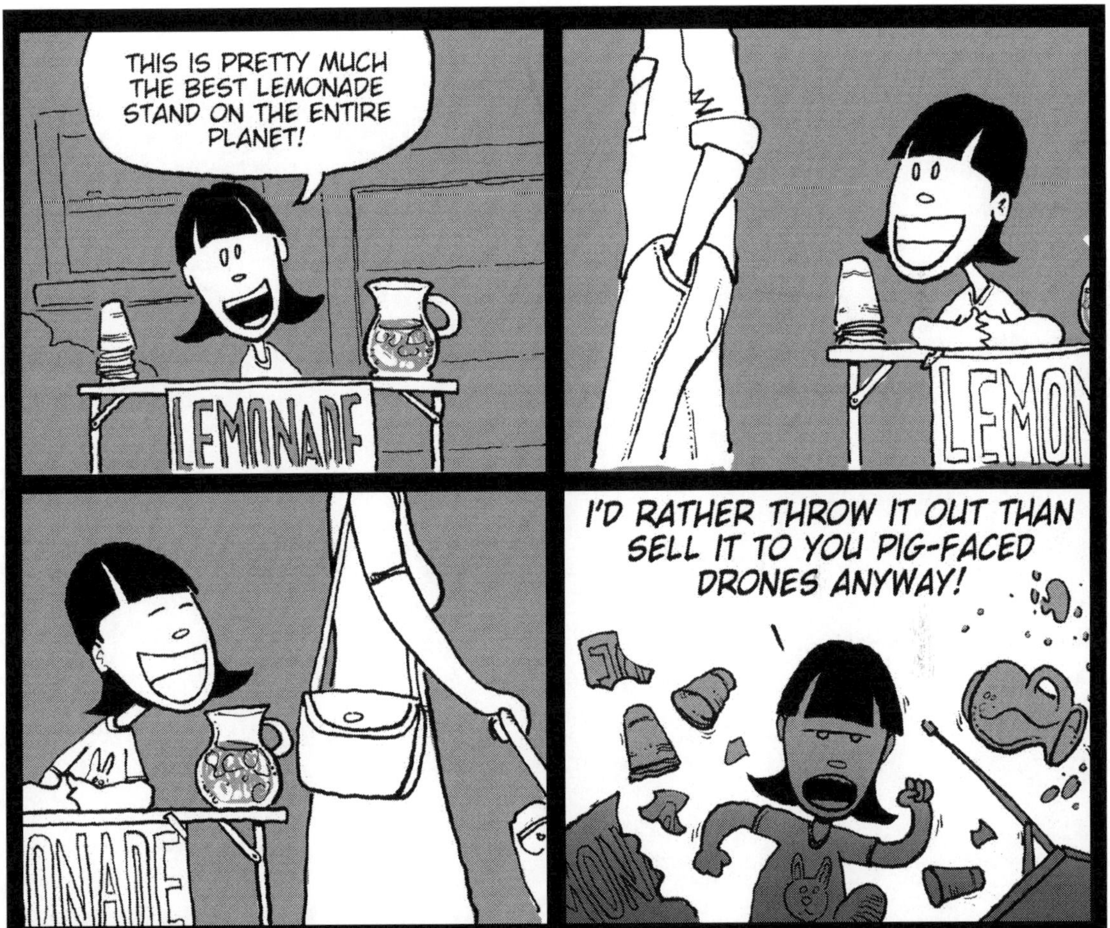
THIS IS PRETTY MUCH THE BEST LEMONADE STAND ON THE ENTIRE PLANET!
LEMONADE
LEMON
ONADE
I'D RATHER THROW IT OUT THAN SELL IT TO YOU PIG-FACED DRONES ANYWAY!

A MINOR INCONVENIENCE

Coop continued, undaunted by her eye-rolling. "So I run in super-fast for a coffee and this one ponytailed hip-dad was totally holding up the line—"

"Wait," Lucy interrupted. "'Held up' like stickup or 'held up' like slow?"

"I think it's pretty obvious," Coop sighed as he stepped behind the counter. In a mournful voice: "He got everything, even my lighter. I'm penniless."

"That's awful," she responded with fake sympathy. The register bleeped as she tried opening the cash drawer. She wiggled the manager's key and tried again. Bleep. "Did you get shot in the face? Cuz you look horrible," she observed, not looking up.

"Anyway," Coop exhaled. "The dude was all complaining about his cappuccino foam or some such shit. I was like dude, get a fucking normal cup of coffee."

"That's an interesting story you've just told me," Lucy said. She slapped the side of the cash drawer. "The fuck?" she demanded of the machine. It did not reply.

"I don't think you actually enjoyed my story. I think you're drenched in sarcastic residue right now. It's like Sarcasm Incarnate has shot a hot load of his spunk all over your hot young college co-ed face."

"Mmmm," she agreed, still pretty much ignoring him. "Why do we keep the bathroom key in the goddamned cash drawer anyway?"

"Because you kept losing it."

"Better to not know where something is when you need it and stand half a chance of finding it than to know exactly where something is when you need it and have absolutely no chance of getting at it."

"What?"

"Just get me the butter knife in the back room. It's in the pencil cup."

"You know, if you bought something, the register would open."

"I don't shop here."

"Well, maybe—"

"I'm going to pee on your shoe."

"Now that's just plain distasteful."

"My question is," Lucy announced, returning from the bathroom with a fashion magazine. "They put beautiful women on magazine covers to attract horny men and image-conscious women as readers, right?"

"Yes," Coop concurred. "Yes, they do." His ass sat on the officially designated employee stool, his torso lay draped across the counter. "I'm failing to see what exactly your question is."

"Well, what's up with *that?*" Lucy demanded, throwing the glossy magazine onto the top of the teetering stack of paper in the bin near the trash can. Coop had never taken out the store's recycling, nor could he ever recall having seen a co-worker empty it. Coop suspected the dense tower of paper pre-dated his employment, and possibly, recycling itself.

"Yes," he agreed again. "I dunno."

"I mean, how about beautiful men on magazine covers for horny women and image-conscious men?" she proposed. "Hah, buddy?" she goaded, punching Coop in the upper arm. "Hah? How bout that, fella?"

Cooper was too tired to feign injury. "Well..." he thought. "What about those weight-lifting magazines—"

"Who reads those? Nobody reads those things. Those magazines suck donkballs!" she declared. A regular perusing the clearance section let out a snort. He always wore a Marlboro hat. Their nickname for him was Marlboro Hat Guy. "Right?!?" she calls to him. "Thank you!" Lucy retrieved the fashion magazine from the recycling pile and began flipping through it again. "I need more of a hot-guy-infotainment-cool-shoes sort of magazine. Aren't I a target audience? Don't I have rights?" she demanded. Without explanation, she licked her thumb, delicately tore a page from the middle of the magazine, folded it into quarters, and slipped it into her jeans pocket. "This magazine is garbage," she muttered, tossing it back onto the pile.

"Then maybe you shouldn't recycle it," Coop suggested from the protective arm-cave he had spelunked his head into.

Coop was closing with Doug. Doug was the sort of fella who would announce how much he loved the Mountain Dew he was drinking or the Camel he was smoking or the Old Navy shirt he was wearing. It was never about mere cola or cigarettes or faux-vintage T-shirts with Doug. No, it was brand loyalty in its purest form. Coop suspected that research analysts and survey conductors and polling people would give free infinite handjobs for a crack at a test subject like Doug. He was the perfect demographic of a perfect consumer. He was the Dougographic. Coop hated Doug. Coop hated Doug because Doug was an idiot.

"Wassup, Cooper?" hailed Doug as he swaggered into the store. "Closing with Cooper!" He wore a very clean baseball cap. All of Doug's baseball caps were very clean.

"Hey, Doug," Cooper nodded, tearing the flesh from his wrists with his teeth,

watching with mild disinterest as his imaginary lifeblood soaked into his rolled-up shirt sleeves. "How's it going." Not a question.

"What are we listening to?" Doug inquired, not bothering to actually listen to the music on the store stereo. He was only aware that he did not immediately recognize it, and would therefore be unable to bob his head up and down to the beat. He began prodding the pile of scratched-to-hell CDs on top of the speaker. Doug loved to fuck with the stereo, and by extension, Coop's sanity.

"It's a band called Nately's Whore," Coop mumbled, mentally preparing himself.

"Nately? Wasn't he one of the guys from The Who? The dude that suffocated on his own puke? UUGGHHHH!!!" Doug snorted with glee, grossing himself out. He took a long pull from his green bottle. "God I fucking love Mountain Dew," he reflected.

"You should rotate the bottle around a little more so the logo faces out," Coop suggested.

"Huh?"

"The singer's name was Daltry, not Nately," Coop smiled.

"I must be thinking of Mama Cass! NAHHAHHAH!" Doug howled. Coop was pretty sure he didn't actually know who Mama Cass was. Or Roger Daltry, or John Bonham, or Bon Scott, or whoever the hell he was thinking of. They were just names tenuously connected to pieces of pop culture trivia, urban legend, and old SNL skits, bumping into each other inside Doug's weird-shaped head. Doug knew Kanye West lyrics. Doug knew Michael Bay movies. Doug knew imported sports cars.

"Subaru BRZ!!!" he shouted, pointing out the window at the blue fiberglass blob cruising past the store. "Ho-shit, you see that?" He jumped from behind the counter and rolled his face against the front window to watch it take the turn at the intersection. "Sick, bro! Thing's sick!"

"Uh huh."

Doug had a weird habit of sometimes putting his gold chain in his mouth. Oral fixation. It dangled from his lips now. "Dude, those things haul balls."

A black wave of dawning horror washed over Coop as he noted that Doug still had his coat on. He looked at the clock and saw that not only was the tortuous evening of working with Doug not anywhere near over yet, but Doug had shown up *fifteen minutes early*. The tortuous evening of working with Doug *had yet to commence*.

"What are you doing here?" demanded Cooper, tapping the plastic face of the clock. "What the fuck are you doing here?" he half-stammered, a sure sign he was about to absolutely fucking lose his shit. He reminded himself he hadn't cried in over seven years.

"Ah, just swung in to drop off my bag," shrugged Doug, oblivious to Cooper's histrionics. He threw his backpack through the back room doorway. "Gotta run up to FasMart and grab some Camels. Want anything?" He left without waiting for an answer.

Coop couldn't construct the proper curse word combination to properly express his feelings. A peculiar choking gurgle escaped from his windpipe. "Roger Daltry's not dead," Coop croaked as he twisted his own head off and stomped it into jelly.

———— ∘⊂◦⊱⊰◦⊃∘ ————

"Wait, *how* awesome was it?" Coop asked for confirmation, eyebrows raised.

"Aw, dude, no fucking contest. It was totally awesome!" Doug declared. "Fucking insane. Truly. The train cars have no floors and they shoot you up, like, 500 feet in the air and drop you like a sack of wet mice and at the last second: WHAM!" He slapped his fist into his open palm. "They slam you into a triple-threat loop! Then these guys come running out on this one slow straightaway part. They're made up like dead zombies all gory and shit."

"Dead zombies, you say?" Coop was just trying to keep himself awake and entertained enough to painlessly ride out the rest of the shift. It was almost time to get ready to start getting ready to prepare to close the store. They had vacuumed an hour earlier and there were no customers.

"And I'm not shitting you Cooper, they start swinging axes and machetes at your fucking head as you ride by! And you're all strapped in and can't duck or anything! It rocked so hard!"

"You paid for this," Cooper non-asked.

"It's like a roller coaster crossed with a haunted house crossed with... I dunno, bungee jumping. I swear I've never been so frightened in my whole fuckin' life!" Doug praised as he chewed on the pen cap. "Like, three people on the ride pissed themselves!"

"So you enjoy this weird, artificial, fear-inducing sort of entertainment?" Coop inquired.

"Artificial, my ass!" Doug defended. "Dude, they almost killed all of us! It was amaaaazing! I'm going back next weekend!"

"You know, Doug..." Coop began, transitioning to his lecturing-a-five-year-old voice. "In other parts of the world—places you don't read about in porn mags or hear on Rock109 or see on 4chan—in those parts of the world, people are being kidnapped and beaten."

"Who buys fuckin' porn mags, Coop?"

"Kidnapped and beaten. Sometimes for their beliefs, sometimes for their race, sometimes just because they're fucking poor. They're tortured. They're shot. They're disfigured."

Doug rolled his eyes and took another extreme chug from his Mountain Dew. He bought the bottles at such a constant rate that Coop had never actually witnessed Doug open or empty one. It appeared that the young man possessed a single, self-replenishing, eternally half-full bottle of green pee. Coop continued in his best Nurse Ratched tone of voice: "You paid money for a thrilling, titillating and ultimately safe re-creation of horrors and fears many many people face every day of their lives. A simulated taste of dangers you'll probably never have to actually worry about." Doug leaned back against the wall and rubbed his temples. "You are an American, Doug. You are a tourist of cruel and barbaric acts. The most frightening and exciting experience of your life took place on a ride at an amusement park in a rented field. You bought a ticket for it, Doug. You following me?" Doug knew better than to respond. "You know Pham? The Cambodian kid that works at FasMart? He told me once that when he was like five, he watched while two of his brothers got dragged out of his house in the middle of the night and shot in their fucking faces."

"Fuck you, Cooper," Doug interrupted with uncharacteristic impatience. "That's too fucking bad about Pham, seriously. But you try to make me feel guilty or stupid for like, everything I do. All I did was go to an amusement park with Carrie, okay? It wasn't a political statement or a symptom of some social injustice or some shit. It was just a roller coaster ride. An awesome one. *Electric Genocide III* was amazingly fun. I'm going to ride it every goddamned weekend for the rest of the summer. So fuck off."

Coop was dumbstruck. He almost trembled in disbelief. Blood shot out of his eyes like an angry lizard. His own voice seemed so very far away.

"What's the ride called?" he whispered.

The rest of the shift was like this.

Every shift they worked together was like this.

———————◦◦◦◦◦———————

"Hey, Pham."

"What's up?"

"Nothing," Coop responded, running a finger across the packets of gum insulating the front of the convenience store counter. "Another morning, another day of item-selling, another delicious breakfast. What's this?" he asked, poking a glass jar with a post-it note taped to it. The post-it note said TIPS.

"Tip jar," Pham confirmed. "Manager said we could put one out."

"Is this in lieu of paying you a living wage?"

Pham shrugged.

"I hate cash register tip jars," Coop said as he strode across the convenience store. "I've never been served by a retail worker to such a high degree of satisfaction that I've ever felt compelled to give 'em extra money. I mean, let's face it: that's what it is. Extra money. Who has extra money? We're capitalists in a capitalist system. There's no such a thing as extra money. Now, incidentally Pham, this is no offense to you. I'm in retail too; I've always been in retail. I just don't get the tip thing, Pham. I just don't."

Pham shrugged again.

Cooper cracked open the refrigerator case and grabbed a Coke. "It's an employer's trick, that's what I think. They're trying to divert their low-paid work force's dissatisfaction away from the company and onto the customer. It's not my fault FasMart pays a crap wage, Pham. It's FasMart's, right?" He slid the bottle onto the counter. "I mean am I right?"

Pham shrugged again. "Want anything else?"

"Nah."

Ding! Lucy strode in, digging through her purse.

"Hey," Coop said. The register bleeped.

Lucy looked up. "Hey." She headed for the lip balm display on the endcap.

"I've been a customer here for like, over a year," Coop reminded Pham. "Old-school regulars don't need to tip, right? There's an understanding amonst civilized retail neighbors, right?" He dug in his pocket for money. "What, do I throw my mom a buck-oh-five for dinner now?"

"What're you guys talking about?" asked Lucy as she tossed an apricot-flavored stick of wax onto the counter. Coop tapped the tip jar with his fingernail.

"Oooh, a tip jar! Why don't we have one at our store?" she scowled at Cooper. To Pham: "I like the ones that say 'for counter intelligence'."

"Why? Why?" Coop cried. "Because we push buttons? Because we put things in bags? We're not craftsmen. We're not skilled artisans. We don't lift or carry or cook or prepare anything! We don't even get off the damned stool most of the time! We're register manipulators, and that's all!" Coop declared. "You!" he pointed at Lucy. "Me!" he pointed at himself. "Pham!" he pointed at Pham.

"Well, a few extra bucks wouldn't hurt."

"Then ask Hal for a raise! Not Marlboro Hat Guy! Not Pardon-Me Lady! Not the customers, Loose!"

"Do *not* call me 'Loose'."

"Customers are supposed to support businesses and the businesses are supposed to support their workers! That's how it's supposed to work!"

"For someone who complains about customers non-stop, you sure are defending their right to consume without care or concern," she pointed out. Lucy leaned over the counter to Pham. "Tell him that if people want to tip us, they should be able to." She patted the tip jar. "A simple receptacle to catch their kindness," she cooed. "Tell him he's an idiot," she added.

Pham looked at Coop. He opened his mouth, paused, and closed it again. "You're an idiot."

Cooper let out a slow exhale. He arched an eyebrow and leaned in over the counter, eye to eye with the young Cambodian. "Waitaminute," Coop scowled. "You don't know my name, do you?"

"No," Pham admitted without any social embarrassment.

"Oh," Coop spun around to address the empty convenience store. Lucy stifled a laugh. "OH!" he barked again. He spread his arms wide, probably reenacting a scene from some Al Pacino movie. "I come in here every goddamned day for a year and Pham doesn't even know my name and I have to tip everybody for doing anything! This is unfuckingbelievable!"

Lucy cracked up. "You lose big, buddy. See ya." She waves at Pham and walks out the door.

Coop hated losing half his audience, but persevered. "Like a knife in my heart, Pham!" he cried to the aisles of high fructose corn syrup. "A knife in my heart!"

"My name's Kim."

Cooper stopped short and turned to the boy behind the counter.

"What, no it's not," Coop denied, perplexed. "It is?"

Kim nodded.

"Fuck me," Coop said, his head cocked at an angle. He stuck a finger absently in his ear and stepped towards the door. "Then who the hell is Pham?" he wondered aloud.

Kim shrugged.

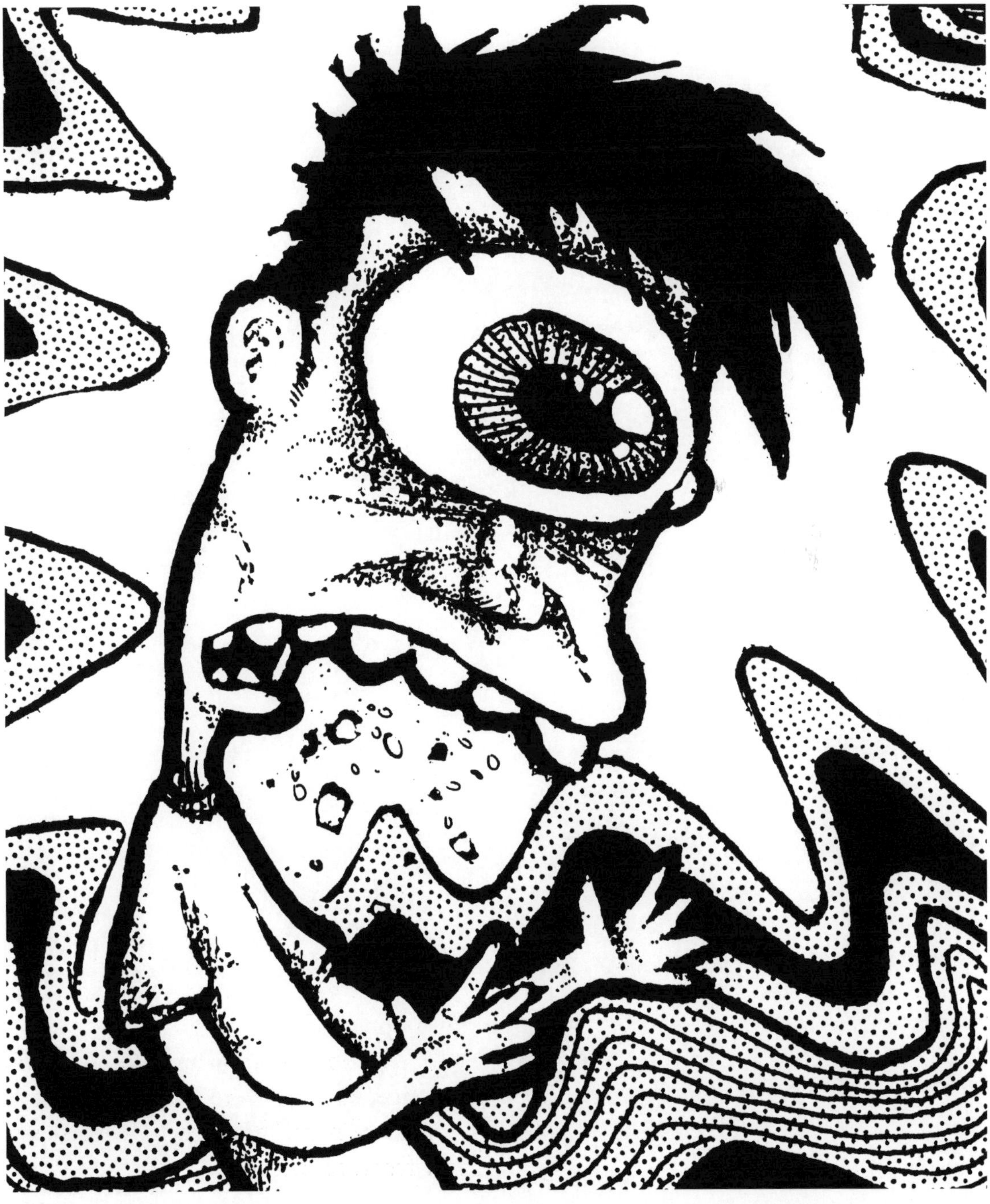

TALK LIKE A PIRATE DAY

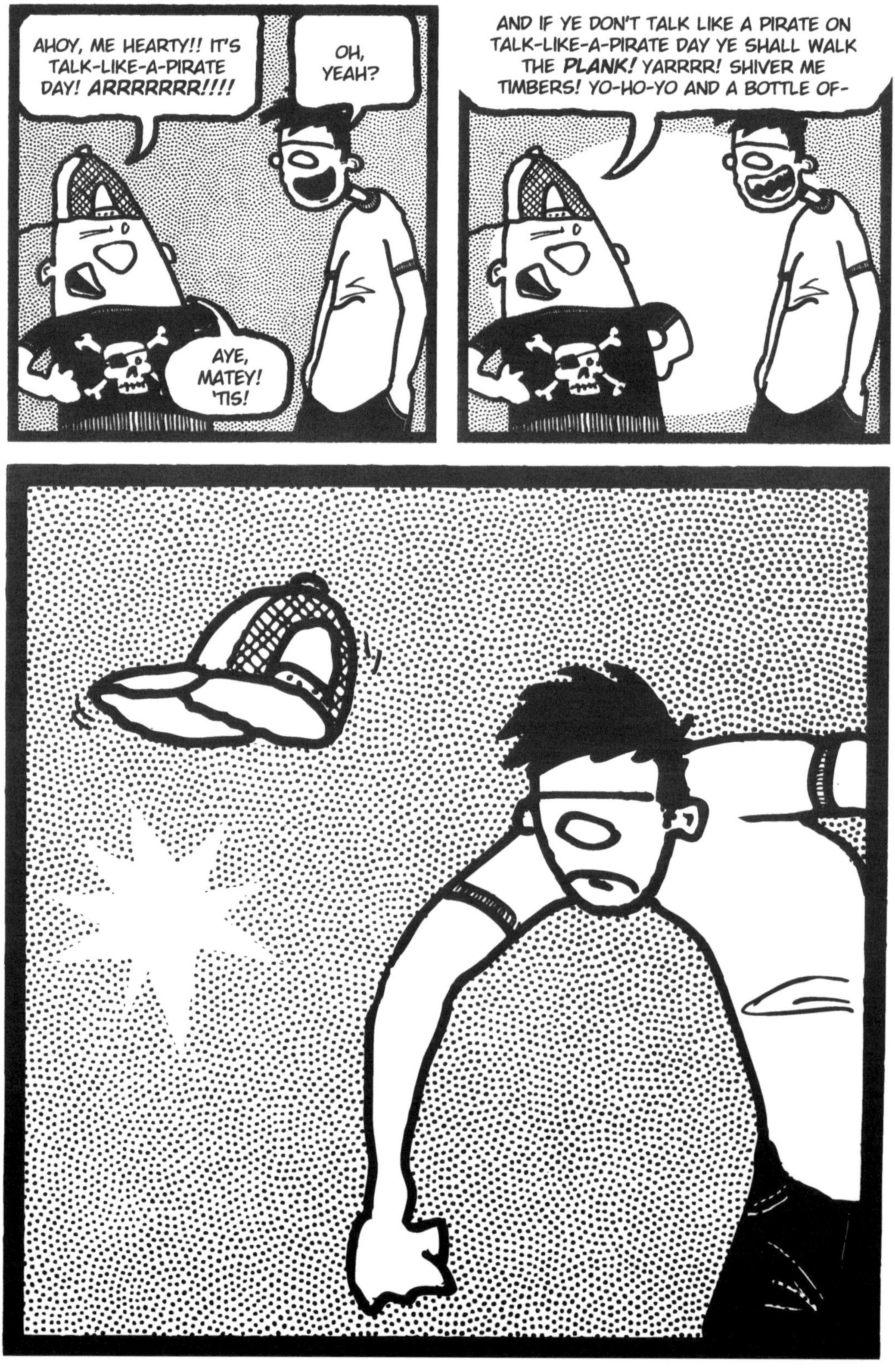
AHOY, ME HEARTY!! IT'S TALK-LIKE-A-PIRATE DAY! ARRRRRRR!!!!
OH, YEAH?
AYE, MATEY! 'TIS!
AND IF YE DON'T TALK LIKE A PIRATE ON TALK-LIKE-A-PIRATE DAY YE SHALL WALK THE PLANK! YARRRR! SHIVER ME TIMBERS! YO-HO-YO AND A BOTTLE OF-

LIGHTS! CAMERA! TERMINOLOGY!

Hollywood! Or maybe Holly*weird* is more like it! AM I RIGHT? But seriously, behind all the glitz and glamour of celebrity life lurks a world of technical jargon and insider lingo! **Let's take a look!**

PLOT - A spot at the cemetery where good stories are buried
SET - What a director says after "READY!" and before "GO!"
PROP - An item used on a set
TURBOPROP- A very fast item used on a set
MALAPROP - The unintentional confusion of a prop with one that has a similar-sounding name
SLATE - The clappy thing
CLAPPY THING- A member of a live studio audience
GOFER - A production assistant
GAFFER - A faux pas assistant
GOLFER - An executive producer
SCORE - Stealing a pair of George Clooney's boxers out of his trailer without getting caught
BEST BOY - That place at the mall where you pay at the cash register, walk ten feet, and then security asks to search your bag and check your receipt
BOOM MIC - A recording device that might explode
MACGUFFIN - A plot device to set things in motion
MCMUFFIN - A breakfast sandwich to set "things" in "motion"
MACGRUBER - A plot device that might explode and/or fail

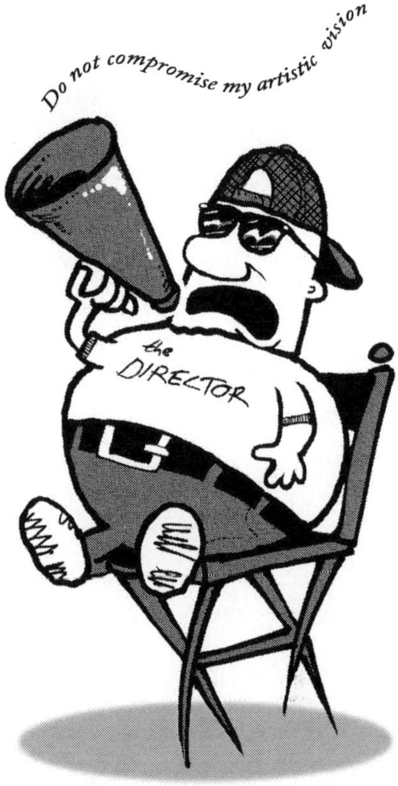
Do not compromise my artistic vision
the DIRECTOR

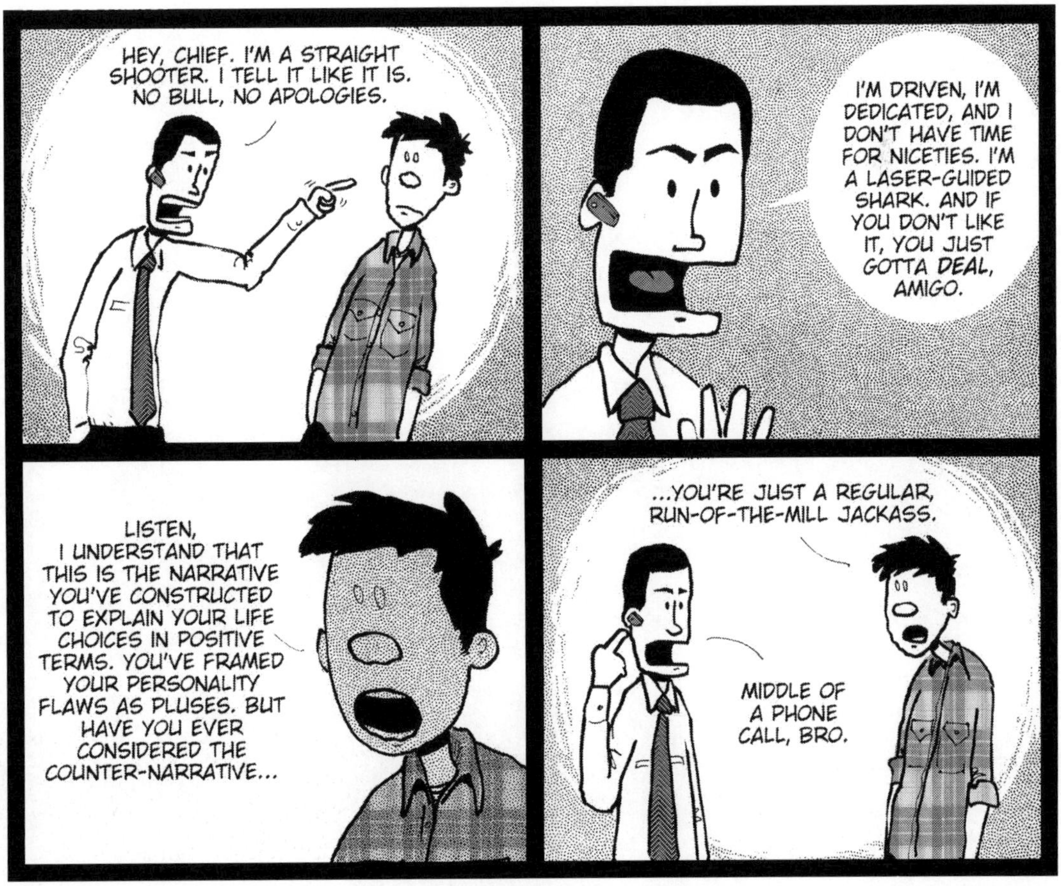
HEY, CHIEF. I'M A STRAIGHT SHOOTER. I TELL IT LIKE IT IS. NO BULL, NO APOLOGIES.
I'M DRIVEN, I'M DEDICATED, AND I DON'T HAVE TIME FOR NICETIES. I'M A LASER-GUIDED SHARK. AND IF YOU DON'T LIKE IT, YOU JUST GOTTA DEAL, AMIGO.
LISTEN, I UNDERSTAND THAT THIS IS THE NARRATIVE YOU'VE CONSTRUCTED TO EXPLAIN YOUR LIFE CHOICES IN POSITIVE TERMS. YOU'VE FRAMED YOUR PERSONALITY FLAWS AS PLUSES. BUT HAVE YOU EVER CONSIDERED THE COUNTER-NARRATIVE...
...YOU'RE JUST A REGULAR, RUN-OF-THE-MILL JACKASS.
MIDDLE OF A PHONE CALL, BRO.

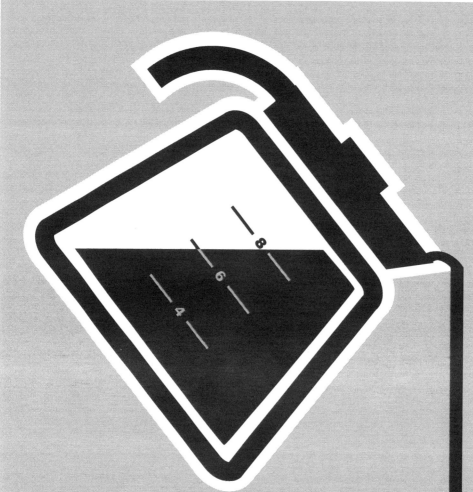

HELLO DARKNESS

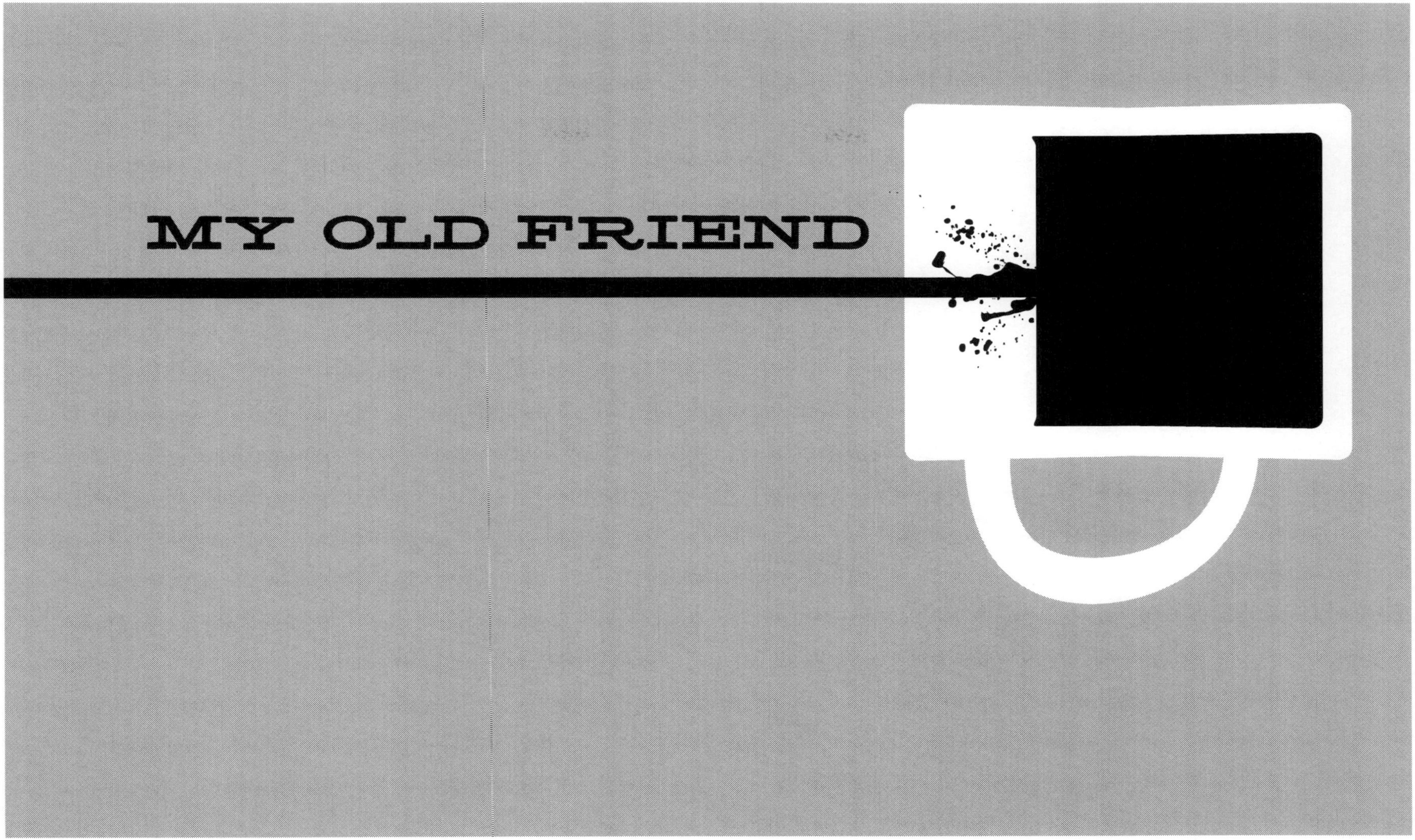
MY OLD FRIEND

Need a new outlook on life?
Tired of hearing bad news?

How to make your own

PINHOLE VIEWER

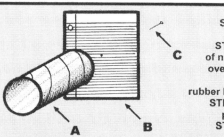

A
B
C

STEP 1: Take cardboard tube (A)
STEP 2: Wrap sheet of notebook paper (B) over one end of tube, securing it with a rubber band (not shown).
STEP 3: Poke hole in paper with pin (C).
STEP 4: Look at life a whole new way!

THE SUN IS ALWAYS SHINING SOMEWHERE!!

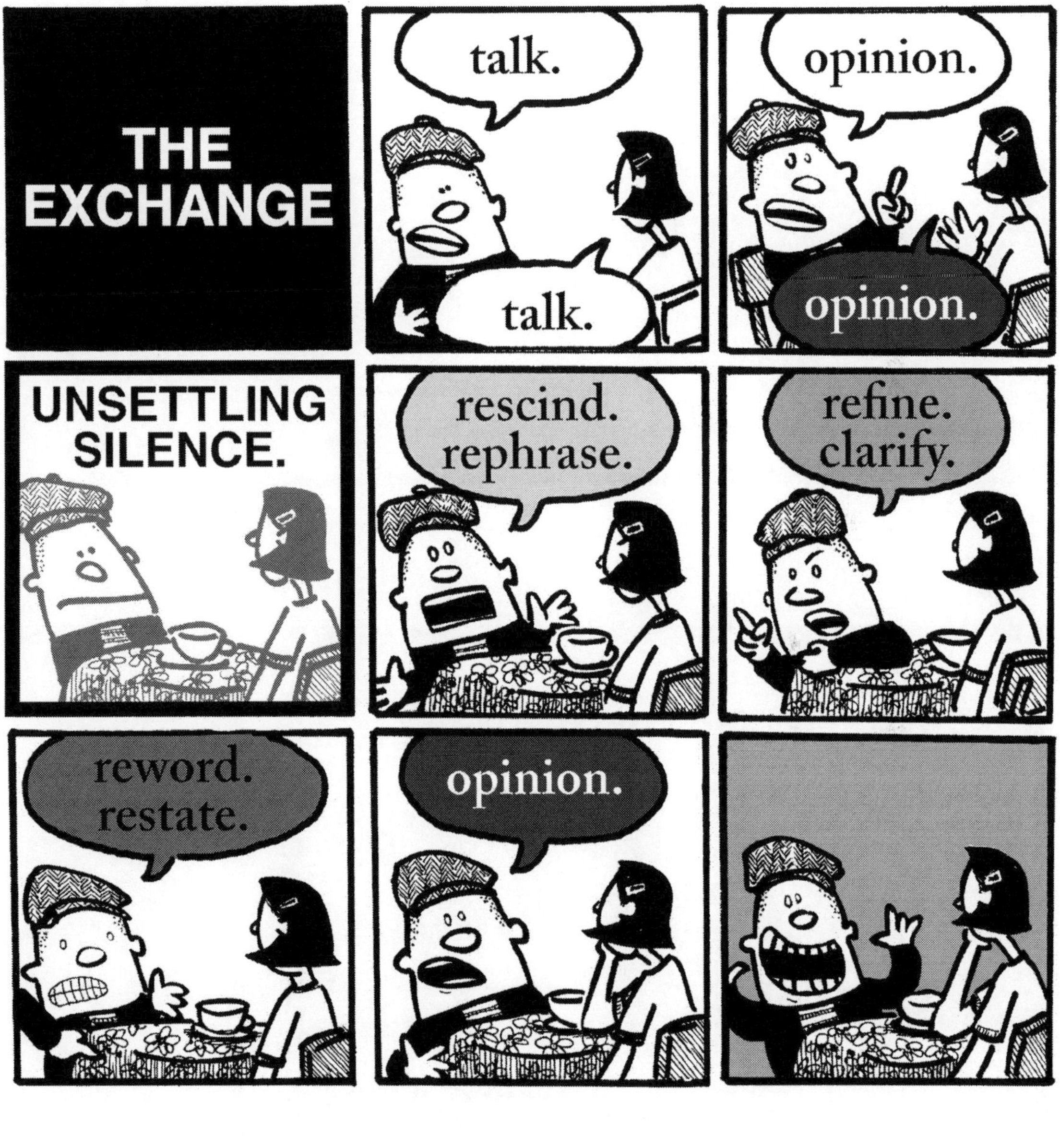
THE EXCHANGE
talk.
talk.
opinion.
opinion.
UNSETTLING SILENCE.
rescind. rephrase.
refine. clarify.
reword. restate.
opinion.

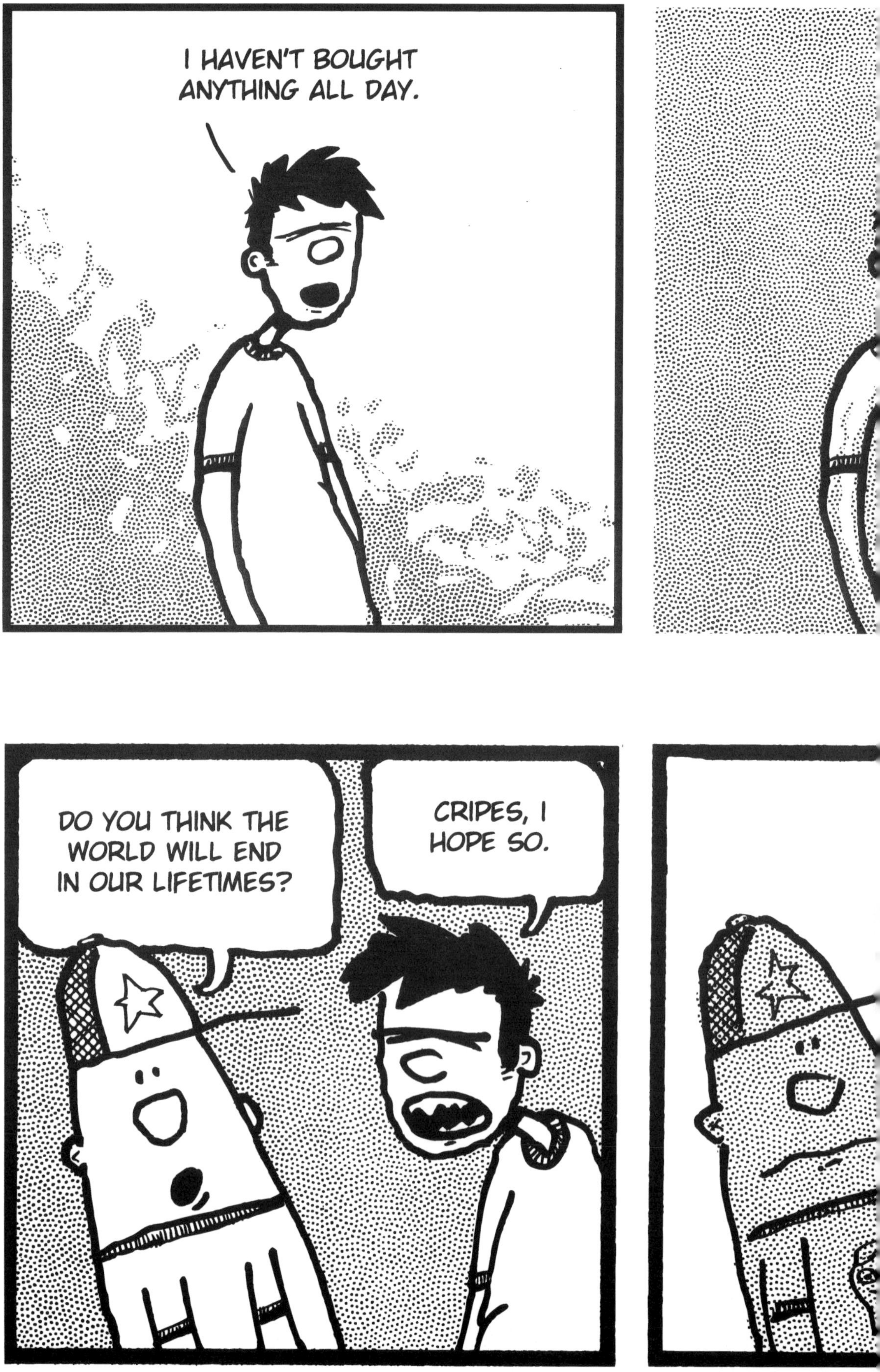
I HAVEN'T BOUGHT ANYTHING ALL DAY.
DO YOU THINK THE WORLD WILL END IN OUR LIFETIMES?
CRIPES, I HOPE SO.

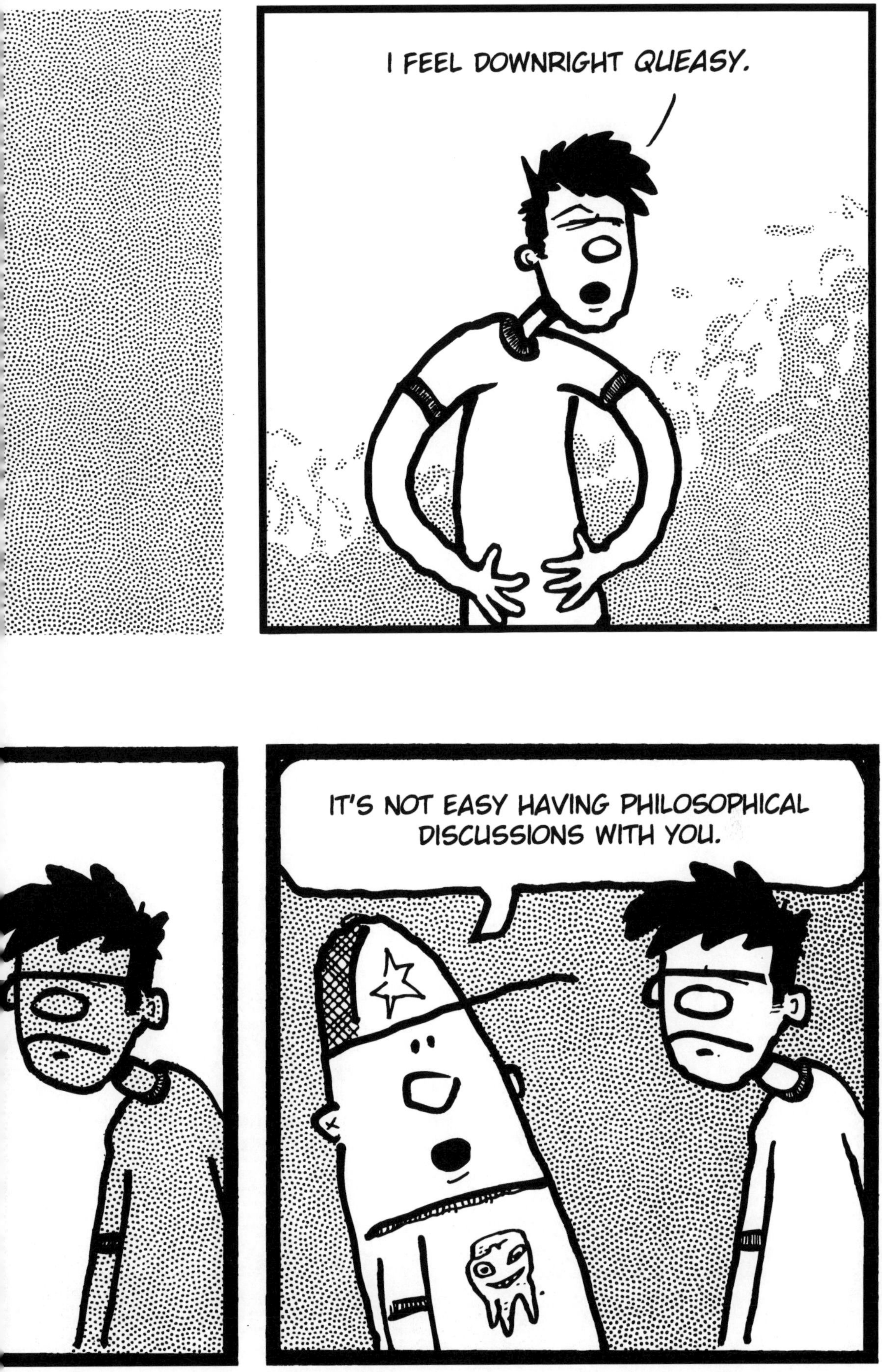
I FEEL DOWNRIGHT QUEASY.
IT'S NOT EASY HAVING PHILOSOPHICAL DISCUSSIONS WITH YOU.

HOUSES & STUFF

GEORGE CARLIN ONCE SAID A HOUSE IS NOTHING BUT A PILE OF STUFF WITH A COVER ON IT. AND HE WAS RIGHT. HOUSES ARE HANDY RECEPTACLES TO PUT ALL OF YOUR STUFF IN. NOW, SOME MIGHT SAY THAT STUFF ISN'T IMPORTANT; THAT RELATIONSHIPS AND HAPPINESS ARE IMPORTANT. I DISAGREE, BECAUSE I AM MATERIALISTIC, AND THEREFORE, SHALLOW AND SOULLESS.

MY HOUSE IS MY PRIVATE LIBRARY, MUSEUM, AND ZOO. I LIKE TO BE IN MY HOUSE, AROUND MY OWN THINGS. I HAVE MY BOOKS, MY CDS, MY TOOLS. MY ART STUFF, MY COMPUTER THINGS, MY MUSIC PARAPHERNALIA. I DON'T LIKE TO SHOW OFF MY POSSESSIONS, AND I'M NOT FOND OF HAVING STRANGERS IN MY HOME. IN FACT, I DON'T EVEN WANT TO DESCRIBE MY STUFF TO YOU, BECAUSE MAYBE YOU WILL WANT TO STEAL IT.

STAY AWAY FROM MY HOUSE.

IS THE DOOR LOCKED?!?!

I FEEL THIS WAY BECAUSE WHEN I WAS A KID, OUR HOUSE GOT BROKEN INTO. THE BURGLARS BROKE OUR STEREO AND STOLE ALL OF OUR CHRISTMAS CANDY. THEY TOOK A LOUSY OLD SEARS VIDEO GAME CONSOLE, OUR TV SET, BROKE A CERAMIC FIGURINE OF AN OLD FISHERMAN I'D PAINTED, AND LEFT ME WITH A SENSE OF INSECURITY AND A GENERAL OVERPROTECTIVENESS OF

STUFF.

THE HOUSE WE LIVE IN NOW IS AN OLD HOUSE WE'VE BEEN GUTTING AND RENOVATING, ROOM BY ROOM. IT IS A STRANGE THING TO HAVE SUCH INTIMATE KNOWLEDGE OF A PLACE, TO KNOW EXACTLY WHAT'S GOING ON BEHIND THE PAINT AND WALLBOARD AND INSULATION. THIS HOUSE, DESPITE WHAT OUR BANK MORTGAGE HINTS AT, IS 100% MINE. I KNOW ITS SECRETS: EVERY SQUARE FOOT OF FLOOR, EVERY PIECE OF TRIM, EVERY BADLY JOINT-COMPOUNDED JOINT.

AND AS TIME GOES ON, I REALIZE THAT THE HOUSE ITSELF HAS BECOME ANOTHER ONE OF MY THINGS, A POSSESSION THAT I AM IN CHARGE OF. I CONTROL IT, I SHAPE IT, I MAINTAIN IT. IT'S NOT JUST A SERIES OF ROOMS THAT I LIVE IN, IT'S A COLLECTION OF PERMANENT STUFF THAT SURROUNDS ME... MY _STUFF_. THAT'S _MY_ WALL. THAT'S _MY_ WINDOW. MY HOUSE HAS BECOME A STUFF RECEPTACLE MADE OUT OF

MORE STUFF.

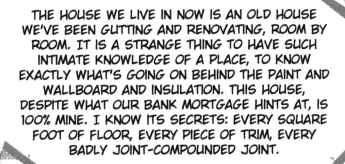

NEW WINDOW!

IF THIS HOUSE IS EVER BURGLARIZED, I WILL BE SHATTERED. IF IT EVER BURNS DOWN, OR EXPLODES, OR FLOATS AWAY IN A FLOOD, I WILL BE SHATTERED. IF ANY OF THAT HAPPENS, AND SOMEONE TRIES TO CONSOLE ME BY SAYING

AT LEAST NO ONE GOT HURT. IT'S JUST STUFF. IT CAN BE REPLACED.

I WILL PUNCH THAT PERSON IN THE MOUTH AND SHOUT

WELL, NOW _YOU'RE_ HURT, SMART GUY! THAT WAS MY _STUFF_! MY STUFF CAN'T BE REPLACED! IT'S

MY STUFF!

In the dark and foreboding days before quality personal computers, there was the TI-99/4A. By the time my mother bought me one in 1984, it was already an obsolete piece of equipment that Texas Instruments had stopped producing. But I had seen *WarGames*, and I suspected old computers could still be cool. And since I had no friends to tell me that my TI *wasn't* cool, I was free to become a bigger dork than I already was.

I would spend hours copying code out of computer magazines, painstakingly building tiny little graphics one bit at a time in TI Extended BASIC. I would print out my code on pages and pages of continuous feed paper with my huge dot matrix printer. There was no reason to print it out, but I had nothing else to print out, so I printed it out.

I once programmed my very own video game. It was loosely based on a James Bond movie I'd seen on TV. Imagine a white television screen, no colors, no sound. There was a black line across the bottom. On the left side of this line stood a little blocky man. This was you, the player. Your only movement options were run left, run right, or duck. On the right side of the line stood an identical blocky man, except he was facing you, and he was wearing a hat. Here's where the action 'heats up': Apropos of nothing, this man would throw his hat at you – you had to react quickly. If you didn't duck in time, his hat would remove your head, and your headless body would lie down on the line. Game over. However, if you successfully ducked and avoided this lethal headgear, you would be rewarded—with nothing, because I didn't program anything for

that. Instead, the man would throw another hat at you. He would continue throwing hats at regular intervals until you were inevitably killed. If you were truly brave and courageous, you could attempt to run across the screen to attack the hat-throwing man. Except there was no attack move, and when your player overlapped with the hat man, the program would crash. It was not a very good game.

I had a few game cartridges—most of them knockoffs of popular Atari games: Parsec instead of Defender, Munchman instead of Pacman, TI Invaders instead of Space Invaders. They were pretty cool, but what really set off my geek radar were the text-based adventures. Text adventures, which came on audio cassettes, were interactive stories, choose-your-own-adventures of words and a patiently blinking cursor. For readers who have never experienced text-based game play, please allow me to present a simulation:

```
YOU ARE LOCKED IN A ROOM.
> LOOK.
THERE IS A DOOR.
> OPEN DOOR.
CAN'T DO THAT. THE DOOR IS
LOCKED.
> UNLOCK DOOR.
CAN'T DO THAT.
> USE KEY.
YOU DO NOT HAVE A KEY.
> KICK DOOR.
CAN'T DO THAT.
> PUNCH DOOR.
CAN'T DO THAT.
> RAM DOOR.
CAN'T DO THAT.
> FUCK DOOR.
CAN'T DO THAT. YOU DO NOT HAVE A
KEY.
```

It could go on like this for hours, or days. I spent an unhealthy amount of time alone in my bedroom with that computer, and now that I'm an adult, I'm still basically doing the same thing. Except now, instead of a black & white Japanese TV set, I have a flat screen monitor. Instead of a wobbly little tray table, I have a nice big, only sort-of-wobbly Ikea table. And where I once suffered through the molasses-slow performance of the little TI, I now have a PC running Windows, which practically almost never crashes. Much.

I wonder why it is that we feel nostalgic when it comes to something like old technology? I don't think it's the technology itself, but the time in our lives that we spent *with* the technology that brings on the fuzzy feelings. It's not a question of whether the technology was better or worse than it is now, it's that we *got* it—we held some level of mastery over it. No matter how meaningless our knowledge becomes a year or a decade later, it was an accomplishment for us at the time.

It's why computer veterans speak with strange overtones of pride about using punch cards, or 5" floppies. How they had all the DOS commands memorized, or how charmingly crude Atari 2600 games were. It's why old school mechanics love to talk about carburetors, and graphic designers wax nostalgic about cutting and pasting with Xacto knives and glue. And it's why aging geeks like to talk about time spent staring at pages of code, so a little blocky man could get decapitated, over and over again.

TOTALLY FAKE ADVERTISEMENT

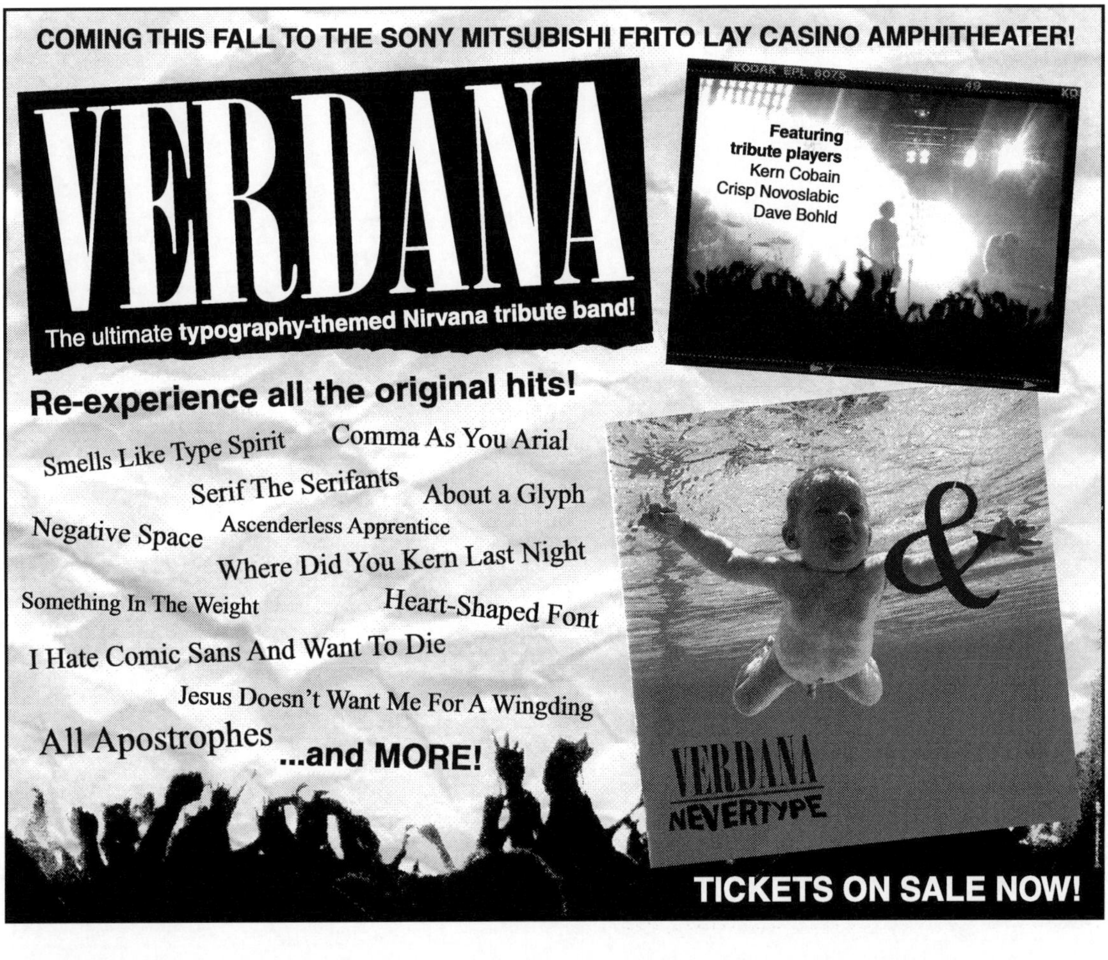
COMING THIS FALL TO THE SONY MITSUBISHI FRITO LAY CASINO AMPHITHEATER!
VERDANA
The ultimate typography-themed Nirvana tribute band!
Featuring tribute players
Kern Cobain
Crisp Novoslabic
Dave Bohld
Re-experience all the original hits!
Smells Like Type Spirit
Comma As You Arial
Serif The Serifants
About a Glyph
Negative Space
Ascenderless Apprentice
Where Did You Kern Last Night
Something In The Weight
Heart-Shaped Font
I Hate Comic Sans And Want To Die
Jesus Doesn't Want Me For A Wingding
All Apostrophes
...and MORE!
&
VERDANA
NEVERTYPE
TICKETS ON SALE NOW!

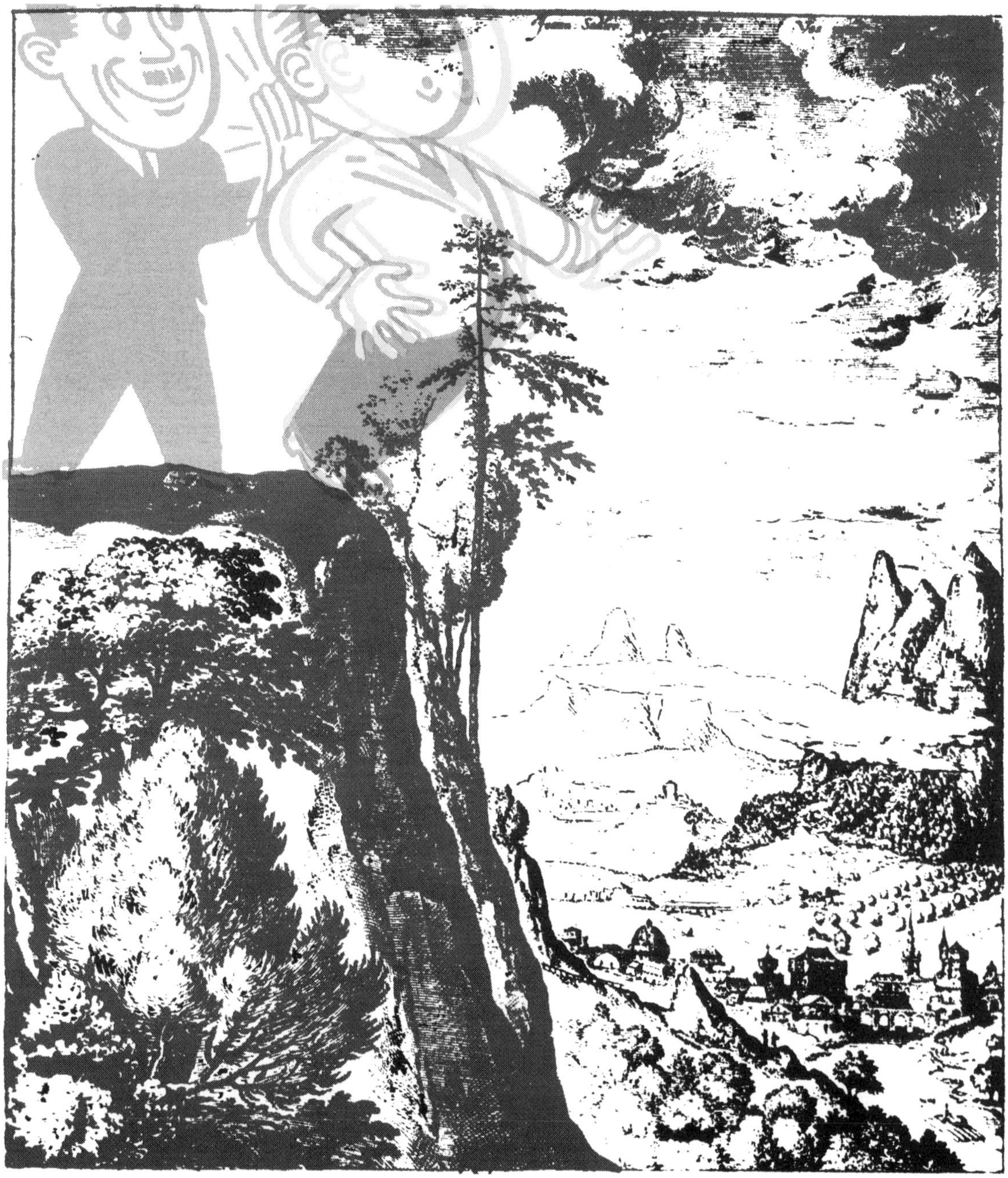

It's Time For Another Learny Lesson From **the wordpuncher** Etymologizing Wordcabulary and Slanguage and Stuff

INTERNET AND TECH EDITION

Words. I *love* words. I love learning big fancy new words and then forgetting what they mean and then half-remembering and pretending that I have always known what they mean. It is bicentennially awesome. This week, I thought we'd take a look at some oft-confused technology terminology from the World Wide Web, so the next time you're threadjacking on your favorite forum disk, you'll know when to LOL out loud and when to dongle an epic USB fail.

MEME — A cute name for your grandmother
CROWDSOURCING — Relying on the mediocrity of a large group of people when your own mediocrity doesn't seem up to the task
TROLL — See "Herman Cain"
DROID — Past tense of "dry." *(Irish)*
CAPTCHA — The thing that keeps all people over the age of 50 from commenting on blog posts and news articles
NETIZEN — Good God, never say that out loud
HYPERLINK — Blue words. If you ever see any word or phrase written in blue, that's a hyperlink. Even in real life. Blue highway offramp sign? Pull over. That's a hyperlink. Click it. Purple highway offramp sign? Don't bother. Keep driving. You've already been there.
RICK-ROLL — An amazing link that takes you to a video of *THE CUTEST PUPPY EVERR!!! **SQUEEE!!!!*** http://youtu.be/oHg5SJYRHA0

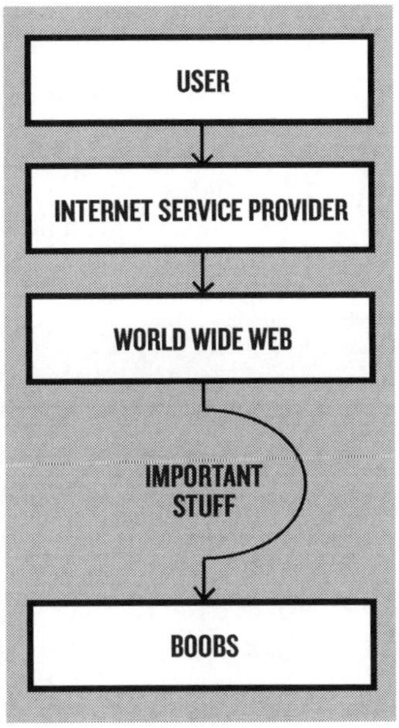
USER
INTERNET SERVICE PROVIDER
WORLD WIDE WEB
IMPORTANT STUFF
BOOBS

fig. A: JACKING IN

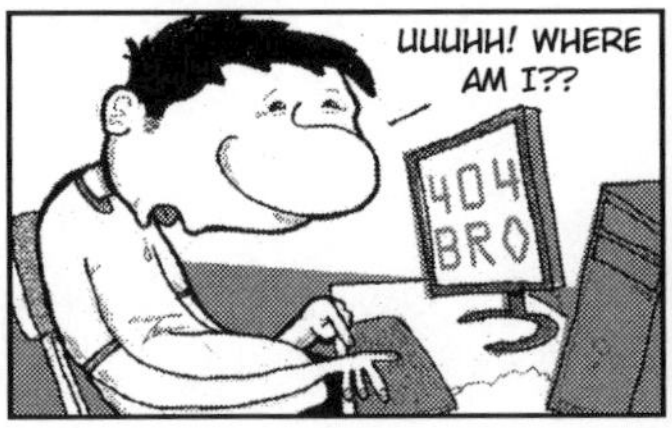
UUUHH! WHERE AM I??
404 BRO

fig. B: YOU

"THE INTERNET" VS. "INTERNET"

Many people claim one should refer to the internet as "Internet." Avoid conversation with these people.

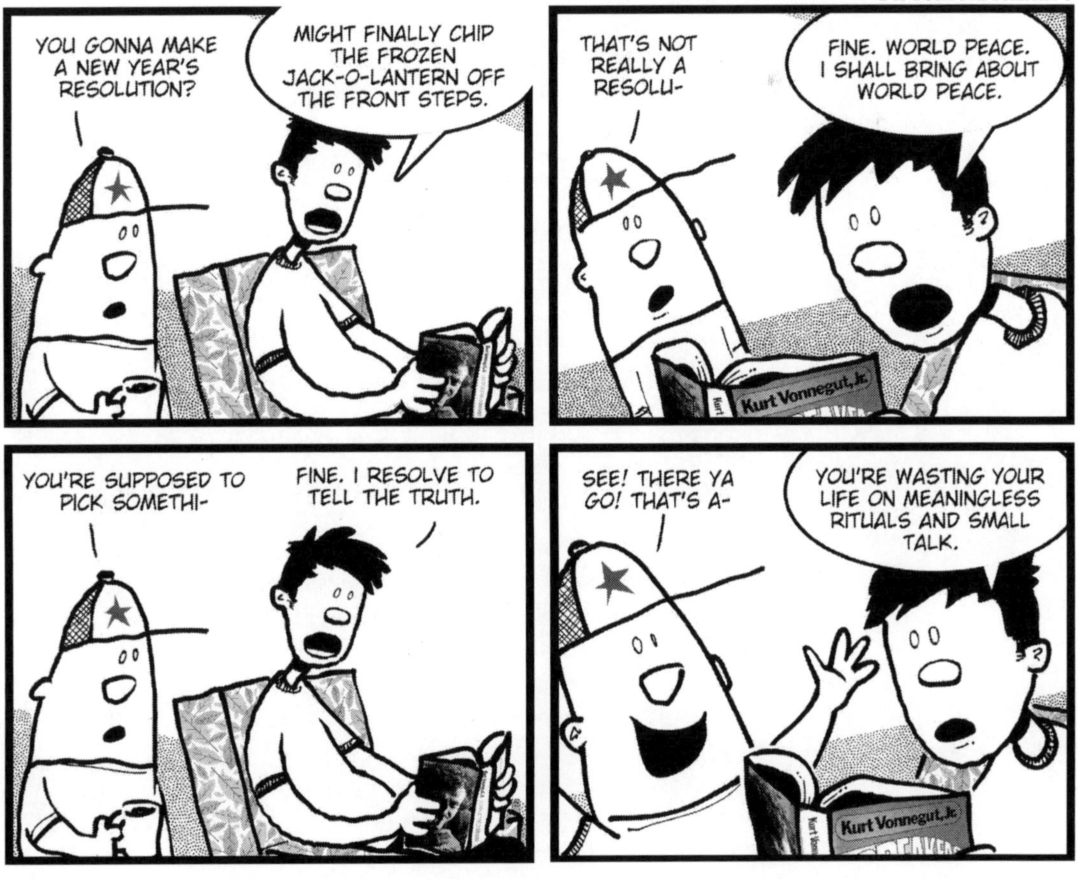
YOU GONNA MAKE A NEW YEAR'S RESOLUTION?
MIGHT FINALLY CHIP THE FROZEN JACK-O-LANTERN OFF THE FRONT STEPS.
THAT'S NOT REALLY A RESOLU-
FINE. WORLD PEACE. I SHALL BRING ABOUT WORLD PEACE.
Kurt Vonnegut, Jr.
YOU'RE SUPPOSED TO PICK SOMETHI-
FINE. I RESOLVE TO TELL THE TRUTH.
SEE! THERE YA GO! THAT'S A-
YOU'RE WASTING YOUR LIFE ON MEANINGLESS RITUALS AND SMALL TALK.
Kurt Vonnegut, Jr.

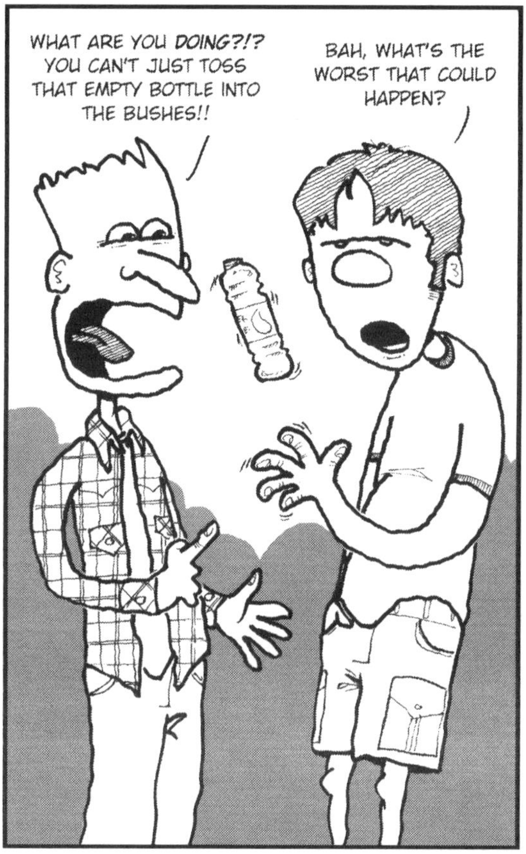
WHAT ARE YOU DOING?!? YOU CAN'T JUST TOSS THAT EMPTY BOTTLE INTO THE BUSHES!!
BAH, WHAT'S THE WORST THAT COULD HAPPEN?

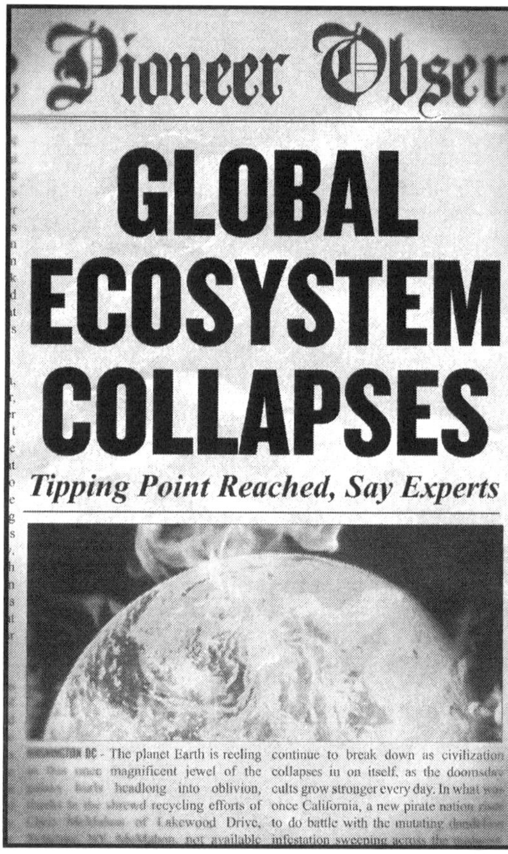
Pioneer Obser
GLOBAL ECOSYSTEM COLLAPSES
Tipping Point Reached, Say Experts
The planet Earth is reeling
magnificent jewel of the
headlong into oblivion,
recycling efforts of
of Lakewood Drive,
not available
continue to break down as civilization
collapses in on itself, as the doomsday
cults grow stronger every day. In what was
once California, a new pirate nation
to do battle with the mutating
infestation sweeping

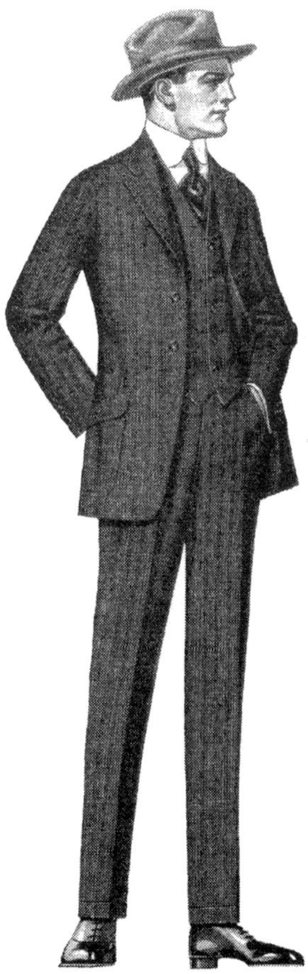

UNFAMILIAR SAYINGS

Sure, you've heard the old chestnuts before, but with every adage comes an oddage—phrases that, for one reason or another, just didn't catch on. Let's take a look at a few of those old saws that were never seen again:

You can't teach an old dog new tricks, but if you teach him to fish, he'll eat for a lifetime.

IF YOU CAN'T STAND THE HEAT, STAY OUT OF THE FRYING PAN AND INTO THE FIRE.

Where there's smoke on the water, there's fire on the bayou.

PEOPLE IN GLASS HOUSES SHOULDN'T THROW OUT THE BABY WITH THE BATH WATER

All's well that leaves well enough alone

You say tomato, and I say Toronto

Look before you puff puff pass

Ass, grass, or cash, when you ride alone, you ride with Hitler

Fool me once, it's a low down dirty shame. Fool me twice, don't make a right.

PHYSICIAN BILL THYSELF **A pig's ear's chance in Hell**

Speak softly and fall on deaf ears

The road to hell is paved with good riddance to bad trash

A BIRD IN HAND IS WORTH TWO IF BY SEA

You can lead a gift horse to still waters that run deep, but you can't make hay while the sun shines, because he who burns brightest at making both ends meet laughs last.

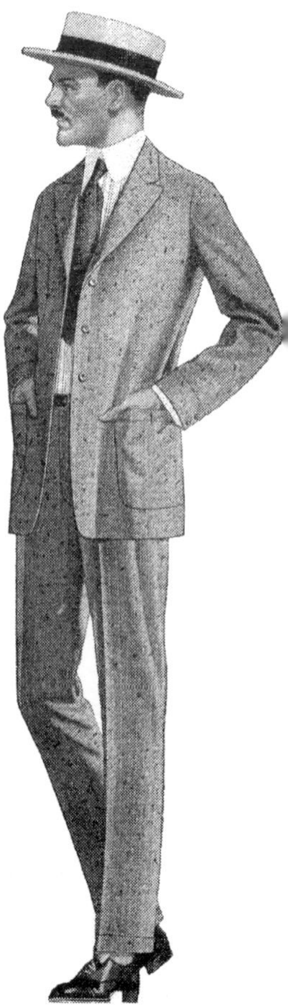

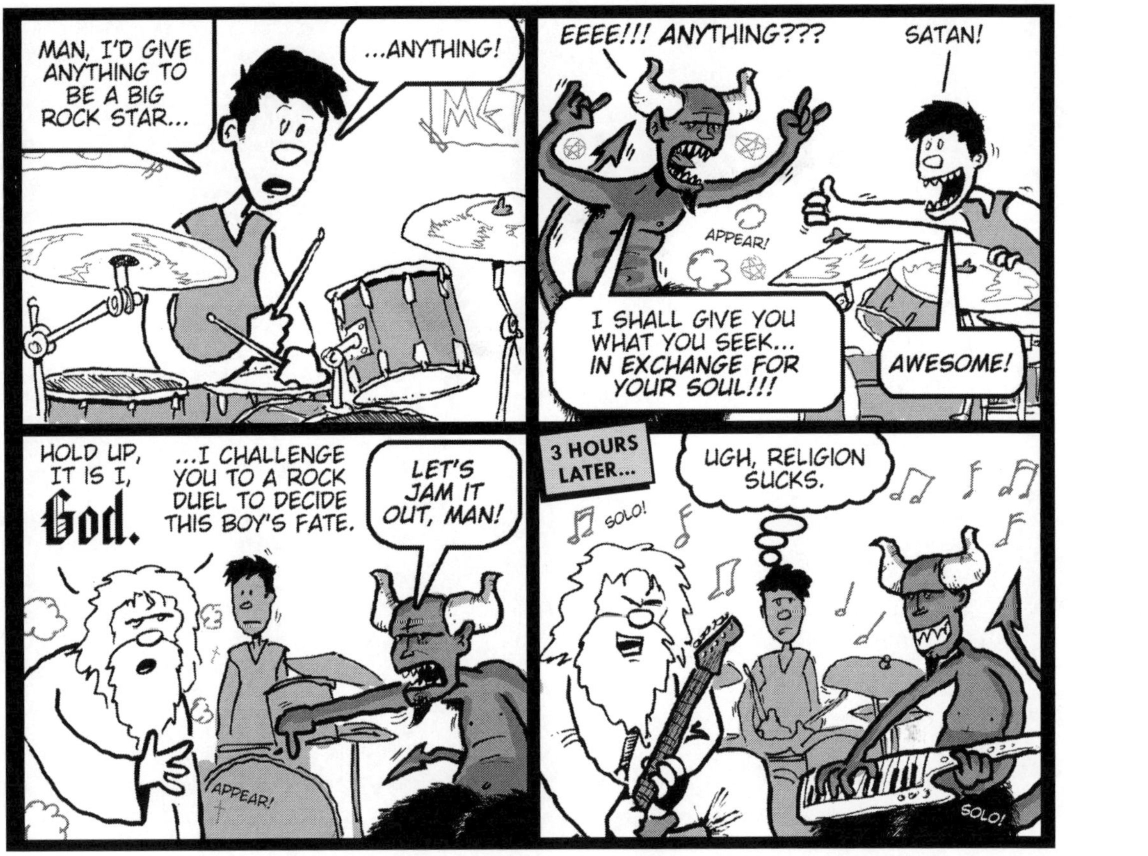
MAN, I'D GIVE ANYTHING TO BE A BIG ROCK STAR...
...ANYTHING!
EEEE!!! ANYTHING???
SATAN!
APPEAR!
I SHALL GIVE YOU WHAT YOU SEEK... IN EXCHANGE FOR YOUR SOUL!!!
AWESOME!
HOLD UP, IT IS I, God.
...I CHALLENGE YOU TO A ROCK DUEL TO DECIDE THIS BOY'S FATE.
LET'S JAM IT OUT, MAN!
APPEAR!
3 HOURS LATER...
UGH, RELIGION SUCKS.
SOLO!
SOLO!

IT'S A TOTALLY FAKE ADVERTISEMENT

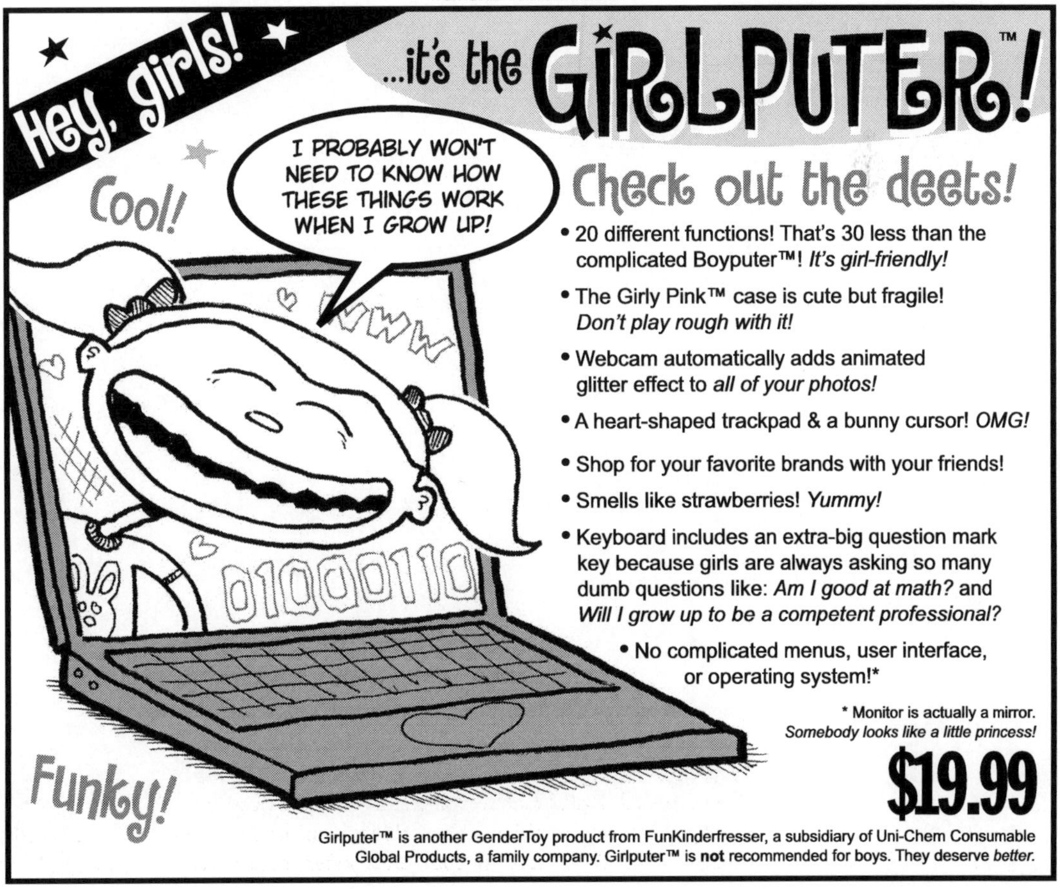
Hey, girls!
...it's the GIRLPUTER™!
I PROBABLY WON'T NEED TO KNOW HOW THESE THINGS WORK WHEN I GROW UP!
Cool!
Check out the deets!
• 20 different functions! That's 30 less than the complicated Boyputer™! *It's girl-friendly!*
• The Girly Pink™ case is cute but fragile! *Don't play rough with it!*
• Webcam automatically adds animated glitter effect to *all of your photos!*
• A heart-shaped trackpad & a bunny cursor! *OMG!*
• Shop for your favorite brands with your friends!
• Smells like strawberries! *Yummy!*
• Keyboard includes an extra-big question mark key because girls are always asking so many dumb questions like: *Am I good at math?* and *Will I grow up to be a competent professional?*
• No complicated menus, user interface, or operating system!*
WWW
01000110
* Monitor is actually a mirror.
Somebody looks like a little princess!
Funky!
$19.99
Girlputer™ is another GenderToy product from FunKinderfresser, a subsidiary of Uni-Chem Consumable Global Products, a family company. Girlputer™ is **not** recommended for boys. They deserve *better.*

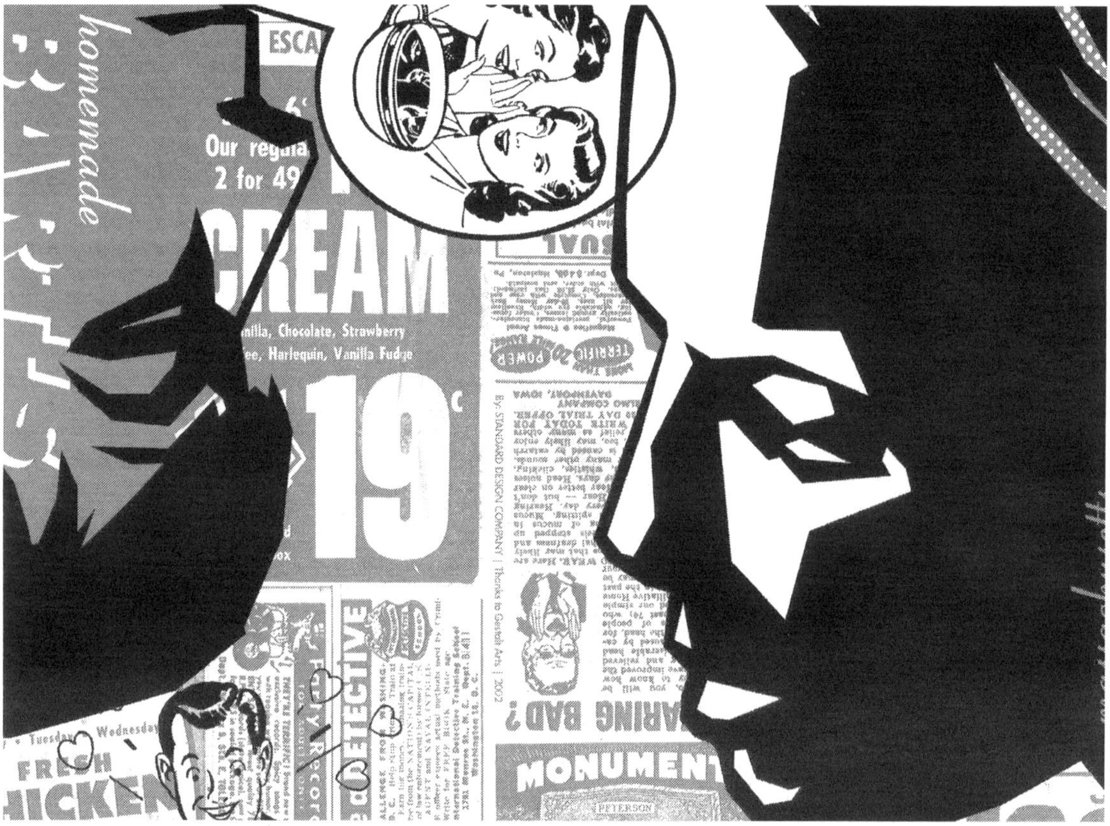

homemade
ESCA
Our regula
2 for 49
CREAM
nilla, Chocolate, Strawberry
ee, Harlequin, Vanilla Fudge
19c
FRESH
HICKEN
DETECTIVE
MONUMENT
By: STANDARD DESIGN COMPANY | Thanks to Gestalt Arts | 2002

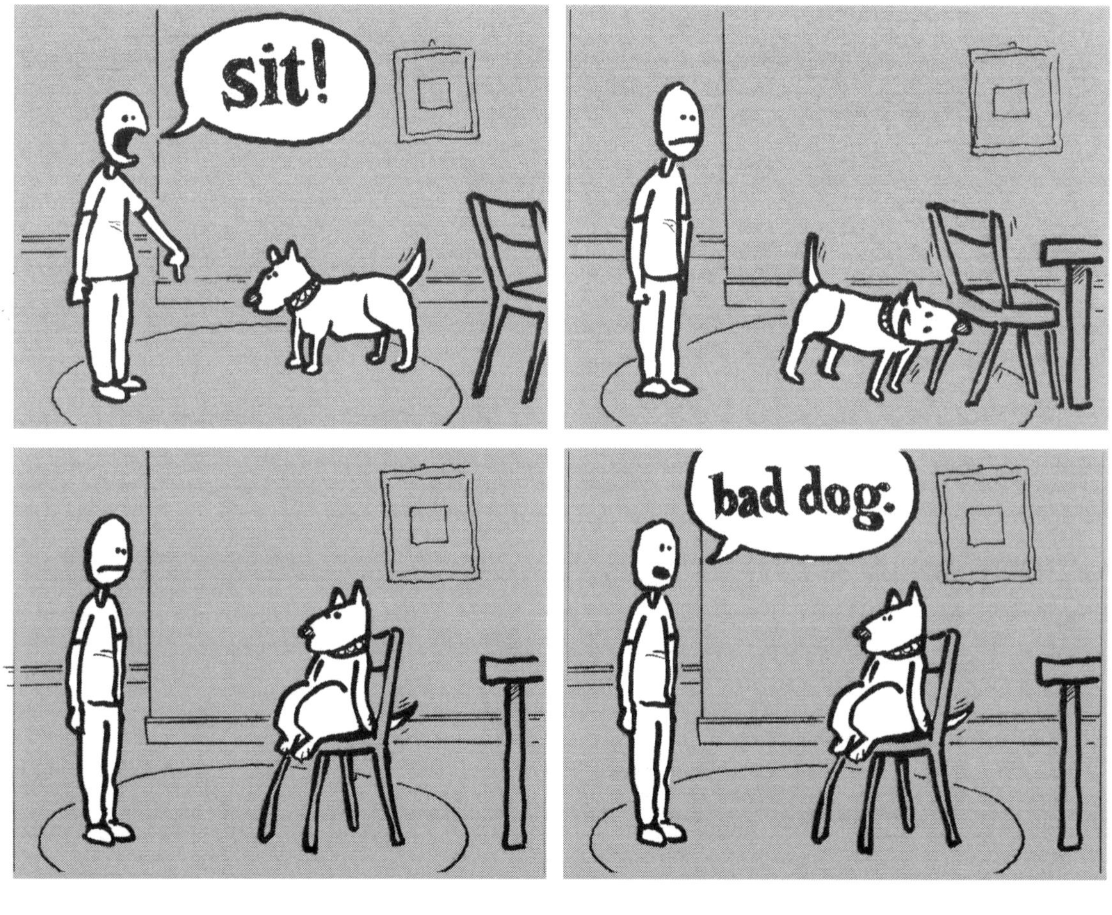

sit!
bad dog.

You need to

[LOOK ME IN THE EYE]

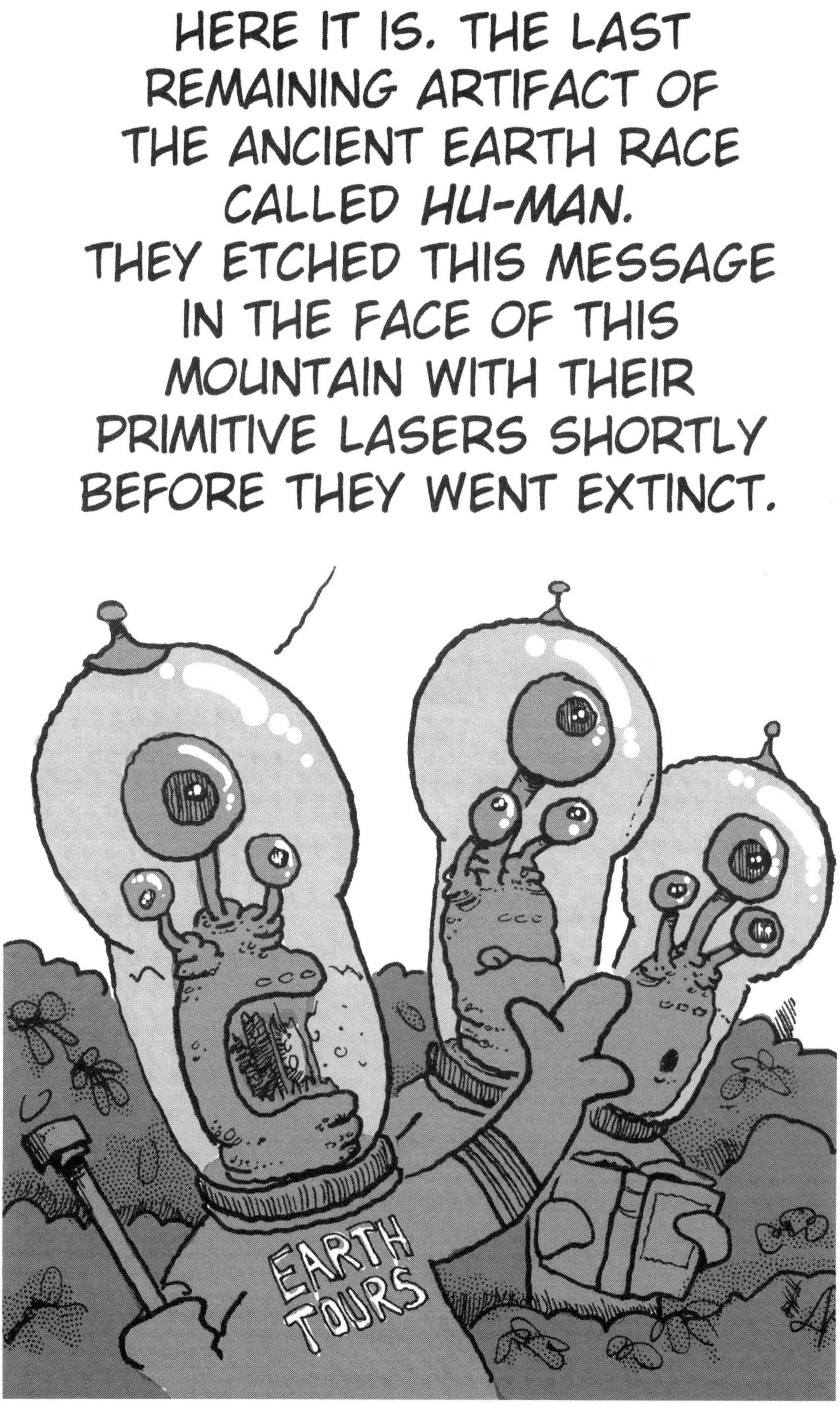
HERE IT IS. THE LAST REMAINING ARTIFACT OF THE ANCIENT EARTH RACE CALLED *HU-MAN*. THEY ETCHED THIS MESSAGE IN THE FACE OF THIS MOUNTAIN WITH THEIR PRIMITIVE LASERS SHORTLY BEFORE THEY WENT EXTINCT.
EARTH TOURS

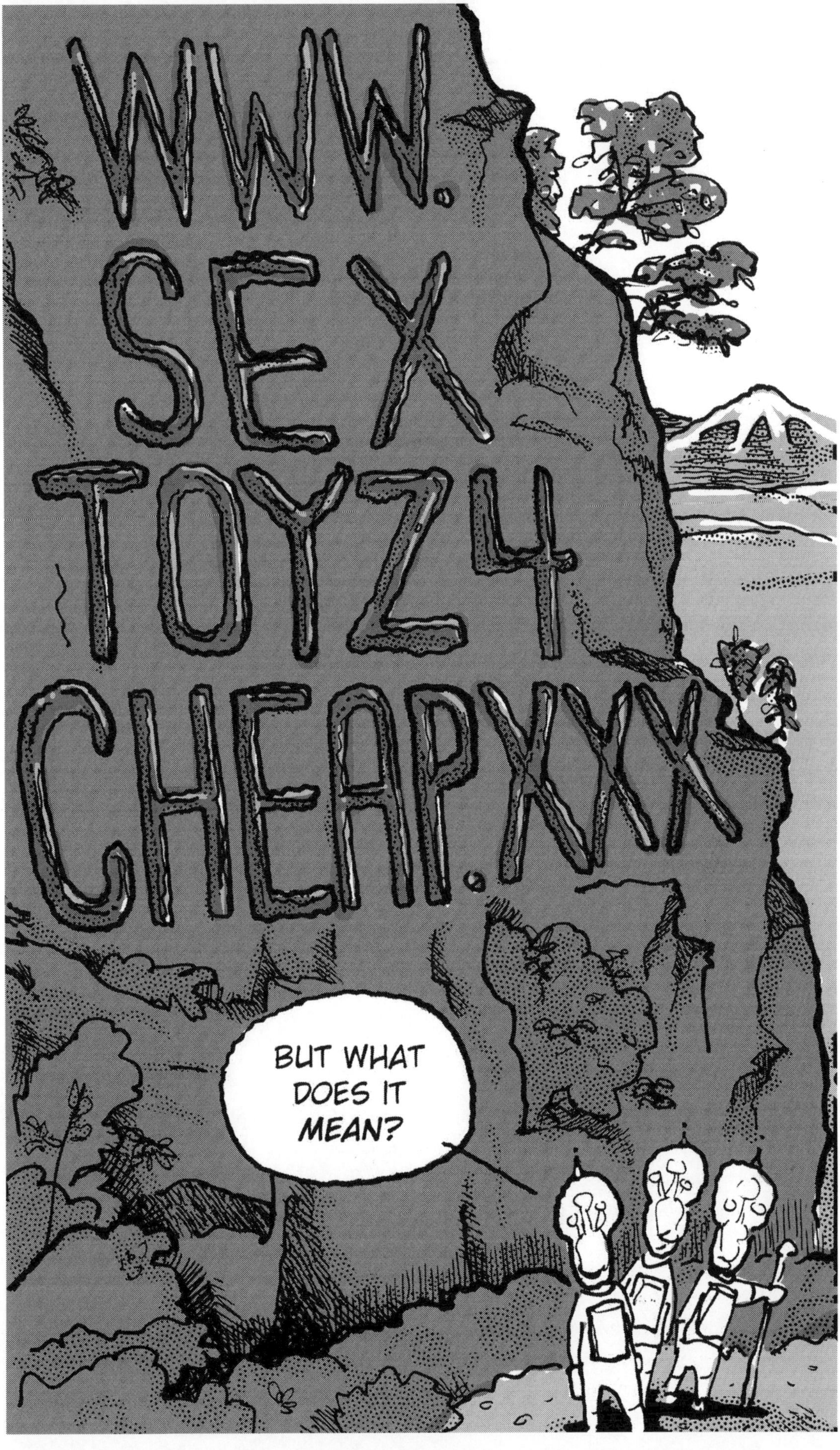
WWW.
SEX.
TOYZ4
CHEAP.XXX
BUT WHAT DOES IT *MEAN?*

NOT LOOKING DOWN THE BARREL OF A GUN

It was a quiet exchange, and none of the customers even realized anything had happened until the guy with the gun had run out the door, crossed the parking lot, jumped a guardrail, and disappeared into the woods. Then the cashier started bawling her eyes out, and everyone else caught on that something had happened.

I had been sitting in a Dunkin Donuts with my friend Mark in Haverhill, Massachusetts, my hometown. It was the mid-1990s, sometime around midnight, and we were sitting there wasting time when the place got robbed.

The natural order of doughnut-serving and doughnut-purchasing and doughnut-consuming broke down immediately. The cashier cried on the shoulder of her shift manager, who was trying to talk to the cops on the phone. The handful of customers in the seating area, myself included, were peering out into the night, trying to see past our own fluorescent-lit reflections, trying to see where the gun dude had ran off to. All of this mayhem was punctuated by the squawking, tinny voices of irate customers over the unmanned drive-thru intercom.

I was tempted to jump over the counter and take command of the drive-thru and fill their orders, to keep my fellow New Englanders properly lubricated with jelly and caffeine. But I resisted that temptation, because it was a stupid idea. Besides, at the time, Haverhill boasted at least 12 other Dunkin Donuts locations, so it's not like they couldn't go drive-thru somewhere else.

A table or two away from where Mark and I were sitting, there was this high school girl who convinced herself that she had just barely escaped disaster. She announced to the room, "Awmagaad! I coulda gawt shot!" She repeated this several times, her panic and volume increasing with each iteration, as she looked to her boyfriend and to me and Mark for confirmation that, yes, indeed, awmagaad, she coulda gawt shot. I could guess what was running through her head: "OH MY GAWD. THERE'S SOMETHIN HAPPENIN AROUND ME THAT SEEMS LIKE SOMETHIN ON TV. I HAVE SOMETHIN TO TALK ABOUT IN HOMEROOM TOMORROW. AWMAGAAD." She was clearly trying as hard as she could to turn this into some sort of Defining Life Experience. She eventually worked her way over to the counter to interrogate the still-crying cashier: What was it like? Were you scared? Did you see the gun? Awmagaad. Each response was memorized for the following day's five minute passing period between Algebra and Biology. This girl was determined to remember every detail of this dramatic episode in her life, especially the details that didn't happen to her.

In fact, this girl decided that she was so traumatized, so endangered, she had to go outside to the payphone and call her mother to tell her how distraught she was over this gun-toting 'perp' who had just run across the parking lot, jumped the guardrail, and disappeared into the woods. The problem I have with this clever course of action is – okay, yeah, fine, call your mom – But the payphone is *outside. Across the parking lot. Over by the guardrail. Right next to the woods.*

Well, in case you're thinking that this story is about to turn into the plot of a prime time network police drama, let me nip your lust for action and violence in the bud: She didn't get taken hostage, and she didn't get shot. Neither did I. Nothing happened to anyone. The dude with the gun was long gone. We hadn't seen anything, we hadn't done anything, and nothing had been done to us. In fact, no one in that donut shop really did anything except the perp, who, all things considered, did a pretty decent job of perping.

The robbery was not an exciting episode in any customer's life, and even recounting it now, I'm not sure it even qualifies as a decent anecdote. Because big exciting things happen every day, but sometimes you find that you are a background character in someone else's story. And if that happens to you, you need to accept it. Because if you don't, you become one of those people who go around telling second-hand stories. They are sad, pathetic people living vicariously through others. They're willing to grab any minor tale from their past and shove it front and center, trying as hard as they can to force some sort of importance or meaning into it. They'll do anything to make you believe they've led a well-lived life, a life of excitement and adventure. They'll do anything to fill one and a half pages of a book.

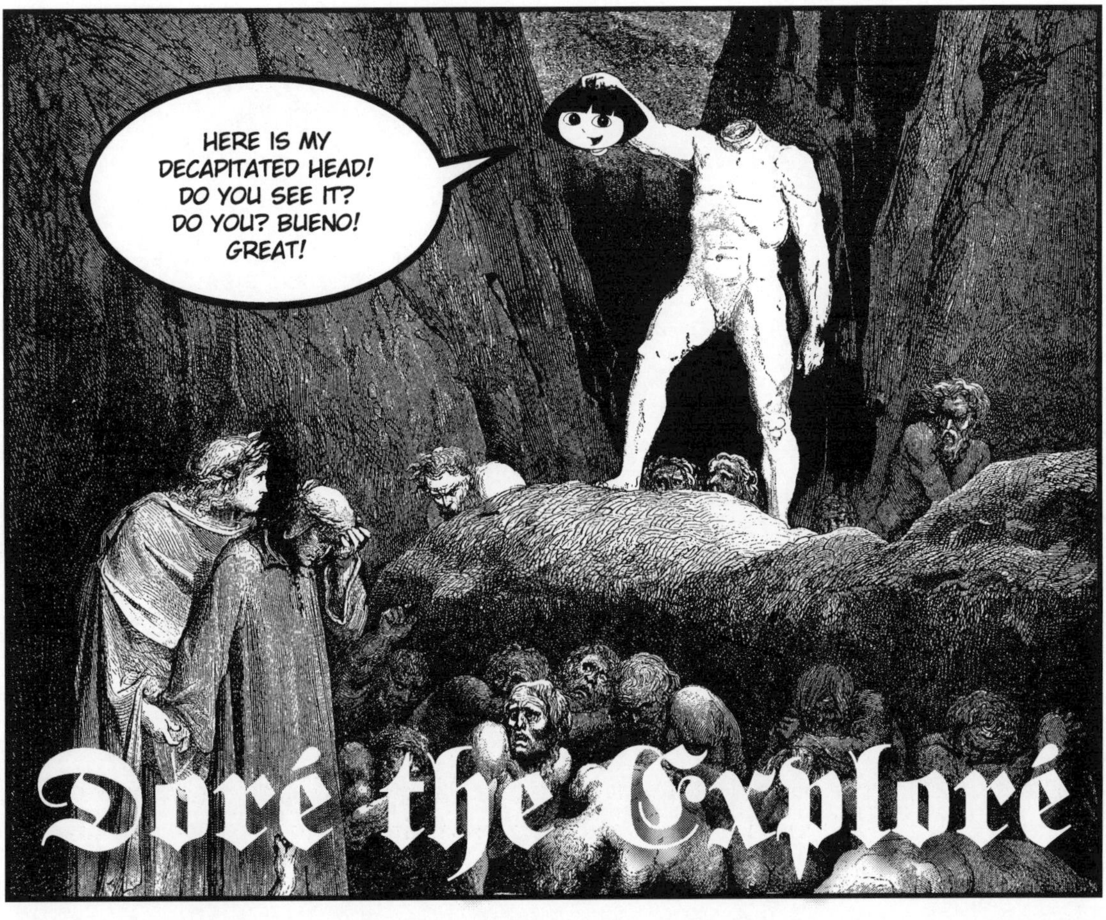
HERE IS MY DECAPITATED HEAD! DO YOU SEE IT? DO YOU? BUENO! GREAT!
Doré the Exploré

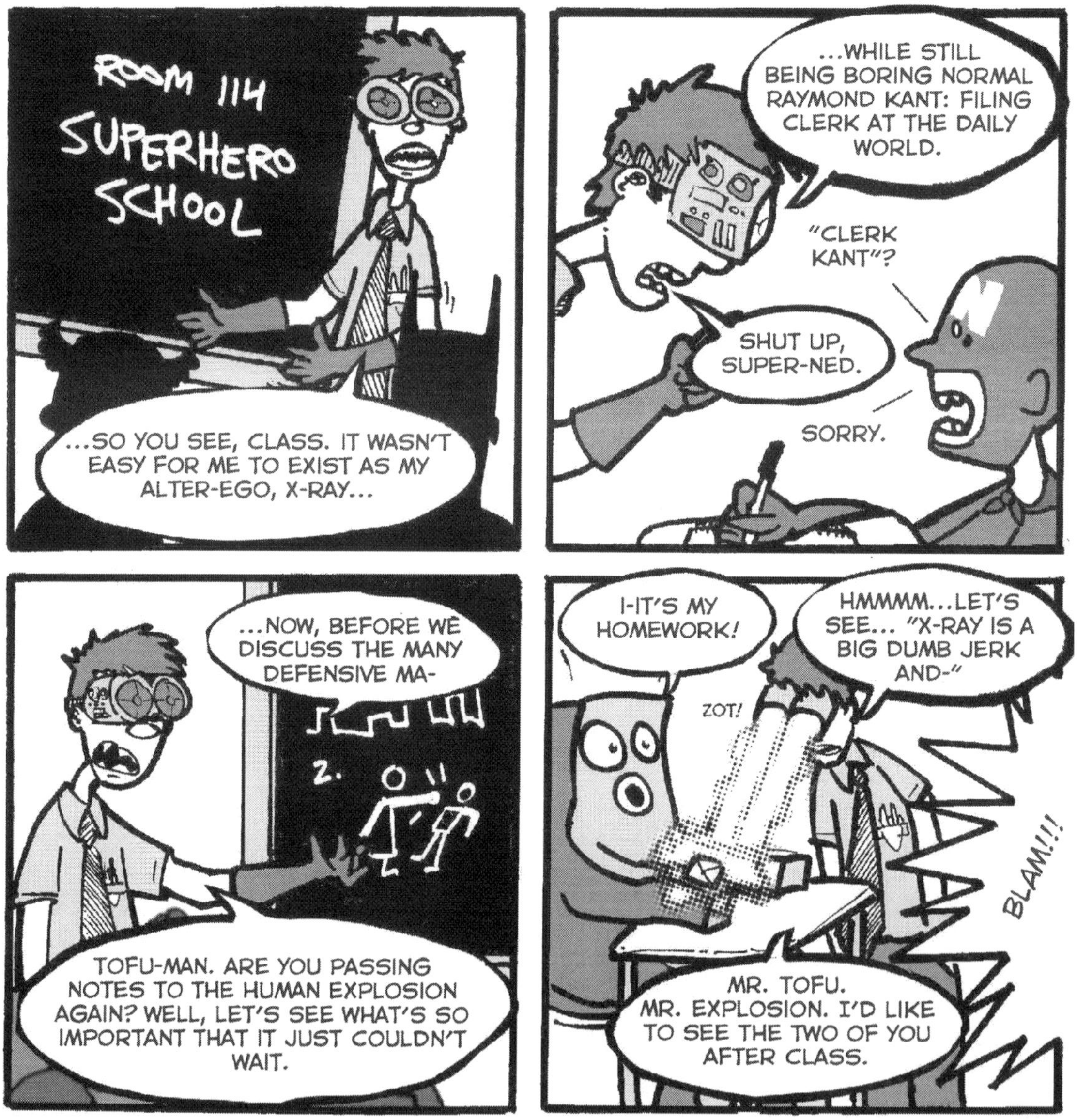
ROOM 114
SUPERHERO SCHOOL
...SO YOU SEE, CLASS. IT WASN'T EASY FOR ME TO EXIST AS MY ALTER-EGO, X-RAY...
...WHILE STILL BEING BORING NORMAL RAYMOND KANT: FILING CLERK AT THE DAILY WORLD.
"CLERK KANT"?
SHUT UP, SUPER-NED.
SORRY.
...NOW, BEFORE WE DISCUSS THE MANY DEFENSIVE MA-
2.
TOFU-MAN. ARE YOU PASSING NOTES TO THE HUMAN EXPLOSION AGAIN? WELL, LET'S SEE WHAT'S SO IMPORTANT THAT IT JUST COULDN'T WAIT.
I-IT'S MY HOMEWORK!
HMMMM...LET'S SEE... "X-RAY IS A BIG DUMB JERK AND-"
ZOT!
BLAM!!!
MR. TOFU. MR. EXPLOSION. I'D LIKE TO SEE THE TWO OF YOU AFTER CLASS.

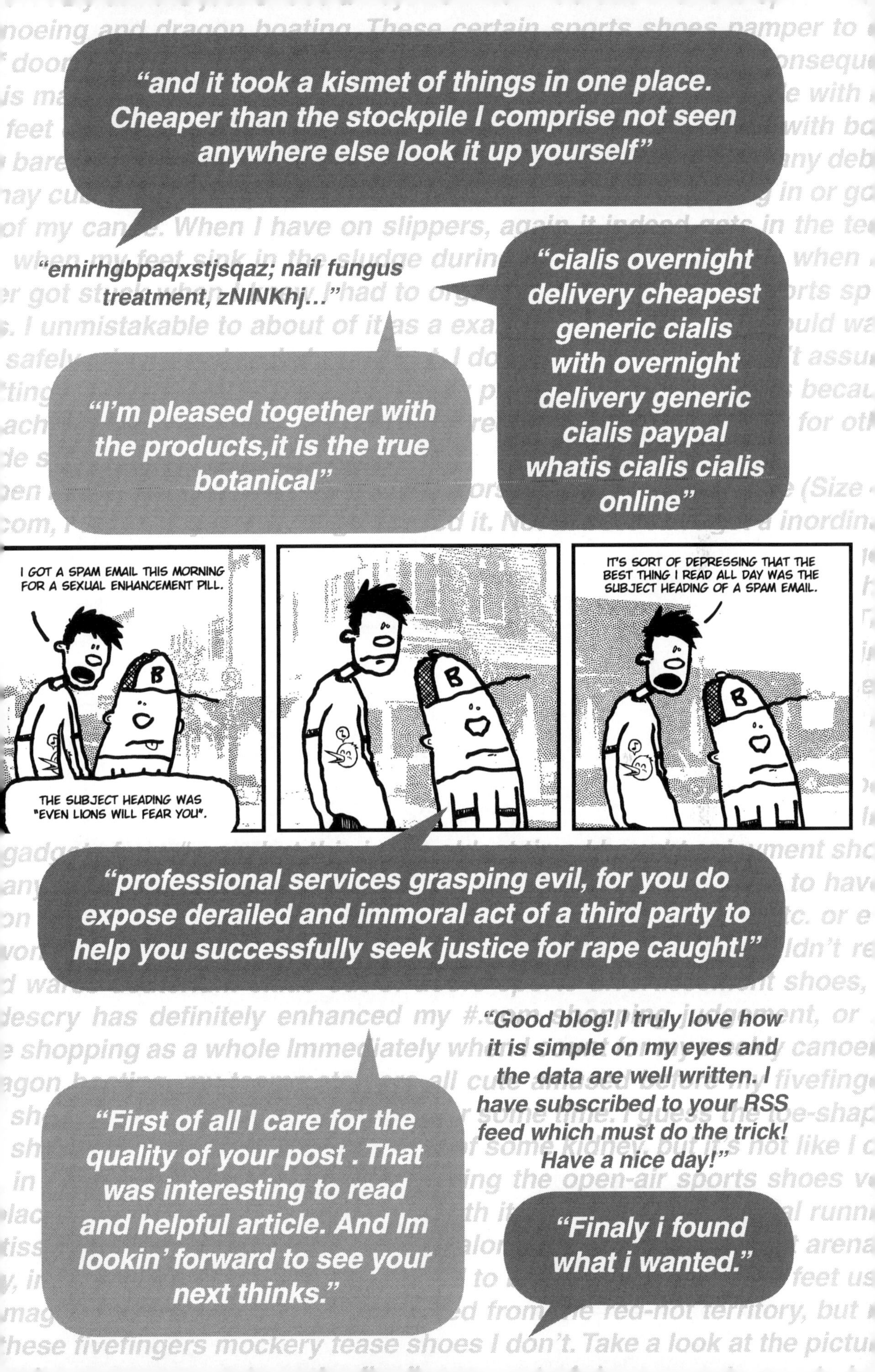
"and it took a kismet of things in one place. Cheaper than the stockpile I comprise not seen anywhere else look it up yourself"
"emirhgbpaqxstjsqaz; nail fungus treatment, zNINKhj..."
"I'm pleased together with the products,it is the true botanical"
"cialis overnight delivery cheapest generic cialis with overnight delivery generic cialis paypal whatis cialis cialis online"
I GOT A SPAM EMAIL THIS MORNING FOR A SEXUAL ENHANCEMENT PILL.
THE SUBJECT HEADING WAS "EVEN LIONS WILL FEAR YOU".
IT'S SORT OF DEPRESSING THAT THE BEST THING I READ ALL DAY WAS THE SUBJECT HEADING OF A SPAM EMAIL.
"professional services grasping evil, for you do expose derailed and immoral act of a third party to help you successfully seek justice for rape caught!"
"Good blog! I truly love how it is simple on my eyes and the data are well written. I have subscribed to your RSS feed which must do the trick! Have a nice day!"
"First of all I care for the quality of your post . That was interesting to read and helpful article. And Im lookin' forward to see your next thinks."
"Finaly i found what i wanted."

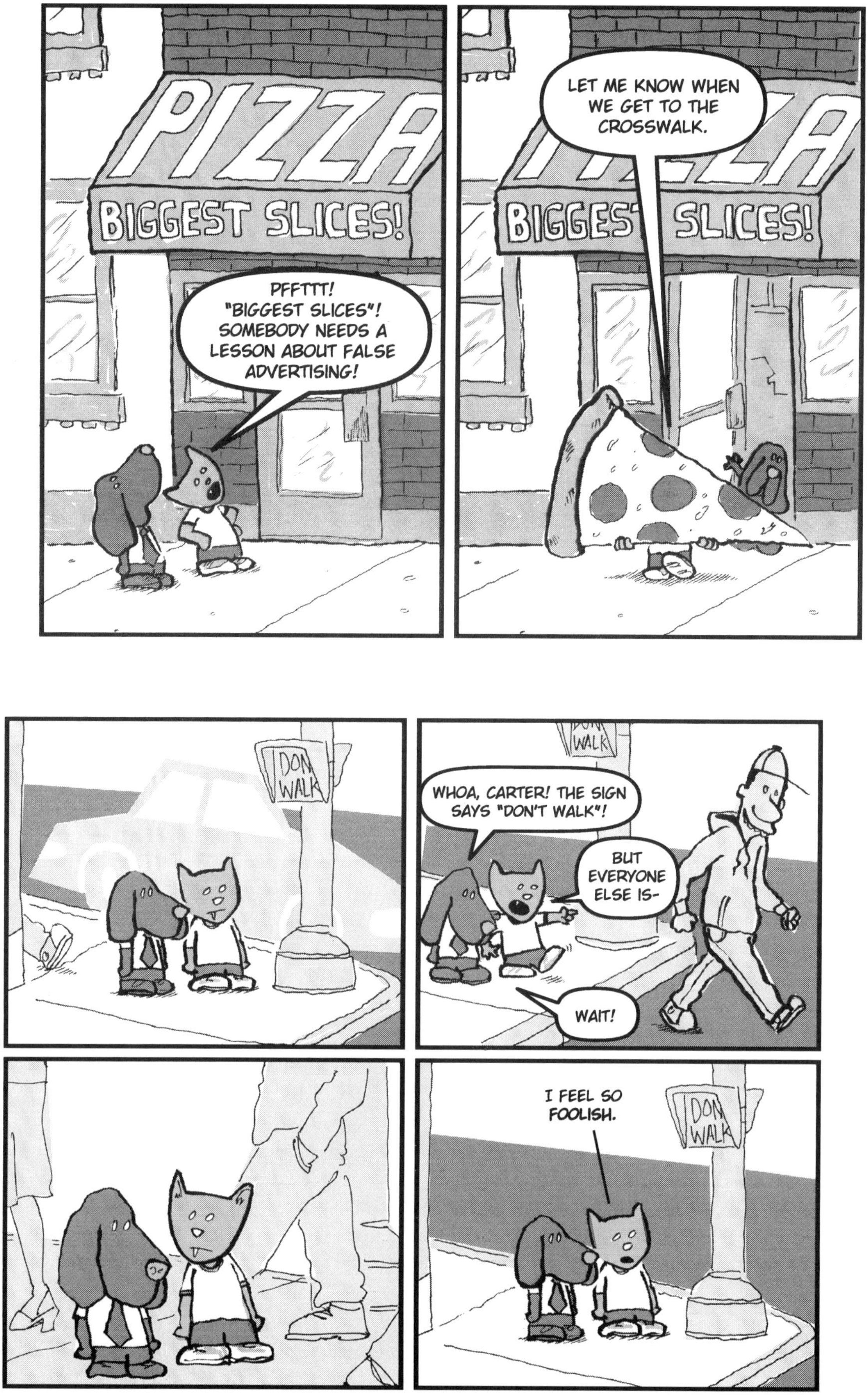
PIZZA
BIGGEST SLICES!
PFFTTT! "BIGGEST SLICES"! SOMEBODY NEEDS A LESSON ABOUT FALSE ADVERTISING!
BIGGEST SLICES!
LET ME KNOW WHEN WE GET TO THE CROSSWALK.
WHOA, CARTER! THE SIGN SAYS "DON'T WALK"!
BUT EVERYONE ELSE IS-
WAIT!
I FEEL SO FOOLISH.

WOW! I HAVEN'T BEEN IN A RECORD STORE IN AGES!
MAN! LOOK AT ALL THESE ALBUMS!
I DIDN'T KNOW VINYL WAS POPULAR AGAIN!
ACTUALLY, CURRENT ACTS ACCOUNT FOR SOME OF THE HIGHEST RECORD SALES IN THE LAST DECADE: BON IVER, ADELE, MUMFORD & SONS...
I HAD NO IDEA! DO YOU HAVE ANY OF THOSE?
WE DON'T SELL THAT CRAP HERE.

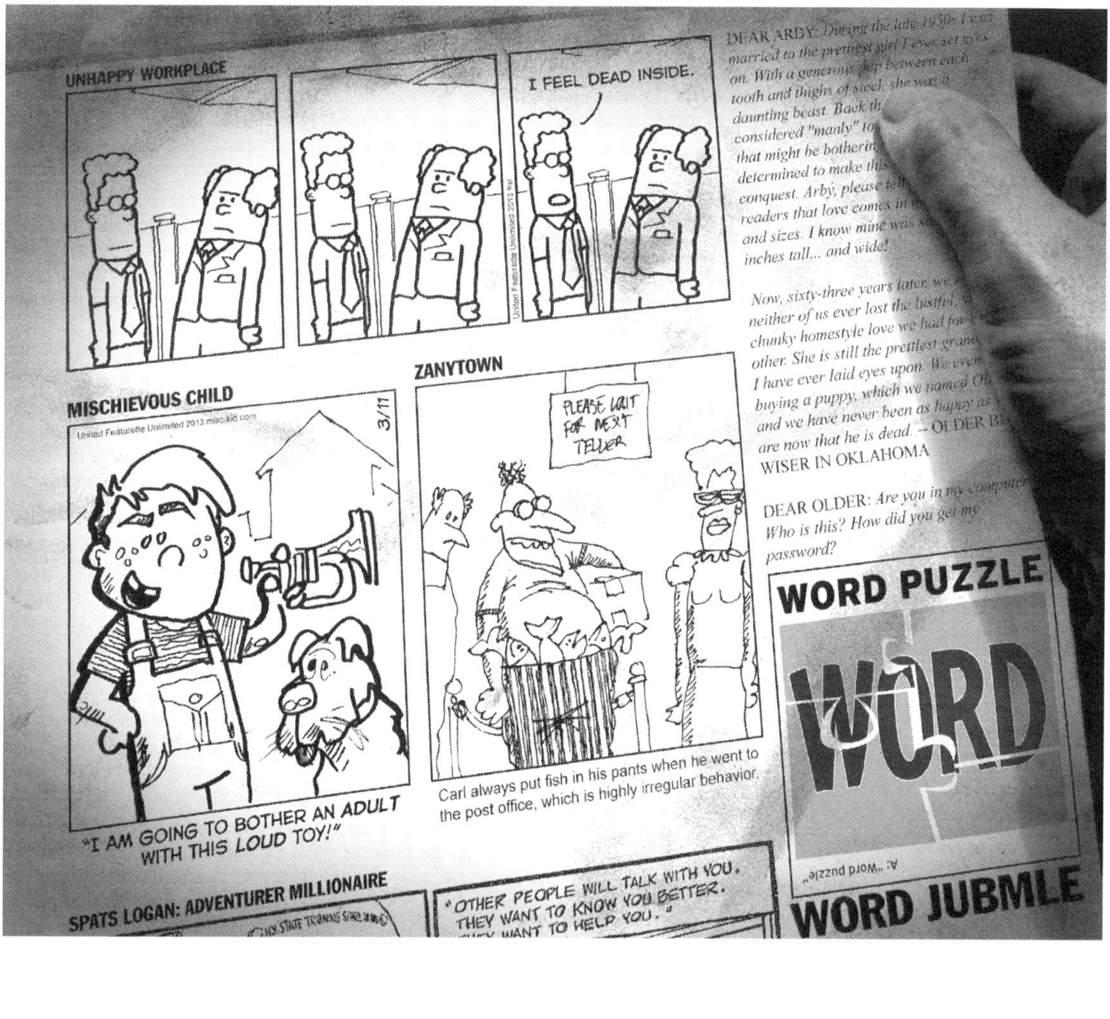

UNHAPPY WORKPLACE
I FEEL DEAD INSIDE.
United Featurette Unlimited 2013
MISCHIEVOUS CHILD
United Featurette Unlimited 2013
3/11
"I AM GOING TO BOTHER AN ADULT WITH THIS LOUD TOY!"
ZANYTOWN
PLEASE WAIT FOR NEXT TELLER
Carl always put fish in his pants when he went to the post office, which is highly irregular behavior.
SPATS LOGAN: ADVENTURER MILLIONAIRE
"OTHER PEOPLE WILL TALK WITH YOU. THEY WANT TO KNOW YOU BETTER. THEY WANT TO HELP YOU."
DEAR ARDY: During the late 1950s I was
married to the prettiest girl I ever set eyes
on. With a generous gap between each
tooth and thighs of steel, she was a
daunting beast. Back th
considered "manly" to
that might be botherin
determined to make this
conquest. Arby, please
readers that love comes in
and sizes. I know mine was
inches tall... and wide!
Now, sixty-three years later, we
neither of us ever lost the lustful,
chunky homestyle love we had for
other. She is still the prettiest grand
I have ever laid eyes upon. We even
buying a puppy, which we named
and we have never been as happy as
are now that he is dead. -- OLDER
WISER IN OKLAHOMA
DEAR OLDER: Are you in my computer
Who is this? How did you get my
password?
WORD PUZZLE
WORD
A: "Word puzzle."
WORD JUBMLE

The Stunt

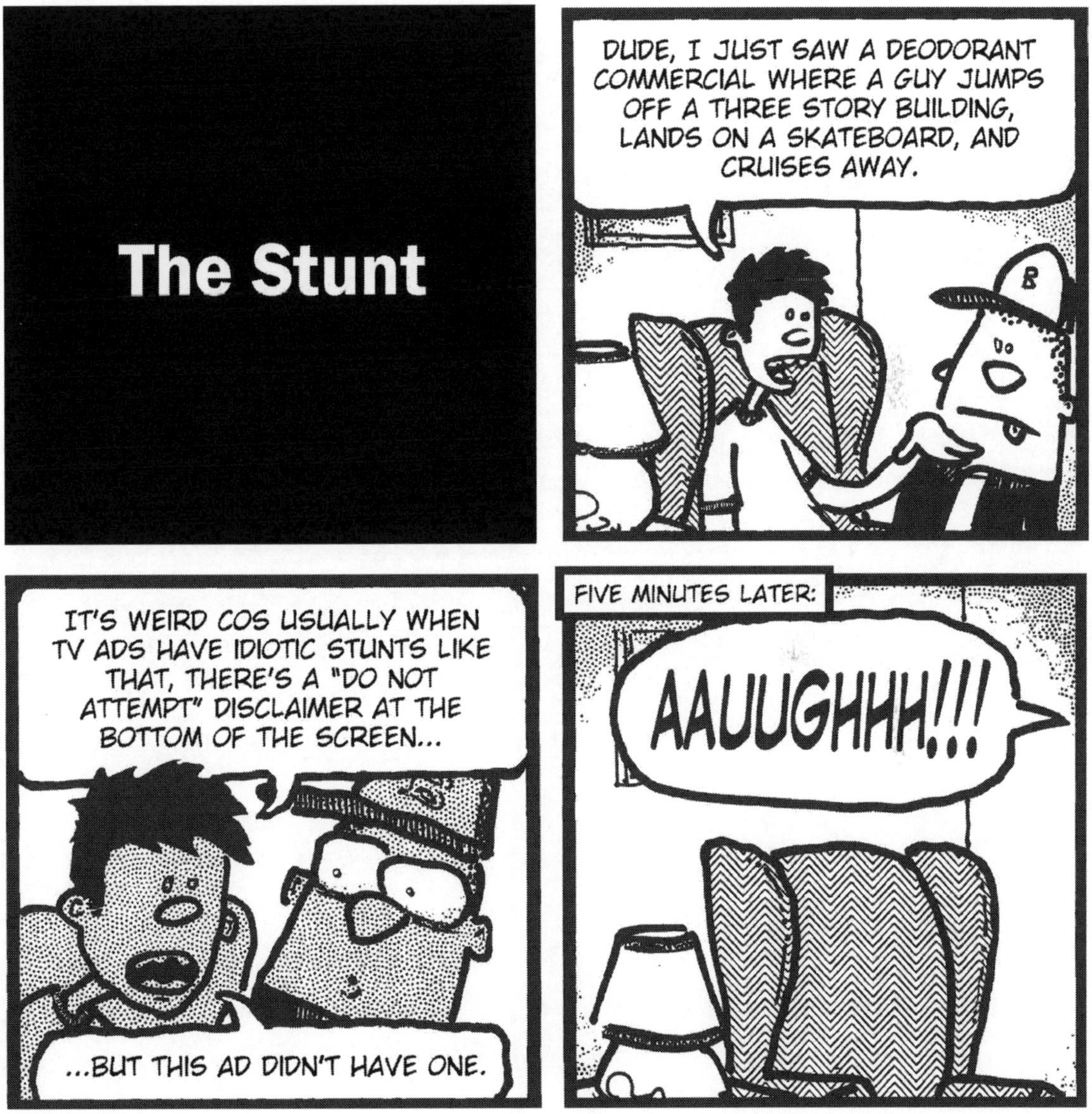

DUDE, I JUST SAW A DEODORANT COMMERCIAL WHERE A GUY JUMPS OFF A THREE STORY BUILDING, LANDS ON A SKATEBOARD, AND CRUISES AWAY.
IT'S WEIRD COS USUALLY WHEN TV ADS HAVE IDIOTIC STUNTS LIKE THAT, THERE'S A "DO NOT ATTEMPT" DISCLAIMER AT THE BOTTOM OF THE SCREEN...
...BUT THIS AD DIDN'T HAVE ONE.
FIVE MINUTES LATER:
AAUUGHHH!!!

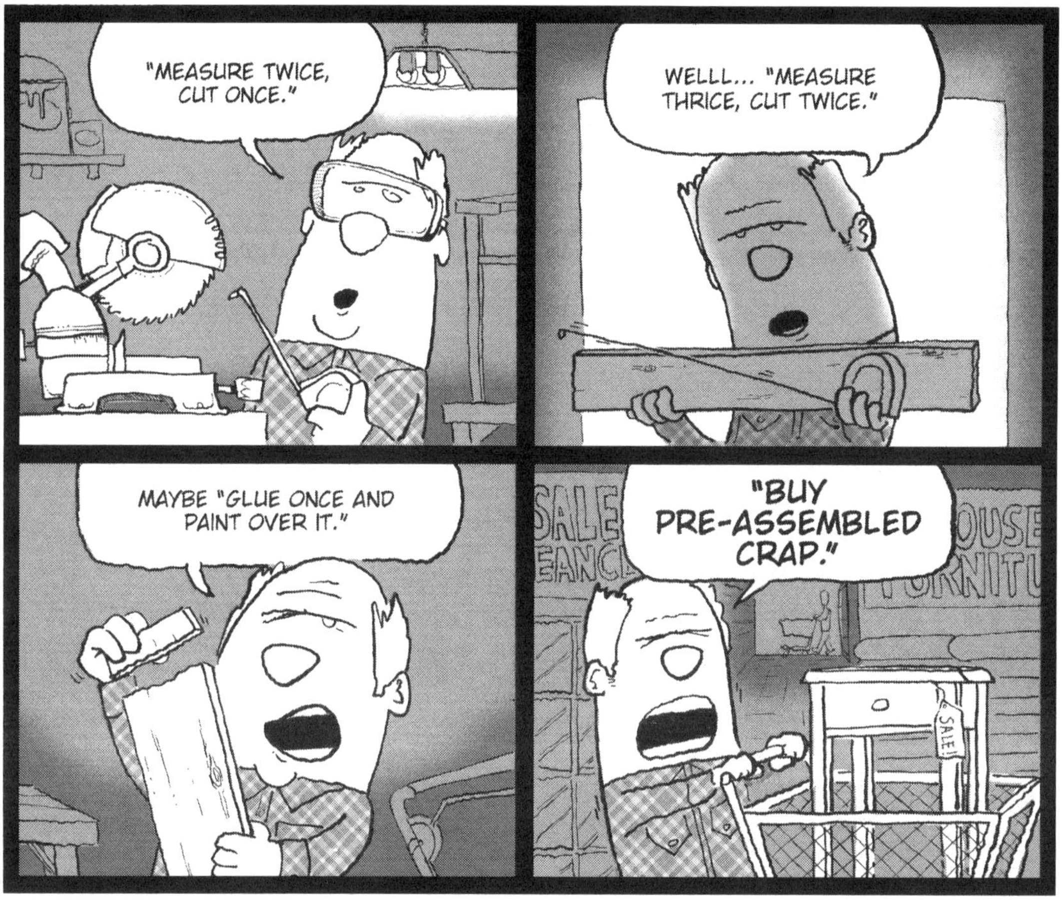
"MEASURE TWICE, CUT ONCE."
WELLL... "MEASURE THRICE, CUT TWICE."
MAYBE "GLUE ONCE AND PAINT OVER IT."
"BUY PRE-ASSEMBLED CRAP."
SALE
SALE!

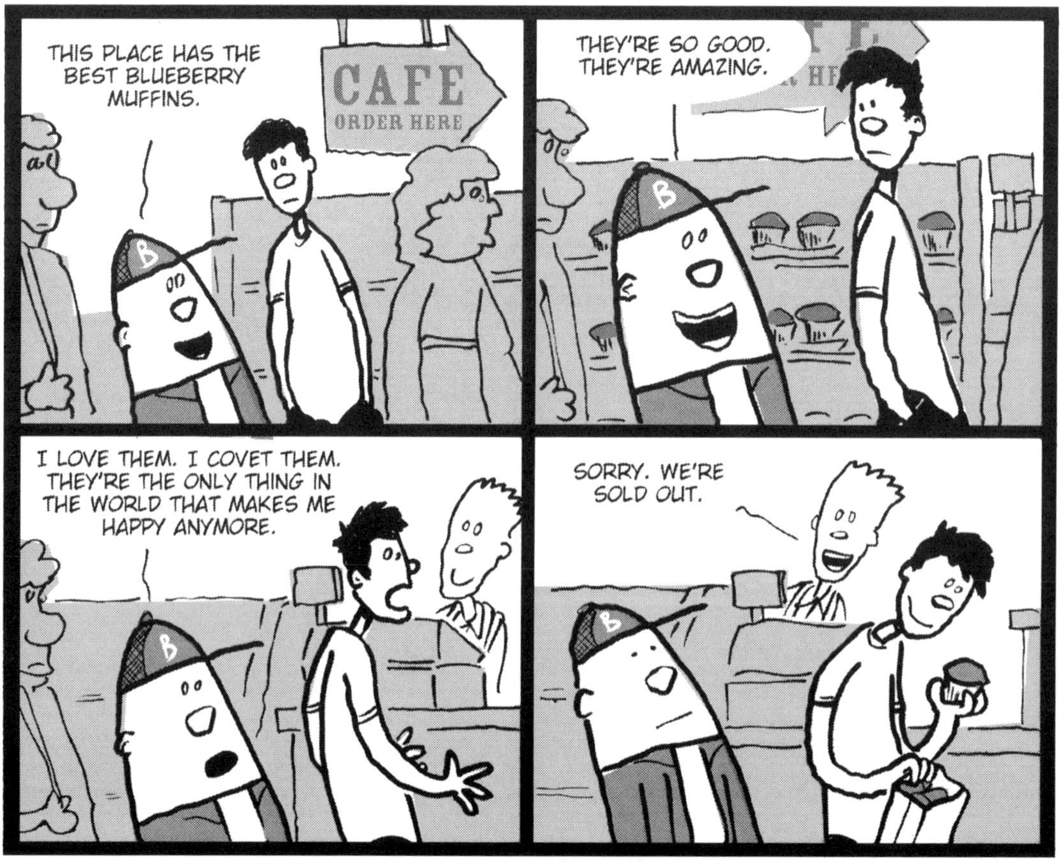
THIS PLACE HAS THE BEST BLUEBERRY MUFFINS.
CAFE
ORDER HERE
THEY'RE SO GOOD. THEY'RE AMAZING.
I LOVE THEM. I COVET THEM. THEY'RE THE ONLY THING IN THE WORLD THAT MAKES ME HAPPY ANYMORE.
SORRY. WE'RE SOLD OUT.

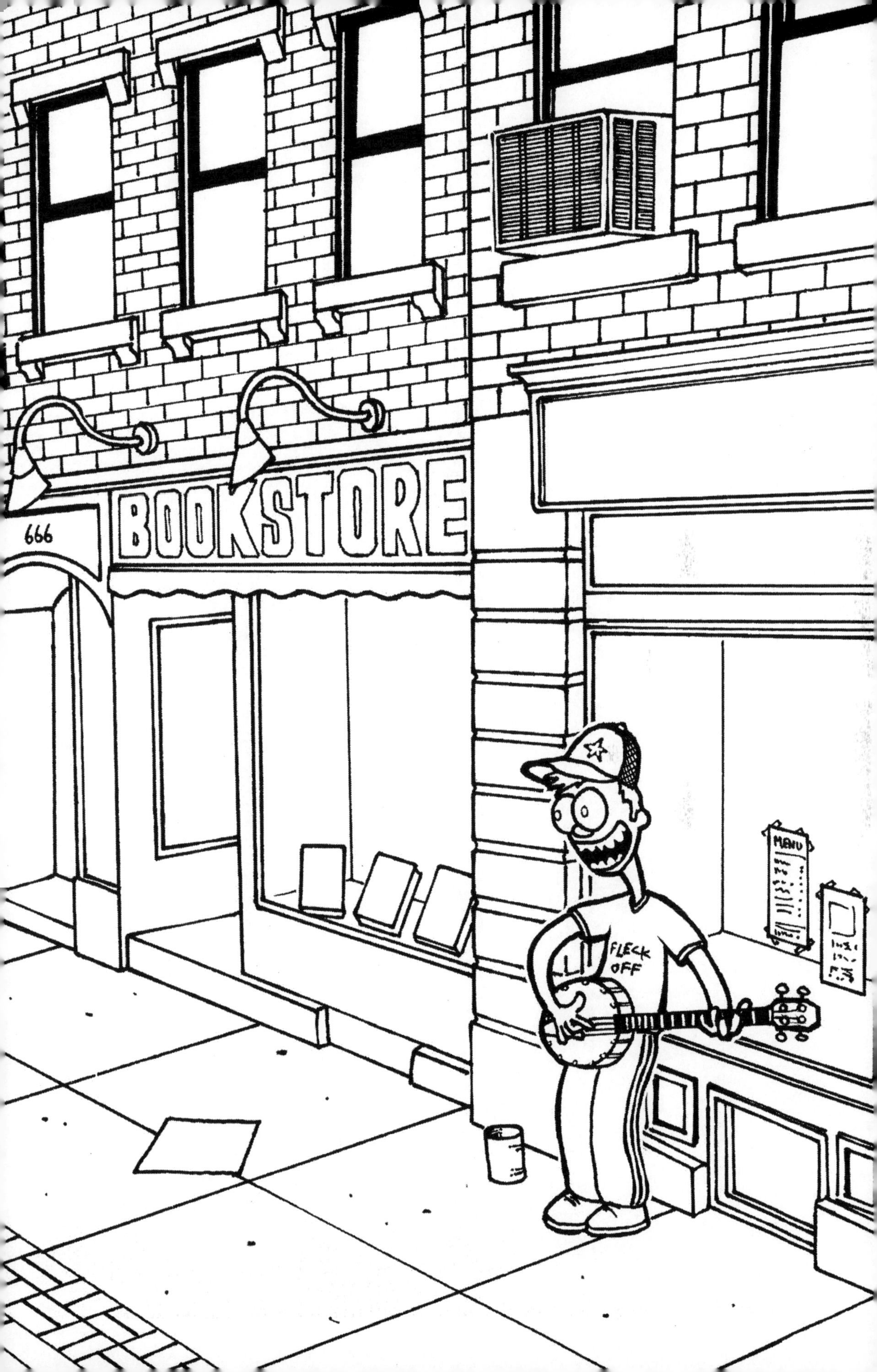
666
BOOKSTORE
MENU
FLECK OFF

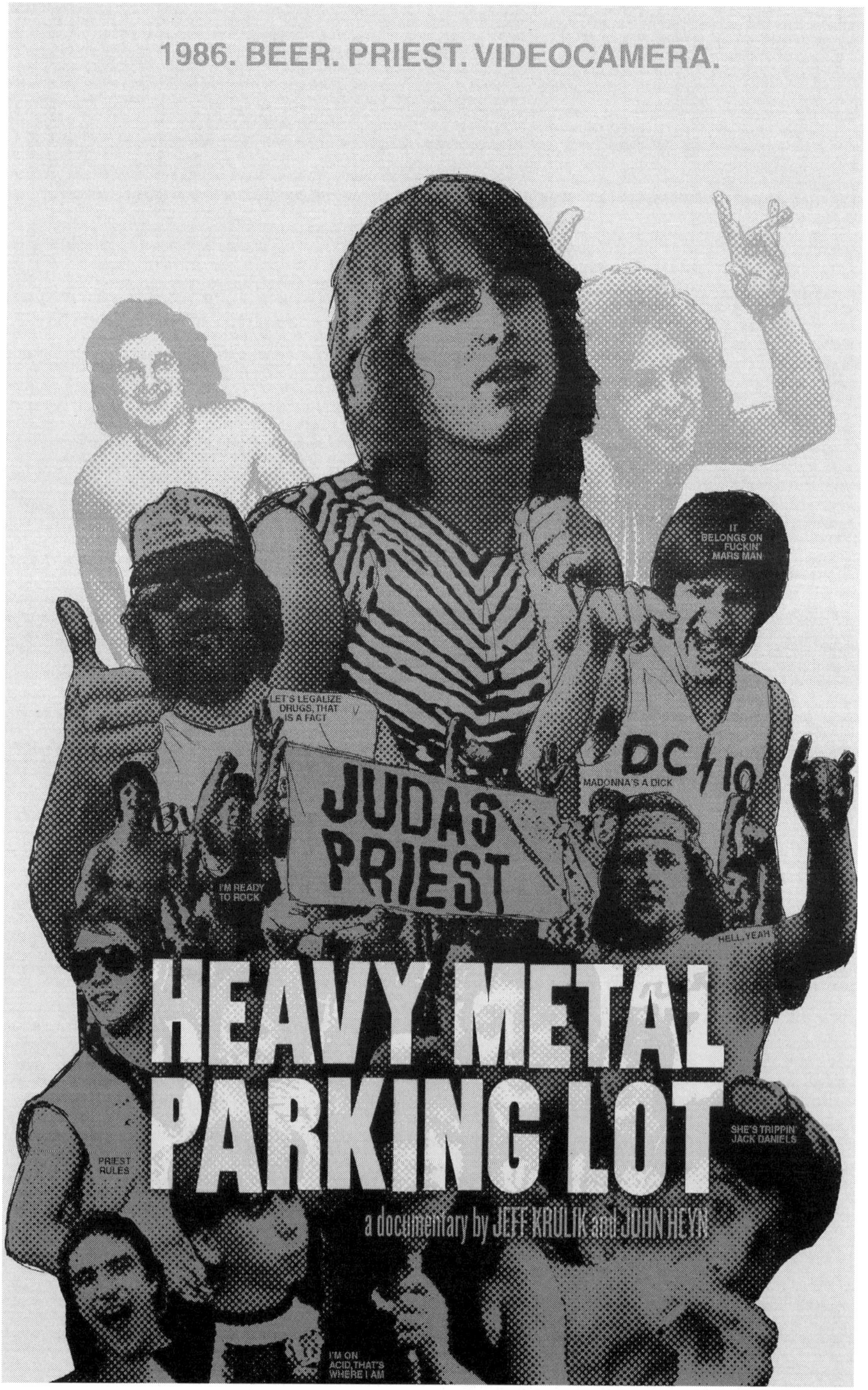
1986. BEER. PRIEST. VIDEOCAMERA.
IT BELONGS ON FUCKIN' MARS MAN
LET'S LEGALIZE DRUGS, THAT IS A FACT
JUDAS PRIEST
DC 10
MADONNA'S A DICK
I'M READY TO ROCK
HELL, YEAH
HEAVY METAL PARKING LOT
SHE'S TRIPPIN' JACK DANIELS
PRIEST RULES
a documentary by JEFF KRULIK and JOHN HEYN
I'M ON ACID, THAT'S WHERE I AM

FUCK YOU-MAN

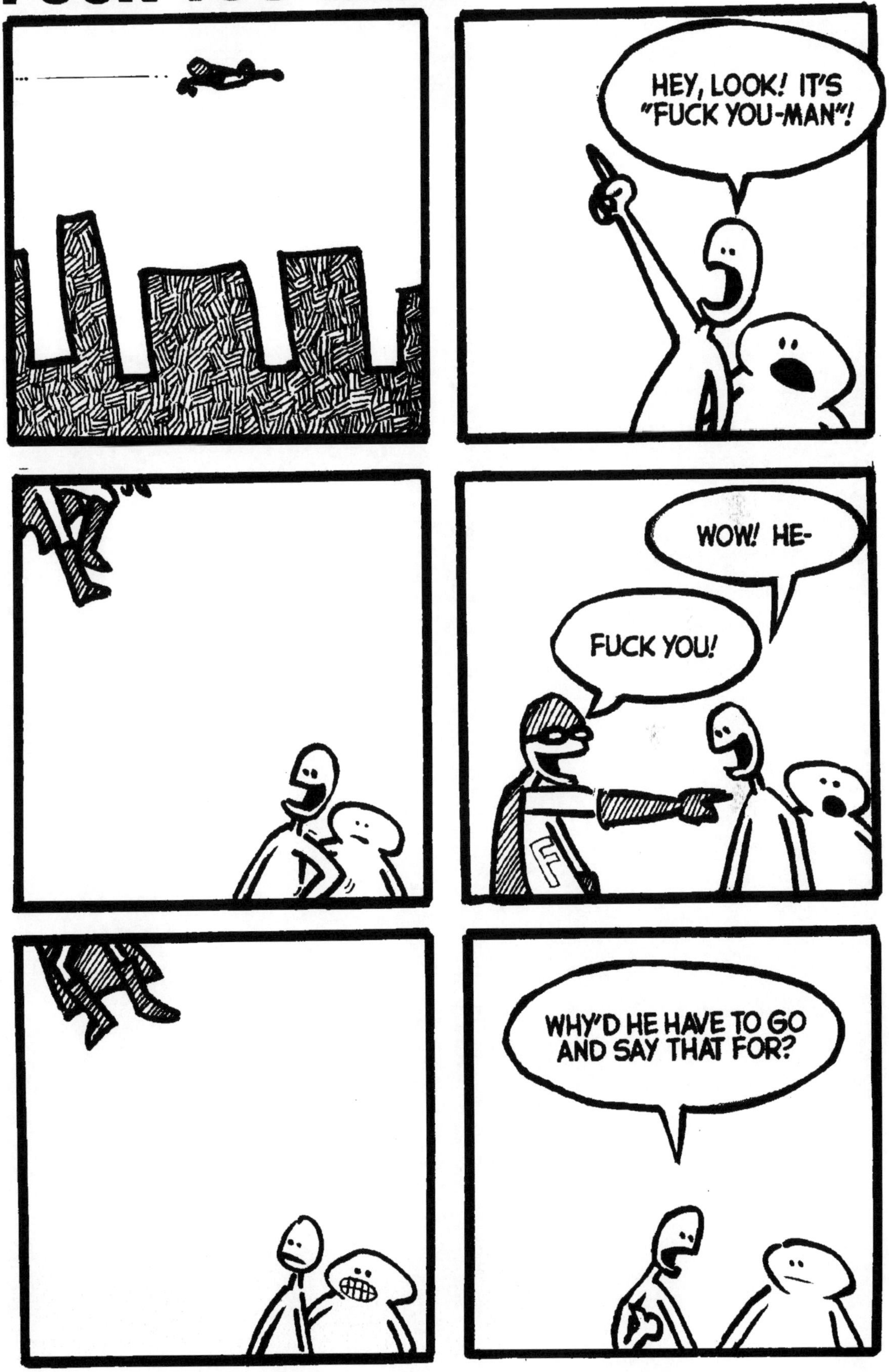
HEY, LOOK! IT'S "FUCK YOU-MAN"!
WOW! HE-
FUCK YOU!
F
WHY'D HE HAVE TO GO AND SAY THAT FOR?

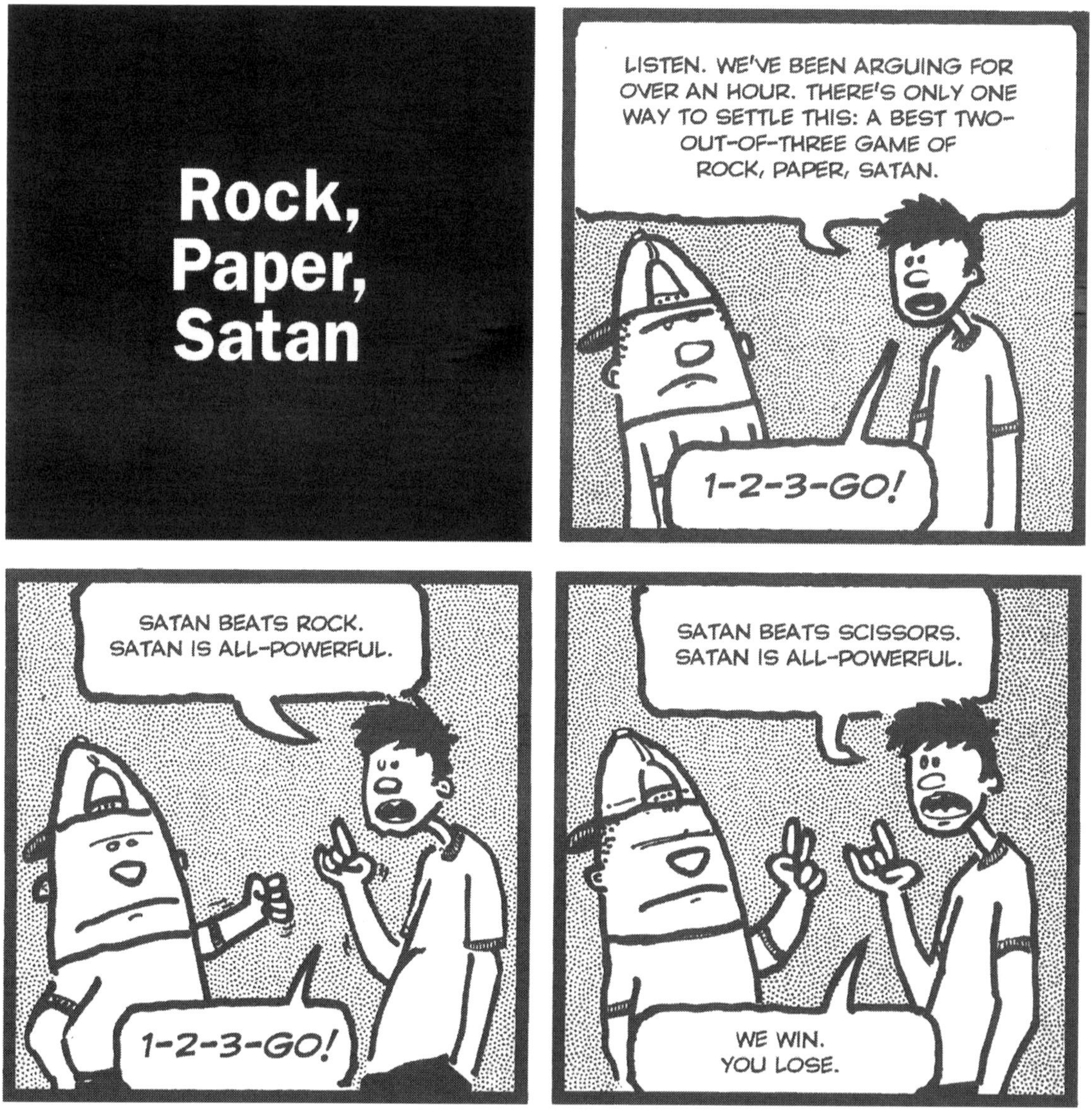
Rock, Paper, Satan
LISTEN. WE'VE BEEN ARGUING FOR OVER AN HOUR. THERE'S ONLY ONE WAY TO SETTLE THIS: A BEST TWO-OUT-OF-THREE GAME OF ROCK, PAPER, SATAN.
1-2-3-GO!
SATAN BEATS ROCK. SATAN IS ALL-POWERFUL.
1-2-3-GO!
SATAN BEATS SCISSORS. SATAN IS ALL-POWERFUL.
WE WIN. YOU LOSE.

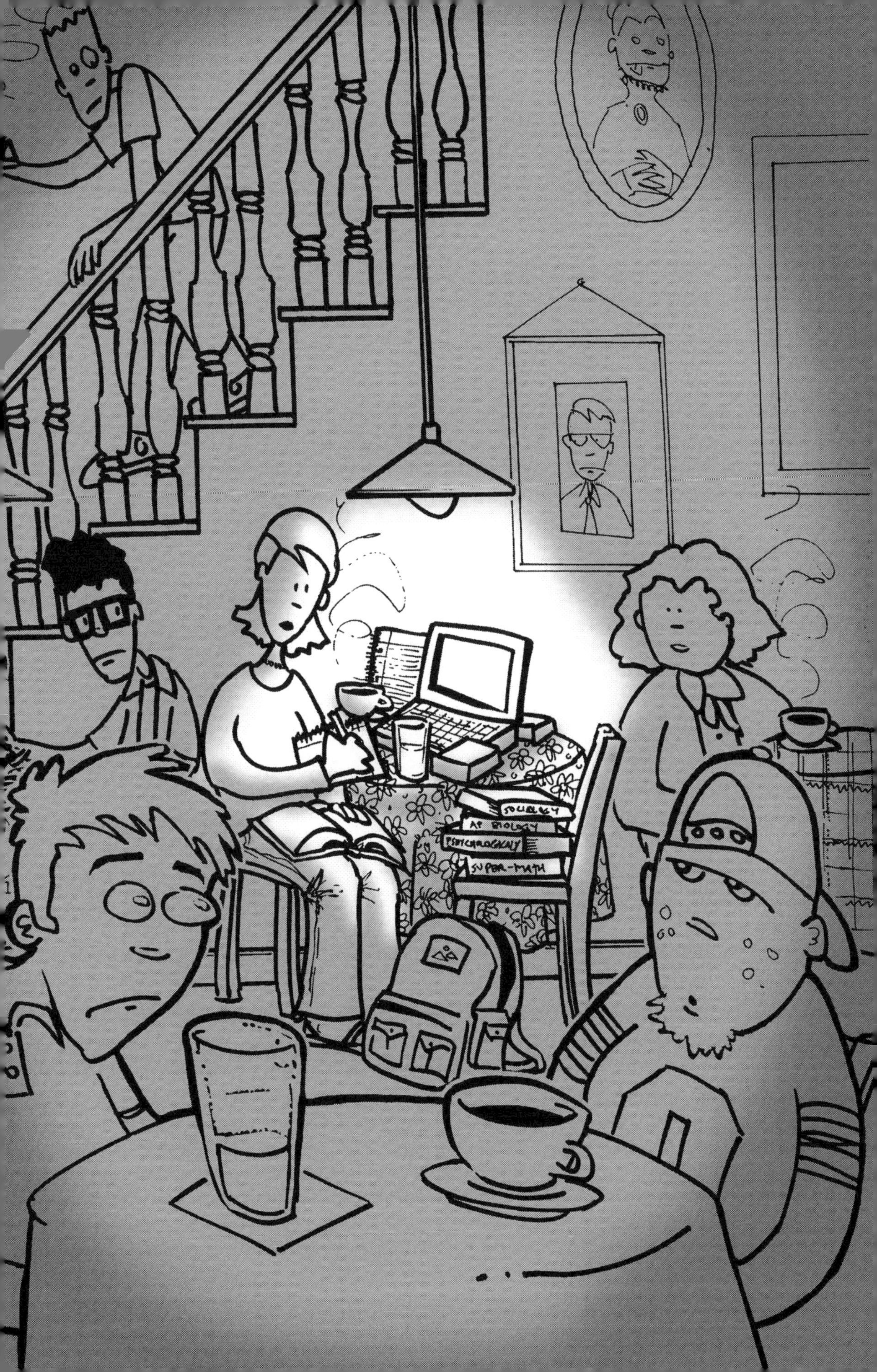
AP BIOLOGY
SUPER-MATH

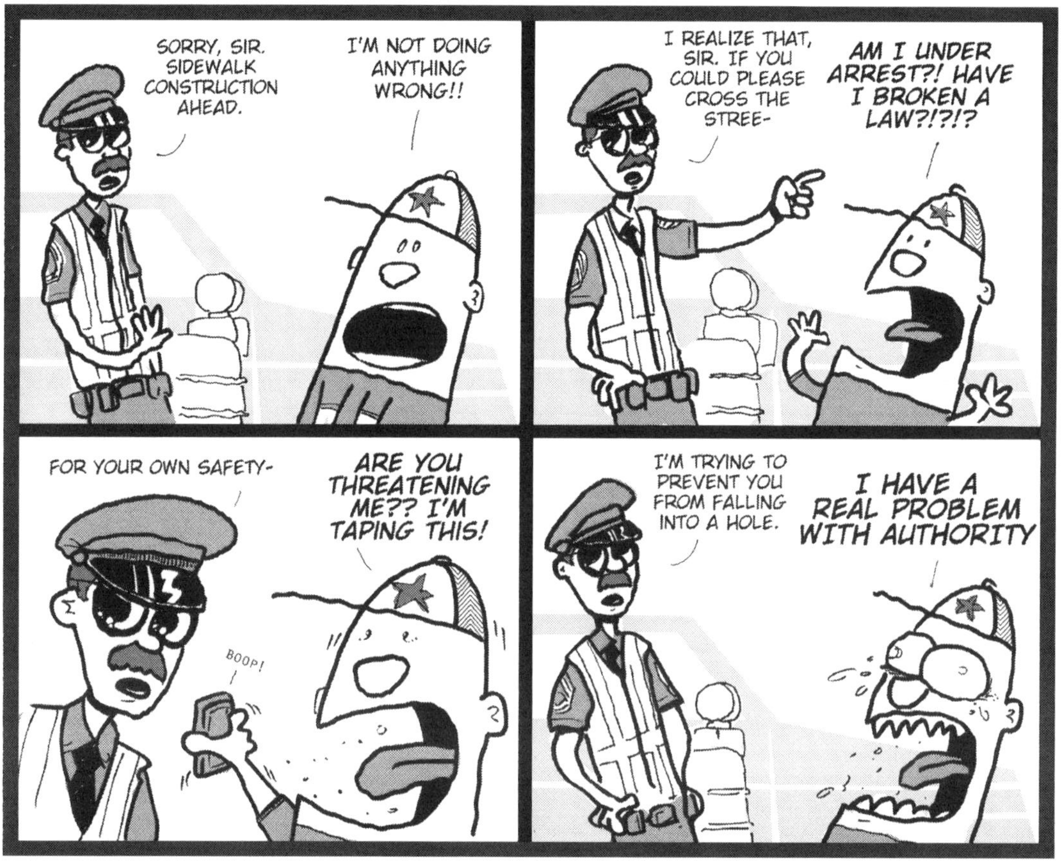
SORRY, SIR. SIDEWALK CONSTRUCTION AHEAD.
I'M NOT DOING ANYTHING WRONG!!
I REALIZE THAT, SIR. IF YOU COULD PLEASE CROSS THE STREE-
AM I UNDER ARREST?! HAVE I BROKEN A LAW?!?!?
FOR YOUR OWN SAFETY-
ARE YOU THREATENING ME?? I'M TAPING THIS!
BOOP!
I'M TRYING TO PREVENT YOU FROM FALLING INTO A HOLE.
I HAVE A REAL PROBLEM WITH AUTHORITY

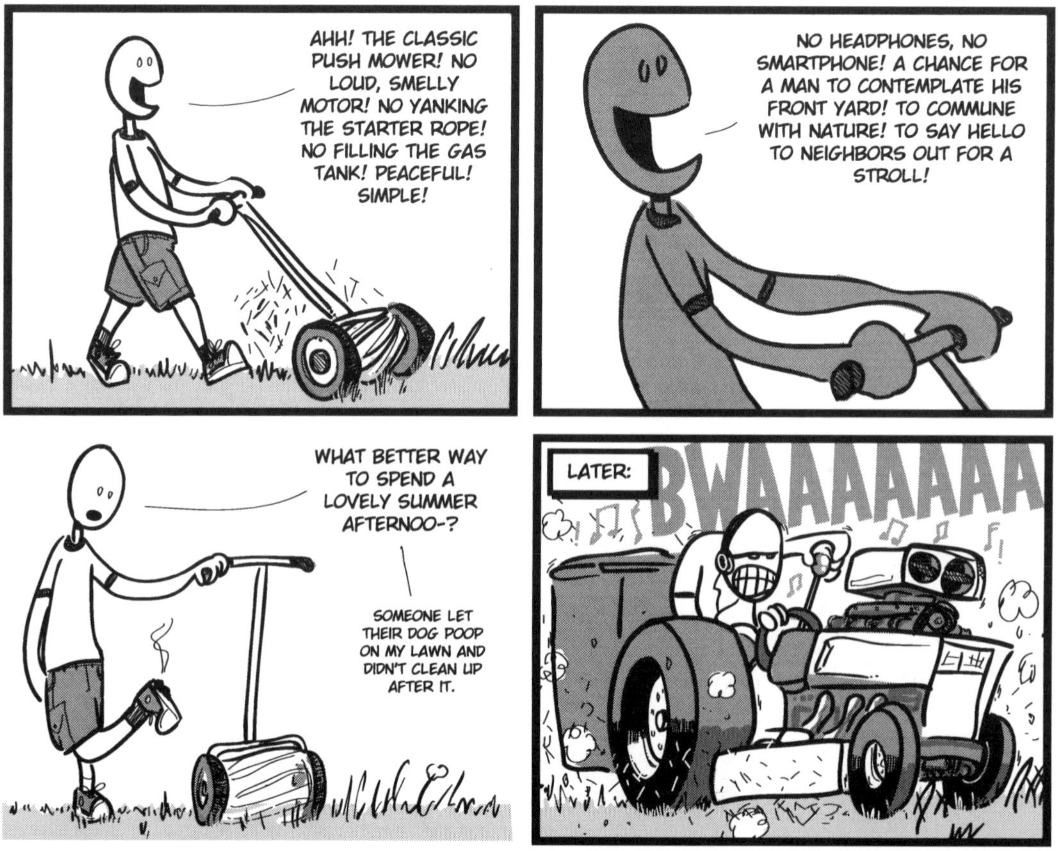
AHH! THE CLASSIC PUSH MOWER! NO LOUD, SMELLY MOTOR! NO YANKING THE STARTER ROPE! NO FILLING THE GAS TANK! PEACEFUL! SIMPLE!
NO HEADPHONES, NO SMARTPHONE! A CHANCE FOR A MAN TO CONTEMPLATE HIS FRONT YARD! TO COMMUNE WITH NATURE! TO SAY HELLO TO NEIGHBORS OUT FOR A STROLL!
WHAT BETTER WAY TO SPEND A LOVELY SUMMER AFTERNOO-?
SOMEONE LET THEIR DOG POOP ON MY LAWN AND DIDN'T CLEAN UP AFTER IT.
LATER:
BWAAAAAAA

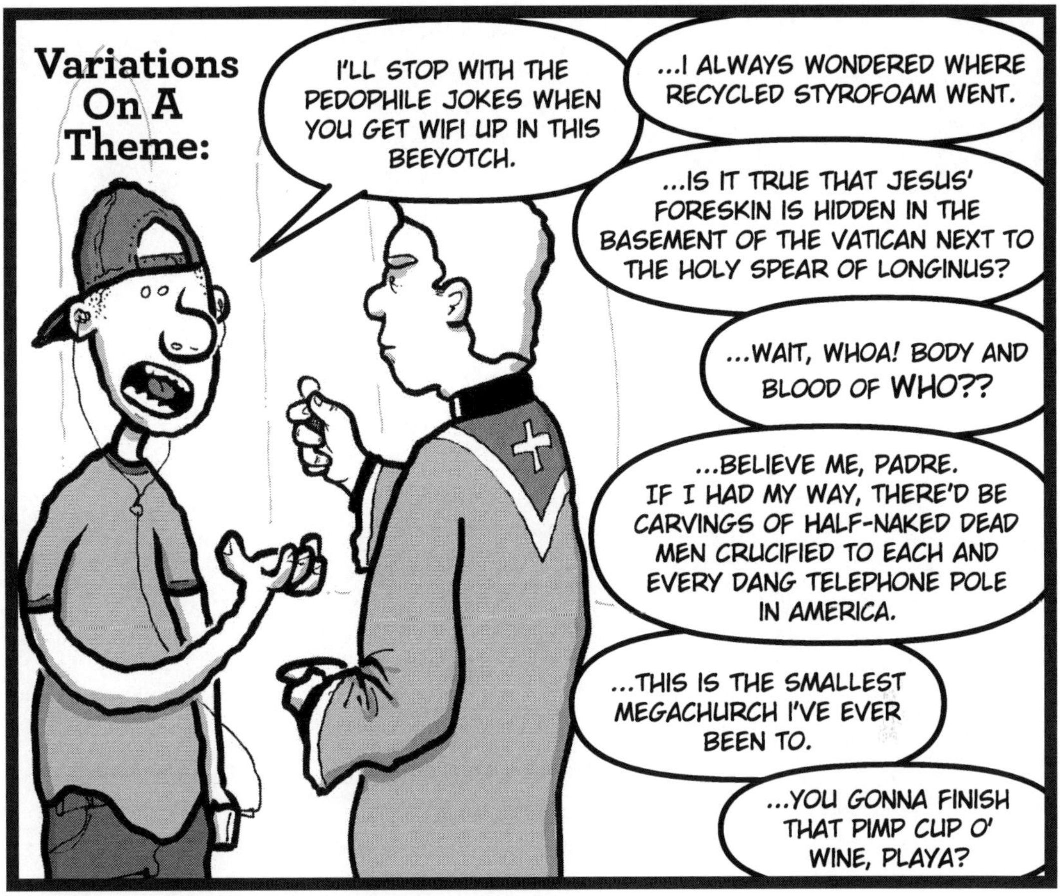
Variations On A Theme:
I'LL STOP WITH THE PEDOPHILE JOKES WHEN YOU GET WIFI UP IN THIS BEEYOTCH.
...I ALWAYS WONDERED WHERE RECYCLED STYROFOAM WENT.
...IS IT TRUE THAT JESUS' FORESKIN IS HIDDEN IN THE BASEMENT OF THE VATICAN NEXT TO THE HOLY SPEAR OF LONGINUS?
...WAIT, WHOA! BODY AND BLOOD OF WHO??
...BELIEVE ME, PADRE. IF I HAD MY WAY, THERE'D BE CARVINGS OF HALF-NAKED DEAD MEN CRUCIFIED TO EACH AND EVERY DANG TELEPHONE POLE IN AMERICA.
...THIS IS THE SMALLEST MEGACHURCH I'VE EVER BEEN TO.
...YOU GONNA FINISH THAT PIMP CUP O' WINE, PLAYA?

"Your cartoon is offensive to me, my God and my religion. A public apology is in order."

"What an empty, thoughtless message."

"The comic is funny and the folks who feel offended are even funnier!"

"What you have done may be considered a Hate Crime, we are looking into that right now."

"This is really offensive."

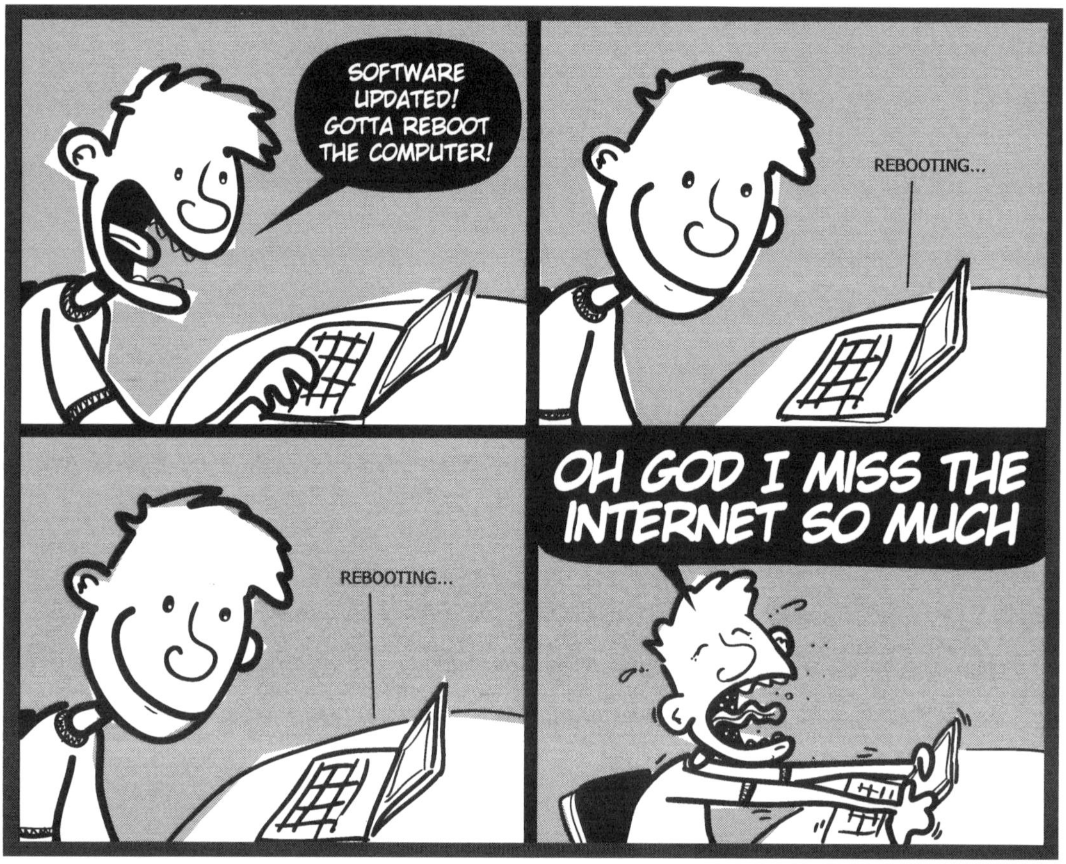
SOFTWARE UPDATED! GOTTA REBOOT THE COMPUTER!
REBOOTING...
REBOOTING...
OH GOD I MISS THE INTERNET SO MUCH

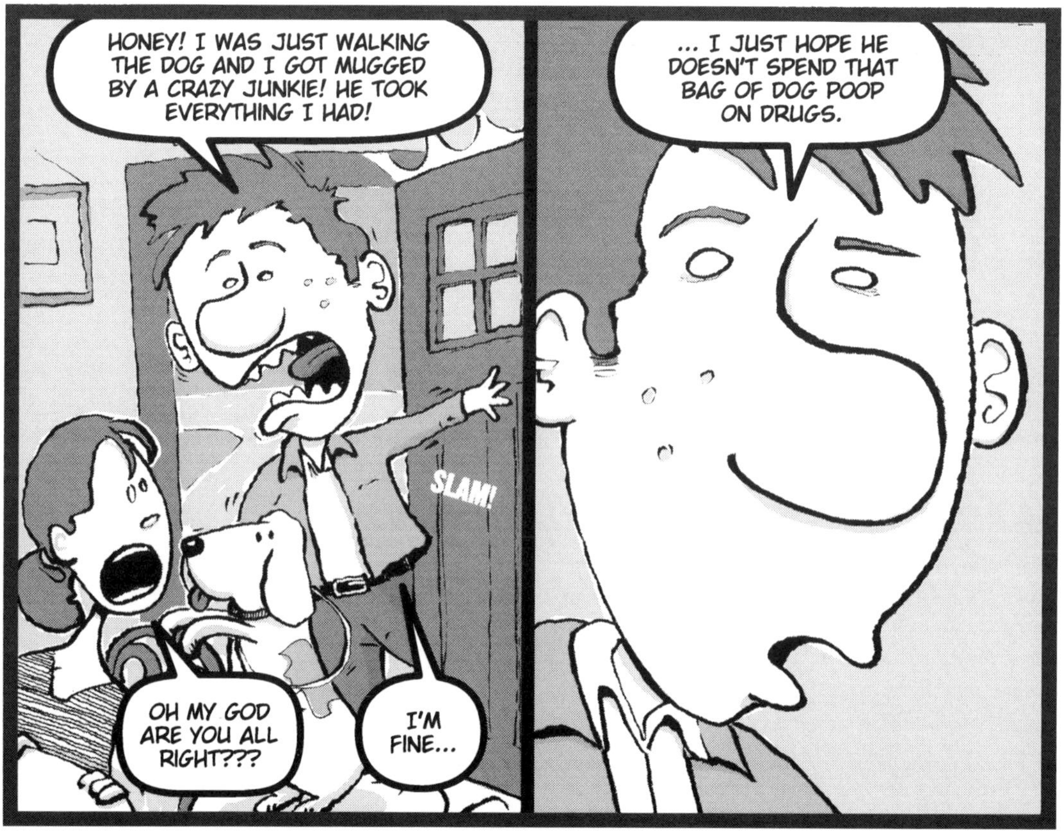
HONEY! I WAS JUST WALKING THE DOG AND I GOT MUGGED BY A CRAZY JUNKIE! HE TOOK EVERYTHING I HAD!
SLAM!
OH MY GOD ARE YOU ALL RIGHT???
I'M FINE...
... I JUST HOPE HE DOESN'T SPEND THAT BAG OF DOG POOP ON DRUGS.

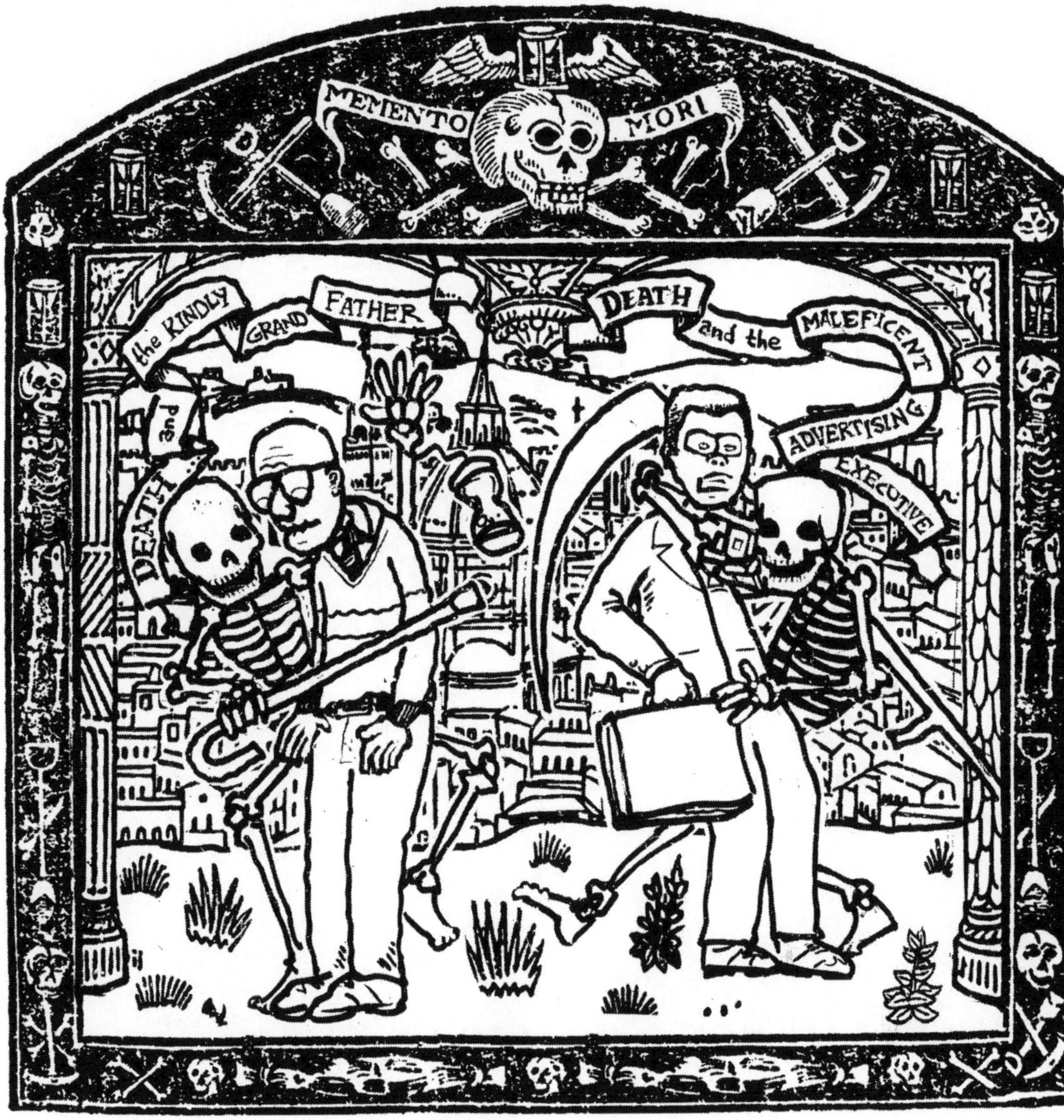
MEMENTO MORI
DEATH and
the KINDLY GRAND FATHER
DEATH and the MALEFICENT ADVERTISING EXECUTIVE

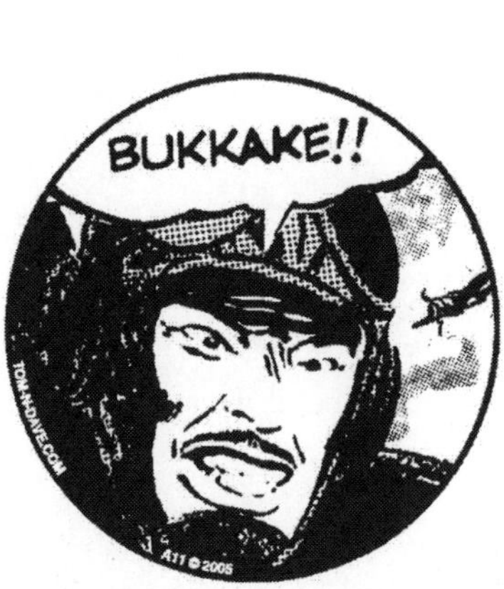
BUKKAKE!!

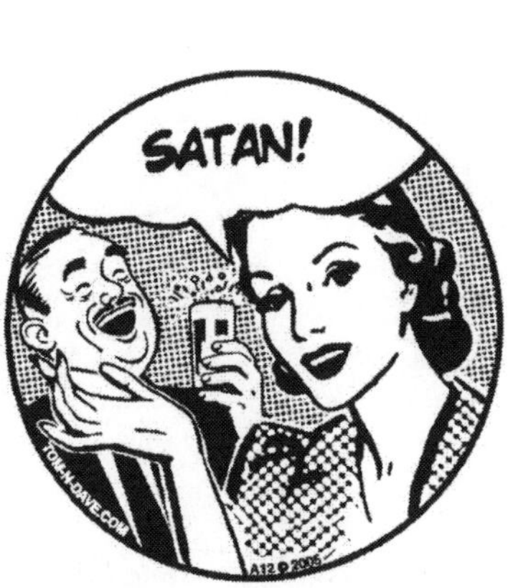
SATAN!

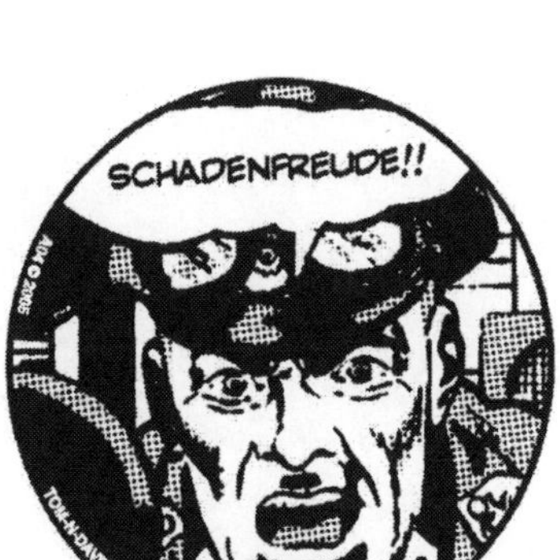
SCHADENFREUDE!!

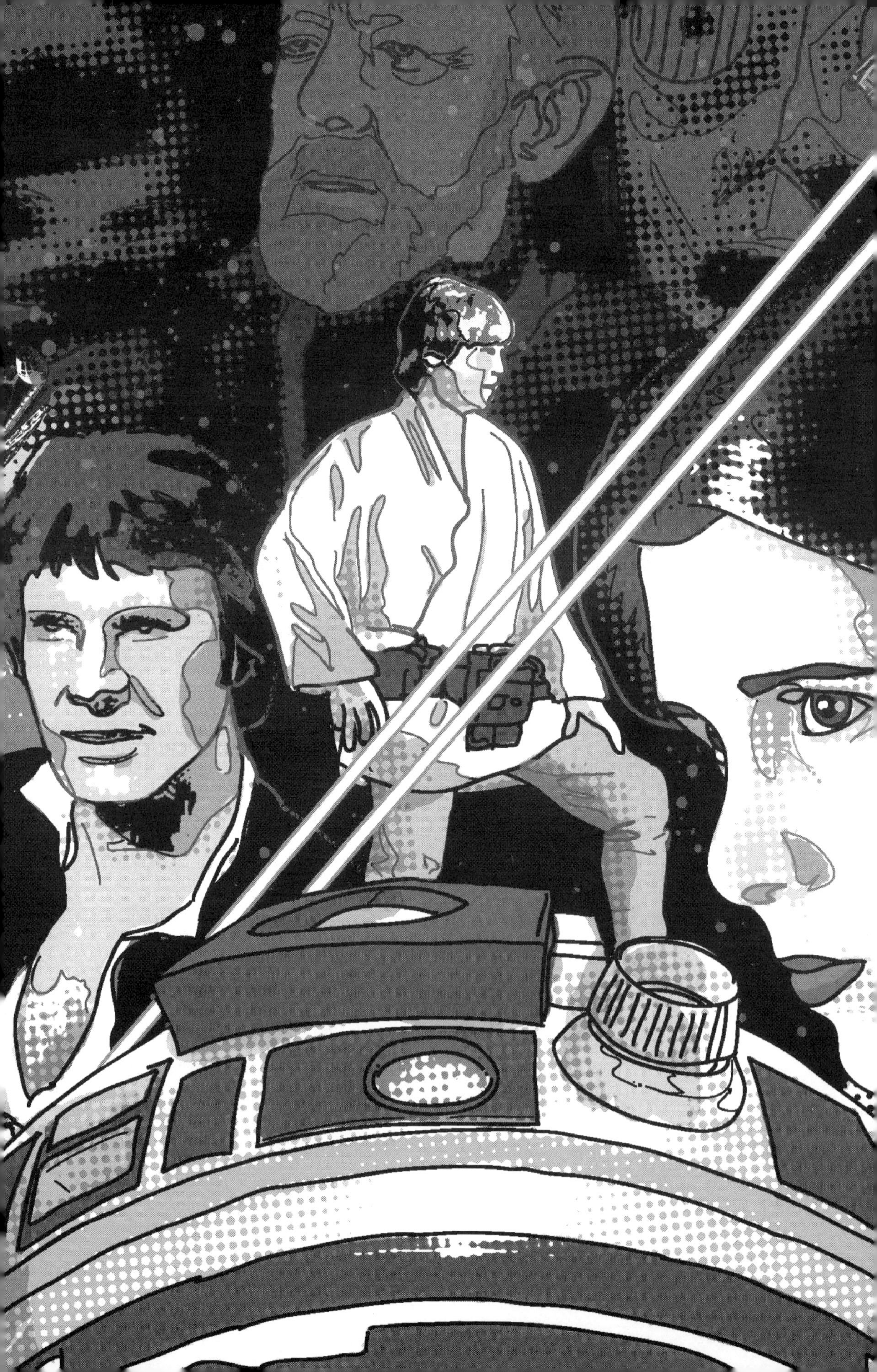

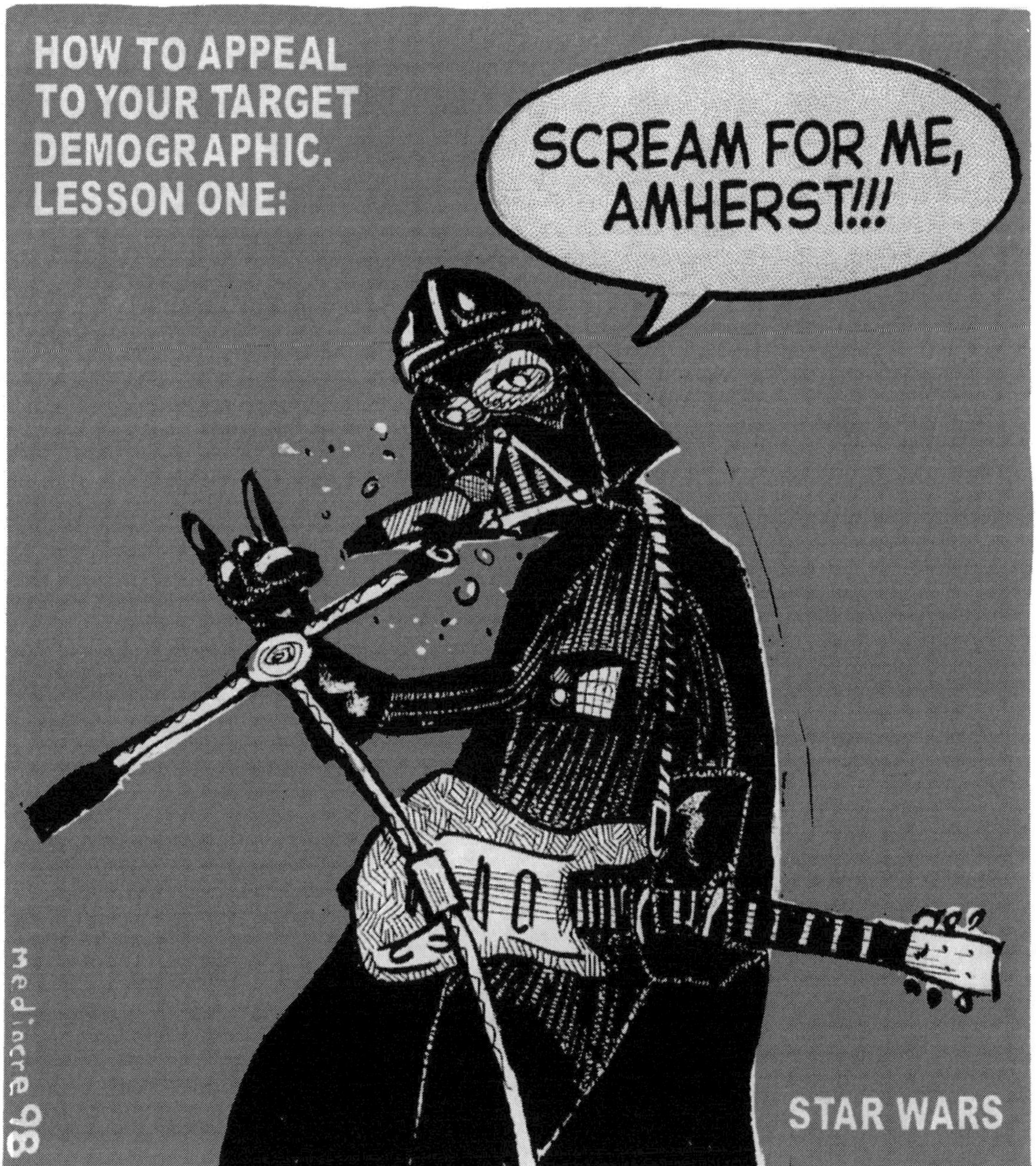
HOW TO APPEAL TO YOUR TARGET DEMOGRAPHIC. LESSON ONE:
SCREAM FOR ME, AMHERST!!!
STAR WARS
mediocre 98

SUNDAY MORNING

We're standing across the street from our house early on Easter morning, surveying our grand 1/8th acre estate and discussing our yard work plans for Spring. I tell Sarah I will be smarter this year and trim the hedge along the fence before it blooms. I realize that the phrase "nip it in the bud" has a real-world literal meaning. It had honestly never occurred to me before.

We watch as a woman and her son push a shopping cart along the sidewalk in front of our house. They stop and begin throwing trash from their cart into our trash barrel, which is at the end of our driveway. Sarah runs over to stop them. There appears to be an amicable exchange of words and the duo heads back up the street. Sarah goes inside while I watch them go. But they don't go far. The woman hands off the boy and the shopping cart to a couple of homeless-looking people and heads back in my direction. I pretend to be doing something, I'm not sure what, as she crosses the street and walks right past me. I feel that adrenaline rush of social anxiety as I avoid eye contact. She says something to me which I don't catch.

"What's that?" I ask.

"Who cut the cheese?" she says. Her tone is flat and menacing. She's vaguely attractive, a pale Irish woman. But her eyes are like black pinholes, something off about them, and honestly she terrifies me. I don't say anything and she walks away.

I hear a cry for help and look down the street. There's a child lying in the street, and another person hunched over her. "Call 911!" I shout towards my house. I run to them, more adrenaline pumping. A young Hispanic girl is lying on her back, eyes wide, breathing shallow. A square Lego-shaped lump protrudes from the side of her neck. She is scared, awake, and absolutely still. "Is she okay?" I ask her father. He looks a little bit like the actor Luis Guzmán, except less frowny-looking.

"She's all right. I called 911." He is calm and in control of the situation.

"Good," I say. "They're coming?" I ask, which is a really stupid question.

"They're coming," he confirms.

"Good," I repeat. I could do an emergency tracheotomy with a pocket knife and an eyedropper if I needed to—I've seen that episode of *M*A*S*H*—but I'd rather not. I hear another cry for help. I look up and realize there is another couple further down the street. Again, one on the ground, one standing. These were the people I had heard calling for help the first time. I'd stupidly stopped at the wrong emergency. I put my hand on the father's shoulder. "Don't worry. They're coming." I run to the second couple. Adrenaline.

A Japanese woman is crouched over an overweight black man, her husband. Even in the rush of the moment, part of my brain is noting what a bizarre multicultural morning I'm having.

"Is he okay?" I ask as I kneel beside him.

"He's not breathing," she replies. She's crying, her palms holding the man's face. She's right. He's not breathing. I don't know jack-squat about CPR.

"Did you call 911?"

She says something I don't understand because of the crying, but I gather the answer is no. I check my pockets but I don't have my phone on me, which is damned unusual, endlessly aggravating, and somehow makes me feel lost. I see her phone and keys on the street next to the man's dead or dying body. I grab the phone. It's not like my phone and it takes me a sec to figure out how to power it up. For the first time in my life, I'm about to hit the "emergency call" button that bypasses the security login screen on a smartphone. I feel anxious about it and there's another rush of adrenaline real adrenaline and I wake up and it's five fucking ten in the goddamned morning, Sunday morning.

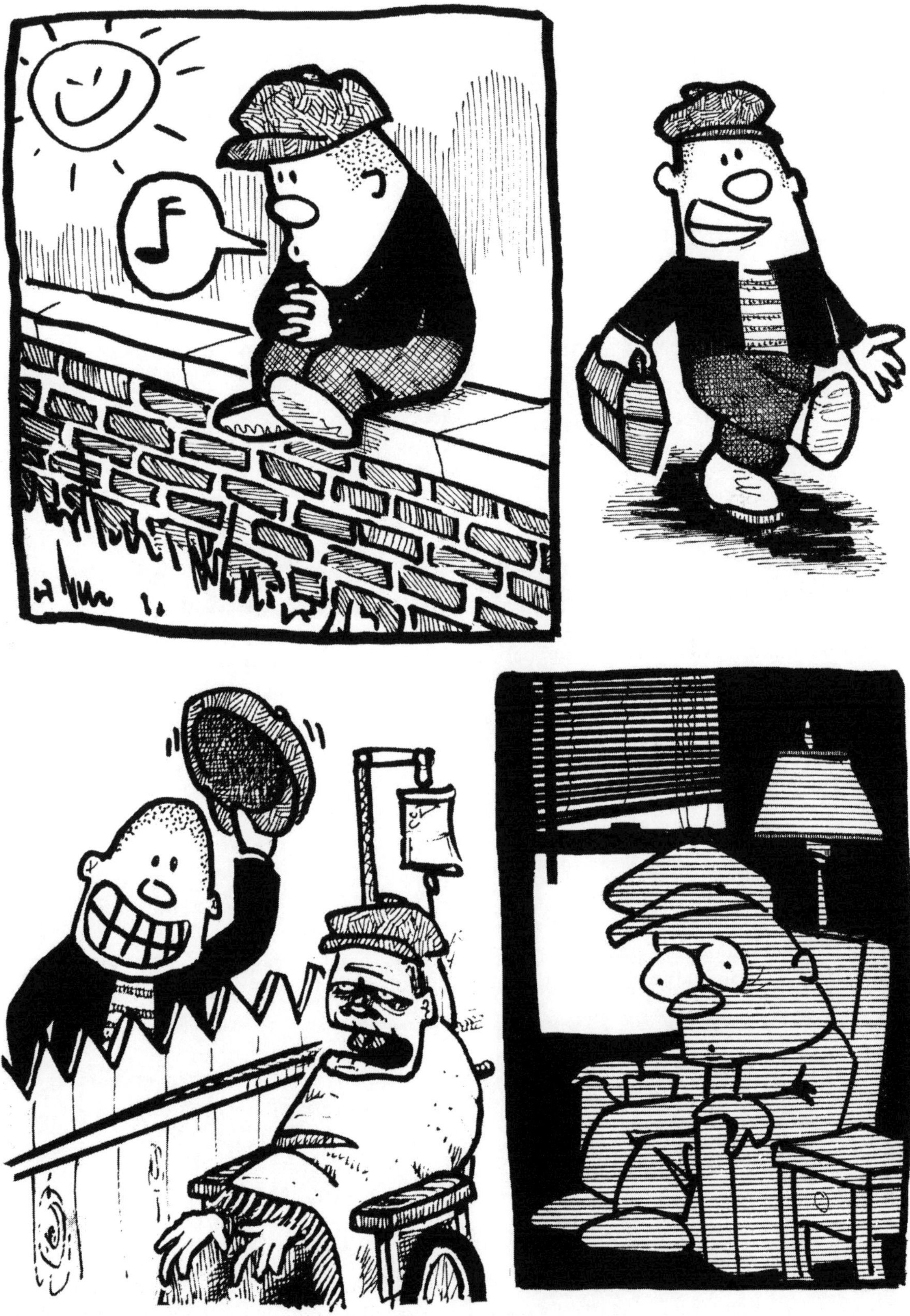

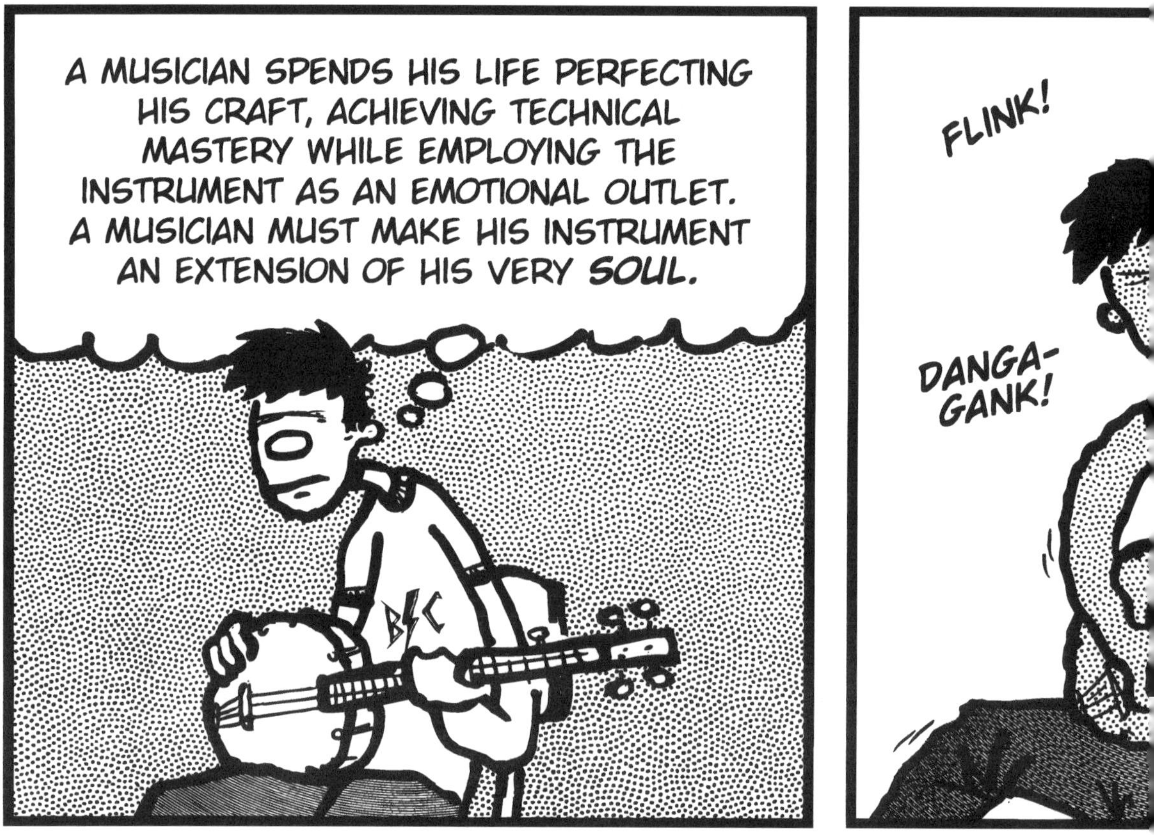
A MUSICIAN SPENDS HIS LIFE PERFECTING HIS CRAFT, ACHIEVING TECHNICAL MASTERY WHILE EMPLOYING THE INSTRUMENT AS AN EMOTIONAL OUTLET. A MUSICIAN MUST MAKE HIS INSTRUMENT AN EXTENSION OF HIS VERY SOUL.
B/C
FLINK!
DANGA-GANK!

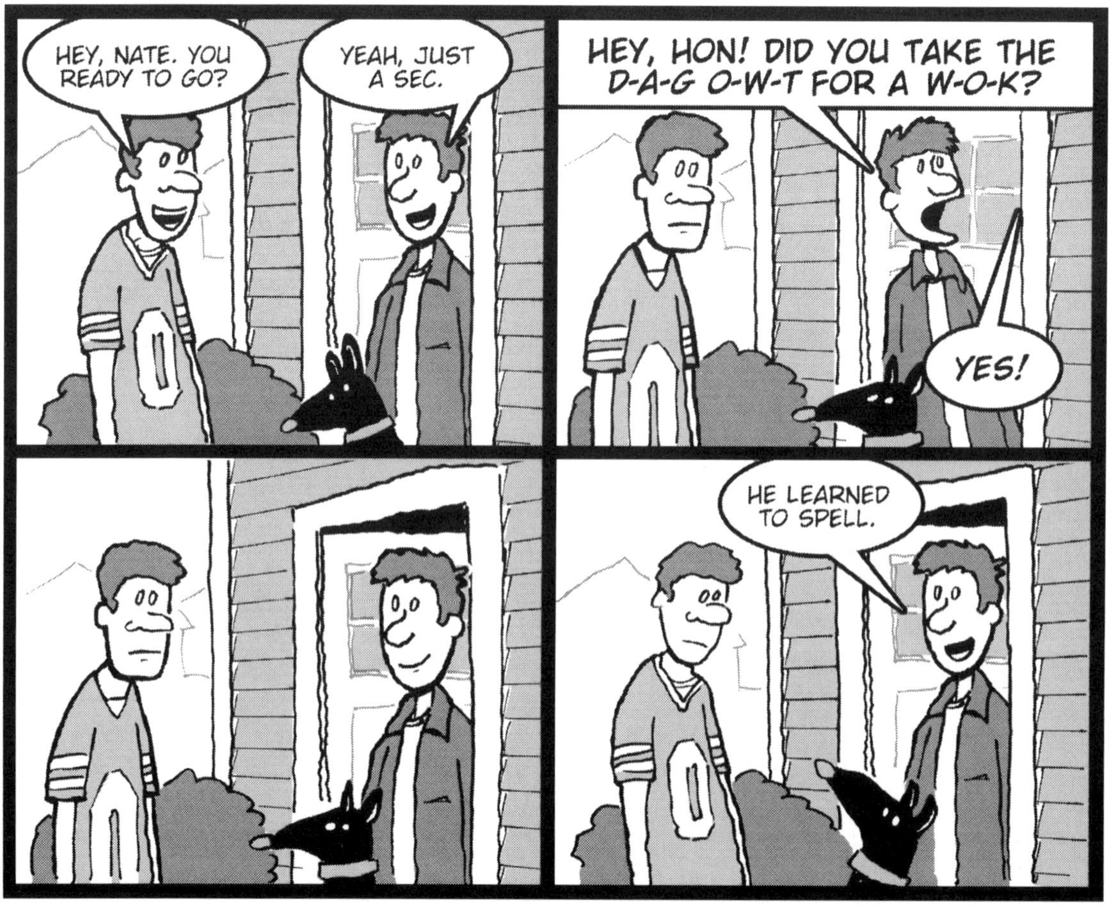
HEY, NATE. YOU READY TO GO?
YEAH, JUST A SEC.
HEY, HON! DID YOU TAKE THE D-A-G O-W-T FOR A W-O-K?
YES!
HE LEARNED TO SPELL.

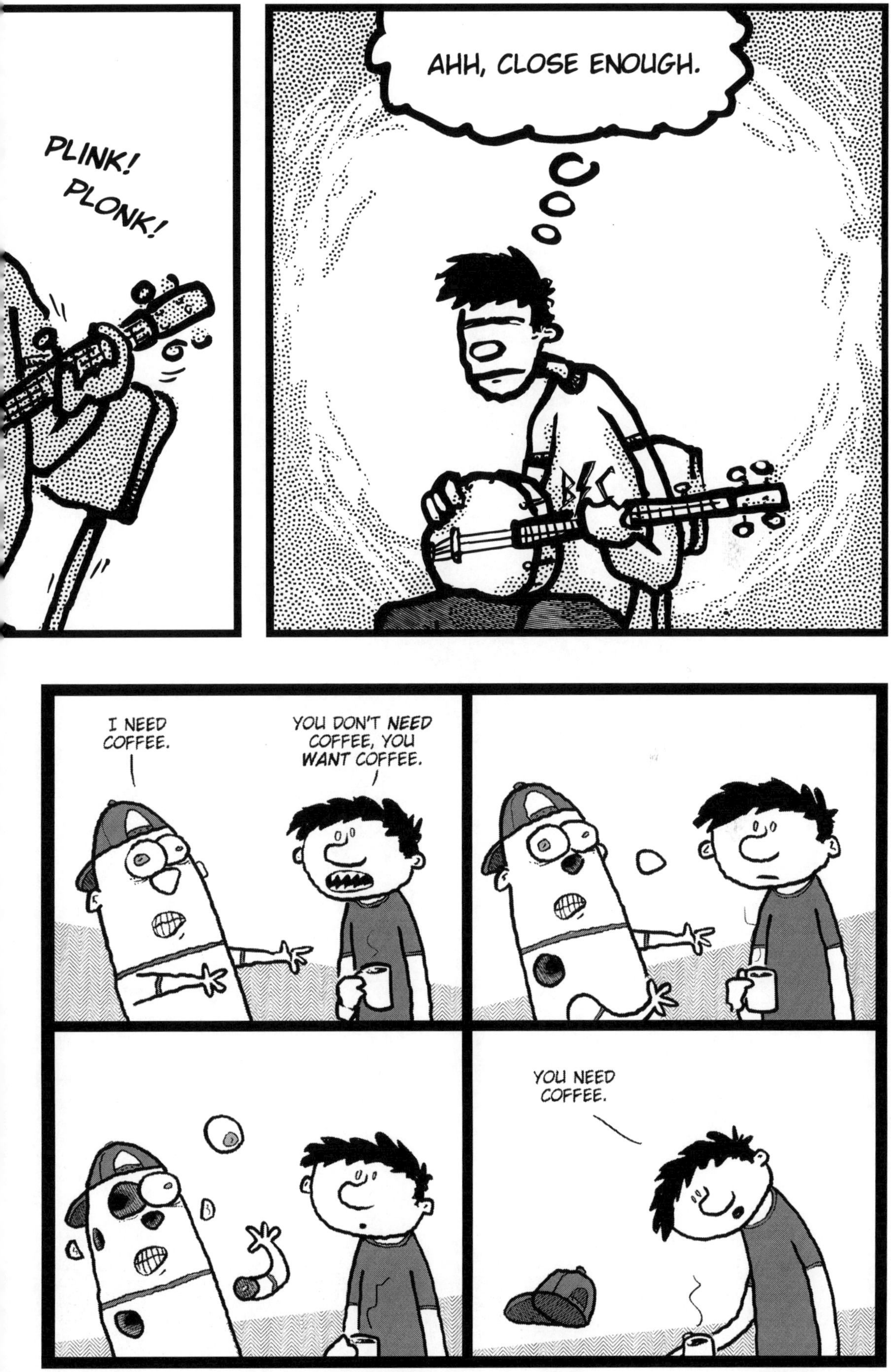
PLINK!
PLONK!
AHH, CLOSE ENOUGH.
I NEED COFFEE.
YOU DON'T NEED COFFEE, YOU WANT COFFEE.
YOU NEED COFFEE.

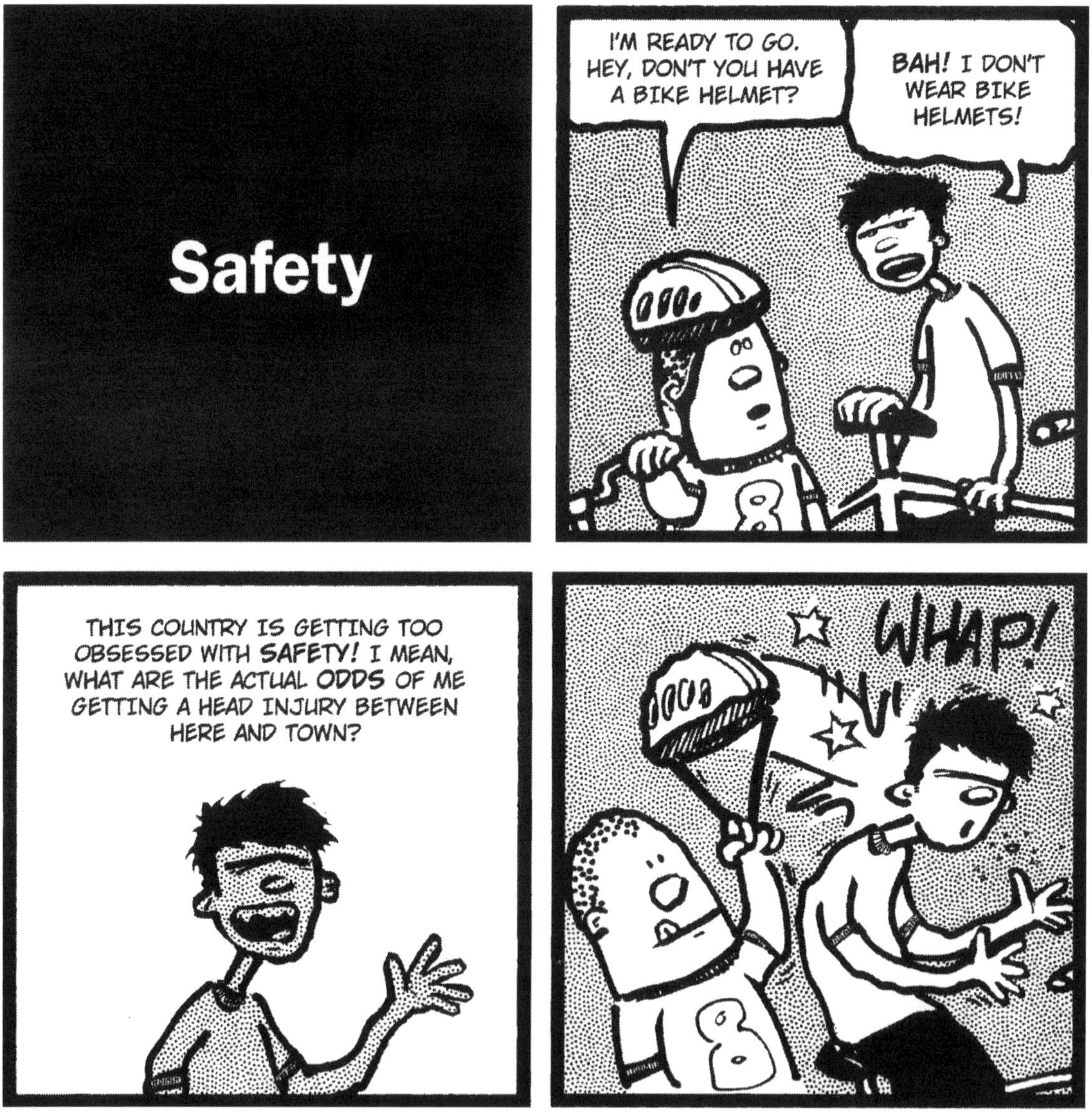
Safety
I'M READY TO GO. HEY, DON'T YOU HAVE A BIKE HELMET?
BAH! I DON'T WEAR BIKE HELMETS!
THIS COUNTRY IS GETTING TOO OBSESSED WITH SAFETY! I MEAN, WHAT ARE THE ACTUAL ODDS OF ME GETTING A HEAD INJURY BETWEEN HERE AND TOWN?
WHAP!

The Artist
MY ART EXPRESSES HOW I FEEL INSIDE.
IS THAT WHY IT SUCKS SO BAD?

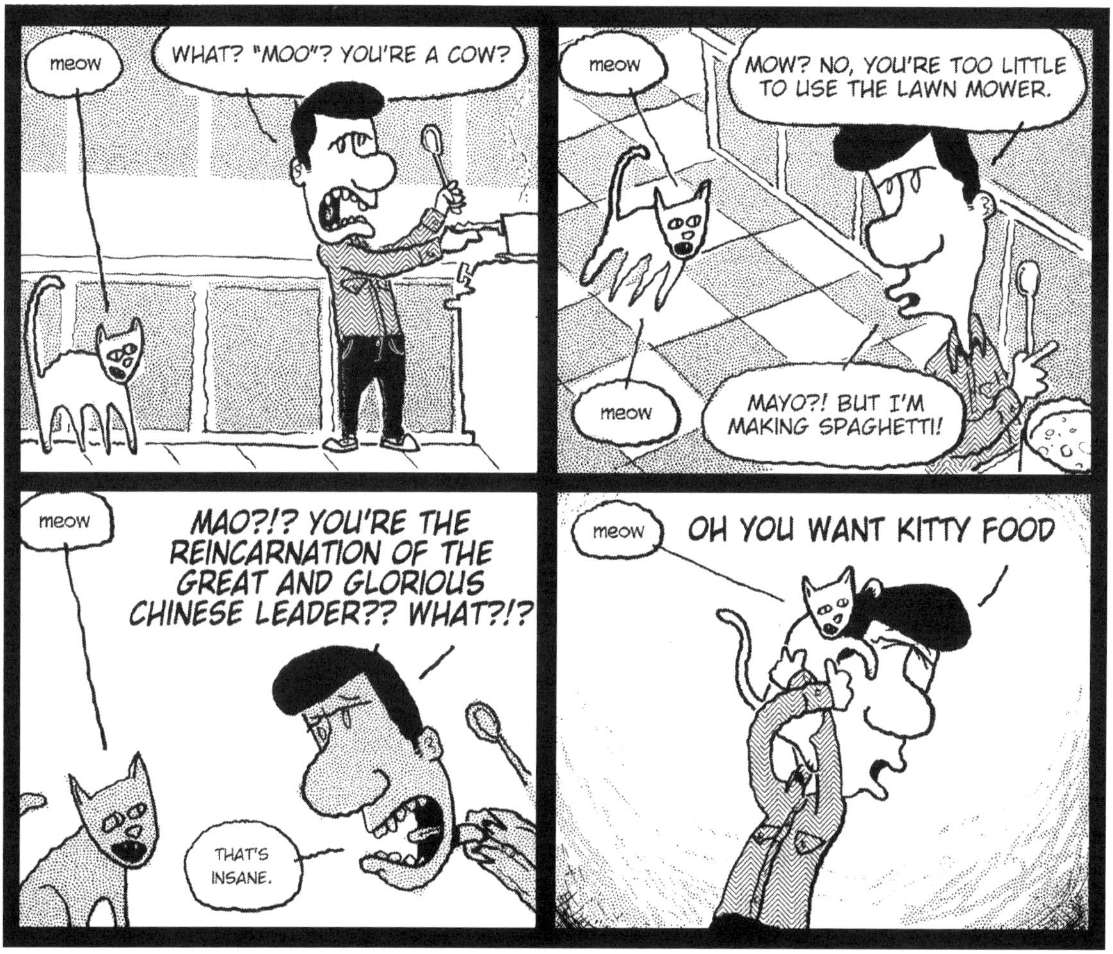
meow
WHAT? "MOO"? YOU'RE A COW?
meow
MOW? NO, YOU'RE TOO LITTLE TO USE THE LAWN MOWER.
meow
MAYO?! BUT I'M MAKING SPAGHETTI!
meow
MAO?!? YOU'RE THE REINCARNATION OF THE GREAT AND GLORIOUS CHINESE LEADER?? WHAT?!?
THAT'S INSANE.
meow
OH YOU WANT KITTY FOOD

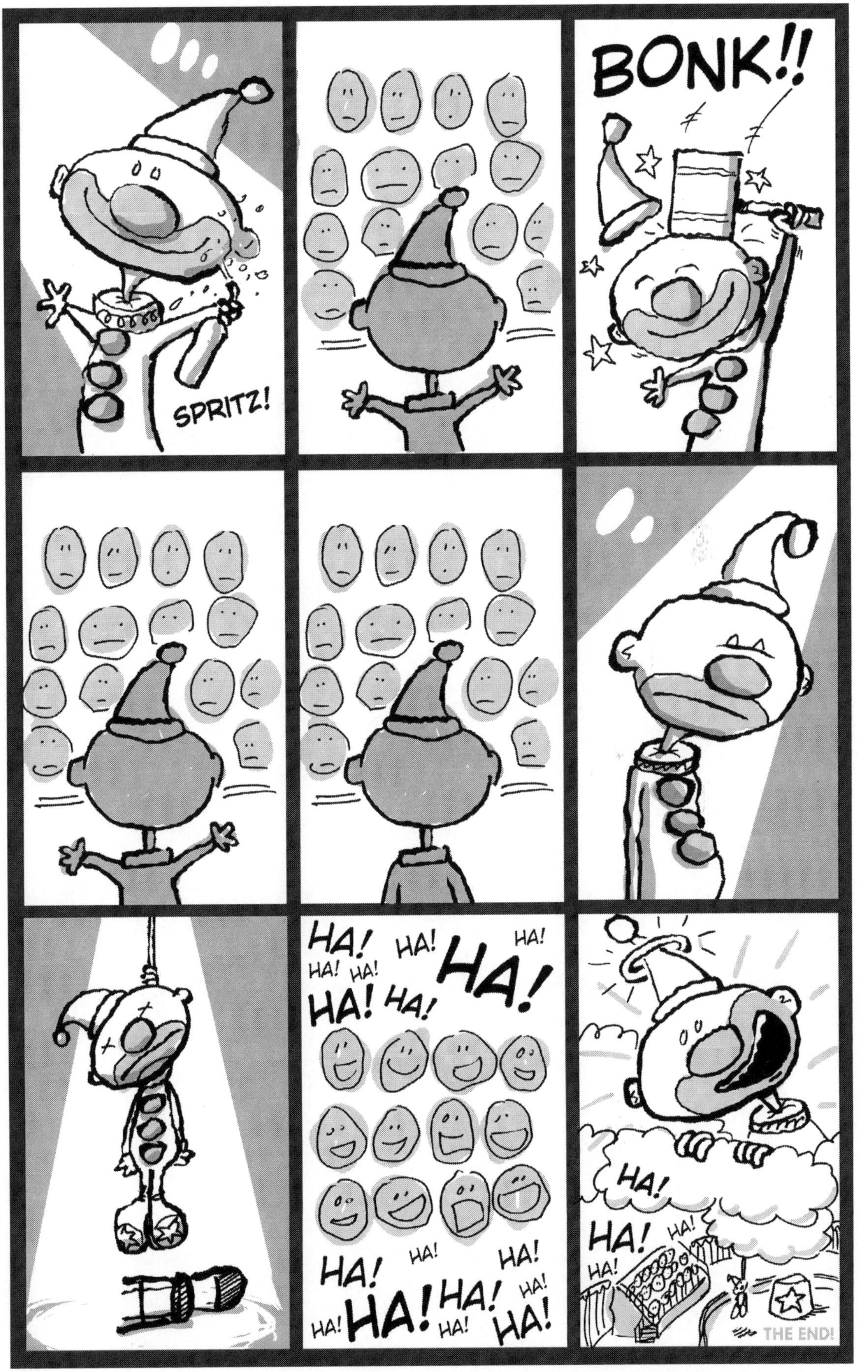
SPRITZ!
BONK!!
HA! HA! HA! HA! HA! HA! HA! HA! HA!
HA! HA! HA! HA! HA! HA! HA! HA! HA!
HA!
HA! HA! HA!
THE END!

34604467R10094

Made in the USA
Charleston, SC
13 October 2014